THE
LIBRARY
OF
SOUTHERN
CIVILIZATION

Lewis P. Simpson,
Editor

A
NEW
COLLECTION
OF
THOMAS
BANGS
THORPE'S
SKETCHES
OF THE
OLD
SOUTHWEST

A
NEW
COLLECTION
OF
THOMAS
BANGS
THORPE'S
SKETCHES
OF THE
OLD
SOUTHWEST

Thorpe, Thomas Bangs, 1815-1878

Edited,
with a Critical Introduction and Textual Commentary,
by
David C. Estes

LOUISIANA STATE UNIVERSITY PRESS
Baton Rouge and London

Copyright © 1989 by Louisiana State University Press
All rights reserved
Manufactured in the United States of America
98 97 96 95 94 93 92 91 90 89   5 4 3 2 1

Designer: Sylvia Malik Loftin
Typeface: Cheltenham Light
Typesetter: G & S Typesetters, Inc.
Printer: Thomson-Shore, Inc.
Binder: John H. Dekker & Sons, Inc.

Library of Congress Cataloging-in-Publication Data

Thorpe, Thomas Bangs, 1815–1878.
    A new collection of Thomas Bangs Thorpe's sketches of the old
Southwest / edited, with a critical introduction and textual
commentary, by David C. Estes.
        p.   cm. — (The Library of Southern civilization)
    Bibliography: p.
    ISBN 0-8071-1457-X (alk. paper)
    1. Southwest, Old—Description and travel.   2. Southwest, Old—
Social life and customs.   3. Frontier and pioneer life—Southwest,
Old.   4. Thorpe, Thomas Bangs, 1815–1878—Journeys—Southwest, Old.
I. Estes, David C., 1950–   II. Title.   III. Series.
F396.T53   1989
976—dc19   88-28642
                                                                  CIP

FOR
C. J. and Lois

CONTENTS

CONTENTS

ACKNOWLEDGMENTS

Milton Rickels' critical biography of Thomas Bangs Thorpe aroused my curiosity to read more of his sketches than those few humorous pieces that have made their way into contemporary anthologies, and I thank Professor Rickels for encouraging me to complete this critical edition of what I found in antebellum newspapers. Benjamin Franklin Fisher IV has also provided wise counsel, for which I am grateful. For patient criticism and willingness to listen to me talk out my ideas, Louis J. Budd deserves my deepest gratitude.

All whose research requires them to read numerous local newspapers know how valuable the interlibrary loan staff is in locating and ordering microfilm reels. Emerson Ford, at Duke University's Perkins Library, helped me obtain them quickly, and I thank him for processing the numerous requests I put on his desk. Newspaper collections at the following libraries were indispensable in my research: Boston Public Library, Howard-Tilton Memorial Library at Tulane University, Library of Congress, Louisiana State University Library, Massachusetts Historical Society, New Orleans Public Library, Perkins Library at Duke University, and Wilson Library at the University of North Carolina at Chapel Hill. For permission to quote from unpublished manuscripts, special thanks are due to Alderman Library at the University of Virginia, Haverford College Library, Historical Society of Pennsylvania, and New-York Historical Society. *American Journalism* and the *University of Mississippi Studies in English* have kindly granted permission for me to include revised portions of articles I have published on antebellum sporting literature.

A Duke University Graduate School Research Award funded a trip to Louisiana in the early stages of this project. Loyola University in New Orleans provided student assistantship funds for Jeanne Pavy to help with the final editing, Jeanice Blancett similarly devoted much time to carefully preparing the final draft of the manuscript, and Nicole Miller assisted with proofreading. All of these students have my thanks for their dedication and good spirits.

PART ONE

Introduction

TRAVELER, SPORTSMAN, HUMORIST

At the beginning of 1837, Thomas Bangs Thorpe, who would be twenty-two on March 1, reached Louisiana from New York City after traveling cross-country by stagecoach and steamboat.[1] Although he made the journey to visit a friend who had been a fellow student at Wesleyan University in Connecticut, he probably also hoped to find employment in the South. By September he was living in Baton Rouge and was corresponding with his friend about plans to establish himself as a painter in New Orleans. Whatever his original intentions, he lived in Louisiana for the next seventeen years and while there wrote the sketches that have earned him a place in American literary history among the humorists of the Old Southwest.

Thorpe arrived in the state shortly before it celebrated the twenty-fifth anniversary of its admission to the Union on April 30, 1812, just nine years after the Louisiana Purchase.[2] This quarter century had been a time of progress and expansion soon to be slowed by the panic of 1837 and falling cotton prices, but only until the early 1840s. Between 1810 and 1820 the total population of Louisiana doubled, to more than 150,000. By 1840 it was over 350,000, having increased by two-thirds in the previous ten years. Nearly half of the residents in 1840 were slaves. Americans emigrated to Louisiana to establish businesses in New Orleans and to raise cotton and sugarcane. Europeans came too, especially after 1830, as a result of revolutions and such difficulties as the Irish potato famine. In 1850 almost 70,000 of the 255,000 whites in the state had been born in foreign countries. New Orleans, where many of these foreigners settled, increased in population from

1. The biographical facts about Thorpe in this section are from Milton Rickels, "Thomas Bangs Thorpe in the Felicianas, 1836–1842," *Louisiana Historical Quarterly,* XXXIX (April, 1956), 169–97; and from his *Thomas Bangs Thorpe: Humorist of the Old Southwest* (Baton Rouge, 1962).
2. The facts about Louisiana in this section are from Edwin Adams Davis, *Louisiana: The Pelican State* (Baton Rouge, 1959); Harry Hansen (ed.), *Louisiana: A Guide to the State* (Rev. ed.; New York, 1971); Garnie William McGinty, *A History of Louisiana* (2nd ed., rev.; New York, 1951); Blake McKelvey, *American Urbanization: A Comparative History* (Glenview, Ill., 1973); Roger W. Shugg, *Origins of Class Struggle in Louisiana: A Social History of White Farmers and Laborers During Slavery and After, 1840–1875* (Baton Rouge, 1939); and Joe Gray Taylor, *Louisiana: A Bicentennial History* (New York, 1976).

17,000 in 1810 to over 100,000 in 1840, when it ranked as the fourth-largest city in the nation, having only about 100 fewer citizens than did Baltimore.

In the same year that Louisiana became a state, the first steamboat traveled from Pittsburgh down the Ohio and Mississippi rivers to New Orleans. Three years later Henry Miller Shreve piloted the first steamboat upstream from New Orleans to Louisville. Arrivals in New Orleans increased rapidly from 21 in 1814 to 1,573 in 1840, when 400 steamboats were traveling up and down the Mississippi. By that time the city had become second only to New York as an American port.

Agricultural production rose rapidly during this period. In 1840 over 380,000 bales of cotton were sent to market, more than double the total of 150,000 in 1834. Largely owing to new settlement in the northern part of the state, the harvest was about 770,000 bales by 1860. Likewise with sugar, the number of hogsheads produced increased from 45,000 in 1825–26 to 110,000 in 1834–35 to 220,000 in 1859–60.

The growing wealth of the state made New Orleans, a city over a century old, seem like a boomtown, since the emphasis everywhere was on making money, and even poor men were able to accumulate fortunes and rise to power. The crime rate, also, was typical for a boomtown, New Orleans reputedly being the most lawless city in the nation. Another sobering fact of life was that in 1850, Louisiana had the highest death rate of any state, and New Orleans the highest of any city. Every summer, yellow fever broke out, killing over 50,000 in New Orleans alone between 1840 and 1860.

The Louisiana frontier contrasted sharply with the New York where Thorpe grew up. He had lived in Albany with his maternal grandparents for a time after the death in 1819 of his father, a Methodist minister in New England and New York City. However, by 1827, his mother had returned to New York City with her children. In "Old Dutch Houses and Their Associations," Thorpe recollected from his childhood the Dutch architecture and the customs of the Knickerbockers, unlike anything he would have found in the Southwest.[3] Thorpe had become a student of the painter John Quidor at his studio in New York in 1830 and first exhibited a painting at the American Academy of Fine Arts three years later. Unable to finance the training in Europe he wanted, his family did send him to Wesleyan University in the fall of 1834. Although he

---

3. Thomas Bangs Thorpe, "Old Dutch Houses and Their Associations," *Knickerbocker Magazine*, XVIII (August, 1841), 150–55.

would have graduated in 1837, he left after the summer term in 1836 because of illness, which may have helped persuade him to travel south that winter.

Thorpe did not succeed in establishing himself as a painter in New Orleans in 1837 and, by the summer of 1839, was living in Jackson in the parish of West Feliciana. The numerous plantations along the Mississippi in that area would have offered him many opportunities for painting portraits. Nevertheless, he returned to New York to marry Maria Hinckley, probably his stepfather's daughter, and in the spring of 1840 she gave birth to their first child. Although he listed himself in the city directory as a portrait painter, Thorpe had not lost his desire to live in the Southwest, and by December he and his family had returned. While living in St. Francisville during the next two years, he continued to paint, and his *A Louisiana Deer* was engraved for the November, 1842, *American Turf Register*. While in St. Francisville he began to write the humorous and sporting sketches set on the southwestern frontier that earned him an international reputation. Undoubtedly, he was a welcome citizen in his adopted state because of his characteristic good humor, as displayed in the acceptance speech he reportedly gave after election to the East Feliciana Parish Police Jury: "Fellow-citizens, we are all broken and gone to ———! Well, I go in for economy and eternal improvements. Our court-house at Clinton is too costly, and the first thing I do in the police jury will be to move that the present court-house be pulled down, and a cheaper one be put up in its place. Boys go and treat!"[4]

In 1843, Thorpe moved to New Orleans, where he began a career as a newspaper editor. The owners of the *Tropic*, in which he had published two humorous sketches that January, engaged him and Robert L. Brenham to edit their new weekly, the *Southern Sportsman*. After twelve issues, Thorpe left in June to become co-editor of the *Concordia Intelligencer* with Robert Patterson in Vidalia, across the Mississippi from Natchez. During the two years of their association, the newspaper came to have the largest circulation of any Louisiana paper outside New Orleans. In May, 1844, Thorpe was appointed postmaster at Vidalia, probably as a reward for his work within the Whig party. After leaving the *Intelligencer* in June, 1845, he spent the summer in New York and Philadelphia, where he prepared for publication *The Mysteries of the Backwoods*, his first collection of sketches. By the

4. New Orleans *Weekly Picayune*, May 23, 1842.

time Carey and Hart released the book in December, he was back in New Orleans, where he had begun publishing the *Commercial Times* on November 1.

Thorpe was becoming dissatisfied with editing newspapers, however, and hoped that Carey and Hart would hire him so that he could devote himself entirely to literary work. By the spring of 1846, his attempts had not resulted in the offer of a position, at least not one he could accept. In the beginning of April, he sold the *Commercial Times*, but instead of devoting himself to literature, he became co-owner of the *Tropic* and traveled to the Mexican War front in May as its correspondent. Immediately upon his return to New Orleans in June, he began writing *Our Army on the Rio Grande*, which Carey and Hart released in October. Meanwhile, Thorpe had sold his share in the *Tropic* at a loss and moved to Baton Rouge, where he published the *Louisiana Conservator*, probably until the following spring. When it did not prove a success, he returned to New Orleans to publish the *Daily National* from June until December, 1847. Carey and Hart released *Our Army at Monterey*, his second book about the Mexican War, late that year, but because of poor sales they refused to consider his projected third volume. Thorpe was once again living in Baton Rouge in 1848 while he worked actively for the Whigs during the presidential election and wrote *The Taylor Anecdote Book*, a campaign biography about Zachary Taylor's leadership during the conflict with Mexico. Unfortunately, after the election Taylor did not give Thorpe a patronage appointment as he had hoped. Following the death of his stepfather and his defeat as the Whig candidate for state superintendent of education, both in 1852, Thorpe must have begun to consider returning permanently to New York. He spent at least the last four months of 1853 there, working on his second collection of sketches, *The Hive of "The Bee-Hunter,"* and his one novel, *The Master's House; A Tale of Southern Life*, both of which were published the next year. Then, sometime in 1854 he moved to New York with his wife and three children, hoping to find a suitable and profitable career.

The list of Thorpe's jobs between his return to the East and the outbreak of the Civil War is varied. He wrote about twenty articles for Harper's *New Monthly Magazine*, worked on the staff of *Frank Leslie's Illustrated Newspaper*, practiced law, painted, lectured, and held a civil service position in the New York Custom House. In February, 1859, he bought part interest in the *Spirit of the Times* and was its co-editor until March 6, 1861, just a few months before financial difficulties and the embargo on mail to the Confederacy caused it to be discontinued. In 1862 he returned to New Orleans with the Union forces and, during the next two years, held various civil service positions, with duties including the supervision of food distribution to the needy and the development of sanitation programs that decreased the incidence of yellow fever. He also represented the second district of the city in the convention that drafted a new state constitution. Yet as a convention delegate and later as appraiser at the New Orleans Custom House, Thorpe was suspected of misappropriation of funds. Stanton Garner has argued that during his four years in New Orleans he was "one of the first, if not the very first, of the carpetbaggers" because of the personal financial gain he tried to realize through his civil service dealings.[5] Garner has also documented the shady dealings in which Thorpe participated after his 1869 reappointment as a weigher in the New York Custom House, one of the most important and also most corrupt organizations in the federal government under the spoils system. After an investigation in December, 1877, he was removed for graft, but his unknown political backer first changed the order to allow him to resign and then worked to gain him a minor clerkship. Only two months after receiving the new appointment, Thorpe died of Bright's disease on September 20, 1878. During these final years of disreputable public service, he had continued to write, publishing columns on art and drama as well as other miscellaneous pieces in *Appleton's Journal*, *Baldwin's Monthly*, and *Forest and Stream*.

Thorpe spent less than one-third of his life in the South and always supported the Union politically. How incongruous, then, that his place in literary history is alongside such ardent southerners as Augustus Baldwin Longstreet, William Tappan Thompson, Johnson Jones Hooper, and George Washington Harris. Yet during the 1830s and 1840s, before political tensions mounted, the scenery, people, and events of the southwestern frontier inspired Thorpe's best writing. He saw the region without a blinding sectional pride and, while not approving of all that he saw, still loved the Southwest and the contributions it alone could make to the growing nation.

While the humorous pieces in this edition are all set on the Southwestern frontier, Thorpe's primary purpose in many others written during his years in Louisiana is clearly to describe the region accurately

5. Stanton Garner, "Thomas Bangs Thorpe in the Gilded Age: Shifty in a New Country," *Mississippi Quarterly*, XXXVI (Winter, 1982–83), 44.

to eastern readers, as the preface to *Mysteries* explains: "An effort has been made, in the course of these sketches, to give to those personally unacquainted with the scenery of the Southwest, some idea of the country, of its surface, and vegetation. In these matters the author has endeavoured to be critically correct, indulging in the honest ambition of giving some information, as well as to lighten the lagging moments of a dull hour."[6] Following Thorpe's return to New York, *Harper's* carried a number of pieces in the 1850s describing southwestern crops and animals, and several others appeared in *Appleton's Journal* after the Civil War.

Travel narratives published by other easterners who ventured into the lower Mississippi Valley during the first decades of the century express a range of viewpoints. Yet despite differing judgments, the accounts generally give attention to the growth of civilization on the frontier and to the promising abundance of natural resources. In *Travels on an Inland Voyage* (1810), one of the first travel narratives written after the Louisiana Purchase, Christian Schultz, Jr., discusses in comparatively greater detail a subject none ignored—the Mississippi River and its importance to the development of commerce. A confident tone characterizes many of these writers. For example, Timothy Flint, a minister whose attitudes toward the region changed greatly during his residence there, notes the beneficial effect of commerce on the cultural life in his *Recollections of the Last Ten Years* (1826). Unlike most other eastern travelers, he argues that experiences on the frontier do not reduce individuals to degenerates, but rather ennoble them by developing high-mindedness and self-respect. Yet Flint's approval of the culture was not typical because travelers, on the whole, regarded the frontiersman as uncivilized. Nor were they generally any less critical of life in the region's principal city. Almost half of Joseph Holt Ingraham's *The South-West* (1835) discusses New Orleans' businesses, buildings, government, society, and entertainments, finding fault with the moral laxity of the people as demonstrated by the Sunday crowds at theaters and gambling houses.

Despite his familiarity with New Orleans as both traveler and resident, Thorpe ignored it in his descriptive sketches until 1869, when he wrote "The 'Levee' of New Orleans" for *Appleton's*. Unlike others who journeyed from the East to the Southwest, he was less interested in the growth of civilization and more concerned with the native character

6. Thorpe, *The Mysteries of the Backwoods; or, Sketches of the Southwest: Including Character, Scenery, and Rural Sports* (Philadelphia, 1846), 8.

types and the unspoiled scenery. The *Harper's* articles "Sugar and the Sugar Regions of Louisiana," "Cotton and Its Cultivation," and "The History and Mystery of Tobacco"—all written in the 1850s—deal with the growth of the economy, and his novel *The Master's House* (1854), set on a Louisiana plantation, takes up the harmful consequences of slavery and of dueling, just as other travelers had done. Nevertheless, the sketches published in the 1840s and then revised for his two collections rarely mention the influx of settlers, the particular changes they were making in the region, or the growing social problems. They show, instead, hunters and backwoodsmen who grew up there, and set forth the untamed natural scenery without reference to its future economic value. Thorpe did not agree with the predominant feeling that the region needed to become civilized. Its greatness did not lie in the future, he believed, but in what was rapidly becoming its past. As the frontier became more densely populated, America was losing the genuine source of its national identity. The preface to *Hive* states that in the Southwest "far removed from trans-Atlantic influences, are alone to be found, in the more comparative infancy of our country, characters truly *sui generis*—truly American." The regional character-types represent the nation as a whole because they demonstrate "what man would be, uninfluenced by contact with the varied associations of long civilization." Thorpe agreed with many writers of his day who, according to Perry Miller, "identified the health, the very personality, of America with Nature" and thought of "the problem of American self-recognition as being essentially an irreconcilable opposition between Nature and civilization."[7]

Thorpe's interest in the region as it existed before the nation began to expand so far westward resembles that of Washington Irving. Irving's *A Tour on the Prairies* (1835) recounts a journey west of Fort Gibson along the Arkansas River in present-day Oklahoma to experience the uncivilized frontier. He found confirmation that the romance of the region was not simply an illusion, despite an unsettling confrontation with nature's overpowering harshness. Thorpe knew this darker side as well and presented it humorously in such pieces as "Letters from the Far West." His descriptive sketches of the southwestern prairies, nevertheless, emphasize the sense of freedom and release travelers could experience there. Generally sentimental and at times ex-

7. Thorpe, *The Hive of "The Bee-Hunter," A Repository of Sketches, Including Peculiar American Character, Scenery, and Rural Sports* (New York, 1854), 6; Perry Miller, *Errand into the Wilderness* (Cambridge, Mass., 1956), 207–208.

cessively melodramatic, the sketches tend to glorify scenes and experiences, and refuse to examine the serious implications of nature's brutality.

The lack of realism in the descriptive pieces is one indication of Thorpe's nostalgia for a time past. They speak of how the rivers and prairies have been for ages, not of how they can begin to serve the nation's commerce. Likewise, they focus primarily on men who grew up there, not on settlers intent on exploiting the natural resources. Yet Thorpe did not always glance backward to find his subjects. His many sporting sketches describe the game of the Southwest, the hunters, and their methods in accurate detail, and the harshest realities of frontier life awaiting settlers find their place in his humorous pieces.

According to Jennette Tandy in *Crackerbox Philosophers in American Humor and Satire*, Thorpe is more precisely a writer of sportsman's stories than a humorist because "wild cats, grizzly bears, turkeys, and opossums are the subjects of his tales. He carefully indicates the habits of each wild beast, and the best methods of coming upon it." Not surprisingly, he once recalled that an invitation to join a fox hunt "was one of the first marked adventures of our Southern life."[8] The interest in hunters and their prey is understandable, given his belief that they embody the uniquely American character. Thorpe was among the first authors to reject the style, tastes, and subjects of the English sporting sketch, and their efforts to Americanize this genre should be viewed in relationship to contemporaneous efforts to create a national literature.

By the early 1840s when Thorpe began writing about field sports in the Old Southwest, two periodicals—the *American Turf Register and Sporting Magazine* (1829–1844) and the *Spirit of the Times* (1831–1861)—were relying on readers across the country to contribute such accounts voluntarily. Many correspondents matter-of-factly told of exaggerated adventures in the tall-tale tradition. For others, however, truthfulness was paramount. They wanted to provide the facts necessary for readers to compare animals and sports from region to region. Yet the best of these sketches are not merely informative, because the authors maintained interest by skillfully handling the narration of the chase. The role of William T. Porter's *Spirit* in the devel-

---

, 8. Jennette Tandy, *Crackerbox Philosophers in American Humor and Satire* (New York, 1925), 77–78; Thorpe, "About the Fox and Fox-Hunters," *Harper's New Monthly Magazine*, XXIII (November, 1861), 750.

opment of American humor is well known, but it is noteworthy that in the first issue he stated a desire to Americanize the sporting sketch:

Have we not in reserve *Fish* stories, *Wild Cat* and *Panther*, and *Bear* stories,—enough in all conscience to set every third person's mouth awry, and contract the muscles of his face, besides making him hold both his sides? . . . We put it fairly to our readers, need we after this go back to the Olympic Games of the Greeks, the Athletæ, the Charioteers, &c.? . . . Is there necessity even to borrow from England the splendor and detail of her far famed Field Sports, in pursuit of *bagged* Foxes, and half domesticated Hares, through a highly cultivated country, upon the backs of the finest horses ever bred?[9]

While Porter did, nevertheless, reprint articles from English magazines, the emphasis in the *Spirit* was clearly on American sports, particularly those of the South and West. One indication of how quickly he succeeded in eliciting excellent sporting articles from unpaid correspondents is his 1846 edition of *Instructions to Young Sportsmen*, the authoritative English manual by Peter Hawker, first published in 1814. Porter deleted the section dealing with English sport and added thirty-eight articles about American field and stream sports by popular writers such as John James Audubon, Henry William Herbert, and Thorpe, as well as other frequent *Spirit* contributors.

Audubon composed sketches in the sporting genre for his five-volume *Ornithological Biography* (1831–1839), which accompanied *Birds of America* (1826–1838). The descriptions of birds, many of which were reprinted in sporting periodicals, include personal hunting experiences along with detailed information about each species' appearance, location, migration patterns, life cycle, diet, flight, and songs. The painter also depicted a variety of rural sports in sixty sketches called "Episodes" or "Delineations of American Scenery and Character," which appeared in the first three volumes, one after every fifth essay on a bird. These are reminiscences of pioneer life between 1808 and 1834, mainly in the Ohio and Mississippi river valleys, where he collected specimens. Unlike many of the local contributors to the *American Turf Register* and the *Spirit* who wrote merely of memorable hunting adventures, Audubon also documented the natural history of the animals and commented on the variety of ways sportsmen chose to pursue them.

The most prolific antebellum sporting writer, Henry William Herbert,

9. William T. Porter, "To Our Friends," *Spirit of the Times,* I (December 10, 1831), 3.

moved to New York from England in 1831, shortly after graduating from Cambridge. Like Audubon, he wrote in detail about animals and hunting methods, completing five books during the 1840s and 1850s. He also published a number of pieces, which might be called sporting novellas or short stories, that simply describe hunters preparing for outings and pursuing game. The seriousness with which Herbert examined sporting subjects, the depth of his knowledge, and his talent as a writer all helped to earn for American sporting literature a respectability it lacked when he first began publishing such sketches in 1839. At that time he used the pseudonym Frank Forester, in order to avoid endangering his literary ambitions as a historical romancer.

Among those who contributed sporting epistles to the *Spirit* were two men remembered today as humorists of the Old Southwest, C. F. M. Noland and Johnson Jones Hooper. In the mid-1830s, Noland began submitting turf reports signed N. of Arkansas and humorous letters signed Pete Whetstone. His reports of sporting events around his hometown of Batesville, Arkansas, often contain brief anecdotes of particular hunts, some of them tall tales rather than factual accounts, and the Pete Whetstone letters show the interest of backwoodsmen in racing, drinking, gambling, fighting, and hunting. In the early 1850s, Hooper, author of *Some Adventures of Captain Simon Suggs* (1845), wrote several sporting accounts under the pseudonym Number Eight for the *Spirit*, accurately describing the game birds of Alabama and including several tall tales about hunting them. He encouraged sportsmen to pay closer attention to the birds they shot and to record their observations precisely. Besides these articles, he published *Dog and Gun; A Few Loose Chapters on Shooting* (1856), a manual for hunters composed not only of articles he had written for the *Southern Military Gazette* in Montgomery and Atlanta but also of excerpts from the works of other sporting writers, such as Herbert. Like Noland and Hooper, Thorpe was both sportsman and humorist, and he treated frontier sports factually as well as fancifully.

Thorpe's response to charges against his "Woodcock Fire Hunting" as a hoax underscores the importance of truthfulness in the sporting sketch genre, a concern that distinguishes it from the tall tale. The piece tells of "a new species of sport, . . . a sport *entirely local* in its character, and confined to a small space of country." Along the Mississippi River for about three hundred miles from its mouth, men were able to shoot woodcock at night by torchlight, much as they went fire-hunting for deer. Usually, the number of birds killed in this manner was large. On his first hunt, Thorpe and a friend killed thirty in two hours, but "with old hunters, the average is always more, and a whole night's labor, if it is a good one, is often rewarded with a round hundred."

Six months after the article's original appearance, when Porter reprinted it in the *American Turf Register*, which he was then editing, he commented that "several persons had unhesitatingly declared their opinion that it was all a *humbug*." He defended Thorpe's account, quoting from Audubon's description of woodcock in the *Ornithological Biography* to prove that this form of hunting was indeed practiced in Louisiana. Nevertheless, almost a year later, a gentleman from Vicksburg, after an unsuccessful attempt at the sport, wrote to the *Spirit* that "shooting woodcock by firelight is all in my *eye*." This public attack on Thorpe's veracity prompted a letter of self-defense that Porter printed in the *Spirit*. He wrote that when "Woodcock Fire Hunting" first appeared, it received little comment in Louisiana because the sport is so common there. The only criticism was by "an advocate for a certain style of cookery, any thing but *anglaise*." Woodcock should not generally be cooked the day after being killed, but "should be hung up by their bills until, they were just on the point of separating their heads from their bodies, from what was stated to be *ripeness*, but I thought to be *decay*." Through a friend who had traveled to New York City, Thorpe learned that Frank Forester had not at first believed the account, but the friend had satisfied his doubts. Not until Thorpe saw Porter's headnote to the *American Turf Register* reprinting did he realize that "my article was more generally misunderstood than I supposed it possible to be." Thus, the letter from the Vicksburg gentleman offered an opportunity for Thorpe to explain that he had written "an unvarnished tale of one of the oldest and most common sports in this section of country." He told again how the sport was practiced and expressed confidence that if his detractor tried once more, he would be so successful he would have "to *measure* the woodcock killed, instead of counting them."[10] Over ten years later, when revising

10. Porter's headnote to Thorpe's "Woodcock Fire Hunting in Louisiana," *American Turf Register*, XII (November, 1841), 633; In the Swamp [pseud.], "Woodcock Shooting by Torchlight," *Spirit of the Times*, XII (September 3, 1842), 319; Thorpe, "A Defence of Woodcock Fire-Hunting," *Spirit of the Times*, XII (October 15, 1842), 385–86. In his next letter to the *Spirit*, "In the Swamp" said that he would try the sport again, since he had not kept behind the torch the first time. However, he was still doubtful ("Sporting Epistle from 'The Swamp,'" *Spirit of the Times*, XII [December 3, 1842], 476).

"Woodcock Fire Hunting" for *Hive*, Thorpe added a new introduction attesting that though many originally did not believe the article, "woodcock fire-hunting is a fact."

Thorpe maintained his interest in writing about sports throughout his life. In the late 1860s he revised the account of the particular hunt in "Woodcock Fire Hunting" and included it in a *Harper's* article entitled "The Woodcock." Of the more than thirty pieces he published in that magazine between the early 1850s and the early 1870s, almost half describe animals or discuss field sports. Although most are much longer than the sporting articles he contributed to the *Spirit*, they contain the same kinds of information about natural history and hunting practices.

Because of his reputation as a sporting writer, Thorpe was selected in 1843 by the proprietors of the New Orleans *Tropic* to co-edit the short-lived *Southern Sportsman* along with Robert L. Brenham. The first issue, eight pages in length, appeared on March 18. Modeled on the *Spirit*, this New Orleans weekly contained original sporting sketches and reports from jockey clubs, in addition to comments on books, paintings, and theatrical productions. Noland of Arkansas and local sporting writers and humorists contributed to its pages. While southern editors responded enthusiastically, Porter considered it a dangerous competitor that could draw both correspondents and subscribers away from his own paper, not only because of its location in the region where he found most of his support, but also because it sold for five dollars a year, half the subscription price of the *Spirit*. In retaliation against this threat, on March 21 he launched another sporting weekly, the *American Sporting Chronicle*, which sold for only two dollars. Regular columns printed information about the turf and field sports, angling, agriculture, and the theater, with most of the items being reprinted from that week's *Spirit*. Because the new paper was just four pages, it carried few sporting sketches, and those that did appear were drawn from the twelve-page *Spirit*. "The Ring," the only new department, was an obvious attempt to create an audience for the paper, because accounts of that sport, viewed as disreputable by genteel society, were not carried regularly in the American press. Despite Porter's contribution to the growth of sports and the development of sporting literature in the nation, he did not wish to go so far as to encourage the establishment of a regional sporting press which might detract from the preeminence of his own *Spirit*. While the *American Sporting Chronicle* continued until January, 1844, the *Southern Sports-*

14

man suspended publication after its twelfth number, on June 5. Thorpe had decided to become co-editor of the *Concordia Intelligencer* in Vidalia, Louisiana, and the loss of him, combined with the astute business sense most probably of John Richards, proprietor of the *Spirit* at that time, meant the failure of the New Orleans paper. Four months later, in October, the owners announced that they would not resume publication as originally planned.[11] Ironically, Thorpe was to end his editing career working on his first competitor, the *Spirit*. In February, 1859, over two years after Porter left the paper and six months following his death, Thorpe became part owner and editor. He did not, however, return to writing sporting sketches for its pages. In March, 1861, he sold his interest, just three months before the last issue of the *Spirit* appeared.

Another indication of Thorpe's interest in sporting literature is his first book, *Mysteries of the Backwoods*, which may properly be called a sporting book. Contemporary readers were aware, as the *Southern Quarterly Review* stated, that its "descriptions of South-western scenery, and of the hunter [*sic*] life and character, possess peculiar attractions, and will be particularly acceptable to all lovers of field sports."[12] Despite the inclusion of this collection in Carey and Hart's Library of Humorous American Works, its contents are not primarily comic. "A vein of humor runs through" it, according to the *Southern Quarterly Review*, but "A Piano in Arkansas" is the only strictly humorous piece. That Thorpe chose not to reprint similar ones, such as "The Big Bear of Arkansas," "My First Dinner in New Orleans," "The Louisiana Law of Cock-Fighting," or "The Little Steamboats of the Mississippi," indicates that the volume, taken on its own terms, does not represent him as a humorist. Instead of reprinting comic sketches, he wrote five dealing with animals and sporting adventures on the southwestern frontier, reworked "Wild Turkey Shooting" into a new piece, and reprinted three

11. When Rickels wrote *Thomas Bangs Thorpe*, he was unaware of the complete file of the *Southern Sportsman* at the Boston Public Library. These are apparently the only extant copies. Francis Brinley's *Life of William T. Porter* (New York, 1860) contains no reference to the *American Sporting Chronicle*. In *William T. Porter and the "Spirit of the Times"* (Baton Rouge, 1957), Norris W. Yates merely states in one sentence that in 1843, Porter was editing this "weekly of the turf" in addition to the *Spirit* and the *American Turf Register*. He offers no comment on the publication history or the content of the *American Sporting Chronicle*. Apparently, the only extant copies of it are in the John Hay Library at Brown University. The file is incomplete and contains only the issues for March 21 through October 10, 1843, and pages three and four of the October 24, 1843, issue. Porter probably continued to print the *American Sporting Chronicle* until mid-January, 1844, when advertisements for it stopped appearing in the *Spirit*. For a more detailed discussion of these papers, see David C. Estes, "The Rival Sporting Weeklies of William T. Porter and Thomas Bangs Thorpe," *American Journalism*, II (1985), 135–43.

12. "Critical Notices," *Southern Quarterly Review*, IX (April, 1846), 528.

articles about hunting—"A Grizzly Bear Hunt," "The American Wild
Cat," and "Tom Owen, the Bee-Hunter." Also among the contents,
"The Disgraced Scalp Lock" is about the skilled marksman Mike Fink,
"The Water Craft of the Back Woods" explains how Indians construct
different kinds of boats, two pieces describe the Mississippi River, and
two are sentimental stories. References to the wild animals of the
Southwest and to shooting and hunting appear in many of the pieces
that are not sporting sketches. Taken as a whole, the collection provides a picture of the region and the character of its inhabitants, a
purpose the subtitle makes clear: *Sketches of the Southwest: Including
Character, Scenery, and Rural Sports*. This sporting book is unique for
the time because it combines an analysis of the character of the frontiersman, who lives removed from the influence of urban civilization,
with descriptions of the game he pursues.

A comparison of *Mysteries* with William Elliott's *Carolina Sports by
Land and Water*, also published in 1846, reveals even more clearly the
distinctiveness of Thorpe's work. The two men present southern sports
from widely different perspectives. Elliott served in the United States
House of Representatives and in both houses of the South Carolina
state legislature before resigning from the state senate in 1832 because
of his unpopular opposition to nullification policies. Under the pseu-
donyms Piscator and Venator, he contributed sporting articles to the
American Turf Register, beginning with its second number in 1829, as
well as to Charleston's newspapers and its *Southern Literary Journal*.
His narrative perspective is that of the southern aristocrat, and the
slave-owning planter's social position is inseparable from the adventures he relates. Classical allusions and Latin phrases appear, suggesting the gentleman's education that both Elliott and his audience had
received. A series of four sketches recounts the adventures of hunting
parties at his plantation Chee-Ha, near Beaufort. Able to hunt wild
animals on his own land, he is rather contemptuous of city sportsmen
in the North who make troublesome preparations for a week's sport to
"bag one brace of grouse, or enjoy a *glorious snap* at some straggling
deer, that escapes, *of course*."[13] The gentleman hunter's dealings with
his slaves receive some attention, as do the class differences among
whites. Elliott and his companions were clearly gentlemen, not backwoodsmen. "The Fire Hunter" describes the disreputable hunting
methods of the lower class. It tells of an overseer who feels he is being

13. William Elliott, *Carolina Sports by Land and Water* (Charleston, S.C., 1846), 107.

treated as one of the slaves, since he is forbidden to shoot deer on Elliott's plantation. Not accepting the master's claims of ownership of the wild animals on his land, the overseer shoots them secretly at night, a crime Elliott strongly argued against both because it abused his own property rights and also because he desired a stringent method of game conservation. Although Thorpe hunted with such wealthy planters—as his "First Hunting Trip of the Steamer 'Nimrod,' of 'Barrow Settlement,' Louisiana" makes clear—the narrator of *Mysteries* takes a democratic perspective quite unlike Elliott's, by praising the backwoods hunter as representative American.

Elliott's style is characterized, as he himself noted, by its *"want of repose"*: *"Celerity of movement* is the play,—whether in the field or in the narrative!" Thus the activity of the chase predominates in his sketches. While Thorpe skillfully depicted similar scenes, adventure was not his single most important goal. He sought to give readers "personally unacquainted with the scenery of the Southwest, some idea of the country, of its surface, and vegetation," as the preface of *Mysteries* states.[14] This intention demonstrates his indebtedness not only to sporting literature but also to popular travel accounts. No other sporting book of the time so consciously combines these two literary genres.[15] Only the "Episodes" in Audubon's *Ornithological Biography* may be compared to it. Influenced by both traditions, then, Thorpe stressed the relationships between the southwestern frontier, its sports, and the character of its inhabitants, in a sporting book that could appeal even to readers who were not themselves sportsmen.

Thorpe's reputation as one of the foremost humorists of the Southwestern frontier rests almost solely on "The Big Bear of Arkansas," a piece that shows his interest in sporting subjects and backwoods hunters. Porter acknowledged its preeminence by naming his first humorous anthology after it, and in this century, too, critics have generally agreed that it is the single best sketch by a writer from what Bernard DeVoto termed the Big Bear school of literature.[16]

Yet Thorpe wrote other humorous pieces that do not deal with sport-

14. *Ibid.*, 100; Thorpe, *Mysteries*, 8.
15. Worthy of note here is Friedrich Gerstäcker's *Streif- und Jagdzüge durch die Vereinigten Staaten Nordamerikas* (1844), which recounts his travels in the Southwest between 1837 and 1843. Gerstäcker, a hunter, spent much time in Arkansas and along the Mississippi River. His book, translated in 1854 as *Wild Sports in the Far West*, is a travel book emphasizing sporting adventures in the same region about which Thorpe wrote.
16. Bernard DeVoto, "Frontier America," *Saturday Review of Literature*, V (June 1, 1929), 1067.

ing subjects, several of them not even set on the frontier. "Cook-a-Doo-Dle-Doo," one of his first publications in the *Spirit*, is an amusing account of the proud, domineering barnyard rooster at his grandparents' farm in New York State, where he spent summers as a child. Irving's influence is unmistakable in "Old Dutch Houses and Their Associations," Thorpe's first piece in the *Knickerbocker*, which describes the old buildings and the typical Dutch customs of the inhabitants. "Bessie Black: or, the Undertaker's Courtship," written after the Civil War, tells of the incongruities at the marriage of a dressmaker to an undertaker in New York City. The bride wears a black gown, the two leave the church in a hearse, and they host a wedding feast in a storeroom using coffins as banquet tables.[17]

Thorpe occasionally set such domestic humor on the frontier, as his "A Piano in Arkansas" shows. Another sketch that focuses on the unfamiliarity of the backwoods settlers with the arts is "The Case of Lady Macbeth Medically Considered." The several humorous touches in it do not disguise Thorpe's interest in writing drama criticism, something he did occasionally for papers he edited. The narrator visits a physician on an isolated bayou who has "an idolatrous love for Shakespeare," in his study they talk at length about the great dramatist, and then he attends the doctor's lecture at the county medical society. Half of the sketch is the lecturer's analysis of *Macbeth*, which gives particular attention to Lady Macbeth's doctor. The audience of about fifteen, most of whom are themselves doctors, listen with gravity and show no surprise at the choice of subject. The humor arises at the end, from the sober remark of the only person who comments to the speaker: "I suppose Mrs. Macbeth lived up in the Scotch settlement, on Alligator Ridge, though I never heard her name before."[18]

The articles Thorpe wrote for *Harper's*, while primarily descriptive, frequently display his love of laughter. For example, "Remembrances of the Mississippi" contains many humorous anecdotes about people associated with river traffic and includes examples of the comic boasts with which the legendary keelboatmen goaded one another to fight. "About the Fox and Fox-Hunters" includes a brief sketch with its own title, "Story of the Imperturbable Witness." Similar in humorous technique to the popular "Cousin Sally Dilliard" by Hamilton C. Jones, it is

17. Thorpe, "Cook-a-Doo-Dle-Doo," *Spirit of the Times*, XI (July 24, 1841), 247; Thorpe, "Old Dutch Houses and Their Associations," 150–55; Thorpe, "Bessie Black: or, the Undertaker's Courtship," *Appleton's Journal*, I (August 7, 1869), 580–84.

18. Thorpe, "The Case of Lady Macbeth Medically Considered, A Western Sketch," Harper's *New Monthly Magazine*, VIII (February, 1854), 391–98.

about a witness with a long, rambling story to tell. He exasperates the patience of the hungry court by starting from the beginning each time the lawyer interrupts to urge him to be more concise.[19] Despite the humor in pieces such as these, Thorpe's novel, *The Master's House*, surprisingly lacks a humorous subplot or even a humorous character. Only a few comic descriptions relieve the sentimentality of this account of a young northern-educated plantation owner who moves to Louisiana from North Carolina and must finally defend his abolitionist principles in a duel. Readers familiar with Thorpe's career were probably surprised that he omitted the comic aspects of southern life that he so greatly appreciated.

Thorpe's reputation as a humorist in his own day rested not only on his publications but also on his love of punning. The frequency of wordplay in "Letters from the Far West" is probably an indication of how he entertained companions in person. One of many funny stories about him in local papers and in the *Spirit* tells how he was once left speechless, unable to think of a pun. His host in the East in 1845 wrote to the *Spirit* that though "I have done my best to keep him out of the way of the Philadelphia punsters," one evening someone interrupted their conversation with such an audacious pun that Thorpe could not think of a reply. When the man went on to top himself, "'The Hunter' immediately fainted."[20]

Probably the most unusual humorous sketch by Thorpe is "A Visit to 'Curnel Pardon Jones,'" which the *Spirit* did not reprint from the New Orleans *Picayune*. Not only does Thorpe write about a character popularized by another humorist, he also atypically focuses on politics and contemporary affairs. Pardon Jones was the fictitious correspondent of the *Picayune* created by Christopher M. Haile, a native of Rhode Island who settled in Louisiana at about the same time as did Thorpe. In December, 1840, Haile started publishing the *Planter's Gazette* in Plaquemine[21] and in the same month began sending the *Picayune* locally popular dialect letters in which Jones tells about his recent arrival in Louisiana from Massachusetts and his plans to set up a school as soon as Jerushy joins him and they are married. Three

19. "Remembrances of the Mississippi," *Harper's New Monthly Magazine*, XII (December, 1855), 25–41; "About the Fox and Fox-Hunters," *Harper's New Monthly Magazine*, XXIII (November, 1861), 756–58.

20. Y. T. [pseud.], "From a Philadelphia Cricketer," *Spirit of the Times*, XV (August 9, 1845), 279. Another reference to Thorpe's interest in punning and its popularity among Philadelphians is in Ginsing-and-so-on [pseud.], "Familiar Epistle from Philadelphia," *Spirit of the Times*, XV (December 6, 1845), 488.

21. "The Planter's Gazette," Baton Rouge *Gazette*, December 26, 1840.

letters also comment on events in the area and inform readers about activities in his old hometown, often satirizing politicians and their electioneering practices. By November, 1842, when Thorpe's article about Jones appeared, the *Picayune* had carried nearly forty of these humorous letters.

For two years Jones had been asserting that he would be a candidate for the first congressional seat to become vacant. When a fourth seat was granted the state, to be filled in the 1843 election, Haile decided to have Jones campaign in earnest. Thorpe's article was the first official notice of his candidacy. It opens with praise for his patriotic defense of America in the disputes with Great Britain over the boundary between Maine and Canada and also over the slave ship *Creole*, which British officials welcomed in Nassau in October, 1841, after the American slaves successfully mutinied. The article records that when Thorpe attracted a great deal of attention on the riverboat while on his way to visit Jones, one man had the impudence to ask if Pardon were related to Shocco Jones, a nationally known playboy and practical joker of the day. At the end of his discussion with the candidate about current issues, Thorpe's offhand comment to Captain Nathan Potter, one of Jones's friends from Massachusetts, about the Santa Fe expedition immediately raises the anger of Jones. He desires to hold office, he claims, in order to make certain that the government will punish Mexico for capturing the members of that expedition organized by the president of Texas in 1841 to open trade with Santa Fe, then under Mexican control. George Wilkins Kendall, founder of the *Picayune*, was among those captured and imprisoned in Mexico City for months. In a rage, Jones vents his anger over the current situation in Rhode Island, where Thomas Dorr had threatened military rebellion. Dorr claimed the governorship in 1842, under a People's Constitution that extended suffrage to those not owning land, but it had not received the approval necessary to become binding. That Thorpe wrote this article to assist another local humorist in his schemes is one indication of his good rapport with fellow editors and writers. Indeed, the only Pardon Jones letter to appear originally in a paper other than the *Picayune* is the one in the *Southern Sportsman* congratulating Thorpe on his new title of colonel and recounting a tall tale about shooting woodpeckers.[22]

22. "Letter from Curnel Pardon Jones," New Orleans *Southern Sportsman*, May 29, 1843. Both Garner and Rickels have argued that Thorpe received the title "Colonel" during the Mexican War. Yet Thorpe's report of the spring agricultural fair in Washington, Mississippi, indicates a source that

Thorpe's only extended humorous production is "Letters from the Far West," a series that burlesques sporting epistles of the sort Porter solicited for the *Spirit*. Twelve letters appeared at irregular intervals between August, 1843, and February, 1844, in the *Concordia Intelligencer*, from which Porter eagerly reprinted them for a national audience. The immediate object of satire is Matthew C. Field, an assistant editor of the *Picayune*, who traveled as a special guest on Sir William Stewart's expedition along the Oregon Trail to the Wind River Mountains in 1843.[23] Stewart, a Scottish sportsman who had made four trips to the region in the 1830s, returned to America as a nobleman after his brother's death left him with a fortune vast enough to finance an elaborate tour solely for the purpose of hunting. John James Audubon, who traveled to the Far West that same summer, for a while considered joining Stewart. Thorpe also declined an invitation to join the group, which numbered over fifty when it left St. Louis in May.[24] By the time the party returned in late October, the *Picayune* had published eight letters by Field, and he had plans for a series entitled "Prairie and Mountain Life." In less than two months he wrote about twenty sketches, and when he died suddenly in November, 1844, thirty-eight had appeared in the *Picayune* and seven in the St. Louis *Reveille*.

Thorpe may have planned to spoof the adventures of Stewart's party even before they set out. In the *Southern Sportsman* of March 27, 1843, the editors wrote that a person in the group "has promised us letters by every opportunity of sending them . . . and also we are to have a *Journal of the Expedition* placed in our hands for publication." Whether this comment was to prepare readers for a hoax remains uncertain, since nothing followed. A great influence on the "Letters from the Far West" series was probably Thorpe's trip to the western Louisiana prairies sometime before the first of August. In reporting his activities, the *Picayune* commented: "We may shortly look for rich returns, derived from his wanderings, in the columns of his clever

---

involved no military service: "Among the honors we received, was the title of 'Colonel,' from the Adams County Agricultural Society" (New Orleans *Southern Sportsman*, May 8, 1843). Thus, it is not surprising that Garner was unable to find either a service record or a pension claim.

23. For information on Stewart's grand hunting trip, see the introduction to Matthew C. Field, *Prairie and Mountain Sketches*, ed. John Francis McDermott and Kate L. Gregg (Norman, Okla., 1957). For critical comments on "Letters from the Far West" see Leland H. Cox, Jr., "T. B. Thorpe's Far West Letters," in James L. W. West III (ed.), *Gyascutus: Studies in Antebellum Southern Humorous and Sporting Writing* (Atlantic Highlands, N.J., 1978), 115–20; John Francis McDermott, "T. B. Thorpe's Burlesque of Far West Sporting Travel," *American Quarterly*, X (Summer, 1958), 175–80; and Rickels, *Thomas Bangs Thorpe*, 77–86.

24. Rickels, *Thomas Bangs Thorpe*, 78.

21

paper.—Eschew politics and give us something in the style of 'the Big Bar of Arkansas.'"[25] When the first letter signed P. O. F.—initials Thorpe never explained—appeared in the *Intelligencer* on August 5, part of the humor was at the expense of the *Picayune*'s own Field, who was termed "the '*sowl*' of the whole party" because of his good humor and practical jokes. Even though Thorpe poked fun at Field and Stewart throughout the letters, he was laughing at all who naïvely traveled the inhospitable frontier for the pleasure of sport. At the same time, he was joking along with the frontiersmen about the surprising ways in which the region threatened their control over their own lives.

Apparently, the editors of the *Picayune* did not immediately recognize the hoax. The postscript to the second letter, which appeared on August 12, states that "Sir William Stuart has put us all under 'martial law,' and some of the 'young uns' make wry faces at it." In the same issue, the editors of the *Intelligencer* referred to reports in the St. Louis *Gazette* of his "overbearing conduct" that some found "insupportable." A few days prior to the publication of these items in Thorpe's paper, the *Picayune* defended Stewart: "We put no faith whatever . . . in the story going the rounds of the papers of the dissensions in the sporting expedition to the West." They must, then, have been puzzled by P. O. F.'s comments on this subject, for they took his remarks at face value. Quoting his statement about Stewart's domineering behavior, they treated the information as factual, even though they still did not want to believe it: "A letter appears in the Concordia Intelligencer from some gentleman in Sir Wm. Stewart's party. It is no later than we have received from our own correspondent, but we find the following item of news in it."[26] According to the St. Louis *Ariel*, the *Picayune* was not the only paper to fall prey to the hoax, because "the Sun and other eastern papers publish as authentic the statement of its fictitious correspondent, that Sir William Drummond Stewart had placed his party under martial law."[27]

Not for another two months did the *Picayune* editors comment on

25. New Orleans *Daily Picayune*, August 2, 1843.

26. New Orleans *Daily Picayune*, August 8 and 16, 1843.

27. The *Intelligencer* reprinted this statement on September 23, 1843. I have been unable to locate a reference to Stewart's expedition in the Baltimore *Sun*, which might be the paper to which the editor of the *Ariel* was referring. The editors of the *Intelligencer* defended Stewart against the attacks appearing in the newspapers: "Sir William is a gentleman of the most exalted honor—loves good order and knows how to maintain it. We have no doubt that he has been obliged to exert his authority, to curb many things that would transpire in the land, where laws have not yet reached, and it is wrong to blame him if persons displeased with his conduct should leave his party. . . . We admire Sir William for his fondness of sport, and the manly manner in which he pursues it" (*Concordia Intelligencer* [Vidalia, La.], November 18, 1843).

Thorpe's series. Shortly before the seventh letter appeared, they acknowledged that "the literary recollections of the editor of the Concordia Intelligencer are very tenacious—very. What's the latest from the Stewart expedition and the Far-West?" Probably because at the appearance of each letter they were being heckled anew for having been taken in, they rather self-righteously accused Porter of reprinting the letters in the *Spirit* without seeing the joke. But Porter was aware of what had happened in New Orleans and quickly reprinted the charge against him with an accusation of his own:

> "*Sold*."—Somebody has been quizzing the editors of the "Picayune."
> Hear them:—
> Our friend T. B. T., of the "Concordia Intelligencer," gets up his letters
> from the Far West very well, even for a backwoodsman. At the North they
> do not appear to take the joke. "The Spirit" has been "done brown" by
> him. They are cut by a *saw*, of which T. B. T. possesses the exclusive
> patent.
> So they don't take the joke at the North! Oh no! We republish another
> of the letters to-day, from the "Intelligencer," and hope "the Pic." will be
> able to publish some half as clever from its exclusive correspondent. No
> wonder they are horribly exasperated, in "the Pic." office, that people at
> the North will not "take the joke" of reading Mat. Field's dull letters, when
> Thorpe's are to be had at the same price. We recollect no Northern editor
> who has been "sold" so cheap![28]

After returning to New Orleans, Field came to his own defense by satirizing Thorpe. In one of the "Prairie and Mountain Life" sketches, he pretended that the *Intelligencer*'s correspondent was traveling with the party. The sketch begins with an exaggerated picture of Thorpe's unattractive appearance and nicknames him Little Woeful because of his "awful face":

> He looked like an animated embodiment, in semi-human form, of a thick
> fog on the Mississippi, at half-past three in the morning, to a man who
> has just lost his last dollar at poker. He claimed to be Irish, but we all
> suspected he was a Dutchman. He was about four feet four in height,
> with a head like the decapitated upper part of a brass andiron, and he
> wore a hat that might have belonged once to Walter Scott; this he made
> tight upon his little odd-looking caput by turning half of the rim inside,
> and stuffing into it, also, a number of old newspapers. His eyes, which
> he concealed, however, in green goggles, were like two faded cherries,
> and his nose! . . . He was decidedly brain-stricken, but quite amiable and
> harmless in his madness. We could never ascertain whether his eye-

---

28. New Orleans *Daily Picayune*, October 13, 1843; Porter, "Sold," *Spirit of the Times*, XIII (November 4, 1843), 426. The charges against Porter appeared in the *Daily Picayune*, October 19, 1843.

brows were cut off or driven in; but no such universally considered necessary portion of the human face divine appeared upon his solemn frontispiece, and Crockett [the nickname of a member of the expedition] declared they must have been scared away by the everlasting gaping upward of his cavernous nostrils. The sight of this nose produced dreadful notions of suicide in the mind such as are awakened sometimes during a long continuance of drizzly weather.[29]

Field continues that though Little Woeful could "say things that would set the company roaring with laughter," he never laughed at his own jokes. His wit could at times have a "sledge-hammer effect," and the men "were all in great terror as to what he might say about us in his letters." However, "beneath all the madness and gloom of his character" was a sympathy for "every thing in life that ever suffered pain; and his favorite amusement seemed to be to pop himself down in the grass, by the head of a dying buffalo, and mournfully soliloquise upon its fate." Field concludes the sketch with an incident poking fun at Little Woeful for being easily frightened. One night, when he had been particularly scared by the bear stories told around the campfire, he was awakened by a drunken member of the party who tumbled down the hill into his shanty. Mistaking the man for a bear, he "put his bandy legs round a tree and ascended, screaming *'bear! bear!'* in blood-freezing tones of terror." Although the men figured out what happened, they let Little Woeful continue to think that "he was the victim of nightmare and a phantom bear!" Thorpe did not let this attack pass unnoticed. With good humor, in the eleventh letter, P. O. F. recalls times when Mat was as easily frightened as was Little Woeful, which he calls himself in that letter.

The "Letters from the Far West" series similarly inspired other New Orleans humorists to spoof the adventures of the expedition, creating the same sort of chain reaction that occurred frequently among correspondents to the *Spirit.* An article entitled "Lost or Stolen," in the December 7 *Tropic,* tells about a horse race with the Indians at the end of which the savages rode off on Stewart's horses. The headnote explains that the sketch was found in a rain puddle and was thought to belong to Field, except the writing was too neat. The editors of the *Picayune* responded the next day with the warning: "We will look out how we furnish you with any more foundation for story telling. The

29. Matthew C. Field, "Prairie and Mountain Life," New Orleans *Daily Picayune*, December 2, 1843. Thorpe printed the first half of this sketch in the *Intelligencer*, December 23, 1843. The entire piece is included in Field, *Prairie and Mountain Sketches*, 220–24.

credit of the expedient belongs to Thorpe, who originally conceived the notion, and made a good thing of it, but we shall not countenance a counterfeit so near home." Yet just a few days later, on December 10, their paper carried a humorous poem by Joseph Field, Mat's brother, entitled "That 'Expedition,'" about how the Flathead tribe captured Thorpe and several others. Thorpe supposedly talked "Their language like a *native*, he / Was raised on tomahawks!" When "things was gettin' *scalpy*," he suggested:

> We should pull off our hats,
> Have all our heads just squeezed at once,
> And "settle" 'mong the *Flats*.

The Indians agreed to this, and Thorpe's

> "letters" prove the sing'lar twist
> They've given to his brains;
> Because, whate'er he *was*, he's now
> A most weracious youth!
> The Flatheads have (a miracle)
> *Squeezed* out of him the truth!

Because this poem pokes fun at the editor of the *Tropic* as well, the next day he playfully reprinted in his paper the warning the *Picayune* had given him not to appropriate Thorpe's successful hoax. Humorous countercharges such as these inspired by the "Letters from the Far West" were a characteristic feature of the local reception of antebellum humor. The newspapers carrying the sketches provided the opportunity for readers to respond in print and thus, as is clear in this case, to influence the content of pieces that followed. Thorpe's decision not to collect any of these letters in his books might have come, at least in part, from a recognition that, while still understandable, they would be less entertaining if removed from the local journalistic context in which readers watched the unfolding contest as humorists matched wits against one another.

Despite the inconsistent characterization of the narrator P. O. F. in the letters, he is one of Thorpe's most important humorous hunters, along with Jim Doggett in "The Big Bear of Arkansas" and Bob Herring in "The Devil's Summer Retreat, in Arkansaw." These men are the antithesis of the hunters presented in Thorpe's sporting sketches because they either fail in the pursuit of game or else kill the game after repeated attempts, raising questions about their reputations. Yet by means of comic boasts and yarns, Doggett and Herring, masters of frontier tall talk, are able to redeem themselves from a lack of verifiable physical skill and to make listeners laugh with them at the uncontrollable mystery of the natural world. P. O. F., on the other hand, remains linguistically powerless, even though he travels as a newspaper correspondent. He can neither adapt to the frontier nor master the language of those who live there. Thus, he becomes the butt of practical jokes and, ironically, the helpless prey in the chase.

P. O. F.'s predicament depicts the frontiersman's nightmare of ultimate impotence in the face of nature's malevolence, a vision absent from Thorpe's sporting sketches. Those works embody the conventional American myth of successful self-reliance on the frontier. His humorous pieces clearly subvert such confidence in the ability of humans to subdue the natural world. "It is told in two sentences—a bar is started, and he is killed," brags Doggett of his prowess. "The thing is somewhat monotonous." However, by the end of his tall tale about the Big Bar, he humbly acknowledges, "I never liked the way I hunted him, *and missed him*. There is something curious about it, I could never understand." In Thorpe's humorous sketches he likewise pondered those dark mysteries of nature that chasten human pride and laughed along with frontier settlers at their surprising survival in such an environment.

BIBLIOGRAPHY AND PUBLISHING HISTORY

Thorpe's career as a writer spanned four decades, beginning in 1839 with the publication of "Tom Owen, the Bee-Hunter" in the *Spirit*. Eager to make a living by his pen after his immediate popularity, he soon began to contribute articles to the *Knickerbocker Magazine*. From 1843 to 1847, he edited six newspapers in Louisiana, and he went on to write six books during the late 1840s and early 1850s: two collections of his southwestern sketches, two histories of the Mexican War, a campaign biography of Zachary Taylor, and a novel in the plantation genre. From his return to New York City in 1854 until his death in 1878, he wrote for periodicals on such diverse topics as the fine arts, natural history, and picturesque scenes, at times making use of his experiences on the nation's southwestern frontier in Louisiana. The bibliography in Milton Rickels' critical biography of Thorpe lists over 150 articles and miscellaneous items from these national periodicals: *Appleton's Journal, Baldwin's Monthly, Forest and Stream, Godey's Lady's Book, Graham's Magazine, Harper's New Monthly Magazine*, the *Knickerbocker Magazine*, the London *New Sporting Magazine*, and the *Spirit of the Times*.[1] For the most part these publications are literary hackwork, yet a careful sifting of those dating from the 1840s in particular is important in assessing Thorpe's place in the history of American literature.

Since the time Rickels completed his research, more issues of Thorpe's Louisiana newspapers have come to light. All twelve issues of the *Southern Sportsman*, none of which Rickels read, are now available, and seventeen issues of the *Commercial Times* from the period of Thorpe's editorship are extant, providing a view of his work on the

---

1. Milton Rickels, *Thomas Bangs Thorpe: Humorist of the Old Southwest* (Baton Rouge, 1962), 257–67. This bibliography first appeared in *American Literature*, XXIX (May, 1957), 171–79. However, the second printing includes one additional listing, "A Squatter's Wife" in *Graham's Magazine*. Rickels determined that Thorpe did not write *A Voice to America*, and Richard Walser earlier argued that the novel *Lynde Weiss* had been incorrectly attributed to Thorpe ("The Mysterious Case of George Higby Throop, 1818–1896; Or, The Search for the Author of the Novels *Nag's Head, Bertie*, and *Lynde Weiss*," *North Carolina Review*, XXXIII [January, 1956], 12–44).

paper that Rickels did not have.[2] Also, only scattered issues of the *Concordia Intelligencer* remain missing.[3] Because of these additional resources, determining the first appearance and the publication history of most of Thorpe's pieces written in the 1840s is now possible. The *Louisiana Conservator* is the only paper Thorpe edited of which no known copies exist. All except one issue of the *Daily Tropic* prior to July, 1843, and copies of the *Daily National* from June through September 9, 1847, are also apparently lost.[4]

The bibliography compiled by Virginia Herron as part of her master's thesis must also be taken into account in revising Rickels' findings. "Thomas Bangs Thorpe and the *Spirit of the Times*: A Study of Southwestern Frontier Life, 1840–1850" lists both sketches and brief anecdotes, but examines only this single periodical.[5] Although she identified several items Rickels overlooked, Herron frequently cast her net too wide for her judgments to stand without scrutiny. The following discussion examines the dubious entries in each of the bibliographies and offers arguments for newly discovered items, including four humorous pieces, found in previously unavailable issues of newspapers, that would tempt any bibliographer to classify them among Thorpe's works.

The major source of error in previous bibliographies was the following of Porter's lead in attributing unsigned and pseudonymous items in the *Intelligencer* to Thorpe. Because his co-editor during those two productive years in Vidalia was Robert Patterson, himself a humorist with a modest reputation, distinguishing between the works of the two is essential. Patterson, a native of Natchez, had been editing the *Intelligencer* since shortly after C. S. Smith founded it on September 4,

2. Copies of the New Orleans *Commercial Times* are available for November 1, December 13, 24, 1845; and January 3, 10, 14, 17, 21, 24, February 7, 11, 18, March 4, 7, 11, 14, 28, 1846. Only the first of these is a copy of the daily paper; the others are all semiweekly issues.

3. Thorpe began co-editing the *Concordia Intelligencer* in mid-June, 1843, and formally ended his association with the Vidalia, Louisiana, paper on June 20, 1845. Apparently, no copies of it are extant for June and July, 1843; April 27, July 12, 19, 26, December 28, 1844; and January 18, April 26, May 10, 1845.

4. Although Thorpe did not become an editor of the New Orleans *Daily Tropic* until 1846, he submitted at least two humorous sketches to that paper during the first months of 1843. See discussion of "My First Dinner in New Orleans" and "The Louisiana Law of Cock-Fighting" later in this chapter. Rickels has suggested that Thorpe "formed a minor connection" with the New Orleans *Tropic* in early 1843 (Rickels, *Thomas Bangs Thorpe*, 72). An October 4, 1842, issue of the *Tropic* at the Library of Congress bears no indication that Thorpe had already begun such an association with the paper at that time. The Library of Congress also has the first two pages of the New Orleans *Weekly Tropic* for January 28, 1843, but they contain nothing attributable to Thorpe.

5. Virginia Herron, "Thomas Bangs Thorpe and the *Spirit of the Times*: A Study of Southwestern Frontier Life, 1840–1850" (M.A. thesis, Alabama Polytechnic Institute, 1953).

1841.[6] Probably his best-known humorous sketch is "Old Singletire, the Man That Was Not Annexed," which Porter included in his *A Quarter Race in Kentucky* anthology. It tells of a desperado, wanted in both the United States and in the nation of Texas, who cleverly avoids prosecution by building his cabin on the boundary line between the two countries. In the *Spirit*, Porter printed two humorous pieces signed Concordia, which are probably by Patterson. "Musketo Bait" opens with a long section praising the American people, particularly the backwoodsmen of the South and the West, and concludes with humorous incidents occurring during a session of the district court in Louisiana. "A New Town in Arkansas" satirizes the crude backwoodsmen who brag of their glorious city of Belleair, even though it has only one house and is still part of a swamp.[7] While Patterson's reputation was not as great as Thorpe's, he was well known because of trips to all sections of Louisiana to attract advertisers and subscribers. These rambles resulted in frequent descriptions of scenes and local customs in the *Intelligencer*. Three months after Thorpe resigned as co-editor, Patterson published this notice:

> For the last two years great injustice has been done the INTELLIGENCER *and its present Editor*, by crediting numerous articles from its columns to *other than the author of them*—a fact arising, we presume, from the circumstance that one of the Editors may have been more generally known to the contemporaries abroad, who so frequently and kindly noticed the Intelligencer. The thing may have been done from kindly motives, yet it was manifestly unjust to the paper, and *more particularly to the author of the articles referred to*.[8]

Rickels clearly disregarded Patterson in the case of "Louisiana Boys and Bear Hunting." He claimed the anecdote for Thorpe, though Porter noted merely that it came from the *Intelligencer*.[9] Since Thorpe was editing the *Southern Sportsman* when the piece appeared in the *Spirit*,

6. New Orleans *Daily Tropic*, April 28, 1846. Thorpe was an editor of the New Orleans *Tropic* at this time and might have written the paragraph announcing the death of his former associate. The earliest extant issue of the *Concordia Intelligencer* to carry Patterson's name as editor is February 11, 1843.

7. "Musketo Bait," *Spirit of the Times*, XIV (August 10, 1844), 279, and *Concordia Intelligencer* (Vidalia, La.), September 7, 1844; "A New Town in Arkansas," *Spirit of the Times*, XIV (March 9, 1844), 13–14, and *Concordia Intelligencer* (Vidalia, La.), April 6, 1844. John Q. Anderson identifies these pieces as Patterson's, in *With the Bark On: Popular Humor of the Old South* (Nashville, 1967), 47.

8. Robert Patterson, "Sharp Practice and Bad Practice," *Concordia Intelligencer* (Vidalia, La.), September 20, 1845.

9. "Louisiana Boys and Bear Hunting," *Spirit of the Times*, XIII (April 15, 1843), 73. Rickels mistitled the piece "Louisiana Bears and Bear Hunting" in his bibliography.

and did not join the *Intelligencer* until two months later, the item should not remain in the bibliography.

Porter's introduction to "A Tall Hunt—Crack Shot—Big Meat" states Thorpe related this anecdote, and on that authority Rickels listed it in the bibliography. However, it appeared anonymously in the *Intelligencer*. In length and style it resembles Patterson's "Southern Sport," which opens with a description of an old raftsman he met on one of his rambles across Louisiana and then, in the raftsman's dialect, relates an alligator hunt.[10] Elated at his success, the hunter exclaims, "Yiock! yiock!—hurray for old Virginny." The same distinctive exclamation appears at the end of "Louisiana Boys," when the slave says, "Yiock!—yock! yock!" laughing at his master's unfortunate shot that brought down a cow instead of a buck. "A Tall Hunt" could well be one of the numerous misattributed articles about which Patterson complained.

Porter placed Thorpe's name under the title "Angling in Lake Concordia, La." and, following the piece, noted that he clipped it from the *Intelligencer*.[11] The issue in which this item originally appeared is not extant. However, items of similar length and content in that paper were never signed. Thorpe may have written this account of a pleasant day of fishing, but Porter's frequent practice of attributing unsigned pieces to him undercuts confidence in the by-line.

Even though Rickels acknowledged that the authorship of the dialect letters signed Stoke Stout is uncertain, he included in the bibliography the three that Porter reprinted in the *Spirit*.[12] Porter later collected the first two, "The Way to Kill Wild Turkeys and Rheumatism" and "Stoke Stout's Adventures with Mr. Stiggins' Bull," in his *Big Bear* anthology. The headnote says that he does not know whether Thorpe or Patterson

10. "A Tall Hunt—Crack Shot—Big Meat," *Concordia Intelligencer* (Vidalia, La.), October 7, 1843, and *Spirit of the Times*, XIII (October 28, 1843), 409; Patterson, "Southern Sport," *Spirit of the Times*, XIII (August 19, 1843), 291. The anecdote begins: "In the absence of our worthy confrerè [*sic*] 'Tom Owen.'" The issue of the *Concordia Intelligencer* in which this appeared is apparently not extant.

11. "Angling in Lake Concordia, La.," *Spirit of the Times*, XIV (May 18, 1844), 140. In his bibliography, Rickels shortened the title to "Angling in Lake Concordia."

12. "The Way to Kill Wild Turkeys and Rheumatism," *Spirit of the Times*, XIII (July 29, 1843), 253; "Extraordinary Case of Mesmerism," *Concordia Intelligencer* (Vidalia, La.), January 13, 1844, and as "Stoke Stout's Adventures with Mr. Stiggins' Bull," *Spirit of the Times*, XIII (February 10, 1844), 589; "Another Letter from Stoke Stout," *Concordia Intelligencer* (Vidalia, La.), March 1, 1845, and *Spirit of the Times*, XV (March 22, 1845), 38. The issue of the *Intelligencer* containing the first of these three letters is not extant. Rickels stated that joint authorship by Thorpe and Patterson is a reasonable explanation (*Thomas Bangs Thorpe*, 89–90), and Herron concluded that their authorship is not definite ("Thomas Bangs Thorpe," 98). However, Anderson attributed these letters to "Concordia" and argued that Patterson used that pseudonym (*With the Bark On*, 49, 47).

wrote them, but it points out that the first letter was addressed to Thorpe soon after he moved from New Orleans to Vidalia. Files of the *Intelligencer* now extant reveal one additional Stoke Stout letter and two other dialect letters, which suggest that Patterson, not Thorpe, used this pseudonym. The previously unknown letter, the second of the four from Stout, concerns the poor cotton and corn crops in the region during 1843.[13] An editorial note in another column, commenting on Stout's correspondence, states that "from our own observation" this situation is true "of too many of our planters throughout the country." The next week's issue of the *Intelligencer* reports that Patterson had recently been on a trip across the state. Quite possibly, he used Stout to report the agricultural news he had learned while absent from Vidalia.

In the *Intelligencer* for June 28, 1845, Patterson stated that Thorpe ended his work with the paper on the fourteenth except for a series of letters he promised to write on his trip east. Despite his departure, dialect humor continued to appear. In the same issue is a letter from Elizabeth Flinn, of "Possum Fork uv Black Bio Nigh upon the Tinsaw in Luzyana." She asks Patterson to print what she has written to the editors of the *Picayune*, taking exception to a comment of theirs about the strength of a woman's will. One week later Patterson printed a report on swamp fevers in a style reminiscent of Stout's, though not as excessive in its misspellings, and commented: "In another column will be found an article in relation to 'SWAMP FEVERS'—it is dressed up by us in the *vernacular*, at the request of 'UNCLE ABLE.' . . . Our worthy and esteemed friend 'STOKE STOUT' must not blame us for poaching on his domain—the *unadulterated vernacular*."[14] These two pieces, which depend on the vernacular and on misspellings for effect, suggest that either Patterson or an unknown correspondent was Stout. While humorous letters in backwoods dialect appeared frequently in newspapers of the day, no such pieces can with assurance be attributed to Thorpe.

Herron's bibliography contributes two items overlooked by Rickels that are unquestionably by Thorpe. She identified the first appearance of "A Grizzly Bear Hunt," published in the *Spirit* at the end of 1841.[15]

13. William T. Porter (ed.), *The Big Bear of Arkansas, and Other Sketches Illustrative of Characters and Incidents in the South and Southwest* (Philadelphia, 1845), 147; untitled, *Concordia Intelligencer* (Vidalia, La.), August 26, 1843.

14. Patterson, untitled, *Concordia Intelligencer* (Vidalia, La.), July 5, 1845.

15. Thomas Bangs Thorpe, "A Grizzly Bear Hunt," *Spirit of the Times*, XI (December 18, 1841), 499–500.

Thorpe later included it in both *Mysteries* and *Hive*. Herron also listed "Epistle from 'Tom Owen, the Bee Hunter,'" dated from Baton Rouge on April 4, 1847.[16] This letter praises Zachary Taylor as "a real specimen of the old school of American citizen." Nevertheless, of the seventeen other miscellaneous pieces and humorous anecdotes listed by Herron but not by Rickels, several are certainly not Thorpe's, and none of the others can be identified as his with as much confidence as can these two.

Internal evidence shows that three humorous items Herron attributed to Thorpe are in fact by Patterson. She erred by accepting without question the validity of Porter's introductory comments when he reprinted them from the *Intelligencer*. In "An Interesting Fix," a slave tells the writer about an unexpected bear fight while guiding him through an extensive canebrake. Twice in relating his tale the slave addresses the writer as "Maus Bob," Patterson's first name. "Catahoula 'Bar Doins'" is an anecdote of a hunter's unusual success in killing four bears, one buck, and a wild hog all within a single hour. Porter refuted his own claim that Thorpe is the author by reprinting another paragraph from the same issue of the *Intelligencer* that says this account "is Bobs' [*sic*] last." "Bear Fight on Tensas" is the third piece Patterson certainly wrote.[17] It opens with a reference to the author's "rambles of the past summer," one of Patterson's duties on behalf of the paper, and he allows an old slave to narrate his hunting adventure just as in "An Interesting Fix."

In an attempt to compile a complete list of Thorpe's writings, Herron included a number of short paragraphs on diverse topics. Porter reprinted six of these, found in the *Intelligencer* without any indication of authorship.[18] Another of these brief items, from the *Commercial*

16. Thorpe, "Epistle from 'Tom Owen, the Bee Hunter,'" *Spirit of the Times*, XVII (May 22, 1847), 141.

17. Patterson, "An Interesting Fix," *Concordia Intelligencer* (Vidalia, La.), September 30, 1843, and *Spirit of the Times*, XIII (October 28, 1843), 414; Patterson, "Catahoula 'Bar Doins,'" *Concordia Intelligencer* (Vidalia, La.), November 4, 1843, and *Spirit of the Times*, XIII (November 18, 1843), 450; Patterson, "Bear Fight on Tensas," *Concordia Intelligencer* (Vidalia, La.), December 16, 1843, and *Spirit of the Times*, XIII (January 27, 1844), 565.

18. The unidentifiable items are: "The Georgia Major—Joseph Jones," *Concordia Intelligencer* (Vidalia, La.), March 9, 1844, and *Spirit of the Times*, XIV (March 30, 1844), 54; "Concordia Trout," *Concordia Intelligencer* (Vidalia, La.), June 15, 1844, and as "Louisiana Trout" in *Spirit of the Times*, XIV (July 6, 1844), 222; "Angling in Concordia Lake," *Concordia Intelligencer* (Vidalia, La.), September 7, 1844, and *Spirit of the Times*, XIV (September 28, 1844), 368; "Prairie Log Book," *Concordia Intelligencer* (Vidalia, La.), January 25, 1845, and *Spirit of the Times*, XIV (February 15, 1845), 606. Two others are apparently not in extant issues of the *Intelligencer*: "Sol. Smith's Last," *Spirit of the Times*, XIV (March 2, 1844), 1; and "Successful Hunting Party," *Spirit of the Times*, XIV (May 25, 1844), 151.

Times, offers general praise for the *Spirit*. Others from the *Conservator* acknowledge gifts, sketch the activities of the local turf enthusiast Duncan Kenner, and report on the Magnolia Course races at Baton Rouge.[19] While these do reflect Thorpe's interests, no copies of that newspaper are extant to indicate whether he had a co-editor in the venture who might have written them. Thus, making an attribution with complete confidence is impossible. In any case, they are insignificant journalistic efforts and would not contribute much to an understanding of Thorpe's character or of his literary ability.

Herron is probably correct in listing several other paragraphs that appear in the *Intelligencer* anonymously, because Porter's attribution may indeed be correct in these instances. In "A Present to Tom Owen the Bee Hunter," the good-humored writer acknowledges receiving a live alligator from an appreciative reader. "The Rival 'Saws' of Thorpe and Field" is Porter's title for an extract from Mat Field's description of "The Intelligencer Man" reprinted along with lines from the *Intelligencer* to introduce it. Thorpe may have written the introduction as well as selected the excerpt from the *Picayune*, since his own "Letters from the Far West" incited Field's hearty counterattack. Finally, Thorpe's interest in painting and his friendship with the artist Charles Loring Elliott suggest that he probably wrote the paragraph entitled "Cattle Pictures," praising Elliott over the more popular Edward Troye for painting thoroughbred horses in action instead of "*always* at a side view, and standing still."[20]

Besides the humorous pieces Patterson probably wrote, the miscellaneous items impossible to identify, and those presumably by Thorpe because they fit his interests, Herron listed one humorous story on the basis of external evidence that merits attention here. "A Deposite Bank" tells of a son who loses his father's money at a faro bank when he goes to town to deposit it. When the father asks which bank has his funds, the son replies that it is the one with a Scripture name. Such clever punning, in this case on the word *pharoah*, is characteristic of

19. Untitled, *Spirit of the Times*, XVI (March 21, 1846), 42; untitled, *Spirit of the Times*, XVII (April 24, 1847), 102; "Sketch of a Louisiana Turfman" and "Baton Rouge Races," *Spirit of the Times*, XVII (May 15, 1847), 134.

20. "A Present to Tom Owen the Bee Hunter," *Concordia Intelligencer* (Vidalia, La.), September 30, 1843, and *Spirit of the Times*, XIII (November 4, 1843), 426; Porter, "The Rival 'Saws' of Thorpe and Field," *Spirit of the Times*, XIII (January 13, 1844), 546 (on December 23, 1844, the *Concordia Intelligencer* carried the excerpt from Field's sketch on the first page; the sentences that Porter used as an introduction appeared on the second page with several differences in wording); "Cattle Pictures," *Concordia Intelligencer* (Vidalia, La.), June 15, 1844, and *Spirit of the Times*, XIV (July 6, 1844), 222.

Thorpe. In the *Spirit* the tale is localized to New Orleans, and the introduction states: "Communicated to 'Spirit' by an acquaintance of the parties." But this evidence is far too weak to support Thorpe's authorship. Herron pointed out that in the same issue of the *Spirit* the letter from Gin-sing-and-so-on, a Philadelphia correspondent, closes thus: "So much for my story, as regards 'The Bee Hunter's,' let him look at the editorial column of last Saturday's Neal's Gazette, where he will find that 'Scriptural Bank' served up as a good thing." *Neal's Saturday Gazette* for August 14, 1845, has a version of the story titled "Pharoh, or Faro."[21] It is also set in New Orleans, but has a much less polished style. Because Thorpe was in both Philadelphia and New York during that summer, arranging for publication of *Mysteries*, he could easily have contributed either of the pieces. He may have told the story to Gin-sing-and-so-on, who was later surprised to see it "served up as a good thing" in written form. One can even imagine that after reading Gin-sing-and-so-on's letter, Porter encouraged Thorpe to publish the version of the tale he was telling his friends. Unfortunately, no external evidence for Thorpe's authorship of "A Deposite Bank" supports such conjectures as these.

Herron omitted one anonymous *Intelligencer* piece that Porter attributed to Thorpe: "Scene in the Picayune Sanctum." It humorously describes George Wilkins Kendall and a former associate from the 1841 expedition to Santa Fe who had dropped by the editor's office unexpectedly. Also not listed in Herron's bibliography is the review of Porter's edition of *Instructions to Young Sportsmen* that the *Spirit* reprinted from Thorpe's Baton Rouge paper, the *Louisiana Conservator*. Although no issues of that paper are extant, the piece is quite probably by Thorpe. The review comments on Porter's additions to the volume: "It is exceedingly pleasant to pass beyond the cultivated hedge, and the stocked park of the English gentleman, to our own western wilds, mingling the aristocratic shooting of the pheasant of Col. Hawker, with the rough and tumble sport of the 'Big Bear of Arkansas.'" Furthermore, Herron omitted "Scene in Gen. Taylor's Tent," which Porter attributed to "Thorpe's N. O. National." This anecdote about Taylor dur-

21. "A Deposite Bank," *Spirit of the Times*, XV (August 23, 1845), 303; Gin-sing-and-so-on [pseud.], "A Story of 'The Gay and the Handsome,'" *Spirit of the Times*, XV (August 23, 1845), 302 (the spelling of this correspondent's name varies slightly from letter to letter; I have regularized it here for convenience); "Pharoh, or Faro," Neal's *Saturday Gazette*, II (August 14, 1845), 2. J. C. Neal, editor of this weekly, was one of those to whom Thorpe sent a complimentary copy of *Mysteries* (Thomas Bangs Thorpe to Carey and Hart, n.d., in New-York Historical Society, New York).

ing the Mexican War could well be by Thorpe, but it is not in *The Taylor Anecdote Book* or in either of his Mexican War histories.[22]

In addition to these items quite probably by Thorpe, overlooked letters, art reviews, and articles by him appear in the newspapers and magazines through which Rickels and Herron searched. Furthermore, the New Orleans *Picayune* and the heretofore unexamined newspapers edited by Thorpe contain several additional sketches of some significance, as well as the first appearance of others already listed in the bibliography. Recently discovered newspapers also contribute to the list of publications.

Five items from the *Spirit* belong in the bibliography. First is a brief letter by Bee Hunter, dated from Concordia, Louisiana, January 12, 1845, describing the skill of two young Mississippians at rifle shooting. Along with it, Thorpe sent their target for Porter to hang in his office "for the examination of the curious." "Houdon's Washington," signed T. B. T., defends Houdon's statue of the first president as superior to a portrait by Stuart, which is "conventional as eggs." An article in the *Spirit* two weeks earlier, depreciating the artistic value of the statue, probably prompted him to publish his views. "Extract of a Letter from Col. T. B. Thorpe" contains praise for the dedicated work of the recently deceased John Richards, who had been proprietor of the *Spirit* since 1842. Rickels listed six letters Thorpe wrote in the fall of 1859 about his journey from Niagara Falls to Montreal, but he omitted the first in the series, which is titled, like the others, "Editorial Correspondence." Last is the lengthy obituary of F. A. Lumsden, one of the editors of the *Picayune*, who drowned in a steamboat accident on Lake Michigan in 1860. The author is presumably Thorpe, because he mentions being friends with Lumsden for almost a quarter of a century. Thorpe moved to Louisiana in 1837, and his comments in his own papers and in the *Picayune* show that he was always on good terms with its editors.[23]

Issues of the *Southern Sportsman*, unavailable to both Rickels and Herron, contain two pieces attributable to Thorpe. "The Last from 'Ar-

22. *Concordia Intelligencer* (Vidalia, La.), March 16, 1844, and *Spirit of the Times*, XIV (April 6, 1844), 63; *Spirit of the Times*, XVII (April 17, 1847), 90; *Spirit of the Times*, XVII (August 14, 1847), 286.

23. "Rifle Shooting in Mississippi," *Spirit of the Times*, XIV (February 8, 1845), 594; "Houdon's Washington," *Spirit of the Times*, XXIV (October 14, 1854), 411–12; "Extract of a Letter from Col. T. B. Thorpe," *Spirit of the Times*, XXVIII (February 5, 1859), 613; "Editorial Correspondence," *Spirit of the Times*, XXIX (September 24, 1859), 385; "The Death of F. A. Lumsden, Esq.," *Spirit of the Times*, XXX (September 15, 1860), 386.

kansaw'" is a humorous anecdote about the liquor-loving backwoodsman Zeb Maiston, which Thorpe later incorporated into the *Hive* version of "The Little Steamboats of the Mississippi." A second item by
him is "Our Visit to Natchez." Although unsigned, it appeared at the
same time as did Thorpe's report on the agricultural fair he attended
near Natchez, the fair at which he received the honorary title Colonel
from the local agricultural society. The first two paragraphs praise the
beauty of Natchez and the surrounding country. The second half, an
anonymous passage recording similar reactions, was clipped from another local paper.[24]

"Broker vs. Banker. Scene in a New Orleans Court" is the only addition to Thorpe's bibliography from the previously unavailable issues of
the *Intelligencer*. This account of an accused exchange broker evading
the direct questions of the prosecutor in court is not signed. However,
in reprinting the piece, the *Picayune* editors commented: "That wag
Thorpe, who was prowling about our city a week or two since, con-
trived to pick up the following humorous story."[25]

The speech Thorpe delivered at the state fair in Baton Rouge on
January 5, 1846, is in the previously unavailable *Commercial Times*,
which he was then editing.[26] This address before the Agriculturists' and
Mechanics' Association encourages development of the state's resources in ways that will strengthen its economy. As a result, in
Thorpe's view, social life in the South will no longer remain inferior to
that in the North. The oration concludes by urging that "the pervading
spirit of our moral culture, should be the necessity of sustaining 'the
Union.'"

Rickels noted that a series of Thorpe's dispatches on the Mexican
War began on June 6, 1846, in the *Daily Tropic*. Those reports are
unsigned but could well be by Thorpe. According to editorial comments, other letters appearing on May 29, June 5, and July 17, signed
The Corporal, are his. The one signed T., printed on June 4, probably
came from him as well.

Miscellaneous publications from later in Thorpe's life were also
overlooked by Rickels. "The New York Custom-House," a *Harper's*

24. Thorpe, "The Last from 'Arkansaw,'" New Orleans *Southern Sportsman*, May 1, 1843; Thorpe,
"Our Visit to Natchez," New Orleans *Southern Sportsman*, May 15, 1843.

25. Thorpe, "Broker vs. Banker. Scene in a New Orleans Court," *Concordia Intelligencer* (Vidalia,
La.), December 14, 1844, *Spirit of the Times*, XIV (January 4, 1845), 531, and New Orleans *Daily
Picayune*, December 18, 1844.

26. Thorpe, "Address, Before the Agriculturists' and Mechanics' Association of Louisiana, January 5, 1846," New Orleans *Commercial Times*, January 14, 1846.

piece, describes the history and organization of the custom house, concluding with anecdotes of daily events there. Rickels listed the first three articles in the series "Glimpses of Indian Life" in *Appleton's*, but overlooked the final one. For that periodical, Thorpe also wrote the descriptive piece "Picturesque America. A Florida Garden, and a Scene in St. Augustine" and the biographical sketch "Thurlow Weed." Appearing in *Baldwin's*, "Triumphs of the Diving-Bell" praises American ingenuity in rescuing the cargo of a sunken ship. Besides these magazine articles, he contributed "Cane Brake" to *The New American Cyclopaedia*, published by Appleton.[27]

Along with these additional entries to Thorpe's bibliography is new information about the first appearance of several sketches. Both "The Water Craft of the Back Woods" and "The Way Americans Go Down Hill" appeared in the *Southern Sportsman* before being reprinted in the *Intelligencer*. Although Rickels found only two issues of the *Intelligencer* containing letters in the "Letters from the Far West" series, all the pertinent numbers have now been located. Thus, "My First Dinner in New Orleans" and "The Louisiana Law of Cock-Fighting" are the only known sketches for which the first appearance remains unrecovered. They were originally printed in the New Orleans *Tropic* during the first two months of 1843, a period for which issues are not available. Rickels knew when and where "My First Dinner in New Orleans" appeared on the basis of reprints, but he did not list it in his bibliography. Unlike "The Louisiana Law of Cock-Fighting," this sketch never appeared in the *Spirit*, though Thorpe reprinted it in an issue of the *Intelligencer* that is now available.[28]

This bibliographic survey reveals that, with the exception of the

27. Thorpe, "The New York Custom-House," *Harper's New Monthly Magazine*, XLIII (June, 1871), 11–26; Thorpe, "Glimpses of Indian Life: IV," *Appleton's Journal*, IV (December 10, 1870), 685–88 (even though Rickels omitted this article, he did know of its existence, according to *Thomas Bangs Thorpe*, 249); Thorpe, "Picturesque America. A Florida Garden, and a Scene in St. Augustine," *Appleton's Journal*, IV (December 31, 1870), 783–85; Thorpe, "Thurlow Weed," *Appleton's Journal*, XII (August 8, 1874), 161–63; Thorpe, "Triumphs of the Diving-Bell," *Baldwin's Monthly*, XII (April, 1876), 5; Thorpe, "Cane Brake," in George Ripley and Charles A. Dana (eds.), *The New American Cyclopaedia* (16 vols.; New York, 1863), IV, 358–59. Despite Rickels' comment that Thorpe wrote "some articles" for this encyclopedia (*Thomas Bangs Thorpe*, 197), the list of contributors assigns only this one to him.

28. Thorpe, "The Water Craft of the Back Woods," New Orleans *Southern Sportsman*, March 18, 1843, and *Concordia Intelligencer* (Vidalia, La.), August 3, 1844; Thorpe, "The Way Americans Go Down Hill," New Orleans *Southern Sportsman*, April 17, 1843 (Rickels saw the reprinting of this latter sketch in the *Concordia Intelligencer* [Vidalia, La.], December 30, 1843.); Thorpe, "Letters from the Far West," *Concordia Intelligencer* (Vidalia, La.), August 5, 12, 19, September 2, 23, 30, October 14, November 4, December 16, 1843; and February 10, 1844 (Rickels saw only the letters in the issues for November 25 and December 30); Thorpe, "My First Dinner in New Orleans," Baton Rouge *Gazette*, February 18, 1843, and *Concordia Intelligencer* (Vidalia, La.), February 1, 1845; Thorpe, "The

Spirit, Thorpe seems to have contributed only a few pieces to newspapers other than those he edited. According to his own reminiscences about the start of his writing career, "Tom Owen, the Bee-Hunter" was rejected by the local editor to whom he gave it before sending it to the *Spirit*.[29] Unfortunately, that paper and its editor remain unknown. "The Louisiana Law of Cock-Fighting" and "My First Dinner in New Orleans" originally appeared in the *Daily Tropic* shortly before his *Southern Sportsman* came out. The *Picayune* is apparently the only other paper not edited by Thorpe to contain the first printing of several items attributable to him. The signature The Bee Hunter identifies the previously overlooked "A Visit to 'Curnel Pardon Jones'" as his. Readers must have enjoyed this description of the *Picayune*'s humorous correspondent, the creation of Christopher M. Haile of the *Plaquemine Gazette*, by another well-known local figure. The other two items in the *Picayune* are letters, both signed T. B. T., reporting on the activities of General Taylor at his home in Baton Rouge during the summer of 1848.[30] While original pieces by Thorpe may someday be discovered in local papers he did not edit, he evidently preferred to use his creative energy filling the pages of his own publications rather than sending off items to other editors as favors that might attract readers and subscribers for them.

Several anonymous articles in Thorpe's newspapers deserve consideration in this discussion of his bibliography because they may in fact be his. Conclusive evidence is, unfortunately, not available, but they do reflect his interests in the arts and in humor. None of the theater or book reviews in the *Southern Sportsman* is signed, but given Thorpe's interest in the fine arts, at least some of them are quite probably by him. Seven issues contain a column entitled "The Drama," which discusses such subjects as the role of drama in society, the history of French drama, and the nature of pantomime, comedy, melodrama,

Louisiana Law of Cock-Fighting," *Spirit of the Times*, XIII (March 4, 1843), 3, and Baton Rouge *Gazette*, March 4, 1843. Both the *Spirit* and the *Gazette* acknowledge the *Tropic* as the source of the last article.

29. Thorpe, "Reminiscences of Tom Owen the Bee Hunter," *Spirit of the Times*, XXIX (February 26, 1859), 30.

30. Thorpe, "A Visit to 'Curnel Pardon Jones,'" New Orleans *Daily Picayune*, November 30, 1842; T. B. T., "Gen. Taylor at Plaquemine," New Orleans *Daily Picayune*, June 1, 1848; and T. B. T., "Letter from Baton Rouge," New Orleans *Daily Picayune*, July 12, 1848. While area newspapers reprinted Thorpe's writings and carried notices about his activities, the issues I have been able to examine in the collections of the following institutions contain no previously unidentified contributions from Thorpe: Duke University, Kansas State Historical Society, Library of Congress, Louisiana Historical Center of the Louisiana State Museum, Louisiana State University, New Orleans Public Library, Tulane University, and University of North Carolina at Chapel Hill.

and farce. These, too, are unsigned but could well be his. Of more importance is the humorous letter "New Orleans Editors" in the April 17 issue, because of the view it provides of prominent local men. It was supposedly written by James Green, a traveler in New Orleans, and then it was printed along with directions that the editor of the *Neutral Partizan* of Sunkhaize, Maine, should reprint it, since the *Southern Sportsman* was "not much circulated about Wiscasset and the Sangamon, and no one will know that it did not appear originally in your paper. To get you a letter, through the post, would cost a broom and two strings of onions, present wholesale prices." Green describes the appearance and character of ten newspaper editors he saw one evening at the theater, poking gentle fun at their idiosyncrasies. He closes with these words about Thorpe:

> Up in the second tier, near the stage, sat Tom Owen the Bee Hunter. We presume he is so used to climbing trees that he would not content himself nearer the earth than sixty feet. Tom wears the tallest kind of whiskers, has a high Roman nose, dark eyebrows, a thin face, and such eyes! to see them roll over on "THE BEE" was beautiful. Tom is a very solemn and sedate fellow, seldom smiles, and in this respect is unlike his coadjutor, R. L. Brenham. He has a deep gash on the left side of his face, which we are informed he got while hunting the "Big Bar of Arkansas."

Thorpe was on good terms with his fellow editors and just a few months later began satirizing Field in his "Letters from the Far West" series. Unfortunately, no external evidence exists to prove the assumption that he wrote this clever letter.

Two items from the *Intelligencer* involve musical performances in Natchez, just across the river from Vidalia. "Music in the Back-Woods" begins with a humorous description of a concert by the violinist Vieuxtemps.[31] The author manages a pun in the second sentence: "Among the audience were some few Concordians, who crossed the Mississippi in a 'dug-out,' determined to give the scraper a fair chance, as they were fond occasionally of a *scrape* themselves." He continues such wordplay in a fashion characteristic of Thorpe: "Vieux Temps brought out airs from his violin, and the venitian [*sic*] blinds of the concert-room, admitted *airs* from the world at large; the ladies present fluttered their fans, and the bow fluttered in the violinist's hand, and the hearts of the *beaux* fluttered beneath fashionable vests." After this

---

31. "Music in the Back-Woods," *Concordia Intelligencer* (Vidalia, La.), April 13, 1844. The acclaimed Belgian violinist Henri Vieuxtemps toured America in 1844, but local papers do not report that he performed in Natchez.

introduction, the article focuses on the behavior of one bachelor upon his return home. Entranced by the music, he attempts to teach a field hand to play classical music on his fiddle. The master seats the slave in the parlor at midnight and tells him to imitate with the bow the movements of the poker in his own hand. As the man shouts directions, the two work themselves into a frenzy, and the violin squeaks and groans: "Twenty calves with their maternal parents absent, could not have made the air more hideous." The bachelor, however, is delighted to think that they have excelled Paganini's "Carnival of Venice." This satire on the low level of culture in the backwoods is similar to that in "A Piano in Arkansas."

The other humorous article about a musical performance is "The Light of Other Days." It first appeared in the *Spirit*, from which Thorpe reprinted it in the *Intelligencer*.[32] In both instances it is attributed to "An Old Louisiana Correspondent." One would expect that Porter would have wanted to distinguish both the article and his paper by naming Thorpe, if it indeed came from him. Nevertheless, because the author's remarks indicate that he is from Vidalia and because the piece treats both cultural and sporting life in the region, it merits consideration as one of Thorpe's. At his recital, the singer named Light of Other Days introduces each piece with pretentious remarks about the acclaim it has received from European musicians and nobility. Yet the listeners, undeceived, easily recognize that local amateurs could surpass him. In the following days, the rumor spreads that the singer is also an artist who is about to publish a book on trout fishing. Knowing this, when they happen to meet, the writer engages him in a long conversation about fishing. When the singer mentions a favorite pond on Long Island, the writer asks for news about Porter. The singer at first mistakes the name for Potter and then, with the help of his servant, decides that he has never heard of Porter or the *Spirit*. In the writer's mind this confession reveals him as a complete impostor, for "a man who sings, and catches trout, and intends to publish a book about it, should know 'nobody else!'" The article concludes with a play on the artist's name: "After this exhibition of character, the 'Light of other Days' hung around the summit of the 'City of the Bluffs' a mere phospherescence [*sic*], for a while and finally went out."

32. "The Light of Other Days," *Spirit of the Times*, XV (March 22, 1845), 39, and *Concordia Intelligencer* (Vidalia, La.), April 12, 1845.

Thorpe was sole editor of the *Daily National*, and Rickels speculated that most of the original work in it is his. "Waiting for a Frost; or Life at a Western River Hotel" is quite possibly one of the pieces Thorpe wrote but did not sign. It describes socially pretentious travelers who have spent the summer in the North. They are now waiting in Ohio for the river to rise sufficiently to permit traffic and also for the first frost to end "the fever" in New Orleans. The wait becomes tedious, and "few of the whole have any spirits—the belles have danced and coquetted theirs away at the watering places, the beaux have drank theirs away where there was no water to be had." The merchants, nervous about their businesses, write their clerks daily and put the letters in the post, which leaves only once a week. No longer do these travelers practice the social graces: "Miss Angelina drops her handkerchief, and Augustus Frederick *don't* rush to pick it up. Even the exquisite Sophthead, who was the late lion at Saratoga, has got his feet above his head on the gallery railing, and is otherwise exceedingly vulg*w*ar [*sic*] in the presence of ladies." In their excitement at seeing a steamboat approaching, all hurry with their baggage to the wharf, but the captain tells them the river is too low to proceed. Disgusted, they pay no attention to whose bags they carry back to their rooms. The servants likewise do not read the names on the trunks and leave "the Mississippi gentlemens' changes of dress and 'shooting irons,' in the nervous old lady's room in the attic story." When the journey to New Orleans finally resumes, the vexation of waiting at a river hotel has "entirely effaced any pleasure that had been enjoyed at the watering places, and procured at so much expense."[33]

The pages of antebellum newspapers are filled with humorous sketches, such as these four, whose authors can never be known with assurance. The bibliography of any humorous journalist is doomed to incompleteness because of the ephemeral nature of the writing and the inadequate preservation of the papers. The foregoing analysis does, however, update Thorpe's bibliography so that it is as exact as possible, given the materials currently available. The deletion of mistaken attributions and the discovery of several new sketches allow a more accurate assessment of his place among contemporary humorists and sporting writers. Furthermore, because the first printing of all

---

33. Rickels, *Thomas Bangs Thorpe*, 267; "Waiting for a Frost; or Life at a Western River Hotel," New Orleans *Daily National*, October 21, 1847.

except two items has been located, it is possible to study the revisions Thorpe made before reprinting sketches in book form, in order to learn more about the craft of writing as he practiced it.

The publication history of Thorpe's writings shows that what began as an amusement during his early years in Louisiana, when he was trying to establish himself as a painter, became the means by which he sought to achieve financial stability. He became a newspaper editor who compiled and wrote books on the side, and his letters to Abraham Hart, of Carey and Hart, reveal an unrealized dream to be engaged by that firm for full-time literary work.[34] Despite attempts to make literature his career, the productions for which he is best known are the sketches contributed without remuneration to the *Spirit* within the first several years after he began publishing his writings.

According to Thorpe himself, he wrote "Tom Owen, the Bee-Hunter" only because of the persistent encouragement of the planter friend at whose home he had met the local figure. Reminiscing about the publication of the sketch twenty years after its first appearance, Thorpe said that he originally gave it to a local editor:

> For weeks the "contribution" remained untouched in the editor's pigeon hole, and after repeated solicitations, a time was specified for its appearance. Unhappily, a sudden excitement was created by a theological discussion, in which the backwoods Boanerges took a most violent interest. People heretofore friends got by the ears on the subject of faith, and baptism, and quarrelled fearfully over the doctrines of Christian charity, or became implacable enemies in considering the necessity of brotherly love. The result was, that our MS. was returned with the remark—
> "That matter more pressing than the hunt of Tom Owen, whom no one cared a fig about, occupied the public mind."[35]

Thorpe's planter friend again encouraged him to publish the sketch, this time in the *Spirit*. Porter printed it on July 27, 1839, with the comment "By a New Yorker in Louisiana." Thorpe's initials and his place

---

34. Thomas Bangs Thorpe to Abraham Hart, December 5, 1845, in New-York Historical Society.

35. Thorpe, "Reminiscences of Tom Owen the Bee Hunter," 30. The sentence preceding the quoted passage creates some confusion: "The sketch, when finished, was placed in the hands of the editor, and published by the local paper, which circulated two or three hundred copies in the vicinity." Nevertheless, "Tom Owen, the Bee-Hunter" was probably not published by this local editor. The account by J. L. C. of a visit with Thorpe says that the editor returned the sketch after three months "as not being sufficiently interesting for publication" ("Men and Things in Louisiana. No. 1.— 'Tom Owen, the Bee Hunter,'" *Spirit of the Times*, XX [July 27, 1850], 270–71). Edward Jones, at the time he was co-editing the *Spirit* with Thorpe and Richard Hays, briefly recalled the arrival of this sketch at the *Spirit* office in "a large and neatly folded letter, postage one dollar and fifty cents, *prepaid*" ("A New Volume of the 'Spirit,'" *Spirit of the Times*, XXIX [February 12, 1859], 1).

of residence, Jackson, Louisiana, appear at the bottom of the article. Porter did not anticipate its enthusiastic reception, as he explained almost fifteen years later: "We were somewhat surprised and gratified at the universal republication of the article; first, in the English magazines; then, on the Continent; and ultimately, as far off as Hindostan."[36] Thorpe recollected that he was ignorant of his international success at the time, though he did know that Louisiana papers were reprinting the piece. When he went to New York "two or three years after these events," he met his old friend Charles Loring Elliott, who inquired if he had ever published anything. Thorpe told him about "the almost forgotten sketch of Tom Owen," and later Elliott went to the *Spirit* office for a copy. Through Elliott, then, Porter discovered the identity of his correspondent and was able to elicit additional contributions. Thorpe said that the effect of his discovery was a second sketch, "The Big Bear of Arkansas." However, his memory here is inaccurate. "The Big Bear of Arkansas" is the sixth of his pieces in the *Spirit*, and several months before its appearance he had also published "The Mississippi" in the *Knickerbocker*. Actually, his second article, "Wild Turkey Shooting," appeared just one year after "Tom Owen, the Bee-Hunter." Rickels' opinion is that Thorpe must have met Porter in the spring or summer of 1840 because "Wild Turkey Shooting" is dated from New York City, July 12, 1840.[37]

By March, 1843, when he first started to edit a newspaper, Thorpe had contributed nineteen original descriptive, humorous, and sporting articles to the *Spirit*, three to the *Knickerbocker*, and one to the *New Sporting Magazine*. At least three others had appeared in New Orleans papers. The *New Sporting Magazine* and the *American Turf Register* had reprinted three sketches each.[38] While Thorpe received no pay-

36. Porter, "The Bee-Hunter," *Spirit of the Times*, XXIII (November 12, 1853), 457. The sketch appeared in the London *New Sporting Magazine*, o.s., XVII (October, 1839), 238–41. From there it might have been reprinted in a British publication in India. However, I have been unable to find the periodical that Porter must have seen. While "Tom Owen, the Bee-Hunter" does not appear in the *Bengal Sporting Magazine*, a Calcutta magazine from which Porter clipped many items for the *Spirit*, that publication did reprint "Wild Turkey Shooting," "The Wild Horses of the Western Prairies," and "The American Wild Cat."

37. Rickels, *Thomas Bangs Thorpe*, 41–43.

38. The following articles by Thorpe are in the *New Sporting Magazine*: "Tom Owen, the Bee-Hunter," o.s. XVII (October, 1839), 238–41; "Wild Turkey Shooting," n.s., III (January, 1842), 34–38; "Woodcock Fire Hunting," n.s., IV (September, 1842), 149–51; and "A Slick Run Down Hill," n.s., VII (March, 1844), 182–87. The last of these articles originally appeared in the New Orleans *Southern Sportsman* under the title "The Way Americans Go Down Hill." The following articles by Thorpe are in the *American Turf Register*: "The Big Bear of Arkansas," XII (May, 1841), 274–80; "Wood Cock Fire Hunting in Louisiana," XII (November, 1841), 633–35; and "The American Wild Cat," XIII (September, 1842), 518–21.

ment for these articles, they had established his reputation as a sporting writer and humorist. He was well known by his own name, and also as either Tom Owen or the Big Bear. The editors of the *Picayune* noted this measure of his popular success: "It has generally been conceded that Thorpe . . . is the only man entitled to tell a '*bar*' story."[39]

The most encouraging praise, however, came from Porter. Several months after violating normal practice by publishing "The Big Bear of Arkansas" in both the *Spirit* and the *American Turf Register*, the "Tall Son of York" wrote: "Aside from his pretensions as an artist, Mr. T. is favorably known on both sides of the Atlantic as one of the most gifted and original sporting writers of the day. Next to the '*Quarter Race in Kentucky*' which was written expressly for this paper, Mr. T. has published in our columns the best original sporting article of a humorous character that ever appeared."[40] While serving as editor of various papers from 1843 to 1847, Thorpe contributed only one original sketch to the *Spirit*. However, Porter kept readers pleased by clipping each installment of the "Letters from the Far West" series and other articles by him. Porter also included his work in the three books he edited. Thorpe's famous sketch supplied the title and leading item for *The Big Bear of Arkansas* (1845) and was one of the few to carry the real name of its author.[41] Porter's second humorous anthology, *A Quarter Race in Kentucky* (1846), reprinted Thorpe's "The Devil's Summer Retreat, in Arkansaw" under the title "Bob Herring, the Arkansas Bear Hunter." In December, 1846, Porter also published the first American edition of Peter Hawker's *Instructions to Young Sportsmen*. Five articles by Thorpe are among the thirty-eight describing American field sports collected there, a compliment to the accuracy and reliability of his descriptions of game and hunting practices in the Southwest.[42]

39. "A Bear Story," New Orleans *Daily Picayune*, January 19, 1844.

40. Porter, "Original Sporting Pictures," *Spirit of the Times*, XI (October 16, 1841), 385.

41. In reviewing *Big Bear*, Edgar Allan Poe stated: "The two first in the volume are, we think, much overrated by the editor—they seem to us dull and forced" (*Broadway Journal*, I [May 24, 1845], 331).

42. Peter Hawker, *Instructions to Young Sportsmen, in All that Relates to Guns and Shooting* (Philadelphia, 1846). The articles by Thorpe are "Woodcock Fire-Hunting in Louisiana," 241–44; "The Wild Cat," 246–50; "Opossum Hunting," 313–18; "The Devil's Summer Retreat, in Arkansaw" under the title "Bear Hunting in Arkansas," 339–50; and "Grizzly Bear Hunting," 368–73. The table of contents incorrectly attributes "Fire-Hunting for Deer" to Thorpe; the introduction to that account of a hunt near Little Rock says that it is by a man from Arkansas. Henry William Herbert also acknowledged the truthfulness of Thorpe's sporting articles when he reprinted "A Grizzly Bear Hunt" in *Frank Forester's Field Sports of the United States, and British Provinces, of North America* (4th ed.; 2 vols.; New York, 1852), II, 286–90. The British sportsman Captain Flack must have recognized the merits in Thorpe's writings, too. However, he did not credit "Wild Turkey Hunting" in *Hive* as the source for his account of a turkey hunt in *A Hunter's Experiences in the Southern States of America* (London,

Because of the encouragement he had received from Porter, Thorpe quite naturally turned to him for assistance when he thought of publishing a book. Thorpe must have mentioned such plans when he sent the manuscript of "The Little Steamboats of the Mississippi" to the *Spirit*, for in the March 2, 1844, issue, Porter acknowledged receipt of the sketch and replied that he would give him "'a lick ahead' with your volume of sketches." One year later, on March 3, 1845, just as his *Big Bear* anthology was being released, Porter sent a letter by Thorpe to Carey and Hart with this introduction: "Thorpe is a man of decided genius. The 'Big Bear' hardly gives one an idea of what he has done or is capable of. . . . Do see what you can do for him. . . . Some of his sketches of *scenery* in the great Valley of the Mississippi, and of the 'characters' encountered there are equal to anything in the language, in my humble opinion. You will see that, like many other young writers, he looks to 'this child' as a sort of 'literary god-father.'"[43]

On March 8, 1845, Thorpe replied to a letter from Carey and Hart that he had "originally contracted to write for A. Ackerman of London '100 pages of writing' at one guinea a page."[44] But the firm failed, and he decided to use an American publisher. He planned for the volume to include "most of my best articles published, corrected and made more perfect." It would also contain a series of sketches on which he had been working during the previous year and a half. He told Carey and Hart: "I have made no definite arrangement regarding the publication of my sketches, and I wrote to Mr. Porter to see on what terms it could be done. A friend of mine who has interested himself much in my favor, has spoken to the Messrs. Appleton of New York and they have expressed a desire to have the M.S."

On April 1, Thorpe wrote Carey and Hart that he hoped to be in Philadelphia on May 15 to confer about "the publication of the

1866), 239–47. Apparently without realizing that Flack merely made wording changes in the section of Thorpe's sketch he plagiarized, Clarence Gohdes republished this very part of Flack's book in *Hunting in the Old South: Original Narratives of the Hunters* (Baton Rouge, 1967), 17–22. Cecil B. Hartley, author of another sporting book, reprinted the *Mysteries* version of "Grizzly Bear Hunting" without giving credit to Thorpe in *Hunting Sports in the West* (Philadelphia, 1859), 273–80.

43. Porter, "To Correspondents," *Spirit of the Times*, XIV (March 2, 1844), 1; William T. Porter to Carey and Hart, March 3, 1845, in New-York Historical Society. Rickels erred in saying that Porter wrote to Carey and Hart the day after publicly offering his assistance (*Thomas Bangs Thorpe*, 96). For an account of Thorpe's dealings with publishers that includes a discussion of his books about the Mexican-American War, see Eugene Current-Garcia, "Thomas Bangs Thorpe and the Literature of the Ante-Bellum Southwestern Frontier," *Louisiana Historical Quarterly*, XXXIX (April, 1956), 199–222.

44. Thomas Bangs Thorpe to Carey and Hart, March 8, 1845, in Simon Gratz Collection, Historical Society of Pennsylvania, Philadelphia.

sketches I am now engaged in writing, together with some already published." However, matters related to ending his co-editorship of the *Intelligencer* delayed his departure for the North. In a letter dated from Vidalia, June 12, he told the publishers, who had not yet seen his manuscript, that Porter's *Big Bear* should "create a wish in the public mind" for the volume he was planning: "My descriptions extend over every department, prairies, swamps, scenes on the Mississippi, scenes inland, with the rural sports peculiar to the South West." On July 27, Thorpe sent Carey and Hart "a number of M.S. which I propose to publish if inducements are offered so to do." Two weeks later, on August 11, he sent the complete manuscript from New York, along with a request to see the proof sheets before his return to the South.[45]

Each of Thorpe's letters to his publisher discusses plans for illustrating the volume. In the letter of March 8 he offered to "furnish illustrations myself drawn from life and consequently correct, a thing not possible when attempted by northern artists unacquainted with this peculiar country." He had a picture for the frontispiece of Tom Owen hunting bees and would supply six other paintings from which the illustrations could be drawn on stone. "The correctness of the pictures would be their chief merit," Thorpe emphasized. The publishers must have mentioned in the next letter that they used woodcuts instead of drawings on stone. On April 1, Thorpe praised the illustration for "Swallowing an Oyster Alive," which had appeared in a recent issue of the *Spirit*, and acknowledged that "my residence in the South has placed me behind the times in these matters, and you must therefore pardon my want of knowledge, in the excellence of wood cuts in illustrating fine works." Nevertheless, Thorpe's interest in the illustrations for his volume continued. He mentioned on June 12 that he considered F. O. C. Darley's work for the *Big Bear* "remarkably fine." Thorpe continued, "With myself at his elbow to give the exact character of our southwestern scenery, I cannot imagine better illustrations." He gave specific instructions in his letter of August 11:

> I want the sketches set up in large type, heads of chapters low down on the pages, thick leads &c &c so that the work may be spread over as much surface as possible, and be in every respect a more readable book. . . . Please have the title page without an illustration, save the little

45. Thomas Bangs Thorpe to Carey and Hart, April 1 and June 12, 1845, and Thomas Bangs Thorpe to Rufus W. Griswold, July 27, 1845, all in Gratz Collection; Thomas Bangs Thorpe to Carey and Hart, August 11, [1845], in New-York Historical Society. In this letter from New York City, Thorpe remarked, "Upon enquiry here I found the offer made me to be 15 percent without any contingencies." This may have been an offer from Appleton.

"Bee" I suggest, which cut would make an appropriate picture to place over the article of "Tom Owen." If Mr. Darley can illustrate the *piano in arkansaw* with success the closing scene will afford I fine subject. I may overate the difficulty but his talents are quite equal to any subject, in fact I have hardly any words to express my admiration of his ability in his particular department.[46]

The publishers followed each of these requests.

In order to publicize the volume, Thorpe asked for proofs from which he could make extracts. However, he requested that Hart not give any newspaper his book in sheets because such practice injures the interests of the publisher and the author.[47]

On August 15, Thorpe sent from New York the words dedicating his book to the American sculptor Hiram Powers. Twelve days later followed the last sections of the manuscript: "Concordia Lake," "Frontier Incident," "The Mississippi," "The American Wild-Cat," and "Tom Owen, the Bee-Hunter."[48] Thorpe also enclosed two drawings of bees: "I should like to have the bee marked No 1, put into the title page, and the bee marked No 2 over the story of Tom Owen or at the end of it as a finis, as the judgement of the printer may decide."

Despite Thorpe's plans to read proof, he had to return to New Orleans before it was ready. Because sending the sheets to the South would have created too long a delay, for assistance he turned to Rufus Griswold, who had been corresponding with him for six months regarding the inclusion of Thorpe's work in *The Prose Writers of America*. He asked Griswold to look over the proofs, or "at least such parts of them as refer to peculiarities of language used in the west."[49]

By November 22, Porter had received a copy of the title page of *Mysteries*, and a few weeks later an advertisement in his paper announced that Carey and Hart would publish the book on December 12. According to the firm's record books, on November 22 it paid $700 for four thousand copies, the same number that it initially printed for each of Porter's humorous anthologies.[50]

46. Thorpe to Carey and Hart, August 11, [1845], in New-York Historical Society. Although Thorpe's letters indicate that he was a poor speller, I have not attempted to correct his spelling or punctuation in any of the quotations used in the introductory chapters. To avoid distracting the reader, no special notes call attention to these frequent errors.

47. Thorpe to Carey and Hart, August 11, [1845], in New-York Historical Society; Thomas Bangs Thorpe to Abraham Hart, August 15, 1845, in Charles Roberts Autograph Letters Collection, Haverford College Library, Haverford, Pa.

48. Thorpe to Abraham Hart, August 15, 1845, in Roberts Autograph Letters Collection; Thomas Bangs Thorpe to Carey and Hart, August 26, 1845, in New-York Historical Society.

49. Thomas Bangs Thorpe to Rufus W. Griswold, September 4[?], 1845, in Gratz Collection.

50. Porter, "New Publications, etc.," *Spirit of the Times*, XV (November 22, 1845), 464; an adver-

The sixteen southwestern sketches that compose *Mysteries* appear in this order: "Traits of the Prairies," "A Piano in 'Arkansaw,'" "Piscatory Archery," "Place de la Croix. A Romance of the West," "Wit of the Woods," "The Water Craft of the Backwoods," "Pictures of Buffalo Hunting," "Scenes on the Mississippi," "The Disgraced Scalp-Lock; or, Incidents on the Western Waters," "Alligator Killing," "A Grizzly Bear Hunt," "Concordia Lake," "A Frontier Incident," "The Mississippi," "The American Wild-Cat," and "Tom Owen, the Bee-Hunter." Five had not appeared previously: "Traits of the Prairies," "Piscatory Archery," "Pictures of Buffalo Hunting," "Alligator Killing," and "Concordia Lake." Although Thorpe revised each of the others, "Wit of the Woods," originally titled "Wild Turkey Shooting," is the only one he reworked into essentially a new piece. In selecting sketches for *Mysteries*, Thorpe omitted nine of those previously published, but he later included them when revising and enlarging the volume in 1854. The most famous of these is "The Big Bear of Arkansas."

Mysteries has six illustrations by Darley, in addition to the two bees Thorpe drew. The frontispiece is a picture of Tom Owen sitting astride a tree limb with his ax and pails. The other drawings illustrate "A Piano in 'Arkansaw,'" "Piscatory Archery," "Place de la Croix," "Pictures of Buffalo Hunting," and "The Disgraced Scalp Lock." A diagram explaining the formation of "dry lakes" and a drawing of the arrow-fisherman's spear accompany "Piscatory Archery." A diagram of a "cut-off" appears with "Concordia Lake." And Thorpe's drawings of bees are on the title page and at the beginning of "Tom Owen, the Bee-Hunter," according to his wishes.

Thorpe was satisfied when he saw a copy of the book. On December 5 he wrote to Abraham Hart: "I return by the mail, the volume of 'Mysteries,' marked in the margin, some few typographical errors have occured not of serious importance save one or two. I am pleased with the book as a whole." Two days later he mentioned that the errors were "most of them perhaps unimportant, save those in the 'Wit of the Woods,'" the piece he considered to be the most significant in the volume.[51]

tisement in *Spirit of the Times*, XV (December 6, 1845), 486; Nelle Smither, "'Library of Humorous American Works': A Bibliographic Study" (M.A. thesis, Columbia University, 1936), 59.

51. Thomas Bangs Thorpe to Abraham Hart, December 5, 1845, in New-York Historical Society; Thomas Bangs Thorpe to Carey and Hart, December 7, 1845, in Thomas Bangs Thorpe Collection (No. 8397), Barrett Library, University of Virginia, Charlottesville.

A short notice of *Mysteries* appeared in the *Knickerbocker* in January, 1846, with special praise for "Wit of the Woods." Complimentary notices ran in several Louisiana newspapers that month. Two southern periodicals, De Bow's *Commercial Review* and the *Southern Quarterly Review*, also included favorable comments. But Thorpe was most interested in how Porter would puff *Mysteries* in the *Spirit*. In the January 17 issue Porter requested that Carey and Hart send him a copy, since "by some unaccountable neglect somewhere," he had not yet received one. Writing to Carey and Hart on January 28, after reading this in the *Spirit*, Thorpe stated: "It is strange indeed, he has been much censured here for his apparent neglect of Tom Owen."[52] Carey and Hart must have sent Porter his copy quickly, for in the January 24 issue he wrote: "Who has not read 'Tom Owen, the Bee Hunter?' and who that has but will seize with avidity upon the present work from the same brilliant pen. Besides that excellent sketch the work contains fifteen more of equal merit, which, illustrated by Darley, are very great for a rainy day."[53] Porter reprinted "A Grizzly Bear Hunt" in the same issue, and "The Mississippi" the following week. Despite this delayed attention, Thorpe felt slighted in comparison with the Alabama humorist Johnson Jones Hooper, who had dedicated *Some Adventures of Captain Simon Suggs* to Porter several months earlier. Thorpe shared his disappointment with Hart on March 2: "I cannot understand why Mr. Porter has treated me so shabily with regard to my book, if it is because I paid him no compliments in the volume, and I see no other reason, he is not the man I gave him credit for, any way he has disappointed me. I had reason to *expect much* from his paper, and have near[?] nothing." In the same letter, Thorpe told his publisher that he would write to friends in the North who were under obligation to him. He hoped they would create some interest in the book they had so far neglected. Two of those friends must have been the *Spirit* correspon-

52. "Literary Record," *Knickerbocker Magazine*, XXVII (January, 1846), 94; New Orleans *Daily Picayune*, January 3, 1846; New Orleans *Weekly Delta*, January 5, 1846; *Concordia Intelligencer* (Vidalia, La.), January 17, 1846; "The Publishing Business," *De Bow's Commercial Review*, I (February, 1846), 191–92; "Critical Notices," *Southern Quarterly Review*, IX (April, 1846), 528–29; Porter, "To Correspondents," *Spirit of the Times*, XV (January 17, 1846), 549; Thomas Bangs Thorpe to Carey and Hart, January 28, 1846, in New-York Historical Society. The oversight may have resulted because Porter's name does not appear on the list of recipients of complimentary copies that Thorpe sent his publishers (Thomas Bangs Thorpe to Carey and Hart, n.d., in New-York Historical Society).

53. Porter, "New Publications, etc.," *Spirit of the Times*, XV (January 24, 1846), 572. Rickels mistakenly stated that Porter did not review *Mysteries* until 1847 (*Thomas Bangs Thorpe*, 140).

dents Acorn (James Oakes) and Gin-sing-and-so-on, for in the *Spirit* of March 21 they both referred to *Mysteries*, but only briefly.[54]

Assessing the lack of immediate popularity of *Mysteries*, Thorpe concluded that the title was an unfortunate choice because it probably kept New Englanders from reading the book. "The book contains I predict some standard literature," he told Hart, "and it will not be ephemeral in its character. According to the present public taste, Irving's Scketch book would be a failure. The day will come when the 'wit of the woods' will be classical, I say it with due reverence."[55] Proud of his book despite its poor reception, Thorpe added, "I fear I can never do better than in my first volume."

In partial justification of Thorpe's hopes, *Mysteries* was reprinted several times during his life by various publishers. In 1848, it was among those publications that Carey and Hart decided to reissue in their Library of Humorous American Works. *Mysteries* became number sixteen in that series, which was started in early 1846. Burgess and Stringer of New York City apparently copublished *Mysteries* with Carey and Hart sometime before 1848, since the names of both publishers appear on the cover of some of the copies. Henry Carey Baird, successor to Carey and Hart, included it in his Library of Humorous American Works in 1850–51. In 1865, over a decade after Thorpe had enlarged and revised the book as *The Hive of "The Bee-Hunter,"* *Mysteries* became one of the volumes in the standard Library of Humorous American Works that T. B. Peterson and Brothers of Philadelphia had begun publishing in 1854.[56]

In his first letter to Carey and Hart, on March 8, 1845, Thorpe mentioned that he was already half-finished with a second book "to follow the 'Tom Owen Sketches,' provided its sale, and merit justifies its being finished, and offers inducement for further literary pursuits." This work was to illustrate "'Western life and manners' as exhibited in 1799 and 1800." Thorpe explained to Rufus Griswold, at about the same time, that it was "a book of novel size, founded on the difficulties of settling a new country, and intended to preserve from oblivion a character

54. Thorpe, "A Grizzly Bear Hunt," *Spirit of the Times*, XV (January 24, 1846), 563; Thorpe, "The Mississippi," *Spirit of the Times*, XV (January 31, 1846), 576–77; Thorpe to Abraham Hart, March 2, 1846, in New-York Historical Society; James Oakes [Acorn], "Sayings and Doings in Boston," and Gin-sing-and-so-on [pseud.], "Matters and Things in Philadelphia," *Spirit of the Times*, XVI (March 21, 1846), 37.

55. Thorpe to Abraham Hart, March 2, 1846, in New-York Historical Society.

56. Smither, "'Library of Humorous American Works,'" 50–57.

almost forgotten in the birth of steam," probably the keelboatman. He sent Griswold an extract from the book, a sketch entitled "A Squatter's Wife," which later appeared in *Graham's Magazine*, but no further reference to this project remains.[57]

He must have discussed plans for a second volume with Hart when they met in the summer of 1845, and Hart probably indicated that the firm would like another volume of sketches. When Thorpe sent the dedication for *Mysteries* to Philadelphia in mid-August, he asked, "Will it be of any advantage to have most of the second book; I have the whole complete, save three or four articles, which I cannot get until I go south." At the end of January he wrote that he had "not been able to work[?] on the subjects for the second volume of sketches as I proposed." In addition to the three half-finished literary projects that occupied him in December,[58] he wanted to prepare a book about northern California, basing it on a manuscript he had purchased that gave an account of an eighteen-month residence there. Such a project would capitalize on the current popularity of that region, he explained, and he hoped to have the manuscript finished in six weeks.[59] However, within six weeks, the disappointing reception of *Mysteries* caused him to agree with Hart that his next volume should be "composed entirely of *humorous sketches*, and nothing else."[60]

Thorpe apparently began working on such a humorous volume rather quickly. In the *Spirit* for April 18 the New Orleans correspondent Piscator announced: "I have promised THORPE to write the concluding story for his new book, but he limits me to something humorous." Nevertheless, Thorpe must not have been too eager to prepare such a

57. Thomas Bangs Thorpe to Rufus W. Griswold, March 19, 1845, in Gratz Collection; Thorpe, "A Squatter's Wife," *Graham's Magazine*, XXIX (December, 1846), 299–301.

58. Thorpe to Abraham Hart, August 15, 1845, in Roberts Autograph Letters Collection; Thorpe to Carey and Hart, January 28, 1846, and Thorpe to Abraham Hart, December 5, 1845, both in New-York Historical Society. The third project might have been a novel. In a later letter to his publishers, Thorpe mentioned: "I have also had for many years an historical novel nearly finished which I think would attract considerable attention as it is original in its design and story" (Thomas Bangs Thorpe to Carey and Hart, December 3, 1847, in New-York Historical Society). Rickels has speculated that this statement refers to *The Master's House*, which Thorpe published in 1854 (*Thomas Bangs Thorpe*, 148). Since events in that novel take place in Thorpe's own day, it is probably more correct to assume that the reference is to the book set at the turn of the century that he mentioned to Griswold in 1845.

59. Thorpe to Carey and Hart, January 28, 1846, in New-York Historical Society. Thorpe kept this project in mind throughout the year. About one month after sending Carey and Hart the last of his manuscript for *Our Army on the Rio Grande*, he wrote that he would send "in the course of sixty days or sooner the M.S. of the best work on California ever written, I have been engaged upon it five months yet accomplished but little for want of time" (Thomas Bangs Thorpe to Abraham Hart, September 15, 1846, in New-York Historical Society).

60. Thorpe to Abraham Hart, March 2, 1846, in New-York Historical Society.

volume. Only two weeks after accepting Hart's advice, he wrote the firm that he had in his possession the correspondence of a revolutionary war general, which he would publish if the terms were agreeable. In fact, he had already taken out a copyright.[61]

In April, 1846, Thorpe became co-owner of the New Orleans *Tropic*, and by May he was on his way to the front to cover the Mexican War for it. Upon his return to New Orleans in mid-June, he decided to write a history of the military campaign. Carey and Hart published *Our Army on the Rio Grande* in October of that year and *Our Army at Monterey* in November, 1847.[62] Thorpe must have sensed the firm's growing dissatisfaction with his books, because on April 5, 1848, when sending the manuscript for *Anecdotes of the War* to Philadelphia, he added a postscript: "I shall devote a large portion of my time hereafter to my pen and will be able to give you a volume for your humorous library soon, if you wish it."[63] In May the publishers rejected the manuscript of *Anecdotes* and cancelled intentions to publish a third volume on the Mexican War, which Thorpe had been writing for almost a year. Thus his association with Carey and Hart ended without the humorous volume they had for years encouraged him to publish.

Not until the spring of 1854 did Thorpe publish a collection of humorous sketches. When the firm of Carey and Hart was dissolved in 1849, Henry Carey Baird, nephew of the deceased Edward L. Carey, received the copyright and plates of *Mysteries*. He wrote to Thorpe in May, 1852, about purchasing the plates, and that summer the two talked when Thorpe was in the East. At the end of August, after investigating the possibility of publishing his sketches, Thorpe realized that only the engravings of Darley's illustrations would be of value and so offered seventy-five dollars for them and the rights to the text. That was unacceptable to Baird. A year later, on September 15, 1853, having made arrangements with Appleton and Company to publish his sketches, Thorpe agreed to the price Baird had apparently named, but

61. Piscator [pseud.], "Extract from a Private Letter from 'Piscator,'" *Spirit of the Times*, XVI (April 18, 1846), 90; Thomas Bangs Thorpe to Carey and Hart, March 14, 1846, in Thomas Bangs Thorpe Collection (No. 8397), Barrett Library. In 1859, Thorpe offered to sell these papers to Edward Everett for $250 (Thorpe to Edward Everett, August, 1859, in Bancroft Papers, Massachusetts Historical Society Library, Boston).

62. For an account of the publishing history of Thorpe's Mexican War books, see Eugene Current-Garcia, "Thomas Bangs Thorpe and the Literature of the Ante-Bellum Southwestern Frontier," 199–222; and Rickels, *Thomas Bangs Thorpe*, 117–28, 147–56.

63. Thomas Bangs Thorpe to Carey and Hart, April 5, 1848, in New-York Historical Society. Eighteen months earlier, Thorpe had written that this volume was completed "so far as matter is concerned" (Thomas Bangs Thorpe to Abraham Hart, October 1, 1846, in New-York Historical Society).

requested credit: "If you will send me the plates I will give you the most responsible house in the city, authority to pay you the hundred dollars for them, from the first moneys due me from the publication of my sketches." Baird refused this offer as well. "I repeat my offer of one hundred dollars for these plates, and if you do not choose to take the amount, I shall proceed to publish my works complete," Thorpe replied just one week later. At the end of October he tried to persuade Baird to come to terms by stressing the errors in *Mysteries*, errors that had not troubled him when it first came out:

> The book was published from M.S. which I got copied from my own, by a *clerk of a court*. I did this as I thought as I could not read the proofs, that such a course would secure the book against mistakes. The very opposite was the consequence. The copyist filled his m.s. full of errors not in the original, and upon some of the pages in the work, there are from five to eight errors, and scarcely a page but has one or more. . . . these mistakes nevertheless destroy the literary as well as the commercial value of the book.

Less than a week later, on November 2, Thorpe accepted Baird's terms for the note and promised to pay the full amount, which is not mentioned in the extant letters, on or before the date due. Baird shipped the plates to New York City at the end of 1853, and within three months Appleton released *The Hive of "The Bee-Hunter," A Repository of Sketches, Including Peculiar American Character, Scenery, and Rural Sports*.[64]

Hoping to achieve financial stability, Thorpe moved back to New York City with his family in 1854. Besides publishing *Hive* that year, he released a novel, *The Master's House; A Tale of Southern Life*, and began writing frequently for *Harper's New Monthly Magazine*. However, after *Hive* had been on sale for almost a year, Thorpe had still not paid the money due Baird. Replying to a letter from him, Thorpe said in March, 1855, that he wanted his publisher to return the plates. Shortly after the death of his wife in October, Thorpe finally acknowledged his inability to pay Baird and promised that "upon receipt of the note held against me, I will relinquish all interest in copyright of 'Mysteries of the Backwoods.'"[65] Thus, when T. B. Peterson and Brothers

---

64. Thomas Bangs Thorpe to Henry C. Baird, May 23, August 31, and September 3, 1852; September 15, 23, October 27, November 2, and December 25, 1853, all in Edward Carey Gardiner Collection, Historical Society of Pennsylvania, Philadelphia.
65. Thorpe to Henry Carey Baird, February 1, March 17, October 22, 1855, all in Gardiner Collection.

added *Mysteries* to its Library of Humorous American Works in 1865, along with other volumes published by Carey and Hart and its successors, Thorpe had no part in the venture.

In collecting sketches for *Hive*, Thorpe included all those in *Mysteries* except three: "Traits of the Prairies," "Concordia Lake," and "A Frontier Incident." He divided the lengthy "Pictures of Buffalo Hunting" into two separate pieces, entitling them "Buffalo Hunting" and "Scenes in Buffalo Hunting." Besides revising each sketch, Thorpe added ten others: "Summer Retreat in Arkansas," "The Big Bear of Arkansas," "Large and Small Steamers of the Mississippi," "A Storm Scene on the Mississippi," "Woodcock Fire-Hunting," "Opossum Hunting," "A 'Hoosier' in Search of Justice," "Major Gasden's Story," "The Great Four-Mile Day," and "The Way That Americans Go Down Hill." One of these, "The Great Four-Mile Day," is not by Thorpe. According to the headnote, it "was elicited from a celebrated but idle pen, by personal friendship for the 'Bee-Hunter.'" It originally appeared in the *Southern Sportsman* on March 27, 1843, as "Reflection of the Turf." The author, who there used the pseudonym A Flat, was A. C. Bullitt, editor of the New Orleans *Bee*. Of the additional pieces by Thorpe, "Major Gasden's Story," originally published under the title "My First Dinner in New Orleans," is the only one that had not previously appeared before a national audience in the pages of the *Spirit* in the 1840s. Also, Thorpe changed the titles "Wit of the Woods" to "Wild Turkey Hunting" and "Louisiana Law of Cock-Fighting" to "A 'Hoosier' in Search of Justice" when revising them. "Enemy in Front and Rear" is the only humorous sketch set in the Southwest known to have been written by Thorpe after the publication of *Mysteries*, and he did not include it in this expanded collection. The publication of *Hive* does not reflect a desire to resume writing humorous and sporting articles. Rather, he chose to offer the public revised versions of the newspaper pieces that established his reputation in the early 1840s.

The twenty-four sketches in *Hive* appear in this order: "Wild Turkey Hunting," "Summer Retreat in Arkansas," "Tom Owen, the Bee-Hunter," "Arrow-Fishing," "The Big Bear of Arkansas," "The Mississippi," "Large and Small Steamers of the Mississippi," "Familiar Scenes on the Mississippi," "A Storm Scene on the Mississippi," "Grizzly Bear-Hunting," "A Piano in Arkansas," "Wild-Cat Hunting," "Mike Fink, the Keel-Boatman," "Alligator Killing," "Buffalo Hunting," "Scenes in Buffalo Hunting," "Woodcock Fire-Hunting," "The Water Craft of the Back-Woods," "Place de la Croix. A Romance of the West," "Opossum

Hunting," "A 'Hoosier' in Search of Justice," "Major Gasden's Story," "The Great Four-Mile Day," and "The Way That Americans Go Down Hill."

All of Darley's illustrations for *Mysteries* are reprinted in *Hive* except the one of Mike Fink asleep at his campfire. Thorpe substituted for that a picture of Fink shooting at Proud Joe. The frontispiece of a wild-turkey hunter is new, as are two other illustrations for the famous sketches "Summer Retreat in Arkansas" and "The Big Bear of Arkansas," neither of which is in *Mysteries*. Thorpe's drawings of bees are no longer on the title page or above the sketch about Tom Owen.

The *Knickerbocker* was the first publication to include a notice of *Hive*. The editor praised Thorpe's "great clearness and simplicity of style, close observation of nature and character, and a certain dry humor of description." He singled out the sketch on hunting wild turkeys just as he had in the earlier review of *Mysteries*, this time reprinting a long section from it. Porter copied this review in the *Spirit* and also printed "The Great Four-Mile Day." Short, complimentary notices also appeared in *Graham's*, the *Southern Literary Messenger*, *De Bow's*, *Harper's*, and the *Southern Quarterly Review*. An indication of the book's popularity was its translation into German in 1856.[66]

Thorpe's inclusion in the standard anthologies of the day helped to sustain the reputation he had achieved by appearing in Porter's publications and by writing his own books. As early as February, 1845, Rufus Griswold wrote Thorpe that he wanted to print something by him in *The Prose Writers of America*, which was published in 1847. "Having almost always written for the 'Spirit,' I have indulged my pen in humorous sketches," Thorpe explained to him. "I should prefer *one extract* of a different character to divercify my style." He sent Griswold "A Squatter's Wife" and also referred him to "Primitive Forests of the Mississippi." Later he sent a copy of "Traits of the Prairies." But Griswold decided to print "Tom Owen, the Bee-Hunter" and four excerpts

---

66. "Literary Notices," *Knickerbocker Magazine*, XLIII (April, 1854), 407–409 (Rickels is mistaken in saying that this review was reprinted from the *Spirit* [*Thomas Bangs Thorpe*, 179–80]; Porter printed his own paragraph of praise in the *Spirit* on June 3); "The Hive of the Bee-Hunter," *Spirit of the Times*, XXIV (April 22, 1854), 111–12; "The Great Four-Mile Day," *Spirit of the Times*, XXIV (June 17, 1854), 208–209; "Review of New Books," *Graham's Magazine*, XLV (July, 1854), 106; "Notices of New Works," *Southern Literary Messenger*, XX (July, 1854), 447–48; "Editorial, Book Notices, Etc.," De Bow's *Commercial Review*, XVII (August, 1854), 217; "Literary Notices," *Harper's New Monthly Magazine*, IX (August, 1854), 425; "Critical Notices," *Southern Quarterly Review*, X (October, 1854), 525–26; T. B. Thorpe, *Tom Owen der Bienenjäger, und andere Geschichten aus dem Südwesten*, trans. W. E. Drugulin (2 vols.; Leipzig, 1856).

from "The Big Bear of Arkansas," which he entitled "Fat Game," "Dogs and Guns," "A Farm in Arkansas," and "Death of the Big Bear." The introduction to these pieces mentions the work of Longstreet and Hooper and explains that Thorpe serves as the only representative of the southwestern writers because of the limitations of space. Biographical facts in the introduction are from an account Thorpe himself sent Griswold.[67] William Gilmore Simms selected "The Disgraced Scalp Lock" for his *Transatlantic Tales, Sketches*, and *Legends*, published in England in 1842, the same year the piece originally appeared. Also in England, Thomas Chandler Haliburton, creator of the popular Sam Slick, the Yankee clock peddler, edited two 3-volume anthologies of American humor in the early 1850s. The first, *Traits of American Humour*, includes "The Big Bear of Arkansas," and "Bob Herring, the Arkansas Bear Hunter" is in *The Americans at Home*.[68] These are the same two sketches that Porter included in his anthologies, from which Haliburton copied them. George and Evert Duyckinck selected "Tom Owen, the Bee-Hunter" for their *Cyclopaedia of American Literature* (1855). The introductory remarks praise Thorpe's recent book, *Hive*, and relate an anecdote about how Sir William Drummond Stewart apparently accepted "Letters from the Far West" as the most truthful account written of his expedition. William Burton's *The Cyclopaedia of Wit and Humor*, another large anthology of the 1850s, selected two stories from *Hive* that had not appeared in other anthologies: "A 'Hoosier' in Search of Justice" and "A Piano in Arkansas." Burton also published an excerpt from *The Master's House*, which he entitled "Cinderella Negrotyped."[69] In it a slave tells her master's children the Cinderella story, adapted to a plantation setting.

Near the end of the century, Thorpe's sketches again began to appear in anthologies. Edward Mason printed "A 'Hoosier' in Search of Justice" in a collection of humorous writing. Edmund Clarence Stedman's eleven-volume *A Library of American Literature* contains "Tom

67. Thorpe to Rufus W. Griswold, March 19 and July 27, 1845, both in Gratz Collection; Rufus W. Griswold (ed.), *The Prose Writers of America* (Philadelphia, 1847), 546–49; Thomas Bangs Thorpe to Rufus W. Griswold, March 19, 1845, in Griswold Manuscripts, Boston Public Library. The unsigned biographical sketch is in the Griswold Manuscripts.

68. William Gilmore Simms (ed.), *Transatlantic Tales, Sketches, and Legends* (London, 1842), 60–65; Thomas Chandler Haiburton (ed.), *Traits of American Humour, by Native Authors* (3 vols.; London, [1852]), I, 18–29; and *The Americans at Home; or, Byeways, Backwoods, and Prairies* (3 vols.; London, 1854), III, 151–71. "The Big Bear of Arkansas" appeared also in England in *Bentley's Miscellany*, XXVII (1850), 35–43.

69. George and Evert Duyckinck (eds.), *Cyclopaedia of American Literature* (2 vols.; New York, 1855), II, 613–15; William Burton (ed.), *The Cyclopaedia of Wit and Humor* (New York, 1858), 372–76.

Owen, the Bee-Hunter," but the two opening and two closing paragraphs are omitted.[70]

The many scholars of southern literary history at the beginning of the twentieth century did not consider Thorpe in their surveys of humorists.[71] Possibly they excluded him because of his birth and long residence in the North, despite the seventeen years in Louisiana during which he wrote of local scenes and characters. Thorpe does not appear in William P. Trent's *Southern Writers* (1905), nor is he mentioned in the multivolume *Library of Southern Literature* (1909–1913), edited by Edwin Anderson Alderman and Joel Chandler Harris. Alexander DeMenil's *The Literature of the Louisiana Territory*, which reprinted "Tom Owen, the Bee-Hunter," is the only work from the first decade of the century to recognize Thorpe as a writer of the region. In 1911, Marshall P. Wilder selected the *Hive* version of "A Piano in Arkansas" for his multi-volume collection *The Wit and Humor of America*.[72]

In 1930, Franklin J. Meine revived interest in Thorpe as a southwestern writer by reprinting "The Big Bear of Arkansas" in *Tall Tales of the Southwest*. Since then "The Big Bear of Arkansas" has become the most frequently reprinted of his pieces. Meine made over thirty changes in wording, spelling, and punctuation from the printing in Porter's *Big Bear* anthology, which he selected as copy-text. One of the most noticeable is the change of Jim Doggett's "prehaps" to "perhaps" throughout. Walter Blair introduced several variants in punctuation when he reprinted Meine's text in *Native American Humor* (1937). Individual words were omitted and numerous accidentals emended, probably to conform to contemporary usage, though the edited text is not uniform. The number of these silent emendations is greatly multiplied in the text Blair and Raven I. McDavid, Jr., prepared for *The Mirth of a Nation* (1983). There they attempted "sympathetic translations" of a wide range of nineteenth-century dialect humor by regularizing punctuation and correcting misspellings not essential to the humor, all with the aim of helping these works remain popular with a general audience. For example, "bar" is spelled "bear" and "Arkansaw" is "Arkan-

70. Edward Mason (ed.), *Humorous Masterpieces from American Literature* (2 vols.; New York, 1887), I, 150–55; Edmund Clarence Stedman and Ellen Mackay Hutchinson (eds.), *A Library of American Literature from the Earliest Settlement to the Present Time* (11 vols.; New York, [1887–90]), VII, 288–90.

71. An exception is Robert Cecil Beale, *The Development of the Short Story in the South* (Charlottesville, 1911). However, Beale merely listed Thorpe's name and did not comment on his sketches.

72. Alexander DeMenil (ed.), *The Literature of the Louisiana Territory* (St. Louis, 1904), 140–43; Marshall P. Wilder (ed.), *The Wit and Humor of America* (11 vols.; New York, 1911), V, 895–902.

sas" throughout. However, the result is that the distinction between Doggett and the narrator is less pronounced, since Thorpe had each use a different form of those words. In addition to the confusion resulting from numerous omitted words and lines, the greatest disappointment is that the editors did not live up to the introductory comment that "choices of words haven't been disturbed." The most flagrant example of their unnecessary liberties with Thorpe's text is the substitution of "haunted" for "hunted" in Doggett's comment that "I would see that bar in every thing I did; *he hunted* me." Although the backwoodsman goes on to compare his prey to a devil, "hunted" is both an acceptable and readily understandable word here—and one Thorpe retained in the *Hive* reprinting. Most of the recent collections copy Blair's *Native American Humor* text, with the variants he and Meine introduced, though several use the *Hive* text, which Thorpe had the opportunity to revise.[73] Only the *Norton Anthology of American Literature* reprints the sketch from the *Spirit*, where it first appeared. However, the editors have followed the *Hive* version by silently emending "big Bar" so that both words are capitalized throughout and also by capitalizing "bowie-knife" in the climactic scene, to indicate that the hunter's dog was present.[74]

"A Piano in Arkansas" and "The Disgraced Scalp Lock" are the most frequently printed pieces after "The Big Bear of Arkansas." However, neither has been anthologized since the 1960s, when they both appeared in Hennig Cohen and William B. Dillingham's *Humor of the Old Southwest* and when "The Disgraced Scalp Lock" appeared in John Francis McDermott's collection of Mississippi River sketches. Editors have reprinted "A Piano in Arkansas" from *Mysteries* and *Hive* but never from the *Spirit* where it originally appeared. Only ex-

73. Franklin J. Meine (ed.), *Tall Tales of the Southwest* (New York, 1930), 9–21; Walter Blair (ed.), *Native American Humor (1800–1900)* (New York, 1937), 337–48; Walter Blair and Raven I. McDavid, Jr. (eds.), *The Mirth of a Nation: America's Great Dialect Humor* (Minneapolis, 1983), 49–59; Harrison Meserole, Walter Sutton, and Brom Weber (eds.), *American Literature: Tradition and Innovation* (Lexington, Mass., 1969), 1626–36. Meserole's anthology follows the *Hive* text, even though it prints 1845, the date of *Mysteries*, below the sketch.

74. T. B. Thorpe, "Big Bear of Arkansas," in Ronald Gottesman *et al.* (eds.), *The Norton Anthology of American Literature* (2 vols.; New York, 1979), I, 1468–78. In the text in this book and its 1985 reprinting, the words *a*, *the*, and *that* have each been dropped once and several punctuation marks have been changed. However, a note explains the decision to emend the puzzling "chickens and rolette" to "checkers and rolotte," following the *Spirit* printing. Brom Weber claimed that the *Spirit* printing served as copy-text for *An Anthology of American Humor* (New York, 1962), 246–55. However, collation indicates that his printing conforms to Porter's *Big Bear* anthology at almost every point where that text differs from the *Spirit*. Quite possibly, Weber referred to the *Spirit* to make some spelling and wording changes in a text indebted to the Blair printing.

cerpts from the *Hive* version of "The Disgraced Scalp Lock" have been printed, but the complete *Spirit* and *Mysteries* texts are in anthologies.[75]

In 1978, Leland H. Cox, Jr., edited the "Letters from the Far West" series for the first appearance of those letters since their newspaper publication in the 1840s. Unfortunately, because not all the issues of the *Intelligencer* were available to Cox, in three cases he used the *Spirit* reprint as copy-text. Mark Keller's 1979 article on "Tom Owen, the Bee-Hunter" contains a reprint of "Reminiscences of Tom Owen, the Bee Hunter" from the *Spirit* of 1859. The piece offers several anecdotes demonstrating the good humor of the local figure Thorpe made famous. Keller calls it "the most detailed piece of contemporary writing about the Southwestern humor that is extant today."[76]

Several other pieces, either in whole or in part, have been gathered by editors over the past fifty years. In a book on Arkansas folklore, Fred Allsopp printed the humorous description of an Irishman from "Opossums and 'Possum Hunting." Arthur Palmer Hudson published "Reminiscences of Seargent S. Prentiss, of Mississippi," a eulogy of the Whig politician. Three short excerpts from "Remembrances of the Mississippi" and two from "Cotton and Its Cultivation," both *Harper's* articles, are in Benjamin Botkin's collection of southern folklore, and his book on Mississippi River folklore includes selections from "Remembrances of the Mississippi," "The Mississippi," "Alligator Killing," and "Piscatory Archery." "Woodcock Fire Hunting" is in Clarence Gohdes's anthology of antebellum hunting accounts. For the first time in this century, John Q. Anderson printed "The Louisiana Law of Cock-Fighting," which was in two nineteenth-century anthologies. He used the less genteel *Spirit* text but made silent changes in wording, punctuation, and paragraphing. In his collection of pieces about the Missis-

75. Hennig Cohen and William B. Dillingham (eds.), *Humor of the Old Southwest* (Boston, 1964), 279–95; John Francis McDermott (ed.), *Before Mark Twain: A Sampler of Old, Old Times on the Mississippi* (Carbondale, 1968), 235–47; "A Piano in Arkansas," Arlin Turner (ed.), *Southern Stories* (New York, 1960), 61–67. Portions taken from the *Hive* version of "The Disgraced Scalp Lock" are in James Daugherty (ed.), *Their Weight in Wildcats: Tales of the Frontier* (Boston, 1936), 3–19, and Arthur Palmer Hudson, *Humor of the Old Deep South* (New York, 1936), 298–300. The *Spirit* printing served as copy-text in Walter Blair and Franklin J. Meine (eds.), *Half Horse Half Alligator: The Growth of the Mike Fink Legend* (Chicago, 1956), 68–82. However, they silently altered punctuation, paragraphing, and several misspellings. McDermott used the *Spirit* as copy-text for that sketch in *Before Mark Twain*. He also silently corrected some misspelled words but did not make changes in the paragraphing or the punctuation.

76. Leland H. Cox, Jr., "T. B. Thorpe's Far West Letters," in James L. W. West III (ed.), *Gyascutus: Studies in Antebellum Southern Humorous and Sporting Writing* (Atlantic Highlands, N.J., 1978), 115–57; Mark Keller, "T. B. Thorpe's 'Tom Owen, the Bee-Hunter': Southwestern Humor's 'Origin of Species,'" *Southern Studies*, XVIII (Spring, 1979), 89–101.

sippi River, John Francis McDermott included "The Little Steamboats of the Mississippi" and "A Storm Scene on the Mississippi," both from the *Spirit*, in addition to the more popular sketches "The Big Bear of Arkansas" and "The Disgraced Scalp Lock." Finally, Eugene L. Schwaab reprinted "Our Visit to Natchez" from the *Southern Sportsman* and "Sugar and the Sugar Region of Louisiana" from *Harper's* in his collection of periodical articles describing life in the Old South.[77]

The desire of scholars during the past half century to identify and preserve indigenous American humor has clearly influenced editors when choosing works by Thorpe. While "The Big Bear of Arkansas" undoubtedly deserves the attention it has received, all save one editor have overlooked Thorpe's serious accounts of rural sports. Also indicative of the change in literary tastes is that "Tom Owen, the Bee-Hunter," equal in popularity with "The Big Bear of Arkansas" during Thorpe's lifetime, has not been reprinted since 1904.

The bias in contemporary anthologies is significant because Thorpe's books are not readily available, and not surprisingly, studies of Thorpe rarely refer to sketches that are not anthologized.[78] The cost of preserving his reputation as a humorist and as a teller of a Big Bear story has been that his factual descriptions of the scenery and rural sports of the Old Southwest are now generally unknown.

77. Fred Allsopp, *Folklore of Romantic Arkansas* (2 vols.; New York, 1931), II, 241; Arthur Palmer Hudson, *Humor of the Old Deep South* (New York, 1936), 188–92; Thorpe, "Mississippi Soil," "The Value of Religious Instruction," "A Flatboat Passenger Finds Excitement," "Samuel Mason," and "Fox-Hunting Fever," all in Benjamin A. Botkin (ed.), *A Treasury of Southern Folklore* (New York, 1949), 48–49, 104–105, 127–28, 219–20, and 610–11; Thorpe, "Bill M'Coy's Honor," "Cut-Offs, Rafts, Sawyers, Snags, and Planters," "Alligator Killing," and "Arrow Fishing," all in Benjamin A. Botkin (ed.), *A Treasury of Mississippi River Folklore* (New York, 1955), 167–68, 271–72, 443–45, 445–47; Gohdes (ed.), *Hunting in the Old South*, 114–19; Anderson, *With the Bark On*, 188–90; Thorpe, "The Little Steamboats of the Mississippi" and "A Storm Scene on the Mississippi," in McDermott (ed.), *Before Mark Twain*, 87–90, 161–65; Eugene L. Schwaab (ed.), *Travels in the Old South: Selected from the Periodicals of the Times* (2 vols.; Lexington, Ky., 1973), II, 367–70, 494–519. Only the first two paragraphs reprinted by Schwaab as "Our Visit to Natchez" are part of the piece Thorpe wrote after attending an agricultural fair in Mississippi. The rest of the article is by an unidentified correspondent who visited Natchez at the same time and signed his letter "Your friend, P."

78. In 1970, Literature House reprinted a facsimile of the first edition of *Mysteries*. In 1960, Lost Cause Press issued *Mysteries* and *Hive* in its microcard series. University Microfilms released the same books on microfilm in its American Culture Series in 1962. *Mysteries*, *Hive*, and *The Master's House* were issued by Research Publications, Inc., in its microfilm series in 1971. Two more studies of unanthologized materials should be mentioned: John T. Flanagan, "Western Sportsmen Travelers in the New York *Spirit of the Times*," in John Francis McDermott (ed.), *Travelers on the Western Frontier* (Urbana, 1970), 168–86; and Daniel F. Littlefield, Jr., "Thomas Bangs Thorpe and the Passing of the Southwestern Wilderness," *Southern Literary Journal*, XI (Spring, 1979), 56–65.

TEXTUAL COMMENTARY

Despite the fact that so few of Thorpe's writings have been in print during the last fifty years, scholars still recognize him as one of the foremost humorists of the Old Southwest. This edition of forty-nine pieces that he wrote about the region offers a broader view of the talents and interests upon which his reputation rests, placing his humorous pieces alongside the descriptive and sporting articles that also received much of his attention. It includes reliable texts for the twenty-five different sketches in his two collections, for the twelve humorous letters and eleven other pieces that appeared only in newspapers in the 1840s, and for the only article by him for which a manuscript is known to exist. All of Thorpe's articles written for the *Spirit* before he moved back to New York in 1854 are included except one, a piece based on reminiscences of his boyhood in the East that he never reprinted.[1] "The Mississippi" and "Place de la Croix," his earliest magazine pieces, are the only writings for national magazines in this edition because, unlike any of the others that appeared in such periodicals, they were later collected in his books. He wrote all of the pieces included here between 1839 and 1848, with the exception of "A Tradition of the Natchez," published in 1855, for which the manuscript survives. This edition, then, makes easily accessible Thorpe's generally unknown writings about the Old Southwest. Furthermore, it presents dependable texts for sketches that he revised and reprinted, and also a list of the significant substantive revisions that he made when preparing for a national book-buying audience what he had written several years earlier for sporting publications and local newspapers.

Since no manuscripts or printer's copies are currently extant for his writings during the 1840s, the earliest available texts are the printed ones. The pieces in this edition first appeared in the *Concordia Intel-*

---

1. "Cook-A-Doo-Dle-Doo," *Spirit of the Times*, XI (July 24, 1841), 247. Also omitted from this edition are a similar sketch, "Old Dutch Houses and Their Associations," *Knickerbocker Magazine*, XVIII (August, 1841), 150–55, and the letter "A Defence of Woodcock Fire-Hunting," *Spirit of the Times*, XII (October 15, 1842), 385–86.

ligencer, the *Daily National*, the *Daily Picayune*, the *Knickerbocker Magazine*, the *New Sporting Magazine*, the *Southern Sportsman*, the *Spirit*, and the *Tropic*, and in the book *Mysteries*. Thorpe reprinted eleven sketches once, eleven twice, and one three times in the *Intelligencer*, *Mysteries*, or *Hive*. The number of substantive variants between first and final versions ranges from around 30 in "Piscatory Archery" to over 150 in "The Disgraced Scalp Lock." "The Devil's Summer Retreat, in Arkansaw," "A Piano in Arkansas," and "Wit of the Woods" also have more than 100 each. "The Big Bear of Arkansas," though lengthy, has just over 50. Besides the many changes in wording, variants resulted from deleting or adding material and from incorporating one sketch into another. Only in the case of "Wild Turkey Shooting" did Thorpe so extensively revise a sketch that what he produced, "Wit of the Woods," must be considered a different piece.

The changes in accidentals deserve only brief comment in this discussion of the differences in the versions of the sketches. As many accidental as substantive variants, if not more, occur in each piece. Yet only in two cases do they alter the meaning of a sentence. In the original *New Sporting Magazine* printing of "The American Wild Cat" the western hunter boasts that he can "keep it up rough, and tumble as long as a wild cat." When Porter reprinted this in his *American Turf Register*, he changed the punctuation so that commas set off the common expression "rough and tumble," and Thorpe followed this revision in subsequent printings. The *Spirit* version of "The Disgraced Scalp Lock" says that after Mike Fink shot off Proud Joe's scalp lock, the Indian's "eye glared upon the jeering crowd around; like a fiend, his chest swelled and heaved, until it seemed that he must suffocate." The printing in *Mysteries* places the semicolon after "fiend," thus making the Indian's fiendish quality his glaring eye rather than his heaving chest. However, because house style so greatly affects punctuation and because only the printed texts are available, analyzing the variants in accidentals from printing to printing cannot lead to trustworthy conclusions about Thorpe's writing style.

Simple revisions in paragraphing are immediately noticeable in the reprintings of most of the sketches. Contrary to current journalistic practice, the newspaper versions usually have lengthy paragraphs. Some of the sketches reprinted in *Mysteries* have more paragraph divisions than do the originals, such as "A Piano in Arkansas," which has twice as many, but most have about the same number. The only exception is "A Frontier Incident," which has ten paragraphs in the

Spirit and only two in *Mysteries*. In *Hive* almost every sketch has four times as many paragraphs as are in its first printing. "The Big Bear of Arkansas" has twenty-four in the *Spirit*, twenty-seven in Porter's *Big Bear* anthology, which served as copy-text for *Hive*, and ninety-five in *Hive*. The *Spirit* version of "The Devil's Summer Retreat, in Arkansaw" has only seven paragraphs. Yet in *Hive* it has sixty, even though Thorpe added no new sections when revising the text. In a few of the sketches the new paragraphing separates speakers' statements in conversation, but usually the divisions seem arbitrary. As with punctuation, Thorpe's control over the changes in paragraphing is impossible to discern on the basis of the printed texts alone.

Substantive variants in several sketches in *Hive* result from the simple reordering of sentences. In the earlier version of "Piscatory Archery" the two sentences explaining the shape of the canoe and the equipment it must contain came before, rather than after, the contrasting descriptions of a novice and a veteran navigator of such a canoe. Shifting four sentences in "Pictures of Buffalo Hunting" similarly creates a more logical progression. When the narrator sees the dwelling of a squatter in northern Texas, he imagines he will pass a comfortable evening there. The *Mysteries* text describes the "lazy, contemptible set of creatures" he unexpectedly meets, before going on to sketch his naïve hopes of enjoying civilized life with them. More effectively, in *Hive* the passage about his illusions precedes any hint of what the narrator will soon find. The sentences in the final paragraph of the original version of "The American Wild Cat" neither logically follow the first sentence nor logically lead into the last. In *Hive*, however, the first sentence mentions the "peculiarities of the cat," and four sentences elaborating on its characteristics come next. The four sentences giving examples of references to the wildcat in the language of the frontier, therefore, are in the last half of the paragraph, where they prepare the reader for the final sentence that mentions Indian traditions and expressions referring to the animal. The desire for greater unity may also have motivated the reordering of several sentences in "Wit of the Woods." However, not enough sentences were shifted, and comments on the wild turkey still interrupt remarks on the character of the turkey hunter.

By far the greatest number of substantive variants are changes in single words or in short phrases; many are inconsequential and could as likely result from house style as from Thorpe's attention. For example, the reprinting of "Opossums and 'Possum Hunting" has "upon" for "on," "ways of doing" for "ways to do," "tree containing" for "tree that contains," and "will you" for "you will." The substitution of "aroused" for "roused" in a later version of "A Grizzly Bear Hunt" is only one instance of revisions that retain the root word. In that sketch, Thorpe also changed "bear" to "bears" and revised passages from singular to plural to maintain consistency. In "Pictures of Buffalo Hunting," the second version has "declared that he would bring" for "declared he would bring," "which" for "that" in several instances, "a token" for "the token," and "rush upon" for "are rushing upon." Other frequent changes in the revised sketches are the substitution or addition of a conjunction, the repetition or deletion of the subject or verb in a compound sentence, and the substitution of a noun for a pronoun or vice versa. While no pattern is apparent in such miscellaneous revisions, other categories do show Thorpe's attention to matters of style and audience. Frequently, he deleted references to contemporary figures, clarified awkward passages, omitted overused words, shaped the sketches for a more genteel audience, and altered the representation of frontier language.

Several of the sketches refer by name to particular acquaintances of Thorpe or to well-known men of the time. In "Concordia Lake" the fisherman Elliott may be Charles Loring Elliott, the painter who was his fellow student under John Quidor. Unidentifiable are Mathews, the skillful storyteller mentioned in "A Frontier Incident," Squire Jones in "The Big Bear of Arkansas," Major Gasden in the revised version of "My First Dinner in New Orleans," and W——, the successful turkey hunter in "Wit of the Woods." Thorpe deleted many specific references to prominent contemporaries in the *Hive* version of the texts. In "Tom Owen, the Bee-Hunter," Davy Crockett's name remains in the first paragraph, but the general term "western hunters" is substituted for it in the conclusion. Similarly, "the great men of the Southern Turf" replaces the specific mention of Colonel Adam L. Bingaman, Natchez racehorse owner and breeder. Nor does the name of Captain John Ross, the Englishman who led an expedition to the North Pole, remain in "The Way Americans Go Down Hill." Besides these changes, the *Mysteries* text of "A Piano in Arkansas" deletes the name of Captain Frederick Marryat and all references to his *Diary in America*.

Many sentences in the sketches are awkward, and Thorpe's prose style has numerous flaws. Yet he did make improvements in later printings. For example, the conclusion of the original version of "A Piano in Arkansas" states that "the seeds of envy, and maliciousness of fash-

64

ion were at that moment sown in the village of Hard-scrabble." In *Mysteries* this confusing sentence opens with "The fashionable vices of envy and maliciousness," making it more intelligible. In "The Disgraced Scalp Lock," Thorpe reworked a sentence about the flatboatmen of an earlier age: "Obscurity has obliterated nearly the actions and the men—a few of the latter still exist, as if to justify their wonderful exploits, which now live almost exclusively as traditions." In *Mysteries* the passage begins: "Obscurity has nearly obliterated the men, and their actions." However, the statement is not precise until the word "death" appears in the *Hive* version: "Death has nearly destroyed the men, and obscurity is fast obliterating the record of their deeds; but a few examples still exist, as if to justify the truth of these wonderful exploits, now almost wholly confined to tradition." Thorpe also avoided awkwardness by integrating his ideas more explicitly. One paragraph in "A Grizzly Bear Hunt" explains how the hunter depends on his improved powers of sight. Its second sentence very abruptly mentions a deaf, dumb, and blind girl in the Hartford Asylum who relies on her heightened sense of touch. The *Hive* version clearly explains the parallel Thorpe had in mind, so that readers need no longer make for themselves the connection between the girl's touch and the hunter's sight. Another way Thorpe improved his writing was by using synonyms for repeated words. In the *Hive* version of "A Grizzly Bear Hunt" other words are substituted for "bear" and "cave" when either appears too frequently within a few lines. Likewise, in "The American Wild Cat" synonyms replace the overworked "hound" and "often." Such revisions give the later texts more polish than many of the sketches have in their first printing.

Other revisions indicate Thorpe's desire to appeal to the tastes of a more genteel, and presumably also a larger feminine, audience than that which his pieces had in their original appearance. In "The Louisiana Law of Cock-Fighting" he changed the boatman's final condemnation of the lawyer from "a dam fool" to the less offensive "an infernal old chuckel-headed fool." In a section of "Wild Turkey Shooting" that Thorpe incorporated into "Wit of the Woods," the Indian hunter explains that he cannot kill a turkey because the animal easily notices "dat damn Indian" approaching. In the revised version the turkey merely thinks, "Indian coming sure," before running away. Although the swear word was left blank in the first version of "A Storm Scene on the Mississippi," in *Hive* "bear on it like ———" reads "bear on it harder." And even the general statement in "Scenes on the Mississippi" that "the crew of the boat yelled and shouted, and swore at the sport" was emended to tell only that they "yelled and shouted." Nevertheless, Thorpe did not revise every instance of such language. In the *Hive* version of "The Devil's Summer Retreat, in Arkansaw," Bob Herring and his friends still tell one another "to go where the occupier of the Retreat in Summer is supposed to reside through the winter months," and they also avoid circumlocution and say "hell" directly.

Furthermore, Thorpe considered some other figures of speech by the narrator inappropriate for his new audience. The book versions omit the reference to Tom Owen's underwear, which says that his linen, "like a neglected penant, displayed itself in his rear." The humor at the expense of Roman Catholics in a sentence from "A Piano in Arkansas" disappeared. The *Mysteries* and *Hive* texts state not that "Cash believed in Mo Mercer with a faith that no Catholic believes in the Pope" but comment instead that Cash believed "with an abandonment perfectly ridiculous." The *Spirit* version explains that when Cash discovered the washing machine on the newcomers' porch, "Mercer turned to the thing as coolly as a toper would to a glass of brandy and water." In both books the comparison is more genteel: "as coolly as a north wind to an icicle."

Even though in *Hive*, Jim Doggett says, "Stranger, it took five niggers and myself to put that carcase on a mule's back," Thorpe omitted every other use of "nigger" in that book. The word "mule" replaces "nigger" in Mike Fink's lament that "the rifle won't make a man a living now— he must turn nigger and work." Tom Owen no longer addresses his assistant as "nigger." The stage driver in "The Way Americans Go Down Hill" uses "darkey" instead. And Bob Herring's expression "like a high pressure nigger camp meeting" becomes "like a high pressure political meeting."

Although Thorpe apparently never sought to present the spoken dialect of the frontier in minute detail, he did incorporate colloquialisms into the dialogue. He also misspelled certain words to suggest local pronunciation. In the revised sketches, some additional words and phrases are in the vernacular, while others, puzzlingly, have been corrected to standard English. In "The Big Bear of Arkansas" the changes of "took" to "tuk," "Kentuck" to "Kaintuck," "I know of" to "I know'd of," and "who had stopped at my place" to "who had drapped in at my place" increase the authenticity of Jim Doggett as a backwoodsman. Thorpe also revised "bar" to "bear" to suggest Doggett's unique pronunciation of the word. Yet in the same printing he says, "I swelled up considerably" instead of "I swelled up considerable," and the spelling "bisiness" is standard. Also in *Hive*, seemingly inconsistent variants appear in "The Devil's Summer Retreat, in Arkansaw." The changes of "nothin'" to "nothing" and of "knowing" to "knowin" occur within twenty lines of each other. While the spellings "malitia," "parfectly," and "prehaps" are regularized, "nigh" becomes "nih," and "sat" becomes "sot." Drawing valid conclusions about whether Thorpe attempted to represent the vernacular more fully in his revisions is impossible on the basis of the printed texts. Some of the changes do seem to be authorial, but others could quite likely be errors by a typesetter who did not recognize the purpose of each misspelling.

Despite the large number of revisions in wording, Thorpe seldom changed his mind about the material that belonged in a sketch once it had been published. He deleted the footnote in "Place de la Croix" and the one in "A Storm Scene on the Mississippi," as well as the first one in "Piscatory Archery," before the second printing of each. The passage in "The Disgraced Scalp Lock" describing the beautiful scenery along the Ohio River is the only lengthy section later omitted. However, in preparing the sketches for *Hive*, Thorpe did add material to several. Immediately following the introductory paragraph in "Opossums and 'Possum Hunting," a new section of approximately 350 words describes the physical characteristics of the animal. The original version tells only about the opossum's habits, before narrating the methods used to capture it on a particular evening's hunt.

Not wanting "Woodcock Fire Hunting" to be considered a hoax, as it had been upon its original publication, Thorpe prepared a new introduction for it in *Hive*. The opening explains that the "legitimists" and the "strait laced" were unwilling to believe the account because such hunting does not follow the rules of the sport. They were horrified to learn how many animals a fire hunter unconstrained by those rules could slaughter so easily. Yet not all who hunt do so merely for sport, the introduction cautions. In the backwoods, people often pursue game "as a necessary of life." The new introduction, then, clarifies the appropriateness of the headnote, "'Tis murderous, but profitable."

In the original version of "My First Dinner in New Orleans" the narrator tells about joining a private party by mistake the first day of his stay in a New Orleans hotel. The introduction to the *Hive* version provides a frame for this tale, thus changing the narrator's point of view. The story is no longer his own. Because he records the reminiscence Major Gasden told to "a happy party" of which he was a member, it is now "Major Gasden's Story." The major "could detail very common-place incidents so dramatically, that he would give them a real interest." Although presenting the tale verbatim, the narrator of the sketch is not taken in by the storyteller, as is the gentleman traveler by Jim Doggett. The "occasional twinkle" in the major's eye causes him to question what he hears. Even though the frame is not very highly developed, it does increase the sketch's complexity by calling attention to the art of the storyteller who entertains by trying to give his exaggerated embellishments the air of truth.

In two instances, Thorpe added material by inserting a previously published piece or part of one. Although he wrote to Rufus Griswold that the last part of "Primitive Forests of the Mississippi" was "much admired," he never republished that sketch.[2] He did, however, revise the last half of the lengthy third paragraph, probably the section that received praise, and incorporated it into the *Hive* text of "The Mississippi" after the explanation of the river's cut-offs, rafts, sawyers, and snags. Since "Primitive Forests of the Mississippi" is a personal reminiscence of a hunting trip, Thorpe had to reword the first-person statements so that the passage would be consistent with the style of the other sketch. He also improved the passage by making it more concise. The description of the forests fits well with the longer sketch because both try to stir up sublime emotions from contemplation of God's control over the wonders of nature. The other instance of such revision is the incorporation of "The Last from 'Arkansaw'" into the *Hive* version of "The Little Steamboats of the Mississippi." Of the few changes, the most noticeable are that the backwoodsman becomes Zeb Marston instead of Zeb Maiston; the unnamed captain becomes Captain Raft, as in the anecdote; and the boat has the name *Emperor* throughout, following the longer sketch.

Finally, Thorpe revised almost half of "Wild Turkey Shooting" from the *Spirit* for inclusion in the *Hive* version of "Wit of the Woods." This combination of previously published material is unique in Thorpe's process of revision because the first printing of "Wit of the Woods" in *Mysteries* is itself an extensive reworking of "Wild Turkey Shooting." Thus, the *Hive* version contains material Thorpe chose not to include when he first published the sketch in book form. "Wild Turkey Shooting" and the *Mysteries* version of "Wit of the Woods" do not agree in

2. Thomas Bangs Thorpe to Rufus W. Griswold, March 19, 1845, in Simon Gratz Collection, Historical Society of Pennsylvania, Philadelphia.

68

specific wordings, but they both lament the disappearance of the wild turkey, describe the wild-turkey hunter, and recount a successful hunt. The sketch in *Mysteries*, twice as long as the *Spirit* version, opens not by praising the wild turkey as a distinctly American species, but by noting its "progressive and certain" extermination. The differences in the conclusion are also significant. Whereas "Wild Turkey Shooting" recounts a hunt in one part of the final paragraph, the entire last half of "Wit of the Woods" describes such a hunt. Emphasizing the turkey hunter and his character, the final sentence of the earlier *Spirit* sketch comments on the satisfaction he feels when successful. Conversely, the focus in "Wit of the Woods" is on the thoughts of the turkey as it is lured to its death, and the sketch concludes with this lament: "The glittering plumage, the gay step, the bright eye, all are gone, without a movement of the muscles, he has fallen a headless body to the earth."

The lengthy section from "Wild Turkey Shooting" that is included in revised form in the *Hive* version of "Wit of the Woods" opens with comments about how skillful hunters lessen the number of wild turkeys each year. It continues with a description of the speed of the birds and then reports that many are killed when fatigued from trying to fly across the Mississippi River. It also includes an anecdote about the Indian who sells game in a frontier town but seldom offers a turkey because, as he explains, "no catch Turkey, *he cunning too much*." Following this section, Thorpe added a paragraph explaining that the true turkey hunter does not use dogs, though some are good at the sport. Like the wild turkey, the hunter prefers solitude. After the publication of *Mysteries*, Thorpe observed to his publisher that most of the errors in the book are "unimportant, save those in the 'Wit of the Woods.'" Several months later, in defense of his literary efforts he commented that "the day will come when the 'wit of the woods' will be classical."[3] The careful attention to further revisions for the *Hive* reprinting attests to the prominence this sketch held in Thorpe's mind.

While major revisions in the sketches are quite likely authorial because of the attention Thorpe gave to the preparation of his books, many of the substantive variants probably resulted from house style and errors in typesetting. Nevertheless, the influence other people may have had on Thorpe's texts deserves consideration. Because he could not remain in the East long enough to read the proof sheets for *Mys-*

3. Thomas Bangs Thorpe to Carey and Hart, December 7, 1845, in Thomas Bangs Thorpe Collection (No. 8397), Barrett Library, University of Virginia, Charlottesville; Thorpe to Abraham Hart, March 2, 1846, in New-York Historical Society, New York.

teries, he asked Rufus Griswold to examine "at least such parts of them as refer to peculiarities of language used in the west."[4] No known record shows that Griswold did so and thereby possibly introduced variants into the text.

Porter, however, probably did introduce variants into the sketches he reprinted in the *Spirit*, and collation reveals that in at least two of them, Thorpe retained those substantive variants in a succeeding printing. As editor of the *Spirit*, Porter could also have revised the nineteen sketches by Thorpe that originally appeared there, but because the manuscripts are unavailable, any such changes can only be conjectured. A way of testing the reliability of these first printings is to examine the accuracy of the reprintings of pieces from Thorpe's newspapers. In the *Spirit* each letter in the "Letters from the Far West" series does have variants in spelling and punctuation, ranging from just a couple to over thirty. Eight of the twelve have changes in wording, but the most in any one letter is six. In no instance is a complete passage deleted or rewritten. The only substantive changes in the first letter, for example, are the printing of "whom" for "who" and "Yaihoo Stunn" for "Yalhoo Stunn," as well as the omission of the final four words in "Mat said it was all a joke, but I think not." The substantive variants are of a similar nature in the rest of the letters and in "The Way Americans Go Down Hill," "Broker vs. Banker," and "Enemy in Front and Rear," the other sketches reprinted in the *Spirit*. The *Spirit* printings probably do not reproduce Thorpe's manuscripts exactly, but major revisions by Porter seem unlikely on the basis of this evidence.

"The Big Bear of Arkansas" is one of the sketches in which several of Porter's changes are identifiable, since he reprinted it from the *Spirit* in his first anthology.[5] The later printing has over 150 accidental variants, some of which result from the house style of changing *-or* endings to *-our*. J. A. Leo Lemay has summarized the changes, commenting on how they damage the sketch: "Porter separated rambling sentences (thus losing part of the mock-oral, monologue effect), frequently added punctuation (with the same unfortunate result), capitalized the 'b' in 'big' when referring to the Arkansan as the 'Big Bar' (thus, regrettably, more clearly distinguishing between the man and the bear), capitalized other proper nouns (e.g., 'hoosier' becomes 'Hoo-

4. Thomas Bangs Thorpe to Rufus W. Griswold, September 4[?], 1845, in Gratz Collection.

5. Porter also reprinted "The Big Bear of Arkansas" in the *American Turf Register*, XII (May, 1841), 274–80. That printing follows the *Spirit* text more closely than does the one in his first anthology. Comparing the variants indicates that Porter probably used the *Spirit* as copy-text for both.

sier'—thus losing some of the appearance of colloquialness, and perhaps of illiteracy), and he even made three substantive changes in the text."[6] The substantive variants are the substitution of "it" for "he" in one of Jim Doggett's references to a wild turkey, as well as the revisions of "until coming" to "until he came" and "then he walked" to "then walked" in the passage describing how the bear climbed into the crotch of a tree. Several additional words belong on Lemay's list. In the last question that the foreigner asks Doggett, the anthology text reads "bears" instead of "bear." The capitalization of "Bowie-knife" in the phrase "taking my gun and Bowie-knife along" is also a substantive change. Porter corrected the spelling of "turkies," "mattrass," and "Sampson's" in statements by Doggett where Thorpe may have hoped these would suggest dialect or illiteracy. Yet Porter changed "diggings" to "diggins" three times. When Thorpe prepared "The Big Bear of Arkansas" for *Hive*, using Porter's anthology as the source for his copytext, he retained all of these substantive variants.

Porter selected five other previously published sketches for his books. "The American Wild Cat" and "Woodcock Fire Hunting" are in his edition of *Instructions to Young Sportsmen*, the texts of both based on earlier reprintings in the *American Turf Register*. Also in *Instructions* are "The Devil's Summer Retreat, in Arkansaw," "A Grizzly Bear Hunt," and "Opossums and 'Possum Hunting," all of them from the *Spirit*. *Scenes in Arkansas*, Porter's second anthology, contains "The Devil's Summer Retreat, in Arkansaw," but its text is collateral to the version in *Instructions*, since collation indicates that the copy-text for both was apparently the *Spirit*. As in the reprinting of "The Big Bear of Arkansas," Porter made many changes in the accidentals but only a few in the substantives. In fact, of all the articles collected in *Instructions*, Thorpe's have the fewest revisions.[7] Yet the changes in several of these pieces are noteworthy because they became incorporated into the *Mysteries* and *Hive* versions when Thorpe used Porter's reprintings as copy-texts.

Collation indicates that the *American Turf Register* printing of "The American Wild Cat," rather than the first one in the *New Sporting*

6. J. A. Leo Lemay, "The Text, Tradition, and Themes of 'The Big Bear of Arkansas,'" *American Literature*, XLVII (November, 1975), 322.

7. See Leland H. Cox, Jr., "Porter's Edition of *Instructions to Young Sportsmen*," in James L. W. West III (ed.), *Gyascutus: Studies in Antebellum Southern Humorous and Sporting Writing* (Atlantic Highlands, N.J., 1978), 81–102. Cox's general conclusions are valid, but he is incorrect in stating that the "only variants to be found [in Thorpe's sketches] all involve minor punctuation changes." Besides the several wording changes Porter made in each sketch, he deleted the final two sentences in "Woodcock Fire Hunting."

Magazine, was the copy-text for *Mysteries*. Besides following Porter's revisions in punctuation and corrections of misspellings, the *Mysteries* text conforms to the reading "to cap the climax" for "to clap the climax." Even though collation reveals that the *Mysteries* printing was in turn the copy-text for *Hive*, the version in *Instructions*, published one year after *Mysteries*, has two additional wording changes with which the *Hive* version agrees: "gave symptoms" for "showed symptoms" and "they say, 'that the lodge . . .'" for "they say, a lodge." Since *Instructions* provided the copy-text for "Opossums and 'Possum Hunting" in *Hive*, Thorpe may have read the printing of "The American Wild Cat" there, noted these differences, and incorporated them along with his own revisions in the *Mysteries* printing; but coincidence is probably a better explanation here.

Of the substantive revisions by Porter that Thorpe followed in the *Hive* version of "Opossums and 'Possum Hunting," three regularize the spelling of "thar's," "bretheren," and "sittin'," which originally indicated pronunciation. On the other hand, the change of "decateful" to "desateful" may have been intended to heighten the suggestion of Irish dialect, even though the spelling does not change the pronunciation. The other significant variant in the *Hive* version attributable to Porter is the substitution of "soared" for "roared" in this passage: "We should have liked very much to have heard 'Elia's' description of a dish of it; . . . where would he have roared to over a dish of 'possum?"

Thorpe did not use as copy-texts Porter's reprintings of the other sketches that are in *Instructions* and *Scenes in Arkansas*. None of the three substantive variants in "A Grizzly Bear Hunt" appears in *Hive*. However, the *Hive* version of "Woodcock Fire Hunting" agrees with four of the approximately twenty substantive changes in the *Instructions* text. They are "during" for "through," "is perfectly" for "is there perfectly," "off" for "off of," and "have" for "has" in a sentence that demands a plural verb. The similarity of these variants may be coincidental. Likewise, in "The Devil's Summer Retreat, in Arkansaw" the *Hive* version agrees with only a few variants from *Instructions* and *Scenes in Arkansas*, and no clear evidence indicates that Porter's reprinting influenced Thorpe.

Even though collating the various printings of the sketches does prove that Porter made revisions in them, those changes are infrequent and, in most cases, unimportant. Such respect for Thorpe's texts confirms the praise Porter offered in a letter introducing him to Carey and

Hart: "Some of his sketches of *scenery* in the great Valley of the Mississippi, and of the 'characters' encountered there are equal to anything in the language."[8]

Readers of recent critical editions of many literary works find not facsimiles of a certain printing but eclectic texts. The basis for such an edition is the copy-text—the text that possesses the greatest original authority because it is either the author's manuscript or the text closest to a lost manuscript. After collating the various forms of the text, an editor emends the copy-text in places where authorial substantive variants occur in later versions. Despite questions about the validity of distinguishing substantives from accidentals, the editor usually accepts the accidentals in the copy-text because each successive printing is likely to introduce errors. According to Fredson Bowers, an edition that "pursues and recovers the author's full intentions wherever found, and correctly associates them in one synthesis, is clearly the only suitable edition that is complete and accurate enough to satisfy the needs of a critic."[9] The eclectic text, then, represents the author's final intentions more faithfully than does any document that preserves a single version of the text.

Nevertheless, an eclectic text does not seem to be an appropriate goal for an edition of Thorpe's sketches of the Old Southwest because substantive variants indicate that he changed his intentions for them in his books. He was aware that the books would have a national audience and could attract a different type of reader than did the newspapers for which he wrote earlier. While the *Spirit* did have a national distribution, most of its subscribers were in the South, where turf and field sports were prominent in the culture. Furthermore, it was a publication for men. In his books, Thorpe aimed at a more genteel audience, an audience unaccustomed to frontier life, by making his language and his subjects more palatable to it. A comment in the New Orleans *Weekly Delta*'s unsigned notice of *Mysteries* suggests the standards of decorum by which Thorpe expected the book to be judged: "The writer is evidently familiar with the originals of his sketches; he posseses a chaste imagination, and writes in an easy style." Quite likely, Thorpe's "chaste imagination," or at least a recognition of such

---

8. William T. Porter to Carey and Hart, March 3, 1845, in New-York Historical Society.

9. Fredson Bowers, "Textual Criticism," in James Thorpe (ed.), *The Aims and Methods of Scholarship in Modern Languages and Literature* (Rev. ed.; New York, 1970), 32.

sensibilities in his audience, guided him in selecting and revising the contents of *Mysteries*. A sketch such as "The Big Bear of Arkansas," with its scatological humor, would probably not have earned the same praise from the *Weekly Delta*'s reviewer, nor from polite easterners. Thorpe was confident that "the New Englanders of all people in the world would like the Mysteries," but, he told his publisher, he realized too late that the title of the volume probably hindered its acceptance.[10]

The humorists of the Old Southwest are significant, in part, for their earthy realism and their vernacular point of view, which subverted the standards of the day's polite literature. Since Thorpe revised his writings with genteel readers in mind, conflating the different versions would obscure both his connection with the other humorists and part of his own achievement. Even the most genteel of these writers, William Tappan Thompson of Georgia, similarly revised his popular Major Jones letters so that their supposed author would appear more refined between hard covers than he had in newsprint. In preparing the 1844, 1847, and 1872 editions of *Major Jones's Courtship*, Thompson not only changed spelling to depict dialect more authentically but also omitted the major's abusive comments that made him, in the original letters, less the gentleman that scholars consider him today. Moreover, one Jones letter printed originally in the *Spirit* was not collected for book publication. In it the Georgia planter angrily defends himself against charges of sexual immorality by making the same insinuations about the *Spirit* correspondent Pardon Jones (Christopher M. Haile), who had playfully baited him.[11] Such decisions regarding the content of a humorous book to be published by Carey and Hart in the same series in which Thorpe's books were marketed suggest the authors shared perceptions about their audience. The textual history of Thorpe's and Thompson's pieces shows that a humorous journalist in the antebellum South had greater freedom in choosing incidents than did an author trying to publish a book in the North at that time. That history thus argues against preparing an eclectic text for a critical edition.

In the absence of manuscripts this edition uses as copy-text the earliest available appearance in print of each sketch and does not cus-

10. Untitled, New Orleans *Weekly Delta*, January 5, 1846; Thorpe to Hart, March 2, 1846, in New-York Historical Society.

11. For a discussion of the textual history of this piece suppressed by Thompson, see David C. Estes, "Major Jones Defends Himself: An Uncollected Letter," *Mississippi Quarterly*, XXXIII (Winter, 1979–80), 79–84.

tomarily emend it where authorial substantive variants occur in later versions, even when the changes are improvements. To say that Thorpe was conscious of standard literary tastes when he made revisions is not to deny that some of his changes enhance the sketches. The decision against preparing an eclectic text comes from the desire to preserve as much as possible the indigenous view of the frontier that characterizes Thorpe's work.

"My First Dinner in New Orleans" and "The Louisiana Law of Cock-Fighting" are the only known items by Thorpe for which the first printing is unavailable. According to the papers that reprinted them, both appeared in the *Tropic* at the beginning of 1843. This edition's copy-text for "My First Dinner in New Orleans" is the printing in the Baton Rouge *Gazette* on February 18, 1843. Porter did not include that piece in the *Spirit*. Both the *Gazette* and the *Spirit* reprinted "The Louisiana Law of Cock-Fighting" on March 4, 1843. The *Spirit* printing is the copy-text for this edition because several of the substantive variants between the two printings seem to be typesetting errors on the part of the *Gazette*. Nevertheless, the Textual Apparatus in this edition lists the seven substantive differences between the two, since the variants in the *Gazette* may be accurate transcriptions of the original, silently corrected by Porter.

In "The Little Steamboats of the Mississippi," the only sketch to appear first in the *Spirit* and then in the *Intelligencer*, the total number of variants between the printings is quite small, and the only two substantive variants could easily be the result of a typesetter's error. Nevertheless, they remain in the *Hive* printing, an indication that Thorpe used the *Intelligencer* as his copy-text. Since the Louisiana paper notes that the sketch is from the *Spirit*, the wiser choice seems to be to use the *Spirit* as copy-text. No evidence exists that Thorpe had type set from a manuscript instead of from the *Spirit*.

Even though "Wit of the Woods" treats the same subject as "Wild Turkey Shooting" and describes some of the same incidents with the same words, the two are distinctly different sketches. This edition does not treat "Wit of the Woods" as simply a later version of "Wild Turkey Shooting" but rather includes both texts.

The signed autograph manuscript of "A Tradition of the Natchez," a sketch in the collection *The Knickerbocker Gallery* (1855), honoring Lewis Gaylord Clark, is evidently Thorpe's only surviving manuscript. Between two and six changes in words and phrases in Thorpe's hand occur on each of the six pages. For example, he substituted "reaching" for "coming to" and "reasons" for "principles." Presumably deciding that the six words at the end of the following sentence were unnecessary, he drew a line through them: "The sun, a female sovereign, was absolute in power, she was the center of all." Only one of the revisions shows Thorpe changing his mind about what information belonged in the sketch. He wrote a sentence at the top of page four, crossed it out, and began on the other side of the sheet. The deleted sentence explains: "Ambassadors from surrounding tribes, were frequently present on these great occasions, and thus learned the custom of keeping up the sacred fire"—a point extraneous to the Natchez account of how French soldiers conquered them because the sacred fire accidentally burned itself out. Even though the story is not one of Thorpe's best, the manuscript provides a more authoritative copy-text for use in this edition than is available for any other piece.

This edition makes few emendations in the chosen copy-text for each sketch because without manuscripts, regularizing the punctuation and spelling would depend on guessing at what Thorpe wrote. Accepting inconsistencies is preferable to introducing errors into the texts under the guise of good intentions. Errors in spelling, capitalization, and punctuation are, however, emended if they were corrected in a later version of the text in which Thorpe was involved. Inaccuracies in subject-verb and noun-pronoun agreement are also corrected on such authority. This edition adopts several revised readings that add necessary words that are missing in the original, delete repeated words, or transpose words obviously out of order. The list of emendations records all changes in the copy-texts except for the infrequent silent insertion of a missing letter for which the printed word has a blank space and the similar insertion of a necessary semicolon or period that did not print on the page of the copy-text. In addition to the small number of emendations, the text of this edition differs from the copy-texts because it does not reproduce all of the visual details of the original typography, pagination, lineation, and spacing of indentions.

Revisions in spelling from printing to printing demand particular attention in these sketches. A change in the spelling of a word spoken by a character is a substantive rather than an accidental variant if the misspelling could be an attempt to represent local pronunciation, suggest differences between standard English and the language of the frontier, or point out the speaker's lack of formal education. Distinguishing between Thorpe's intentions for a word and the effects of printer's error or of house style is very difficult, especially when a re-printing of a sketch regularizes some dialectal spellings and at the same time introduces others. Therefore, the policy for emending spelling is conservative. The spelling of words in dialogue follows the copy-text, since authorial and nonauthorial revisions in later printings cannot be distinguished with confidence. The list of significant post-copy-text variants does, however, include the revised forms of these words in order to present the history of the text.

While authority for emending many apparently accidental misspellings in the narrative passages comes from the texts in Thorpe's books, annoying misspellings also occur in the sketches he did not reprint. For example, "buffaloe" and "skilful" appear in "Wild Turkey Shooting" in passages of description not dialogue. "Sporting in Louisiana" has "tressel-work" and "aligators," as well as two errors in punctuating possessives. Throughout "Broker vs. Banker" runs the spelling "defendents." Such errors and the confusion of plural and possessive forms are extremely numerous in "Letters from the Far West." Since elementary misspellings frequently appear in Thorpe's correspondence, which of the nonstandard spellings might be deliberate? Those in "Letters from the Far West" contribute to the characterization of P. O. F., the supposed writer of the letters, as an easily duped tenderfoot. The errors and inconsistencies in that series, therefore, remain in this edition, since Thorpe could have included them intentionally. The errors in the other pieces are usually in passages where they inconsistently undermine confidence in the narrative voice. Retaining them simply because they might conform to Thorpe's manuscript is not justifiable in light of his poor spelling. This edition corrects a small number of misspellings and mispunctuated possessive forms that clearly do not represent forms of frontier language and includes them in the list of emendations.

That Thorpe misspelled almost twenty different words in the manuscript of "A Tradition of the Natchez," a sketch in which he makes no attempt to represent frontier language, supports the decision to emend mistakes occurring in descriptive passages in other pieces. He must have relied on editors or typesetters to make necessary corrections. This edition emends the spelling errors in "A Tradition of the Natchez," citing as authority the printed version in *The Knickerbocker Gallery*. The number of errors in Thorpe's manuscripts is quite possibly a reason why the first printing of "The American Wild Cat" in the *New Sporting Magazine* has so many more misspellings and run-on sentences than do sketches that first appeared in other publications. The London typesetter may very well have followed the manuscript more closely than did the others who set Thorpe's sketches in America.

Unlike misspellings, sentences that make little sense because of missing words must remain unemended unless Thorpe corrected them in a subsequent printing. Some words are missing from the copy-text of the first Far West letter because the only known copy of the *Intelligencer* containing it is damaged, so this edition follows the *Spirit* reading for those words, noting them in the list of emendations.

This edition prints the sketches in chronological order according to their first appearance. The Far West letters are grouped together, even though "The Little Steamboats of the Mississippi" appeared before the series was completed.

The Textual Apparatus includes a list of significant post-copy-text substantive variants for the twenty-three sketches that Thorpe reprinted and for "A Tradition of the Natchez." The list does not contain every substantive variant because many of them are inconsequential and may quite likely reflect house style. Preparing a list of variants from which the reader can completely reconstruct each printed state of a sketch would be a pedantic exercise here. Completeness is not in itself a worthwhile goal for the Textual Apparatus in this edition. Rather, the list of substantive variants is designed to be useful as a critical aid in analyzing how Thorpe revised his writings for a new audience and in assessing the accuracy and fullness of his presentation of the frontier.

The list of significant substantive variants generally omits (1) changes in prepositions, pronouns, articles, and conjunctions, and in tense, voice, and mood of verbs; (2) changes from plural to singular and vice versa; (3) substitutions of nouns and pronouns for each other; (4) repetition or deletion of a subject or verb within a compound sentence; and (5) revisions in word order alone. A high proportion of these changes could well be nonauthorial. The variants classified as significant include (1) additions or deletions of single words, phrases, sentences, and lengthy passages; (2) substitutions that provide different information, improve clarity, or avoid unnecessary repetition; (3) changes in words whose spelling represents the language of the frontier; and (4) changes in punctuation that affect the meaning of a sentence. Variants between the manuscript and the printed version of "A Tradition of the Natchez" are listed, since no evidence exists showing whether Thorpe himself made changes in the proof sheets. The decision to treat a variant as significant was difficult in many instances, especially when a large number of the variants in a sketch belonged on the list. Despite the editor's desire not to produce cumbersome lists preserving relatively worthless data, exceptions to the principles of exclusion were frequently made in order to present whatever might prove helpful. Although another editor would undoubtedly have made different decisions in some cases, this editor hopes he has included the necessary textual information for further study of Thorpe's writings about the Old Southwest.

The texts of the sketches in this edition are based on microfilm copies of the *Concordia Intelligencer*, the *Daily Picayune*, and the Baton Rouge *Gazette* from the Louisiana State University Library and the Mississippi State Historical Society Library. Files of the *Daily National* are in the Louisiana Historical Center of the Louisiana State Museum in New Orleans. The Boston Public Library provided a microfilm copy of the *Southern Sportsman*. The microfilm of the *Spirit* prepared by the New York Public Library in 1948 was used, and unclear spots in the film were checked against the file of the newspaper in the Rare Book Room at the Library of Congress. Texts of other Thorpe sketches were examined in the *New Sporting Magazine* at the Library of Congress, in the original printing of Porter's edition of *Instructions to Young Sportsmen* in the library holdings of the University of Tennessee–Knoxville, and in the American Culture Series microfilm copy of the *American Turf Register*. Perkins Library at Duke University has the copies of the *Knickerbocker Magazine*, *The Knickerbocker Gallery*, Porter's humorous anthologies, and Thorpe's two collections that were used in establishing the textual history of the sketches. All are original printings. Collating the copies of the original printings of *Mysteries* and *Hive* at Duke and those at Wilson Library, University of North Carolina at Chapel Hill, revealed no textual differences, though one illustration is bound into *Mysteries* at a different place in each copy. The manuscript of "A Tradition of the Natchez" is in the Alderman Library, University of Virginia.

PART TWO

Sketches
of the
Old
Southwest

TOM OWEN, THE BEE-HUNTER

As a country becomes cleared up and settled, Bee-hunters disappear; consequently they are seldom or ever noticed. Among this backwoods fraternity have flourished men of genius in their way, who have died unwept and unnoticed, while the heroes of the Turf and the common chase have been lauded to the skies, for every trivial superiority they have displayed in their respective pursuits. To chronicle the exploits of sportsmen is proper and commendable; the custom began as early as the days of the antedeluvians, for we read that "Nimrod was a mighty hunter before the Lord." Familiar, however, as Nimrod's name may be, or even Davy Crockett's, what does it amount to, when we reflect that TOM OWEN, the Bee-hunter, is comparatively unknown? Yes, the mighty Tom Owen has "hunted" from the time he could stand alone until the present, and not a pen has inked paper to record his exploits. "Solitary and alone" has he tracked his game through the mazy labyrinths of the air, marked "I hunted," "I found," "I conquered" upon the carcasses of his victims, and then marched homeward with his spoils, quietly and satisfiedly sweetening his own path through life, and by its very *obscurity* adding the principal element of the sublime.

It was on a beautiful Southern October morning, at the hospitable mansion of a friend, where I was staying to drown dull care and court the roseate hue of health, that I first had the pleasure of seeing Tom Owen. He was straggling on this occasion up the rising ground that led to mine host's hospitable mansion, and the difference between him and ordinary men was visible at a glance; perhaps it showed itself as much in the perfect contempt he displayed for fashion in the adornment of his outward man, as it did in the more elevated qualities of his mind, that were visible in his face. His head was adorned with an outlandish pattern of a hat, resembling somewhat an ancient hive; his nether limbs were ensconced in a pair of inexpressibles, beautifully fringed by the briar bushes, through which they were often drawn; part of his "linen," like a neglected penant, displayed itself in his rear. Coats and vests he considered as superfluities; hanging upon his back were a couple of pails, and an axe in his right hand, formed the varieties that represented the corpus of Tom Owen. As is usual with great men, he had his followers, and with a courtier like humility, they depended upon the expression of his face for all their hopes of success. The usual salutations of meeting were sufficient to draw me within the circle of his influence, and I at once became one of his most ready followers. "See yonder!" said Tom, stretching his long arm into infinite space, "see yonder—there's a bee." We all looked in the direction he pointed, and that was the extent of our observations. "It was a fine bee," continued Tom, "black body, yellow legs, and went into that tree," pointing to a towering oak, blue in the distance. "In a clear day I can see a bee over a mile easy!" When did Coleridge ever "talk" like that? And yet Tom Owen uttered such a saying with perfect ease.

After a variety of meanderings through the thick woods, and clambering over fences, we came to our place of destination, as pointed out by Tom, who selected a mighty tree, whose top contained the sweet, the possession of which the poets have likened to the possession of other sweets, that leave a *sting behind*. The felling of a mighty tree is a sight that calls up a variety of emotions, and Tom's game was lodged in one of the finest in the forest. However, "the axe was laid at the root of the tree," which to Tom's mind was made expressly for bees to build their nests in at the top, that he might cut them down, and obtain possession thereof. The sharp sounds of the axe, as it played merrily in the hands of Tom on the butt of the tree, was replied to by a gigantic negro on the opposite side from Tom, and the rapidity of their strokes fast gained upon the heart of their lordly sacrifice. There was little poetry in the thought, that long before this mighty empire of States was founded, Tom Owen's "bee-hive" had stretched its brawny arms to the winter's blast, and grown green in the summer's sun. Yet, such, no doubt, was the case, and I know not when I should have ceased my moralizing reflections, had not the enraged buzzing about my ears satisfied me that the occupants of the tree were not going to give up their home and treasure without showing considerable practical fight. No sooner had the little insects satisfied themselves that they were invaded, than they began one after another to descend from their airy abode, and fiercely pitch into our faces; anon a small company, headed by an old veteran, would charge with their entire force upon all parts of our body at once. It need not be said that the better part of valor was displayed in a precipitate retreat from such attacks. At last the tree began to tremble with the fast repeated strokes. There was a "bee-hive" of stingers seen precipitating themselves from above, and landing on the unfortunate hunter beneath. Then it was that Tom shone forth in his glory. His partizans, like too many hangers-on about great men, began to desert him upon the first symptoms of alarm; but when the trouble thickened, they one and all took to their heels, and left only our hero and Sambo to fight their adversaries. Sambo, however, soon dropped his axe, and fell into all kinds of contortions: first he would seize the back of his neck with his hands, then his shins, and then he would yell with pain. "Don't holler, nigger, till you get out of the woods," said the sublime Tom, consolingly; but grunt and writhe he did, until he broke, and left Tom "alone in his glory." Cut—thwack, sounded through the confused hum at the foot of the tree, marvellously reminding me of the interruptions that occasionally broke in upon the otherwise monotonous hours of my schoolboy days. A sharp cracking finally told me that the chopping was finished, and as I looked aloft, I saw the mighty tree, balancing in the air. Slowly and majestically it bowed for the first time towards its mother earth, gaining velocity as it descended, shivering the trees interrupting its downward course, and falling with thundering sound, splintering its mighty limbs, and burying them deeply in the ground. The sun, for the first time in at least two centuries, broke uninterruptedly through the chasm made in the forest, and shone with splendor upon the magnificent Tom, standing a conqueror among his spoils. As might be expected, the bees were very much astonished and confused, and by their united voices, they proclaimed death, had it been in their power, to all their foes, not, of course, excepting Tom Owen himself. The wary hunter was up to the tricks of his trade, and knew how easily an enraged mob could be quelled with smoke, and smoke he tried, until his enemies were completely destroyed. We, Tom's hangers-on, now approached his treasure. It was a rich one, and as he observed, "contained a smart chance of plunder." Nine feet by measurement of the hollow of the tree was full, and afforded many pails of pure honey. Tom was liberal, supplied us all with more than we wanted, and "toted," by the assistance of Sambo, his share to his own home, soon to be devoured, and replaced by the destruction of another tree, and another government of bees; exhibiting within himself an unconquerable genius, which would have immortalized him had it been directed in following the sports of Long Island, or New-market. We have seen Col. Bingaman, the Napoleon of the Southern Turf, glorying amid the conquests of his favorite sport; we have heard the great Crockett detail the soul-stirring adventures of a Moose hunt; we have listened with almost suffocating interest to the tale of a Nantucket seaman, while he portrayed the death blow he gave the mighty whale. And we have seen Tom Owen triumphantly engaged in a bee-hunt. We beheld and wondered at the exploits of the Turf, the Field, and the Sea, because the objects acted upon by man were terrible when their instincts were aroused. But in the "Bee hunt" of Tom Owen, and its consummation, the grandeur *visible* was imparted by the mighty mind alone of Tom Owen himself.

WILD TURKEY SHOOTING

The discovery of America by Columbus resulted, among other great events, in the addition of the Turkey to the table of the poor man and the epicure, and in adding to the list of game the most remarkable bird that presents itself to the notice of the sportsman. The Wild Turkey stands entirely alone, altogether unrivalled, and is unquestionably more *American* than anything else of which we can boast. The Americans are charged with being *rather complacent* when they touch upon their peculiar advantages, and are apt to claim the honor of being a little the *tallest* young people that ever breathed. They do believe, we have no doubt, that they have rivers the longest, mountains that stick up the highest, valleys that squat the lowest, horses that run the fastest, politicians that talk the loudest, and girls that are the prettiest, of any other in creation. But the Englishman, Frenchman, or any other European, have all these things in kind, and they will vaunt about the Thames, the Seine, and the like, and thereby grow very self-conceited and satisfied; but they knock under when you mention the Wild Turkey, and willingly admit that America is a great country: indeed, Franklin knew all this, and with a wisdom that eclipsed himself, wished to have this bird of birds introduced upon our national emblem, instead of the Eagle. The idea was enough to have immortalized him if he had not been a philosopher, or a modern Ajax, defying the lightning.

The Eagle, after all, is no great shakes of a bird, if we look into Audubon for its history, being own cousin to the Turkey Buzzard, and the most respectable of the family are fish thieves, and the like. Besides, an Eagle is no more peculiar to America than rats and mice are, it being common to all countries, and anything but a democratic bird to boot. Cæsar enslaved the world with his eagle banners borne in front of him; Russia, Prussia, and Austria all exalt the Eagle as the ensign of royalty, and we think that a bird thus favored by emperors and autocrats ought to be very little respected by the sovereign-people-democrats. So Franklin thought, and so we think, and we shall always go for the Turkey as the most appropriate national emblem of our country, even if we can have no other *stripes* associated with it than those given by a gridiron.

The Turkey, in its domesticated state, though he may be, and is, the pride of the festival dinner and the farm-yard, gives but an indifferent idea of the same bird when wild, both as regards its appearance and flavor. To see the bird in all his beauty, he must be visited in the wild regions of the South and West: there, free and unconstrained, he grows up in all the perfection of his nature, with a head as finely formed as the game-cock's, and elevated, when walking, perpendicular with his feet, much larger in the body than the tame Turkey,* possessed of a never-varying plumage of brownish black, that glistens in the sun like bronze, he presents at the same time the *ne plus ultra* of birds for beauty and for game, ranking with the Indian and Buffalo as the three most remarkable living productions of the Western world. The haunts, too, of the wild Turkey are in harmony with the same character as the Aborigines and the Buffalo. In the deep recesses of the primitive forest, on the shores of our mightiest rivers, or buried in the midst of our vast prairies of the West, only is the Turkey to be found. In these solitudes the Turkey rears its young, finding in the spontaneous productions of the soil a never-failing supply of food, and always occupying the same section of a country in which they are found; their disappearance from their peculiar haunts is indicative of total extinction. Thus it is that their numbers are irreparably lessened yearly by the sturdy arm of the pioneer and the hunter, and a comparatively few years more are re-quired to give a traditionary character only to the existence of the wild Turkey upon the borders of our very frontier settlements. At present the traveller in the far West, while wending his solitary way through the trackless forests, sometimes very unexpectedly meets a drove of Tur-keys in his route, and when his imagination suddenly warms with the thought that he is near the poultry yard of some hearty backwoods-man, and while his wearied limbs seem to labor with extra pain as he thinks of the couch, compared with the cold ground as a resting place, he hears a whizzing in the air, a confused noise, and his prospects of civilization and comfort vanish as the wild Turkey disappears, telling him the painful truth, that he meets with these birds to him so familiar

*The writer of this article was told by a naturalist recently, from the Columbia river, that the Wild Turkey had been shot in that region, weighing over twenty-eight pounds. We have now the tail of a Wild Turkey in our possession, which is used as a fan, measuring over twenty inches in width, being stretched only to its natural dimensions; they are frequently much larger. The magnitude of this tail, compared with the common farm-yard Turkey, will give some idea of the difference in the size of the wild and the tame birds.

in a wild state, because he is far from the haunts of men and his home. Skilful indeed is the shot that stops the Turkey in his flight of alarm, and yet the wing is little used by the bird; like the quail, and the partridge, he depends upon running more, and their speed is wonderful, and we doubt if the hounds could match them in a race even if their wings were clipped, and they could not resort to heights to elude their pursuers. So little indeed does the Wild Turkey depend on the wing, that they find it difficult to cross rivers moderately wide, and the weakest of the birds are often sacrificed in the attempt. We have seen the wild Turkey gathering upon some tall cotton wood on the Mississippi, and we have known by their preparations that they intended to cross the river; after mounting the highest tree they could find on the banks of the river, and stretching out their necks once or twice as if for a long breath, they would start for the nearest point on the opposite side of the stream, descending constantly until they reached it, and frequently very many would find their strength overtasked and would light in the water and be drowned. The Squatter on the banks of the Mississippi often notices these gatherings, and makes preparations to meet the bird with a warm reception, and often with a club and a canoe, he supplies himself with a quantity and quality of game that royalty cannot command, and from the hardy health he acquires by wood-chopping and exposure to the air, he eats the bird with a relish, and digests it with an ease which, if the luxurious resident of a city life could realize, he would consider a rich reward for the Backwoodsman's privations and toils.

In hunting the wild Turkey there is unfortunately too little excitement and *too much luck* to make it a favorite sport. Could the bird be as surely started as the fox, or deer, and chased in the same manner and with the same chances of success, the value of the bird would make its hunting the greatest sport in the world. But, the uncertainties of meeting with the bird even if you know its haunts, the word and blow sort of manner necessary if you do meet with it, confines its hunters to a very few individuals indeed. The cautiousness of the wild Turkey is wonderful, excelling that of the deer or any other game whatever, and nothing but stratagem and the most intimate knowledge of its habits will command success. We once knew an Indian who gained a living by bringing game into a town in the west, who always boasted exceedingly if he could add a wild Turkey to his common load of deer, and as the bird was in greater demand than he could supply, he was taunted by the disappointed epicures of the village for want of skill in hunting. To this charge he would always reply with great indignation, and claim the character of a good hunter from the quantities of venison that he disposed of. "Look here" he would angrily say, "I see deer on the prairie, deer look up and say maybe Indian, maybe stump, and deer eats on, come little nearer, deer look up again, and say maybe Indian, maybe stump, and first thing deer knows he dead. I see wild Turkey great way off, creep up very slowly, Turkey look up, and say first time he see me, dat damn Indian any how, and off he goes, no catch Turkey, *he cunning too much*."

I never knew but one really successful Turkey hunter, and as might be imagined, he was a genius. The talent that pitches into a deer or fox-hunt, argues nothing in favor of making a Turkey hunter, on the contrary, it is against it, on account of the want of exercise and bustle, which to a real deer or fox-hunter, is as necessary as horses and hounds. A Turkey hunter on the contrary, must be a man possessed of the anomalous character of being very lazy, and yet very fond of rising early in the morning; he must also be a shot most unquestionable, for he can have but *one* as the reward for his morning exertions,—the game never waiting for a second notice to quit their feeding grounds, so as to be entirely secure for that day at least. A wild Turkey hunter must also be something of a musical and imitative genius; for unless he can gobble turkey-like, so as to deceive the bird itself, he can seldom succeed. The imitation, however, is frequently perfect, and can be acquired with practice. The large bone of the turkey's wings, cut off at one end, and properly used in the mouth, will produce the plaintive sound exactly of the female, who in the mornings of the Spring seems to be calling to her notice her proud lord and master, who like most dandies, employs himself in the presence of his mistress in strutting himself poor. The hunter armed with one of these turkey calls, and the sure rifle, starts for the woods where he knows the turkey frequents, long before the sun shows the least light in the eastern horizon; silent, and generally alone, he places himself under some previously marked tree, and waits patiently for the light. Sometimes he is fortunate in placing himself directly under a *roost*, and when he can discern objects, he sees his game asleep over his head; but if this is not the case, he at least finds his game in the vicinity of his hiding-place, and here concealed by brush, he listens until he hears the gobble of the morning begin. The first sound from the old gobblers the hunter answers by the plaintive note of the female, and the male bird is ready to search

90

out a mistress with becoming gallantry. Pup, pup, lisps the hunter,—gobble, gobble, utters the proud bird,—and here the interest of the hunt commences. Then is to be seen the alluring on of the gobbler, his struttings and prancings, and a thousand gallant airs for his lady love; anon, his suspicions get the better of his love, and the coward is plainly visible, in his suddenly contracted body, and air of ready flight. The hunter warily plies his music, and the bird comes on, until the sure rifle finds the beautiful bird in its range,—its sudden report, and the breaking of the dried brush in the bushes beyond, tells of the death throes of the bird, while his companions frightened by the sudden noise, scatter like lightning; but not unfrequently until a second rifle, held by veteran hands, careens another bird o'er as he speeds by on the wing. Here the hunt of the day generally ends, and if success has crowned the efforts of the hunter, he feels that he has acquired game and glory enough for that day at least; and no man goes home better satisfied with himself and the world, than the successful wild turkey hunter.

PRIMITIVE FORESTS OF THE MISSISSIPPI

The very name of primitive forests, excites feelings of a singular character, and presents to the mind many images suggested under no other circumstances. It would seem if there was a place in the world that was pure, it must be those forests; and I have always conceived a person entering their lone solitudes, in the same light as a discoverer, and as carrying on the work that Columbus had the honor to begin. That there is something noble in it, I believe every one feels; and the consciousness that we are the first to place our feet upon the soil, the first to break its long silence, gives a feeling of mingled self-importance and gratified curiosity nowhere else to be had, at least I thought so; and I anticipated the expedition that was to introduce me to this new scene with unusual delight.

The opportunity of gratifying my curiosity occurred when in Louisiana, by my being permitted to become one of a little party bound on a hunting excursion; I acting the part in the affair of a *greenhorn*, who was astonished at the ordinary things of life, and one who, as an old backwoodsman of the company observed, "walked into rather tall language when I spoke of the trees, and the growth of the country thereabouts." About noon of a fine day, the party started, and when the sun was going down we reached the edge of the "settlements," and began to find ourselves off of the wagon roads, and threading our way through footpaths, and I could perceive the country was at almost every step growing more wild and broken, for it was but seldom I could get a glimpse of the stars that shone over head, brightly as they only can shine in a Southern sky; and even these spare openings ceased, and I was satisfied by the sudden darkness that surrounded us, that I was in the densest woods. Our party now came to a halt, the cocking and snapping of rifles were heard, powder flashed, but the "report" that followed was a brisk blaze, from a number of pine-knot torches, whose smoky lights curled upwards, disclosing one of the most mysterious and singular exhibitions I ever beheld; every form and shape the mind can conceive of, started magically into being, the wildest fancy was tame in its creations, compared with the surrounding reality; the unmeaning eyes of the owl glared wildly from above upon us for an instant, and then with a whoop he would flounder in his confused flight into the deepest darkness; the bittern screamed, and as the lights were changed from one point to another, the whole scene seemed a moving panorama,—a wild, unearthly sight. The wonderful novelty of my situation, and the confidence I reposed in my guides, made me indifferent about the direction and the hour I was travelling, and with a sturdy step I groped on, my companions in the dim light ahead resembling troubled ghosts, flitting among the ruins of some old cathedral. Soon after the hour of midnight we halted, and to my surprise I found myself in an opening in the forest,—a long avenue as regular as if made by art was before me, for in the west the moon in its first quarter was suspended like a diadem, with its accompanying jewels reflecting down their cold blue light upon the scene, while our torches and our night fires sent upwards a red glare from the earth, their blood-stained colors making them look impure and unholy as they contrasted with the lights of heaven. The preparations for repose for the night were soon made; my companions were used to such adventures, and acted like true philosophers, for each arranged things to best suit number one, and with as much unconcern as if they were individually the only beings in existence. Salvator Rosa only, could have painted the group, and had he done it justice, his reputation would have been increased by the addition of the wildest production of his pencil.

The morning was far advanced when I awoke from my slumbers. A rude tent, plenty of blankets, and much fatigue operated to keep me asleep the latest of any inhabitant of the woods; my companions were all gone, and the occasional report of a distant rifle, and the baying of dogs, told me that they had long been employed in their business and sports. The day thus opened was one of the finest of the spring,—one of those days which disposes the body to languidness, and the mind to those soft musing feelings which comported well with the mysterious orgies I fancied I should behold in the new world that surrounded me, and a new world indeed it was. Down the "wind-row" in the far distance might be seen the baleful cypress towering upwards against the sky—that singular tree that springs out of the dismal swamps that hide themselves in these dark solitudes, those vegetable charnel houses where decay grows luxurious, where venomous reptiles revel in gigantic fungi and poisonous plant, where the alligator and rattlesnake gorge themselves with prey, and sleep out a long life of security and repose. In such places, the cypress finds its sustenance and foot-hold, its roots bracing themselves in the soft bottom by a hundred "knees" that here and there protrude out of the dark red water of the swamp; out of such foul places the cypress towers above all other trees, its dark bony looking trunk, its delicate and almost impercep-tible foliage, suggesting to the mind that before it is the vampire of the forest. Near me, the wonderful magnolia rose in beautiful proportions, that pride of the South, a mighty forest tree that is for months covered with flowers as superior for their fragrance and size, as the tree is for its height, and forming by their brilliancy of white, the most beautiful contrast to the evergreen leaf. Here also were the tall quick growing cotton wood, the oak, and the beech, all apparently vieing to overtop each other, and prove the reigning monarch of the crowd, while the larger species of vines, more numerous than the botanist has con-ceived, tangled their majestic folds in such wild confusion, that the whole forest grew solid to my wondering eye, and seemed a mountain vegetation. Into these solitudes I penetrated, and I started at the unex-pected appearances that met my view; here were lightning-cloven trees distending their wide jaws as if to swallow me, anon, some excres-cence on the oak would turn me aside as it rounded out in the form and attitude of a grisly bear. Dark, sombre,—I followed no path, and it was finally with difficulty I could get foothold in the underbrush which extended about my feet like netting. The silence became more and more profound, until the breaking of a twig as I passed on seemed to echo with a loud report; my voice grew distinct, and a whisper would have been sufficient to have carried on an audible conversation. The sun, although now in its meridian splendor, but occasionally sent a ray through the surrounding gloom, and only tended to make the twilight that rested on every thing more visible. Gigantic trees ob-structed my path, and as I cast my eye upward, my head grew dizzy with the height; here, too, might be seen dead trunks shorn of their mighty limbs, and whitening in the blasts of years, that appeared, dead as they were, as mighty as the pillars of Hercules; and I could not help comparing them to those lone columns of fallen temples, that occa-sionally protrude themselves above the ruins of Chœops and Thebes. Grape vines were here larger than my body, which would for some distance creep along the ground, when suddenly you would see where they appeared to have sprung a hundred feet into the air, grasped some patriarch of the forest, pressed its aged limbs in its folds, crushed, mutilated, and destroyed its life, then, as if to make amends for its destructiveness, throw over its deadening work the brightest green, the richest foliage, filled with fragrance and the clustering grape. Here the squirrel will sit and cast his eye down with complacency upon the common fowling piece, and chatter out his derision as report after report sends the shot rattling harmlessly below his perch. Upon the ground were long hillocks of crumbling mould, distinguished from the earth around them, as they stretched along the ground, with flowers more various than the imagination can conceive. One of these long hillocks nearly reached above my head, while the end opposite to the one near me, insensibly mixed with the grass upon which it rested. This immense pile was but the remains of a single tree, that, some hundred years before, startled the silence that now reigned so profoundly, and, with its headlong crash, sent through the green arch above sounds that for a time silenced the echoing thunder that loaded the hurricane that prostrated it; here was a ruin of the new world, one of the mouldering antiquities of America. How unlike the antiquities of the old world. Omnipotence, not man, had erected this wonderful monument of greatness, with no other tears than the silent rain, no other slavery than the beautiful laws that govern nature in the ordering of the seasons; and yet this monument, erected in so much innocency, amid so much beauty, and at the expense of so much time, was wasting into nothingness. God alone in his power could erect it, hold it suspended for centuries in the air, breathe upon it, and turn it into dust. Awful, indeed, are the feelings suggested, as one wanders in the primitive forests that cover this vast continent. No wonder that the savage as he treads them alone, pours out his feelings in adoration to the Great Spirit. No wonder he turns from the temples of art to his own native temples, and laughs to scorn the beauties of the corinthian column, when he remembers the dizzy height, the god-like proportions and majesty of those pillars that seem to his burning imagination to support the clouds, and form the resting place for the foot of Deity; worthy, indeed, are yon mighty forests to line the shores of the "Father of Waters."

With a mind filled with the sublimest emotions, equal to those suggested upon the highest Alps, or amid the thunders of Niagara, or by any other of the mightiest exhibitions of nature, I returned to the little camp of my companions, their joyous back-woods mirth, their quaint jokes, and rejoicings at the entire success of their hunting expedition, did not expel the solemn feelings of my mind excited by my first visit to the primitive forests of the Mississippi, and those feelings, thus excited, will be among the last effaced from my memory.

A FRONTIER INCIDENT

A frontier military post, in peace or war, to a great number of persons, is a place of much fun and frolic. We are obliged to such a place for much past pleasure, and many pleasing recollections. The soldier's life is one of incident, few of them indeed are dull talkers, and although all of them may not tell a story as well as Mathews, still the poorest of them in this way can detail events so thrilling in their character, that the manner is unnoticed in the interest of the subject itself. Then again, these military posts have some good fellows, as hangers on, that are no where else to be met with,—gentlefolks that at College were remarkable for their low standing with the Faculty, and for their popularity with the boys. Mad scape-graces that after graduating as doctors, or lawyers, lost all their practice at home, the one by quoting too largely from the imagination instead of the "statutes," the other by some unfortunate propensity to feel ladies' hands instead of their pulses, in an unprofessional manner. Good dogs indeed, but unsuited to the times, and where else could they find a field for gibes and jests, like a new country? or more fit companions than the officers of a frontier garrison? Beside, the officers are so glad to meet with such refined company where they least expected it, and the hangers on are so delighted to meet with champagne and *pate de foie gras*, where they least expected it. Thus, both parties are always pleased, always ready to be happy, and to do their best to make all around them so, and a frontier garrison is a jolly place.

Major Freeman, was the name of the commander of one of these military posts; he possessed the most generous and warmest of hearts, and as is the consequence sometimes with such persons, he was exceedingly passionate. Educated in a camp from his infancy, he had learned to command even in his boyhood, as naturally as he learned to grow, without knowing any thing about the matter, except that he grew, and commanded, and took one as much as a matter of course as the other. As manhood and middle age came on, as might be expected, his influence among his equals amounted to the highest respect, and with his inferiors it was wonderful; they would quail before his angry eye, and tongue, as if they saw lightning, and heard thunder, and yet Maj. Freeman was loved, almost idolized, by all who knew him, and the helpless injured innocent, though the humblest being under his command, would from him receive redress and protection. In early life the Major had won the fame of a brave and prudent man, but many years of inglorious ease, had made him the master spirit in feats of the trencher; in this active service he told the best story, had the "choicest brands," the best cook, and with a delicacy almost unknown, always turned his back, or shut up his eyes, whenever you drank at his table or sideboard. In him we had a frontier lion, and the way said lion and his companions used to destroy the beasts of the forest, including a considerable number of the fowls of the air, was a "huckleberry above the persimmon" of any native in the country, and astonished said natives beyond anything else, save the idea of a "man's keeping two varmints in a grass patch, when he might shoot a dozen by going a little way into the woods." These "varmints" were two beautiful deer, which the Major had purchased when they were fawns, from some wandering Indians; he had fed them with milk from his own hand, and now that they were full grown, they adorned the garrison park, the favorites on which he bestowed those affections, which would most probably under other circumstances, have been lavished on a wife and children. These deer in fact were sacred; if the roe eat up the dahlias, jessamines, or other choice flowers of the neighboring gardens,—if the buck kicked over every child he met, and then half kicked out its eyes—for these things were their constant pastimes—the Major would pleasantly observe that, "flowers were made for Fanny to eat, and Dick's heels were perfectly harmless if the young ones were out of the way;" all was wrong, if so the deer were right.

On a fine summer evening, the jolly good fellows of the garrison, as they were wont, headed by the Major, were whiling away the time in the most agreeable manner, by turns humorous and pathetic, the feelings softened by choice wine, the mind disposed to quiet, until we had arrived at that point of all others the most agreeable,—that hallucination, when one is entirely satisfied with himself, and feels at peace and good will with all mankind. In this humor, for the first time in our memory, we were interrupted. A tall, scape-gallows looking fellow, thrust a strange face in at the door without notice or ceremony; the

Major's eye flashed for a moment, but grew mild as he discovered it was "one of the people" (the soldiers were under better discipline) that had interrupted us, and at the same time demanded what the fellow wanted. The reply was prompt, and as follows. "I comprehend that you are fond of venison in thish-ere place; well, I have a fine buck to sell,—a ra'l smasher, and you can have him for precious little plunder, and no mistake." The name of venison acted upon our senses like a charm, and we congratulated each other with a friendliness and cordiality, that would have done honor to friends meeting after a long separation. While this was going on, the Major bargained for the buck, provided he liked its appearance on sight, and purse in hand, and followed by his gallant companions in knives and forks, went out to see the carcass.

Oh horror! who shall describe the scene that ensued? On the grass before us lay a magnificent buck, slightly wounded, with his feet bound, and panting from fear, as if his heart would fly out of his mouth, and "big round tears were rolling down his dappled cheeks." In this affecting plight the Major discovered his favorite Dick; speechless with rage, he looked at the poor prisoner, and then at its keeper, and choking like a drowning man, he at last exclaimed with the voice of thunder—

"Damnation, fellow, where did you get that deer!"

The astonished countryman knew the man he was dealing with, and his anger appalled him; and in choking accents he replied, as soon as his fright would let him speak,—"I caught the thing in the river below, I did."

"You are a liar!" roared the Major,—"you have been robbing my premises, and you shall rot in prison, you shall ———!" then drawing a knife, he stepped forward, and with one dash unloosed the deer, which struggled upon its feet and limped away; then turning as we thought to unloose the robber's windpipe, who had, on the appearance of the knife, broke, and made good his escape before he could be molested. The Major in his rage, gasped convulsively for a moment, and then giving utterance to the wildest imprecations, disappeared. The effect of all this on our party was dreadful; it was the first time in his life that he had ever left his guests without a smile, and an invitation to "walk in and be at home." We viewed each other with rueful countenances, and returned unbidden to the room we had so recently left. Here we found the Major, moody and dispirited, and this humor increased upon him as we heard the report of a rifle, which deposited its contents in the unfortunate deer's head, by the Major's orders, to release the poor creature from its sufferings. In the midst of this embarrassing situation, there burst into the room, contrary to all military etiquette, a "regular," his eyes staring and his mouth open. This piece of ill manners, and second interruption, and that too, from one of his own corps, was too much for the Major, as he then felt, and probably taking advantage of this event to give loose to his pent-up feelings, he leaped across the table, seized the poor private by the throat, and hurled him to the floor, exclaiming—

"You poltroon, and will *you too*, without a single mark of respect, enter into the presence of your superiors? Do you think I will pardon your impertinence as I did that scoundrel of a countryman's, on the score of ignorance?"

"No, no!" cried the poor soldier, "forgive me, your two deer are safe, and the one just shot is"—

The man said no more; the Major reeled for a moment like one about to faint, then throwing his purse at the poor soldier's head, gave three cheers, in which all present joined as loudly and heartily, and with such unison, that the tumblers and decanters on the table chimed like the ringing of distant bells. Happiness was most singularly and unexpectedly restored to our little party, and the poor deer which had caused the only unwelcome interruption in our long social intercourse, apologised to our entire satisfaction, in the richest steaks and haunches that ever graced our board, and as we paid our *devoirs* to these delicious viands, there flashed the brightest wit, and passed the happiest hours, that ever blessed the old campaigners of the Frontier Garrison.

THE
MISSISSIPPI

'I have been
Where the wild will of Mississippi's tide
Has dashed me on the sawyer.'
BRAINERD.

The North American continent, in its impenetrable forests, its fertile prairies, its magnificent lakes, its variety of rivers with their falls, is the richest portion of our globe. Many of these wonderful exhibitions of nature are already shrines where pilgrims from every land assemble to admire and marvel at the surpassing wonders of a new world. So numerous indeed are the objects presented, so novel and striking is their character, that the judgment is confused in endeavoring to decide which single one is worthy of the greatest admiration; and the forests, the prairies, the lakes, the rivers, and falls, each in turn dispute the supremacy. But to us, the Mississippi ranks first in importance; and thus we think must it strike all, when they consider the luxurious fertility of the valley through which it flows, its vast extent, and the charm of mystery that rests upon its waters. The Niagara Falls, with its fearful depths, its rocky heights, its thunder, and 'bows of promise,' addresses itself to the ear, and the eye, and through these alone impresses the beholder with the greatness of its character. The Mississippi, on the contrary, although it may have few or no tangible demonstrations of power, although it has no language with which it can startle the senses, yet in a 'still small voice' it addresses the mind, with its terrible lessons of strength and sublimity, more forcibly than any other object in nature.

The name MISSISSIPPI was derived from the aborigines of the country, and has been poetically rendered the 'Father of Waters.' There is little truth in this translation, and it gives no idea, or scarcely none, of the river itself. The literal meaning of the Indian compound Mississippi, as is the case with all Indian names in this country, would have been much better, and every way more characteristic. From the most numerous Indian tribe in the South-west we derive the name; and it would seem that the same people who gave the name to the Mississippi, at different times possessed nearly half the continent; judging from the fact that the Ohio in the north, and many of the most southern points of the peninsula of Florida, are from the Choctaw language. With that tribe the two simple adjectives, *Missah* and *Sippah*, are used when describing the most familiar things; but these two words, though they are employed thus familiarly when separated, when compounded, form the most characteristic name we can get of this wonderful river. Missah, literally *Old big*, Sippah, *strong*, OLD-BIG-STRONG; and this name is eminently appropriate to the Mississippi.

The country through which this river flows is almost entirely alluvial. Not a stone is to be seen, save about its head waters; but a dark rich earth 'looks eager for the hand of cultivation,' and in its wildness sports with its own strength; for vegetation lies piled upon its surface with a luxuriant wastefulness that beggars all description, and finds no comparison for its extent, except in the mighty river from which it receives its support. This alluvial soil forms frail banks to confine the swift current of the Mississippi; and as might be imagined, they are continually altering their shape and location. The channel is capricious and wayward in its course. The needle of the compass turns round and round upon its axis, as it marks the bearings of your craft, and in a few hours will frequently point due north, west, east, and south, delineating those tremendous bends in the stream which nature seems to have formed to check the head-long current, and keep it from rushing too madly to the ocean. But the stream does not always tamely circumscribe these bends: gathering strength from resistance, it will form new and more direct channels; and thus it is that large tracts of country once on the river, become inland, or are entirely swept away by the current; and so frequently does this happen, that 'cut-offs' are almost as familiar to the eye on the Mississippi as its muddy waters. When the Mississippi, in making its 'cut-offs,' is ploughing its way through the virgin soil, there float upon the top of this destroying tide thousands of trees, that covered the land, and lined its caving banks. These gigantic wrecks of the primitive forests are tossed about by the invisible power of the current, as if they were straws; and they find no rest, until with associated thousands they are thrown upon some projecting point of land, where they lie rotting for miles, their dark forms frequently shooting into the air like writhing serpents, presenting one of the most desolate pictures the mind can conceive.

These masses of timber are called 'rafts.' Other trees become attached to the bottom of the river, and yet by some elasticity of the roots they are loose enough to be affected by the strange and powerful current, which will bear them down under the surface; and the tree, by its own strength, will come gracefully up again, to be again engulphed; and thus they wave upward and downward with a gracefulness of motion which would not disgrace a beau of the old school. Boats frequently pass over these 'sawyers,' as they go down stream, pressing them under by their weight; but let some unfortunate child of the genius of Robert Fulton, as it passes up stream, be saluted by the visage of one of these polite gentry, as it rises ten or more feet in the air, and nothing short of irreparable damage, or swift destruction ensues, while the cause of all this disaster, after the concussion, will rise above the ruin as if nothing had happened, shake the dripping water from its forked limbs, and sink again, as if rejoicing in its strength. Other trees will fasten themselves firmly in the bottom of the river; and their long trunks, shorn of their limbs, present the most formidable objects to navigation. A rock itself, sharpened and set by art, could be no more dangerous than these dread 'snags.' Let the bows of the strongest vessel come in contact with them, and the concussion will drive through its timbers as if they were paper; and the noble craft will sometimes tremble for a moment like a thing of life, when suddenly struck to its vitals, and then sink into its grave.

Such are the 'cut-offs,' 'rafts,' 'sawyers,' and 'snags' of the Mississippi; terms significant to the minds of the western boatman and hunter, of qualities which they apply to themselves and their heroes, whenever they wish to express themselves strongly; and we presume the beau ideal of a political character with them, would be one who would come at the truth by a 'cut-off,' separate and pile up falsehood for decay, like the trees of a 'raft,' and do all this with the politeness of a 'sawyer,' and with principles unyielding as a 'snag.'

The vast extent of the Mississippi is almost beyond belief. The stream which may bear you gently along in mid-winter so far south that the sun is oppressive, finds its beginnings in a country of eternal snows. Follow it in your imagination thousands of miles, as you pass on from its head waters to its mouth, and you find it flowing through almost every climate under heaven: nay more, the comparatively small stream on which you look, receives within itself the waters of four rivers alone; Arkansas, Red, Ohio, and Missouri; whose united lengths, without including their tributaries, is over eight thousand miles: yet this mighty flood is swallowed up by the Mississippi, as if it possessed within itself the very capacity of the ocean, and disdained in its narrow limits to acknowledge the accession of strength.

The color of this tremendous flood of water is always turbid. There seems no rest for it that will enable it to become quiet or clear. In all seasons, the same muddy water meets the eye; and this strange peculiarity, associated with the character and form of the banks, strikes the mind at once as the dark sediment which has for centuries settled upon the river's edge, and thus formed the 'ridges' through which it runs; or in other words, it has *confined itself:* and in this we behold one of its most original features. On the Mississippi we have no land sloping down in gentle declivities to the water's edge; but a bank just high enough, where it is washed by the river, to protect the back country from inundation, in the ordinary rises of the stream; for whenever, from an extensive flood, it rises above the top of this feeble barrier, the water runs down into the country. This singular fact shows how all the land on the Mississippi, south of the thirty-fourth degree of latitude, is liable to inundation, since nearly all the inhabitants on the shores of the river find its level, in ordinarily high water, running above the land on which they reside. To prevent this easy and apparently natural inundation, there seems to be a power constantly exerted to hold the flood in check, and bid it 'go so far and no farther;' and but for this interposition of divine power, here so signally displayed, the fair fields of the south would become sand-bars upon the shores of the Atlantic, and the country which might now support the world, would only bear the angry ocean wave. Suppose, for an instant, that an universal spring should beam upon our favored continent, and that the thousands of streams which are tributary to the Mississippi, were to become at once unloosed: the mighty flood in its rushing course would destroy the heart of the north-western continent. But mark the goodness and wisdom of Providence. Early in the spring, the waters of the Ohio rise with its tributaries, and the Mississippi bears them off, without injuriously overflowing its banks. When summer sets in, its own head waters about the lakes, and the swift Missouri, with its melting ice from the Rocky Mountains, come down, and thus each, in order, makes the Mississippi its outlet to the Gulf of Mexico. But were all these streams permitted to come together in their strength, what, again we ask, would save the Eden gardens of the south?

In contemplations like these, carried out to their fullest extent, we may arrive at the character of this mighty river. *It is in the thoughts it suggests*, and not in the breadth or length, visible at any given point to the eye. Depending on the senses alone, we should never think of being astonished, or even feeling the least degree of admiration. You may float upon its bosom, and be lost amid its world of waters, and yet you will *see* nothing of its vastness; for the river has no striking beauty: its waves run scarce as high as a child can reach: upon its banks we find no towering precipices, no cloud-capped mountains. All, all is dull—I might say tame. But let us float day after day upon its apparently sluggish surface, and by contemplation and comparison, once begin to comprehend its magnitude, and the mind is overwhelmed with fearful admiration. There seems to rise up from its muddy waters a spirit, robed in mystery, that points back for its beginning to the deluge, and whispers audibly: 'I roll on, and on, *altering*, but *not altered*, while time exists!' Here, too, we behold a power terrible in its loneliness; for on the Mississippi a sameness meets your eye every where, without a single change of scene. A river incomprehensible, illimitable, and mysterious, flows ever onward, tossing to and fro under its depths, in its own channel, as if fretting in its ordered limits; swallowing its banks here, and disgorging them elsewhere so suddenly, that the attentive pilot, as he repeats his frequent route, feels that he knows not where he is, and often hesitates fearfully along in the mighty flood, guided only by the certain lead; and again and again is he startled by the ominous cry, 'Less fathom deep!' where but yesterday the lead would have gone down 'where never plummet sounded.' Such is the great Aörta of the continent of North America; alone and unequalled in its majesty; proclaiming in its course the wisdom and power of GOD, who only can measure its depths, and 'turn them about as a very little thing.'

SPORTING
IN
LOUISIANA

The citizens of Louisiana may with propriety be called a sporting people, and the remark holds good particularly with regard to the chase. The planters in the country are men who can command their time, and are from their youth practised sportsmen; a sufficient number of them to form a pleasant hunting party, promiscuously brought together, have only *to will*, and a hunting party is formed, all good shots, and all possessed eminently of qualifications for refined pleasure. Accidental meetings of friends in the evening, frequently result in arrangements for the chase in the morning. And as the party in the grey dawn scour through the country, the cheerful cry of the hounds, and the music of the mellow horn, will be answered by *volunteers*, who will thus at a moment's warning, mount their chargers, and dash off with the crowd, as well prepared for the fun as if they had had a month's warning. Of such a character was the party of eight or nine, whose adventures we would describe, and yet in no other country in the world, could the same number of persons be selected who were possessed of more excellent qualifications as sportsmen, and gentlemen. In this respect Louisiana excels all other parts of the United States, and was never equalled, except in the "Old Dominion" in those ancient days when the chivalrous knights of the Golden Horse Shoe, under the guidance of Gov. Spottswood, made the Blue Ridge ring with their sports.

The place our party selected for their hunt, was about the mouth of Red river, the last great tributary of the Mississippi above its mouth, though there are below this river a number of small streams that empty into the "father of waters," that are larger than the Danube, Thames, or the Seine, but in this country, such small streams are of "no account." The place was a favorite one, consisting of a large section of country in the vicinity of the most thickly settled *interior* of the state, and yet it offers no inducement to the settler, as it is low, and frequently overflowed with water, and thus it remains comparatively wild and unknown.

106

Our hunting party consisted of three gentlemen of West Feliciana, and the remainder were residents in the vicinity of the hunting grounds. The whole party having collected together at the mouth of Red river, proceeded up that stream in a couple of skiffs, rowed by stout negroes; after navigating for a few miles, a narrow strait presented itself of some fifty yards wide, which formed the entrance to one of the most romantic little lakes in the world, presenting a silvery sheet of water some four miles long, and three fourths wide, reflecting the trees that lined its banks, with as perfect an outline in the water as they formed against the clear southern sky. The Oak and Persimmon tree, festooned with a thousand flowing vines, disposed in draperies and tressel-work, made the whole scene like a fairy land, of perfect natural beauty in repose. In this delightful place the party "camped," which means simply building a fire, and spreading a few blankets on the ground, as the climate seldom makes such simple arrangements uncomfortable. Before, however, these preparations were completed, a deer was shot within a quarter of a mile of the camp, which formed the basis of a hearty supper, and with an infinite quantity of laughing at jokes, new and old, witty and dull, the hunters "laid down in their lair," to be ready for the sports which were to follow in the morning.

On Tuesday morning long before Phœbus unbarred the gates of rosy morn, while the wood nymphs of the night were still at their gambols, and the wise owl, like some misery-portending politician, saw sights in the dark, the hounds that formed the pack of our party, were, with trumpet tongued notes, disturbing the solitudes. At one time they would be yelping forth the cry of suppressed indignation, as they discovered some cold trail, or screaming with delight as fresh marks of deer came upon their senses. The huntsmen too, no less eager for the chase, were posted, like eagle-eyed sentinels, at the different *stands*, or were far off in the *drive* with the pack; and when the sun had marked upon the great dial of the heavens the hour of noon, and was already descending in the west, our party scarcely dreamed the day had fairly begun, so exciting were the sports in which they engaged.

To one of this party, however, the time went heavily. Gun in hand, and often within the sound of the distant echoes of the hounds, he was listless, and had care marked on his countenance. A sportsman in this fix, and under such circumstances? Is it possible? Was the man a disappointed office seeker? No. Was he a victim of speculation in the stocks? No. Was he in love? No, no. Then in the name of the mighty

107

Nimrod, what ailed him? Why he was LOST.—Under such circumstances, although a good shot and an enthusiastic sportsman, yet the uncertainty of his "peculiar position," rendered him most uncomfortable indeed. But, even in this situation, he took the advantage of a good shot, and killed a fine doe that came within range of his gun, and although he despaired of bringing the carcass to the camp, he being only ambitious to take his own there, still he preserved a trophy of his prowess in a "scalp lock," cut from directly the opposite end which an Indian would have chosen of a fallen enemy—viz., the tail. It was late in the evening before our lost friend got into the camp, his difficulties through the day confessed upon his looks. But a good fire, a hearty supper, and the hilarity which is always the accompaniment of a hunting party, restored our hero to himself, his adventures only proving a subject for excellent wit, in which he received his share of the enjoyment. Towards midnight the jest grew less and less frequent, and sleep, hard and heavy, the result of the day's exercise, came upon the camp. But while its members were thus situated, they seemed inclined to renew the sports of the day in their dreams, though evidently with little success, if the way they sounded their horns, (noses) was intended to call in the pack that accompanied them in their dreamy sports.

Wednesday morning opened with all the excitement of Tuesday, but the day proved an entirely unsuccessful one, so far as shooting deer was concerned, yet many little incidents occurred full of interest, showing the plentifulness, and variety of game with which the party was surrounded, one of which we will relate. Two of the gentlemen from West Feliciana, were returning to the camp in the evening, when one of them for something better to do, shot his gun into a school of little fishes, that were visible in the lake, and killed eight or nine. His companion, who was a most enthusiastic disciple of Izaac Walton, finding among the odds and ends that had accumulated in his pockets, a fishing line, gathered up the "minnows," cut down a small sapling, trimmed off its limbs, and soon found himself possessed of a very respectable fishing tackle and bait. These implements, the gentlemen who shot the bait, took possession of, and his friend, acting the part of a painter to keep the boat in which they sat, fixed to the shore. Within ten minutes after the fishing commenced, six most beautiful bass were caught, of a species the finest in the world; the seventh was an extraordinary fine one, but in the haste to detach the fish from the line the *hook broke*.—Nothing could have been more unfortunate than this, nearly all the bait was still preserved, and with a hook any quantity of the bass could have been taken. Richard cried "A kingdom for a horse," owing to the peculiarity of his situation, and we believe our sportsman at this trying moment would have given an equally high reward for a hook. But the thing was up, the feast had to be deserted, though Tantalus like, it seemed within grasping distance, yet was for the time, irrecoverably beyond reach.

Thursday, off again before day, the hounds opened at once in first style, the echoing reports of the guns as they vibrated through the forests, the character of the parties using them, guaranteed success, and showed that the sport was fine. In the course of the day an uncommonly fine buck was fired upon from a *stand*, but he ran on with redoubled speed, although his shaking antlers and quivering tail, signified that the lead had taken effect. Yet on he went, passing almost through the very camp and plunging with a graceful bound into the lake. Now, indeed, was a beautiful and exciting scene presented. The noble buck sped through the quiet water so swiftly that it foamed at his breast and spread out behind him in widening waves that laved the shore he was leaving. Behind him came the trusty pack of hounds, their blood up, and fairly exulting in loud cheers at the sport, so joyous and animated appeared their cry. Wild geese, duck, and heron, that filled this region, started with screams into the air, at this intrusion into their quiet retreats; while alligators rolled about on the surface of the lake, as the dogs came in contact with them, like so many logs.*
Everything was redolent with life, and excitement. The noble deer reached the opposite side of the lake, but found the brush that lined the shore too thick for him to make an entrance into the forest; leaping back into the lake, he would try another point, and another. The chase was the most beautiful that could be conceived. The beauty, the graceful leaps, the noble strength, the deer exhibited in eluding pursuit, the cry of the hounds, the shouts of the sportsmen, kept the woods ringing with a thousand reverberations. Meanwhile, two of the party were nearing the victim of the chase with a boat, the gun was raised, and while its sharp report confused the echoes already sounding on every side, the heart's blood of the deer was coloring the lake, and with glazed

---

*In the warm season a pack of hounds in water inhabited by alligators, would be almost instantly caught by the reptiles and devoured. Persons to amuse themselves with shooting alligators, are in the habit of taking a dog down to the water where they frequent, and making it hollow there, when this noise is heard they will bob their heads out of the water to seek for the prey. But in the winter they are perfectly torpid, and seem to float upon the water as if they were destitute of life; in this respect alligators resemble the frog, snake, and other reptiles.

eye, and powerless form, and not till then, did his relentless pursuers find him in their possession. This singular chase varied by being thus carried on in the water, as well as on land, closed the sports of the day.

Friday morning early, the camp was broken up, a negro boy in one of the two skiffs that accompanied the expedition loaded the baggage and venison, and started for the plantation nearest in the vicinity, belonging to a gentleman of the party. This was done that every advantage might be taken of a favorite *drive* which the party would pass on their return home.

The term *drive*, it might be well to say, means a place where deer are known to frequent, and as they always in running select the clearest places, the eye of a practised sportsman can detect the various openings in the forests, where deer would rush out to gain the open country, or to hide in the swamps. These places are called *stands*. Some of these openings are so situated that they form the only entrance to a large tract of country, and when this is the case, of course a person at it would be able to shoot every deer the hunters in the *drive* might alarm, and cause to fly from its haunts. The particular *drive* to which our party now directed their attention, was remarkably adapted for this purpose. A lake inland, ran about a mile parallel with the river, thus forming a narrow strip of land only one-quarter of a mile in width. The hunters as they came down the river in the remaining skiff, landed three of their party with the hounds, at the head of the narrow strip of land. Those remaining in the boat, intending to proceed to the foot of the drive; in thus doing they would of course be able to secure all the deer on the guarded territory. No sooner, however, had the trio landed, than they discovered fresh signs of deer. The dogs were on the track in an instant, and before the party in the boat had proceeded three hundred yards, they heard the cry of the hounds, and the report of "fire barrels" following each other in the quickest succession. The party in the skiff could not stand this, but turned the boat towards the shore,—but so long did it seem to accomplish this manœuvre, that one of the party like another Charles XII., leaped into the water, to his middle, and waded ashore. I need hardly add that his companions *in arms* followed him. No sooner had they landed than they too had occasion instantly to fire; killing three deer, one of which, in its death-leap, fell into the lake and sunk. The two parties now came together at the foot of the drive, and they found they had five deer in

110

their possession, the result of comparatively a few minutes' work. Not yet content, a party with the dogs went up the drive on the lake side, and there spreading themselves out, came down again; only one deer was left to run the gauntlet, and although it was fired upon, it escaped, whether with a whole skin, or to die a lingering death from wounds, none of the party could tell. This was the consummation of the hunt, and a glorious one it was. The party would now have gone immediately to the house of their companion, where their baggage had preceded them, had not the hounds run off, and detained them until evening, blowing their horns, and shouting to get them together again. But in spite of this detention, they reached "the plantation" in time to secure a good night's rest, and an early start for their different homes in the morning. Thus ended the week. The number of the deer killed and secured being fifteen. Making on the whole, one of the most pleasant and successful expeditions of the kind that had been got up for a long time; and that too, in a country where hunting in parties is so common, and success almost always the reward.

THE
BIG
BEAR
OF
ARKANSAS

A steamboat on the Mississippi frequently, in making her regular trips, carries, between places varying from one to two thousand miles apart; and as these boats advertise to land passengers and freight at "all intermediate landings," the heterogeneous character of the passengers of one of these up-country boats can scarcely be imagined by one who has never seen it with his own eyes. Starting from New Orleans in one of these boats, you will find yourself associated with men from every State in the Union, and from every portion of the globe; and a man of observation need not lack for amusement or instruction in such a crowd, if he will take the trouble to read the great book of character so favorably opened before him. Here may be seen jostling together the wealthy Southern planter, and the pedlar of tin-ware from New England—the Northern merchant, and the Southern jockey—a venerable bishop, and a desperate gambler—the land speculator, and the honest farmer—professional men of all creeds and characters—Wolvereens, Suckers, Hoosiers, Buckeyes, and Corn-crackers, beside a "plentiful sprinkling" of the half-horse and half-alligator species of men, who are peculiar to "old Mississippi," and who appear to gain a livelihood simply by going up and down the river. In the pursuit of pleasure or business, I have frequently found myself in such a crowd.

On one occasion, when in New Orleans, I had occasion to take a trip of a few miles up the Mississippi, and I hurried on board the well-known, "high-pressure-and-beat-every-thing" steamboat "Invincible," just as the last note of the last bell was sounding, and when the confusion and bustle that is natural to a boat's getting under way had subsided, I discovered that I was associated in as heterogeneous a crowd as was ever got together. As my trip was to be of a few hours' duration only, I made no endeavors to become acquainted with my fellow passengers, most of whom would be together many days. Instead of this, I took out of my pocket the "latest paper," and more critically than usual examined its contents; my fellow passengers at the same time disposed of themselves in little groups. While I was thus busily employed in reading, and my companions were more busily still employed in discussing such subjects as suited their humors best, we were startled most unexpectedly by a loud Indian whoop, uttered in the "social hall," that part of the cabin fitted off for a bar; then was to be heard a loud crowing, which would not have continued to have interested us—such sounds being quite common in that *place of spirits*—had not the hero of these windy accomplishments stuck his head into the cabin and hallooed out, "Hurra for the big Bar of Arkansaw!" And then might be heard a confused hum of voices, unintelligible, save in such broken sentences as "horse," "screamer," "lightning is slow," &c. As might have been expected, this continued interruption attracted the attention of every one in the cabin; all conversation dropped, and in the midst of this surprise the "big Bar" walked into the cabin, took a chair, put his feet on the stove, and looking back over his shoulder, passed the general and familiar salute of "Strangers, how are you?" He then expressed himself as much at home as if he had been at "the Forks of Cypress," and "prehaps a little more so." Some of the company at this familiarity looked a little angry, and some astonished, but in a moment every face was wreathed in a smile. There was something about the intruder that won the heart on sight. He appeared to be a man enjoying perfect health and contentment—his eyes were as sparkling as diamonds, and good natured to simplicity. Then his perfect confidence in himself was irresistibly droll. "Prehaps," said he, "gentlemen," running on without a person speaking, "prehaps you have been to New Orleans often; I never made *the first visit before*, and I don't intend to make another in a crow's life. I am thrown away in that ar place, and useless, that ar a fact. Some of the gentlemen thar called me *green*—well, prehaps I am, said I, *but I arn't so at home*; and if I aint off my trail much, the heads of them perlite chaps themselves wern't much the hardest, for according to my notion, they were *real know-nothings*, green as a pumpkin-vine—couldn't, in farming, I'll bet, raise a crop of turnips—and as for shooting, they'd miss a barn if the door was swinging, and that, too, with the best rifle in the country. And then they talked to me 'bout hunting, and laughed at my calling the principal game in Arkansaw poker, and high-low-jack. 'Prehaps,' said I, 'you prefer checkers and rolette;' at this they laughed harder than ever, and asked me if I lived in the woods, and didn't know what *game* was? At this I rather think I laughed. 'Yes,' I roared, and says, 'Strangers, if you'd asked me *how we got our meat* in Arkansaw, I'd a told you at once, and given you a list of varmints that would make a caravan, beginning with the bar, and ending off with the cat; that's *meat* though, not game.' Game, indeed, that's what city folks call it, and with them it means chippen-birds and shite-pokes; maybe such trash live in my diggings, but I arn't noticed them yet—a bird any way is too trifling. I never did shoot at but one, and I'd never forgiven myself for that had it weighed less than forty pounds; I wouldn't draw a rifle on anything less than that; and when I meet with another wild turkey of the same weight I will drap him."

"A wild turkey weighing forty pounds?" exclaimed twenty voices in the cabin at once.

"Yes, strangers, and wasn't it a whopper? You see, the thing was so fat that he couldn't fly far, and when he fell out of the tree, after I shot him, on striking the ground he bust open behind, and the way the pound gobs of tallow rolled out of the opening was perfectly beautiful."

"Where did all that happen?" asked a cynical looking hoosier.

"Happen! happened in Arkansaw; where else could it have happened, but in the creation State, the finishing up country; a State where the *sile* runs down to the centre of the 'arth, and government gives you a title to every inch of it. Then its airs, just breathe them, and they will make you snort like a horse. It's a State without a fault, it is."

"Excepting mosquitoes," cried the hoosier.

"Well, stranger, except them, for it ar a fact that they are rather *enormous*, and do push themselves in somewhat troublesome. But, stranger, they never stick twice in the same place, and give them a fair chance for a few months, and you will get as much above noticing them as an alligator. They can't hurt my feelings, for they lay under the skin; and I never knew but one case of injury resulting from them, and that was to a Yankee: and they take worse to foreigners anyhow than they do to natives. But the way they used that fellow up! first they punched him until he swelled up and busted, then he sup-per-a-ted, as the doctor called it, until he was as raw as beef; then he took the ager, owing to the warm weather, and finally he took a steamboat and left the country. He was the only man that ever took mosquitoes at heart that I know of. But mosquitoes is natur, and I never find fault with her; if they ar large, Arkansaw is large, her varmints ar large, her trees ar large, her rivers ar large, and a small mosquitoe would be of no more use in Arkansaw than preaching in a cane-brake."

This knock-down argument in favor of big mosquitoes used the hoosier up, and the logician started on a new track, to explain how numerous bear were in his "diggings," where he represented them to be "about as plenty as blackberries, and a little plentifuler."

Upon the utterance of this assertion, a timid little man near me enquired if the bear in Arkansaw ever attacked the settlers in numbers.

"No," said our hero, warming with the subject, "no, stranger, for you see it ain't the natur of bar to go in droves, but the way they squander about in pairs and single ones is edifying. And then the way I hunt them—the old black rascals know the crack of my gun as well as they know a pig's squealing. They grow thin in our parts, it frightens them so, and they do take the noise dreadfully, poor things. That gun of mine is a perfect *epidemic among bar*—if not watched closely, it will go off as quick on a warm scent as my dog Bowie-knife will; and then that dog, whew! why the fellow thinks that the world is full of bar, he finds them so easy. It's lucky he don't talk as well as think, for with his natural modesty, if he should suddenly learn how much he is acknowledged to be ahead of all other dogs in the universe, he would be astonished to death in two minutes. Strangers, that dog know a bar's way as well as a horse-jockey knows a woman's; he always barks at the right time—bites at the exact place—and whips without getting a scratch. I never could tell whether he was made expressly to hunt bar, or whether bar was made expressly for him to hunt; any way, I believe they were ordained to go together as naturally as Squire Jones says a man and woman is, when he moralizes in marrying a couple. In fact, Jones once said, said he, 'Marriage according to law is a civil contract of divine origin, it's common to all countries as well as Arkansaw, and people take to it as naturally as Jim Doggett's Bowie-knife takes to bar.'"

"What season of the year do your hunts take place?" enquired a gentlemanly foreigner, who, from some peculiarities of his baggage, I suspected to be an Englishman, on some hunting expedition, probably, at the foot of the Rocky Mountains.

"The season for bar hunting, stranger," said the man of Arkansaw, "is generally all the year round, and the hunts take place about as regular. I read in history that varmints have their fat season, and their lean season. That is not the case in Arkansaw, feeding as they do upon the *spontenacious* productions of the sile, they have one continued fat season the year round—though in winter things in this way is rather more greasy than in summer, I must admit. For that reason bar with us run in warm weather, but in winter they only waddle. Fat, fat! it's an enemy to speed—it tames everything that has plenty of it. I have seen

115

wild turkies, from its influence, as gentle as chickens. Run a bar in this fat condition, and the way it improves the critter for eating is amazing; it sort of mixes the ile up with the meat until you can't tell t'other from which. I've done this often. I recollect one perty morning in particular, of putting an old he fellow on the stretch, and considering the weight he carried, he run well. But the dogs soon tired him down, and when I came up with him wasn't he in a beautiful sweat—I might say fever; and then to see his tongue sticking out of his mouth a feet, and his sides sinking and opening like a bellows, and his cheeks so fat he couldn't look cross. In this fix I blazed at him, and pitch me naked into a briar patch if the steam didn't come out of the bullet hole ten foot in a straight line. The fellow, I reckon, was made on the high-pressure system, and the lead sort of bust his biler."

"That column of steam was rather curious, or else the bear must have been *warm*," observed the foreigner with a laugh.

"Stranger, as you observe, that bar was WARM, and the blowing off of the steam show'd it, and also how hard the varmint had been run. I have no doubt if he had kept on two miles farther his insides would have been stewed; and I expect to meet with a varmint yet of extra bottom, who will run himself into a skin full of bar's-grease: it is possible, much onlikelier things have happened."

"Where abouts are these bear so abundant?" enquired the foreigner, with increasing interest.

"Why, stranger, they inhabit the neighborhood of my settlement, one of the prettiest places on Old Mississippi—a perfect location, and no mistake; a place that had some defects until the river made the 'cut-off' at 'Shirt-tail bend,' and that remedied the evil, as it brought my cabin on the edge of the river—a great advantage in wet weather, I assure you, as you can now roll a barrel of whiskey into my yard in high water, from a boat, as easy as falling off a log; it's a great improvement, as toting it by land in a jug, as I used to do, *evaporated* it too fast, and it became expensive. Just stop with me, stranger, a month or two, or a year if you like, and you will appreciate my place. I can give you plenty to eat, for beside hog and hominy, you can have bar ham, and bar sausages, and a mattrass of bar-skins to sleep on, and a wildcat-skin, pulled off hull, stuffed with corn-shucks for a pillow. That bed would put you to sleep if you had the rheumatics in every joint in your body. I call that ar bed a *quietus*. Then look at my land, the government ain't got another such a piece to dispose of. Such timber, and such bottom land, why you can't preserve anything natural you plant

116

in it, unless you pick it young, things thar will grow out of shape so quick. I once planted in those diggings a few potatoes and beets, they took a fine start, and after that an ox team couldn't have kept them from growing. About that time I went off to old Kentuck on bisiness, and did not hear from them things in three months, when I accidentally stumbled on a fellow who had stopped at my place, with an idea of buying me out. 'How did you like things?' said I. 'Pretty well,' said he; 'the cabin is convenient, and the timber land is good, but that bottom land ain't worth the first red cent.' 'Why?' said I. ''Cause,' said he. ''Cause what?' said I. ''Cause it's full of cedar stumps and Indian mounds,' said he, 'and *it can't be cleared.*' 'Lord,' said I, 'them ar "cedar stumps" is beets, and them ar "Indian mounds" ar tater hills,'—as I expected the crop was overgrown and useless; the sile is too rich, *and planting in Arkansaw is dangerous.* I had a good sized sow killed in that same bottom land; the old thief stole an ear of corn, and took it down where she slept at night to eat; well, she left a grain or two on the ground, and lay down on them; before morning the corn shot up, and the percussion killed her dead. I don't plant any more; natur intended Arkansaw for a hunting ground, and I go according to natur."

The questioner, who thus elicited the description of our hero's settlement, seemed to be perfectly satisfied, and said no more; but the "big bar of Arkansaw" rambled on from one thing to another with a volubility perfectly astonishing, occasionally disputing with those around him, particularly with a "live sucker" from Illinois, who had the daring to say that our Arkansaw friend's stories "smelt rather tall."

In this manner the evening was spent, but conscious that my own association with so singular a personage would probably end before morning, I asked him if he would not give me a description of some particular bear hunt—adding that I took great interest in such things, though I was no sportsman. The desire seemed to please him, and he squared himself round towards me, saying, that he could give me an idea of a bar hunt that was never beat in this world, or in any other. His manner was so singular, that half of his story consisted in his excellent way of telling it, the great peculiarity of which was, the happy manner he had of emphasizing the prominent parts of his conversation. As near as I can recollect, I have italicized them, and given the story in his own words.

"Stranger," said he, "in bar hunts *I am numerous*, and which particular one as you say I shall tell puzzles me. There was the old she devil I shot at the hurricane last fall—then there was the old hog thief

I popped over at the Bloody Crossing, and then—Yes, I have it, I will give you an idea of a hunt, in which the greatest bar was killed that ever lived, *none excepted*; about an old fellow that I hunted, more or less, for two or three years, and if that ain't a *particular bar hunt*, I ain't got one to tell. But in the first place, stranger, let me say, I am pleased with you, because you ain't ashamed to gain information by asking, and listening, and that's what I say to Countess's pups every day when I'm home—and I have got great hopes of them ar pups, because they are continually *nosing* about, and though they stick it sometimes in the wrong place, they gain experience anyhow, and may learn something useful to boot. Well, as I was saying about this big bar, you see when I and some more first settled in our region, we were drivin to hunting naturally; we soon liked it, and after that we found it an easy matter to make the thing our business. One old chap who had pioneered 'afore us, gave us to understand that we had settled in the right place. He dwelt upon its merits until it was affecting, and showed us, to prove his assertions, more marks on the sassafras trees than I ever saw on a tavern door 'lection time. 'Who keeps that ar reckoning?' said I. 'The bar,' said he. 'What for?' said I. 'Can't tell,' said he, 'but so it is, the bar bite the bark and wood too, at the highest point from the ground they can reach, and you can tell by the marks,' said he, 'the length of the bar to an inch.' 'Enough,' said I, 'I've learned something here a'ready, and I'll put it in practice.' Well, stranger, just one month from that time I killed a bar, and told its exact length before I measured it by those very marks—and when I did that I swelled up considerable—I've been a prouder man ever since. So I went on, larning something every day, until I was reckoned a buster, and allowed to be decidedly the best bar hunter in my district; and that is a reputation as much harder to earn than to be reckoned first man in Congress, as an iron ram-rod is harder than a toad-stool. Did the varmints grow over cunning, by being fooled with by green-horn hunters, and by this means get troublesome, they send for me as a matter of course, and thus I do my own hunting, and most of my neighbors'. I walk into the varmints though, and it has become about as much the same to me as drinking. It is told in two sentences—a bar is started, and he is killed. The thing is somewhat monotonous now—I know just how much they will run, where they will tire, how much they will growl, and what a thundering time I will have in getting them home. I could give you this history of the chase with all the particulars at the commencement, I know the signs so well. *Stranger, I'm certain.* Once I met with a match,

118

though, and I will tell you about it, for a common hunt would not be worth relating.

"On a fine fall day, long time ago, I was trailing about for bar, and what should I see but fresh marks on the sassafras trees, about eight inches above any in the forests that I knew of. Says I, them marks is a hoax, or it indicates the d——t bar that was ever grown. In fact, stranger, I couldn't believe it was real, and I went on. Again I saw the same marks, at the same height, and *I knew the thing lived*. That conviction came home to my soul like an earthquake. Says I, here is something a-purpose for me—that bar is mine, or I give up the hunting business. The very next morning what should I see but a number of buzzards hovering over my corn-field. The rascal has been there, said I, for that sign is certain; and, sure enough, on examining, I found the bones of what had been as beautiful a hog the day before, as was ever raised by a Buck-eye. Then I tracked the critter out of the field to the woods, and all the marks he left behind, showed me that he was *the Bar*.

"Well, stranger, the first fair chase I ever had with that big critter, I saw him no less than three distinct times at a distance, the dogs run him over eighteen miles, and broke down, my horse gave out, and I was as nearly used up as a man can be, made on *my* principle, *which is patent*. Before this adventure, such things were unknown to me as possible; but, strange as it was, that bar got me used to it, before I was done with him,—for he got so at last, that he would leave me on a long chase *quite easy*. How he did it, I never could understand. That a bar runs at all, is puzzling; but how this one could tire down, and bust up a pack of hounds and a horse, that were used to overhauling every thing they started after in no time, was past my understanding. Well, stranger, that bar finally got so sassy, that he used to help himself to a hog off my premises whenever he wanted one;—the buzzards followed after what he left, and so between *bar and buzzard*, I rather think I was *out of pork*. Well, missing that bar so often, took hold of my vitals, and I wasted away. The thing had been carried too far, and it reduced me in flesh faster than an ager. I would see that bar in every thing I did,—*he hunted me*, and that, too, like a devil, which I began to think he was. While in this fix, I made preparations to give him a last brush, and be done with it. Having completed every thing to my satisfaction, I started at sun-rise, and to my great joy, I discovered from the way the dogs run, that they were near him—finding his trail was nothing, for that had become as plain to the pack as a turnpike-road.

119

On we went, and coming to an open country, what should I see but the bar very leisurely ascending a hill, and the dogs close at his heels, either a match for him this time in speed, or else he did not care to get out of their way—I don't know which. But, wasn't he a beauty though? I loved him like a brother. On he went, until coming to a tree, the limbs of which formed a crotch about six feet from the ground,—into this crotch he got and seated himself,—the dogs yelling all around it—and there he sat eyeing them, as quiet as a pond in low water. A green-horn friend of mine, in company, reached shooting distance before me, and blazed away, hitting the critter in the centre of his forehead. The bar shook his head as the ball struck it, and then he walked down from that tree as gently as a lady would from a carriage. 'Twas a beau-tiful sight to see him do that,—he was in such a rage, that he seemed to be as little afraid of the dogs, as if they had been sucking pigs; and the dogs warn't slow in making a ring around him at a respectful dis-tance, I tell you; even Bowie-knife himself stood off. Then the way his eyes flashed—why the fire of them would have singed a cat's hair; in fact, that bar was in a *wrath all over*. Only one pup came near him, and he was brushed out so totally with the bar's left paw, that he en-tirely disappeared; and that made the old dogs more cautious still. In the mean time, I came up, and taking deliberate aim as a man should do, at his side, just back of his foreleg, *if my gun did not snap*, call me a coward, and I won't take it personal. Yes, stranger, *it snapped*, and I could not find a cap about my person. While in this predicament, I turned round to my fool friend—says I, 'Bill,' says I, 'you're an ass—you're a fool—you might as well have tried to kill that bar by barking the tree under his belly, as to have done it by hitting him in the head. Your shot has made a tiger of him, and blast me, if a dog gets killed or wounded when they come to blows, I will stick my knife into your liver, I will ——.' My wrath was up. I had lost my caps, my gun had snapped, the fellow with me had fired at the bar's head, and I expected every moment to see him close in with the dogs, and kill a dozen of them at least. In this thing I was mistaken, for the bar leaped over the ring formed by the dogs, and giving a fierce growl, was off—the pack of course in full cry after him. The run this time was short, for coming to the edge of a lake the varmint jumped in, and swam to a little island in the lake, which it reached just a moment before the dogs. I'll have him now, said I, for I had found my caps in the *lining of my coat*—so, rolling a log into the lake, I paddled myself across to the island, just as the dogs had cornered the bar in a thicket. I rushed up and fired—at the same time the critter leaped over the dogs and came within three feet of me, running like mad; he jumped into the lake, and tried to mount the log I had just deserted, but every time he got half his body on it, it would roll over and send him under; the dogs, too, got around him, and pulled him about, and finally Bowie-knife clenched with him, and they sunk into the lake together. Stranger, about this time I was excited, and I stripped off my coat, drew my knife, and intended to have taken a part with Bowie-knife myself when the bar rose to the surface. But the varmint staid under—Bowie-knife came up alone, more dead than alive, and with the pack came ashore. Thank God, said I, the old villain has got his deserts at last. Determined to have the body, I cut a grape-vine for a rope, and dove down where I could see the bar in the water, fastened my queer rope to his leg, and fished him, with great difficulty, ashore. Stranger, may I be chawed to death by young alligators, if the thing I looked at wasn't a *she bar, and not the old critter after all*. The way matters got mixed on that island was on-accountably curious, and thinking of it made me more than ever convinced that I was hunting the devil himself. I went home that night and took to my bed—the thing was killing me. The entire team of Arkansaw in bar-hunting, acknowledged himself used up, and the fact sunk into my feelings like a snagged boat will in the Mississippi. I grew as cross as a bar with two cubs and a sore tail. The thing got out 'mong my neighbors, and I was asked how come on that individ-u-al that never lost a bar when once started? and if that same individ-u-al didn't wear telescopes when he turned a she bar, of ordinary size, into an old he one, a little larger than a horse? Prehaps, said I, friends—getting wrathy—prehaps you want to call somebody a liar. Oh, no, said they, we only heard such things as being *rather common* of late, but we don't believe one word of it; oh, no,—and then they would ride off and laugh like so many hyenas over a dead nigger. It was too much, and I determined to catch that bar, go to Texas, or die,—and I made my preparations accordin'. I had the pack shut up and rested. I took my rifle to pieces, and iled it. I put caps in every pocket about my person, *for fear of the lining*. I then told my neighbors that on Monday morning—naming the day—I would start THAT BAR, and bring him home with me, or they might divide my settlement among them, the owner having disappeared. Well, stranger, on the morning previous to the great day of my hunting expedition, I went into the woods near my house, taking my gun and Bowie-knife along, just *from habit*, and there sitting down also from habit, what should I see, getting over my fence, but *the bar!* Yes, the old varmint was within a hundred yards of me, and the way he walked *over that fence,*—stranger, he loomed up like a *black mist,* he seemed so large, and he walked right towards me. I raised myself, took deliberate aim, and fired. Instantly the varmint wheeled, gave a yell, and *walked through the fence* like a falling tree would through a cobweb. I started after, but was tripped up by my inexpressibles, which either from habit, or the excitement of the moment, were about my heels, and before I had really gathered myself up, I heard the old varmint groaning in a thicket near by, like a thousand sinners, and by the time I reached him he was a corpse. Stranger, it took five niggers and myself to put that carcase on a mule's back, and old long ears waddled under his load, as if he was foundered in every leg of his body, and with a common whopper of a bar, he would have trotted off, and enjoyed himself. 'Twould astonish you to know how big he was,—I made a *bed spread of his skin,* and the way it used to cover my bar mattrass, and leave several feet on each side to tuck up, would have delighted you. It was in fact a creation bar, and if it had lived in Sampson's time, and had met him, in a fair fight, it would have licked him in the twinkling of a dice-box. But, stranger, I never liked the way I hunted him, *and missed him.* There is something curious about it, I could never understand,—and I never was satisfied at his giving in so *easy at last.* Prehaps, he had heard of my preparations to hunt him the next day, so he jist come in, like Capt. Scott's coon, to save his wind to grunt with in dying; but that ain't likely. My private opinion is, that that bar was an *unhuntable bar, and died when his time come.*"

When the story was ended, our hero sat some minutes with his auditors in a grave silence; I saw that there was a mystery to him connected with the bear whose death he had just related, that had evidently made a strong impression on his mind. It was also evident that there was some superstitious awe connected with the affair,—a feeling common with all "children of the wood," when they meet with any thing out of their every day experience. He was the first one, however, to break the silence, and jumping up he asked all present to "liquor" before going to bed,—a thing which he did, with a number of companions, evidently to his heart's content.

Long before day, I was put ashore at my place of destination, and I can only follow with the reader, in imagination, our Arkansas friend, in his adventures at the "Forks of Cypress" on the Mississippi.

WOODCOCK
FIRE
HUNTING

" 'Tis murderous,
but profitable."
—ORIGINAL.

The face of a country, and the climate, give the character to hunting. Sports which abound in India are unknown to the Americans, or Europeans; even localities might be marked out, where particular game frequent, and of course the sport connected with hunting this particular game is confined to the locality where it resides. The Sportsman of America must go to England for the Pheasant, while the British Sportsman must come to America for the Wild Turkey, and Buffalo. The reader therefore will not be surprised if he finds here recorded a new species of sport, which we designate for want of a better name, as Woodcock (*scolopax minor*) Fire Hunting, which we find pursued in a particular section of the United States, a sport *entirely local* in its character, and confined to a small space of country. The reasons for which, we will endeavor to analyze, while we attempt a description.

Woodcock fire hunting is almost entirely confined to a narrow strip of country running from the mouth of the Mississippi, up the river about three hundred miles. This narrow strip of country is the rich and thickly settled land, that borders on the river, and varies from one to three miles in width; it is in fact nothing but the *ridge*, or high ground, that separates the Mississippi from the interminable swamps that compose most of the state of Louisiana, bordering on the Gulf of Mexico. The habits of the Woodcock make it entirely a nocturnal bird; it retires into these swamps that border on its feeding grounds through the day, and is there perfectly safe from interruption, hid among the tangled vines, cane-brakes, and boggy land, it consults its pleasure with safety, finds convenient places for its nests, and raises its young, with the assurance of being undisturbed. As a matter of course, it increases rapidly, until these solitudes become alive with their simple murmuring note, and when evening sets in they fill the high land, which we have described, in numbers that can scarcely be imagined by any one

123

except an eye witness. Another cause probably of their being so numerous in this section of the country, may be owing to their migratory habits, as the bird is seen as far north as the river St. Lawrence in summer, and we presume these very birds return for their winter residence to Louisiana, in the very months when "fire hunting" takes place, which is the latter part of December, January, and the first of February. Yet a resident in the vicinity, or among the haunts of these birds, may live a life through, and make *day hunting* a business, and be unconscious that woodcock inhabit his path; so much is this the case, that I do not know of the birds ever being hunted in the common and universal way in the places where fire hunting them is practised. This novel sport we presume originated among the descendants of the French, who originally settled on the whole tract of country, bordering on the Mississippi as high up as it favors this kind of sport. Here it is, that "Beccasse," forms a common dish when in season, in which the wealthy, and the poor indulge as a luxury, too common to be a variety, and too fine not to be always welcome. With these preliminaries, let us prepare for the sport.

Provide yourself with a short double-barrelled fowling piece, of small bore; let your powder be first-rate, and have something the size of a small thimble to measure out your load of *mustard shot*. Let your powder be in a small flask, but keep your shot loose in the right-side pocket of your shooting jacket, with your measure—and, astonished sportsman! leave thy noble brace of dogs shut up in their kennels, for we would hunt Woodcock, incredible as it may seem, without them. In the place of the dogs, we will put a stout negro, who understands his business, burdened with what resembles an old fashioned warming-pan, the bottom *punched* with holes, instead of the top; in this pan are small splinters of pine knot, and we denominate this the torch. Then put on this broad-brimmed palmetto hat, so that it will shade your eyes, and keep them from alarming the birds. Now follow me down into any of the old fields, that lie between the river and the swamp, while the ladies can stand upon spacious galleries, that surround the house, and tell by the quick report of our guns, our success, and the streaming light from "the torch" will to them, from the distance, look like an *ignis fatuus*, dancing the cachuca in the old field. It is in the middle of January, the night is a favorable one, the weather rather warm, the thermometer, says "temperate," and the fog rolls off of the cold water in the river like steam; an old "fire hunter" says "this is just the night."

124

Whiz—whiz—hallo! what's here? Sambo strike a light and *hoist it over your head*. Now friend, place yourself behind the torch, on the right side, while I will do the same on the left, both of us in the rear, to court the shade. Now torch-bearer, lead on. Whiz, bang—whiz, bang—two woodcock in a minute. Bang, bang—Heavens, this is murder! Don't load too heavy, let your charges be *mere squibs*, and murder away, the sport is fairly up. The birds show plainly from three to ten paces all around us, and you can generally catch them on the ground, but as they rise from the glare of the light in a sort of flickering motion, slowly and perpendicularly, you can bring them down before they start off, like an arrow, in the surrounding darkness. Thank the stars, they do not fly many paces before they again alight, so you can follow the same bird, or birds, until every one is destroyed. Bang, bang—how exciting—don't the birds look beautiful, as they stream up into the light; the slight reddish tinge of their head and breast shining for an instant in the glare of the torch like fire. Ha! see that stream of gold, bang—and we have a meadow lark, the bright yellow of its breast being more beautiful than the dull colors of the woodcock. And I see, friend, you have bagged a quail or two. Well, such things occasionally happen. Two hours' sport, and killed between us nearly thirty birds. With old hunters, the average is always more, and a whole night's labor, if it is a good one, is often rewarded with a round hundred.

Practice, and experience, as a matter of course, have much to do with success in this sport, but less than in any other, for we have known tyros, on one or two occasions, to do very well with clubs; the birds being so thick, that some could be brought down even in this way, in their confusion to get out of the glare of the torch. This fact, and the quantity of birds killed, attest to the extraordinary numbers that inhabit this particular section of country. Let the birds, however, be less numerous than we have described—and they are on some days more plentiful than others—and a good shot, in the ordinary way of hunting the bird, has only to overcome the astonishment, and we will add, *horror*, at the mode in which he sees his favorite game killed, to be a perfect master of woodcock fire-hunting under all circumstances. It is common with some who are fond of sport, and have some sentiment about them, never to fire until the bird rises, and then to bring down a bird with each barrel. This requires quick shooting, as the torch only sheds an *available* light in a circle of about twenty yards in diameter. Parties are frequently made up, who hunt a given number of hours, and the destruction of the bird on these occasions is almost beyond belief. These parties afford rare sport, and it is often kept up all night. When this is the case, this nocturnal excitement is followed by heavy sleep, and the sportsman not unfrequently sleeps to so late an hour in the day, that he has only time to rise, sip a strong cup of coffee, and leisurely dress for dinner, when it is announced as ready, and woodcock, plentiful to wasting, are smoking on the table before him. That such a dinner is a brilliant repast, both for sense and soul, the dullest intellect can imagine, for woodcock and wit are synonymous. As the dinner has been served, and the popping of champagne that follows it, is already heard, we will leave our sportsmen, and the reader, (if this article has paid him for the perusal) to dream of WOODCOCK FIRE HUNTING.

AN EXTRA DEER HUNT IN LOUISIANA

Parks for deer are not common in Louisiana at present, the animal being too frequently met in the native forests to be thus preserved; yet in those parts of the country long settled, a park may occasionally be seen. A fine one flourished for a long time in our neighborhood, on the edge of the town of ———. Some time since, however, it was broken up, the deer were sold and moved off, save one fine old buck, who, resenting the liberties taken with his person in trying to catch him, leaped over the double fence of the park with a prodigious bound, and soon buried himself in the forests, in which his ancestors had found a home before him. But, true to his instinct, he soon returned to his old haunt, the park where he would browse about, until run off by some cur dog, only to return again, when his momentary alarm had subsided. These visits were frequent, and could be anticipated, and some good shots made such preparations to meet him, that on a moment's warning they could give him a brush. An opportunity soon occurred, for his white tail, like a feather, was seen flying through the very streets of the town, as if in defiance of dogs and destruction. The alarm was given, and two or three hunters turned out, the dogs were let loose, and as they opened on the trail, every village cur, of high and low degree, caught up the cry, and answered it back in a thousand discordant sounds, and all this racket and confusion in the town itself. The report of a rifle was soon heard, "a shot," that never missed, warranted a wounded buck, and the report that the deer was seen rolling down a ravine, and then running into a thicket, satisfied all that the lead had taken effect. But the crowd and the dogs were at fault as to the buck's location after he hid himself. Some said he ran off into a neighboring swamp, others that he had taken to the woods, while the knowing ones contended that he was hid in the blackberry bushes that so plentifully grew round the town. This discussion was suddenly stopt by the buck's breaking from his lair, almost running down the dogs, the blood streaming at every leap down his left fore leg; off he went like the wind, taking to the open fields, the dogs hard after him. Now was "fun a heap." An old bull, who reigned monarch of this field, not liking the intrusion of a pack of dogs, gave a fierce bellow, and straightening up his tail *a la* pump-handle, pursued the dogs; the cows, with laudable female curiosity, followed up the bull to see what was the matter, and the calves, knowing their anxious mothers wouldn't like to have them out, followed the cows, while the crowd generally, and a sprinkling of niggers, brought up the rear. Here was a chase new under the sun, and down it went through the main street of the village. The slamming of windows, the braying of mules, the rattling of carts, the shouts of the crowd, the lowing of the bull, all combined, with the dust that rose in clouds, made a hubbub very much resembling hell broke loose. Old "Durham short-horn" was the first of the interlopers to give out; probably finding he was off his own ground, he turned down a bye street, and his "kine" along with him. The cur dogs and the niggers gave out with the cattle, the pack and one or two hunters only keeping near the deer, who, faint with the loss of blood, rolled head over heels nearly opposite the Court House, and expired.

SCENES ON THE MISSISSIPPI

It has been the policy of the United States Government to remove the Indians west of the Mississippi. There, there is still a vast extent of country unoccupied, in which he can pursue, comparatively unrestrained, his inclinations, and pluck a few more days of happiness before his sun entirely sets. Occasionally may be seen in the southwest a large body of these people, under the charge of a "government officer," going to their new homes provided for them by their "white father." These "removals" are always melancholy exhibitions. The Indians, dispirited and heart-broken, entirely unconscious of the future, with dogged looks, submit to every privation that is imposed on them, and appear equally indifferent as to the receipt of favors. Throwing aside every mark of etiquette among themselves, the chief, who, among their native haunts, is almost a sacred person, lies down, or takes food promiscuously with the noblest or most degraded of his people; all distinctions of ages, as well as caste, are thrown aside, and they seem a mere mass of degraded humanity, with less seeming capability of self-preservation than the brute.

Some two or three years ago, we took passage on board of a boat bound from New Orleans to St. Louis, which boat the government had engaged to carry, as far towards their place of destination as practicable, near four hundred Seminoles, who with their chiefs had agreed to emigrate west of the Mississippi. We were not particularly pleased with our numerous and novel passengers, but the lateness of the season lessened the chances of getting a boat, and as most of the Indians were to remain in a tender, lashed to the side of the steamer, we concluded that a study of their manners and habits would beguile away the time of a long trip, and thus pay us for the inconveniences we might be put to. Unfortunately the novelty of our situation too soon passed away. The Indians, who on first acquaintance kept up a little display of their original character, gradually relapsed into what appeared to be a mere vegetable existence, and slept through the entire twenty-four hours of the day. Of all the remarkable traits of character that dignify them in history, we could not discern the least trace; yet,

129

among the brutal, insensible savages at our feet, were many daring spirits, who had displayed in their warfare with the whites dangerous talents, and taken many a bloody scalp. The girls were possessed of little or no personal charms, while the women, the laborers of the tribe, were as hideous as any hags than can be imagined.

The heat of the weather and the confinement of the boat had a dreadful effect on these poor wretches; sickness rapidly broke out among them, and as they stoutly refused to take the white man's medicine, their chances of recovery were poor indeed. The tender was turned into a perfect Lazar-house, and nothing could be seen but the affecting attentions of the old squaws to their friends and relatives, as they wasted away before their eyes. The infant and patriarch lay side by side, consuming with slow fever, while the corpse of some middle aged person lay at their feet, waiting for the funeral rites and the obscurity of the grave. Vain were the prescriptions of the "medicine man" of their tribe, he blew his breath through a gaudy colored reed upon the faces of his patients, and recited his incantations without success. He disfigured his person with new paint, and altered his devices daily, still his patients would die, and at every landing where the boat stopped some poor Indian was taken ashore and hastily buried. No one mourned over the corpse but the females, and they only when intimately related to the deceased. The father, son, or husband, as they saw their relatives falling around them, scarce turned their glazed eyes upon the dead, and if they did, it was only to exclaim in gutteral accents, "Ugh!" and then turn away to sleep. Not an article belonging to the dead but was wrapped up with it or placed in the coffin; the infant and its playthings, the young girl and her presents, the squaw with her domestic utensils, and the "brave" with his gun and whatever property there was in his possession. A beautiful custom, indeed; one that brings no crocodile tears to the eyes of the living heir, or gives the lawyer a chance for litigation.

Among those who died was one old veteran warrior, who had particularly attracted our attention by his severe looks and loneliness of habit, and we watched attentively his exit from the world. He seemed, as near we could judge, to have no relatives about him; no one noticed him but the doctor, who was markedly attentive. The old man was a chief, and the scars that covered his body told of many a dreadful encounter with man and beast. His huge skeleton, as he moved about in his ill-concealed agony, looked like the remains of a giant, exaggerated by its want of flesh. His hands were small, and of feminine delicacy, occasionally he would move them about in mute eloquence, then clutch at the air, as if in pursuit of any enemy, and then fall back exhausted. Recovering from one of these fits, he tried to stand, but found it impossible, he got however upon his elbow, and opening his eyes for the first time in a long while, stared wildly about him. A smile lit up his features, his lips moved, and he essayed to speak. The sun, which was at this time low in the west, shone full upon him, his smooth skin glistened like burnished copper, his long-neglected hair, of silvery whiteness, hung over his head and face, while the scalp lock displayed itself by its immense length, as it reached his shoulder. His muscles, shrunken by age and disease, moved like cords in performing their offices. A very old man was dying. As his mouth opened a faint chant was heard, the doctor, at the sound, bent his head, and assumed an air of reverence. The chant, as it continued to swell on the evening breeze, reached the ears of the slumbering warriors that lay about, and as they listened to the sounds, I could discern their sottish eyes open and flash with unearthly fires, sometimes exhibiting pleasure, but oftener ferocity and hatred. The old man sang on, a few raised to their feet, and waved their hands in the air, as if keeping time, and occasionally some aged Indian would repeat the sounds he heard. The old man ceased, turned his face full to the setting sun, and fell back a corpse. The Indians cast a look in the direction of their homes, gave an expression of malignity, as well as sorrow, and then silently and sluggishly sank into repose, as if nothing had happened. "That old fellow brags well of his infernal deeds," observed one of the white men accompanying the Indians, "and the red skinned devils about here drink it in as a Cuba hound would blood."

The intense heat of the weather, and the quietness that reigned so profoundly among the Indians, broken only by the saw and hammer of the carpenter at the capstan, making coffins, made us sigh for a landing place, and a separation from such melancholy scenes. This desire was encouraged from the well-known fact, that the savages grew every hour more discontented and troublesome, and the song of the dying old chief, had not allayed their feelings, or made them more comfortable.

The morning following the death of the old chief had been preceded by one of those nights, in which the fog rose from the water so thick, that in the hyperbolical language of the boatmen, you could make feather beds of it. The pilot had "felt his way along" for many hours, until the sudden crash that shook every thing in the boat, convinced us that we were aground. The engine stopped, and left us in perfect silence and obscurity. Long after our accustomed late hour of rising, we dressed and went on deck. The fresh mist blew in our faces with sickening effect, and the sun—then two hours high—was invisible. The shore, which was so near that the breaking of twigs could be heard, as cattle or game moved about on it, was undiscernible. Even the end of the boat opposite to the one on which we stood was in obscurity. A deep, damp, opaque Mississippi river fog, had swallowed us up. As the sun continued to rise and gain strength in its ascent, its rays penetrated through the gloom, and we at last discovered it, looking about as brilliant as an illuminated cheese. On it came, working its way through the fog by its rays, reaching them out as a debilitated spider would his legs, and apparently with the same caution and labor. With the growing heat a gentle breeze sprang up, and the fog rolled about in huge masses, leaving spots of pure atmosphere, and then closing them up; gradually it became more and more rarified, and things at a distance began to appear, all magnified and mysterious. On came the sun, brightening and enlarging, until his streaming rays dipped into the water, and shot up to the zenith. The fog, no longer able to keep its consistency, retired before its splendor in little clouds, which would sometimes rally, and spread over the surface of the river, then breaking asunder, vanish away into air, with a splendor that rivalled the dying dolphin's tints. Now, for the first time, could we learn our whereabouts. The broad bosom of the Mississippi stretched far to the front of us, while at the stern of our boat was discovered one of those abrupt banks that denote a sudden bend in the river. This had deceived the pilot. On our right, within a few hundred yards, lay the shore, lined with huge trees, tangled with gigantic vines, and waving with festoons of moss, giving them a sombre appearance that was singular and repulsive. Wild ducks and geese went screaming by, heron and crane innumerable would come near us, but discovering the dark form of our boat, fly precipitately away. The water glistened in the sun, and there would rise from its quiet surface little columns of mist, that would ascend high in the air and sail along on the surface of the water, until striking the distant shore, they would roll over the landscape, enveloping parts in momentary obscurity, and not until near noon did the fog entirely disappear. Then the sun, as if incensed with the veil that had for a time kept him from his scorching work, poured down its heat with more intensity, leaving a foggy day, hotter before its close, than if the sun had been unobscured in its first appearance in the morn.

While sitting in the cabin, congratulating ourselves on the prospect of getting off the bar, on which we had so long been detained, the report of a rifle was heard, fired from the deck, accompanied by a loud yell. Another rifle was discharged, and a loud Indian whoop followed, that made our blood run cold. The ladies present turned pale, and the commanding officer who had charge of the Indians, somewhat astonished, left the cabin. A momentary alarm seized upon us all. Could the old warrior's death song have incited mutiny? Crack! went another rifle outside, and another shout; we could stand it no longer, but rushed on deck. What a scene! Not an Indian that was able but was upon his feet, his eyes sparkling with fire, and his form looking as active as a panther's. The sluggards of yesterday were as sleek and nervous as horses at the starting post, so perfectly had a little excitement altered them. Their rifles, however, thank Heaven, were not turned upon the white man—their enemy was between the boat and the shore—in the water—in the form of a very large black bear. It was a beautiful sight to see the savage springing with a graceful bound on some high place in the boat, and raise his rifle to his eye, and before the report was heard you could mark a red furrow on the head of the bear, where it was struck by the ball as it passed its way through the skin and flesh, without entering the bone. While the bear, at these assaults, would throw himself half out of the water, brush over the smarting wound with his huge paw, and then dash on for life. Another shot, and another yell brought the bear on the defensive, and showed he was dangerously wounded. While this firing was going on, some Indians, armed only with knives, launched a canoe that lay among their moveables, and paddled hurriedly out to the bear. No sooner was the canoe within his reach than he put his huge paws on its side, in spite of the thrusts aimed at his head, and turned his enemies, with a somerset, into the water. Loud shouts of laughter greeted this accident; the little "papooses" and women fairly danced with joy, while the crew of the boat yelled and shouted, and swore at the sport as much as the savages themselves. The bear turned from the boat, and looked for his victims, but they were not to be seen; precipitated so suddenly into the water, they sank below the surface, like the wild duck when much alarmed, and then thrust out their shining polls far from the friendly hug of the bear. Laying their plans of attack at once (for the firing of rifles was

133

suspended), one of the Indians attracted the bear's attention, and made towards him; they met, the floating canoe between them, and while thus skirmishing, the unoccupied Indian came up behind the bear, raised his knife, and drove it deeply into his side, and then disappeared, as a lump of lead would have done about his own weight. The bear turned in the direction of this new attack, snapped and clawed in the water in the greatest agony. Another stab was given in the same way, and as the Indians again disappeared, a "white hunter," who had been looking on, rifle in hand, quite coolly, sprang upon the guards of the boat, and singing out "red devils, look out below," fired. The bear leaped entirely out of the water, fell upon his back, and after a convulsive kick or two, floated a dead body on the water. This exploit of the white man, so sudden and unexpected, was greeted by a loud shout from all parties. "You see," said the hunter, as he coolly laid down his rifle—"you see, the Bar has feeling, strangers, and whar is the use of tormenting the varmint? my old shooting iron never misses, but if it had hit a red skin, by accident, I should not have been ashamed of the shot—for the Bar is the best of the two, and a perfect Christian, compared with the best copper skin in the tender *thar*."

The Indians in the water, at this last shot, expressed a significant "ugh," and approaching the Bear, gave him repeated thrusts with their knives, that showed they thought him a hard lived, and dangerous animal. In a few minutes they recovered their canoe, and were towing the dead carcase ashore. Fifty Indians at least, now threw their blankets aside, and leaping into the river, swam after the Bear ashore. The tearing off of the huge skin, and jerking the meat, was despatched so rapidly, that it indicated an accustomed work.

This little incident, relieved the monotony, of all others the most disagreeable, that of being aground in the Mississippi, and the hours of labor which were spent in releasing the boat, passed quickly away, and by the time the Indians on shore returned to their friends in the tender, the bell sounded; *we moved*; and the steamer pursued its way.

THE FIRST HUNTING TRIP OF THE STEAMER "NIMROD," OF "BARROW SETTLEMENT," LOUISIANA

"A Louisiana Sportsman.—The ardent enthusiasm with which Field Sports are almost universally regarded in Louisiana, by the intelligent and spirited gentlemen of that State, forcibly characterizes the American portion of the population. A great majority of the planters are gentlemen of character and fortune, and their devotion to the chase is only paralleled by their hospitality. One of them, well known on the Turf, has recently ordered a steamboat built expressly for sporting expeditions to the remote rivers and lakes with which Louisiana and Mississippi abound, where the game being rarely disturbed is plentiful to a degree that can hardly be realized anywhere else. The boat is to be about seventy-five feet long, having permanent stable accommodations on deck for twelve horses, and also for two packs of hounds. She will be a curiosity when completed, and we hope at some future period to have the pleasure of "touching knees under mahogany," with her high spirited owner and his friends, in her spacious cabin. An expedition up the Sunflower river, with such a party as the *Nimrod* will carry, would add years to the existence of a 'Frank Forester' or a 'Cypress.'"

EDITORIAL, "SPIRIT OF THE TIMES," July 10th.

The Nimrod is finished, and there is no prettier craft afloat. The wealth and taste of the owner of the boat would guarantee this. The Mississippi, that river of steamboats, was never honored with any thing so perfect. It looks like some exquisite yacht, with a sublimated engine in it. What an improvement this boat is upon the lumbering craft of a few years ago, so appropriately termed by a sleepy Dutchman "floating saw-mills." Just see her under way, passing that flat boat; they rival each other in the grace of their movements as would Taglioni and a goose. "Go it, old ark," you are as much behind the Nimrod in perfection, as the flood was behind it in time. No sordid commerce, is to lumber up its decks—its comfortable cabin is not devoted to traffic—each revolution of its engine adds nothing in the way of business speculation. No! Thanks to Diana, its purposes are for SPORTING. The money changer, and the eternal talker of stocks, take no passage in the Nimrod. The very atmosphere of the boat would kill off such characters. Liberal-minded, and high-minded men, only, have a berth; men who can strip off the sordid cares of the world as easily and pleasur-

135

ably as a tired traveller would his pack, and devote their whole souls to a pleasure excursion.

The idea of having a costly boat built entirely for hunting trips, is original, IT'S A GREAT IDEA. Its magnitude is sufficient to cause congestion of the brain in common men. The thing is worthy of the large scale on which the South West is laid out!

Imagination in Europe is not up to reality in America, and that's the reason poetry is so tame in this country. Milton couldn't conceive of the Mississippi; he sang of the *mighty Thames!* The "Big Bear of Arkansaw," if he should see the Thames, would designate it, as *"that creek, thar."* The decks of the Nimrod have accommodations for ten or twelve horses, and hounds to match. Isn't it beautiful? What can be finer than all this? in a country, where a few hours sail will take us into an almost unexplored country, carrying into the wilderness the comforts of refined life, thus mixing up the life of a perfectly wild hunter, and the associations of the drawing room. Then such a company as can be gathered together on board of the Nimrod. Every man with a soul extending from his head to his feet. But enough, we must get under weigh.

Sound the horn "commodore," to notify all the passengers—bah— the sportsmen, that every thing is ready for the start. There sounds the horn again, and the hounds are yelling in answer to it, like so many devils.—We are under weigh, now, puff, puff. The Nimrod is on the high pressure principle. The low muddy banks of the river seem to be giving us the slip. There comes a steamer, bound for New Orleans. She smells of business, ding-dong, ding-dong, the pilot gives the usual passing signal, and we answer with the horn—what a staring it excites, particularly in that youth on the wheel house—his anxious mother don't know he's out, so we will excuse him. Now go into the cabin and look about; were there ever more comfortable cushions, better rifles, fowling pieces, and fishing tackle, or better hands to wield them? The bar, too, I must not forget to mention. This important appendage in the Nimrod has no great merit about its architecture, save in its extensiveness; but Chancellor Brougham would get down on his knees to *practice* at it. The rules observed at that bar are unexceptionable, they would even suit loafers, as well as lawyers, for it is an open bar. Its ends circle outwardly, so that the practitioner is encompassed by them, on the right and left, the bottles glisten, while the bouquets of mint throw over the whole a kind of vernal charm. And then those ancient wine bottles, those untasted and living testimonials of the care of great-grandfathers. *There is no money drawer in that bar!* A negro replenishes, and keeps the tumblers like crystal, but only changes, empty bottles for full ones; no other *change* is permitted. What an invention!!!

"Fuel out, Commodore?" "Yes, don't you see we are making for that wood yard." "Out with the hawser." "Where is this boat from," enquires the chopper. "From the 'Barrow Settlement,' you old fool, can't you tell that from its fixins." "Never heard of that ar port in my life," said the chopper. "Well prehaps, massa, you never heered of Heaven," replied one of the niggers, at which piece of wit, Sambo laughed so loud, that he alarmed that part of the company ashore with an idea that the scape pipe had collapsed.

The chopper was soon on board of the Nimrod; he was used to boats, but this one puzzled him. "What trade is this boat in?" "Principally in the fish, deer, and bear business." This made the poor fellow stare more than ever, and when he entered the cabin, he seemed to be in a trance. Everything was new to him, and wrong. He recognised the bar, however, and instinctively patronised it. When his money was refused for the liquor, he rushed off the boat, murmuring something about having nine children dependent on his exertions. He thought his day was come, but he reached the shore in safety, and detailed his visit thus—

"Thar's a boat, something un-natural 'bout it—*too comfortable for this world, by half*—all the crew with long-tailed coats on, and tights—no cargo, save arms, ammunition, ten horses, and a raft of hounds;—*the bar made backwards*—and they don't take pay for liquor!—no certificate of a safe biler from the appointed authority—it's a bust-up sure,—niggers at the furnace too sassy by half—the bar turned backwards, and no pay taken at it.—Well, God bless the craft, hit or miss; they have paid for their wood, and they do the *liquoring* in a christian manner—they are too good looking to be very bad. I take them to be the 'me-li-o-ra-tors, or the Fiscal Agent, the papers speak of. No bell either—off at the braying of the horn—bar turned backwards, and no pay taken at it."

The Nimrod was no sooner out of sight of the chopper, who probably finished his exclamations of surprise to a Cincinnati business man, who was seized with an apoplexy at the astonishment he was thrown into, because the "commodore" of the Nimrod refused to take a load of "bulk pork" at the one hundred and twenty-fifth part of a cent in *advance* of the regular rates.

A happy set of fellows, truly, are the party on the Nimrod; only one fault, *everybody wants to be captain*, particularly if the weather is pleasant, and as the responsibility of managing the boat is so divided out, I fear she will, some of these days, make a *rayther* short trip of it. On the morning of our first day out, C. D. insisted on being pilot while his companions went to breakfast; it's plain sailing on the Mississippi if you keep the *channel*. Breakfast was half discussed, when some one suggested that the cabin swung round rather singularly; this eccentric motion was noticed by all, and in the midst of the speculations of the whys and wherefores, the bow of the steamer, while under full head-way, imbedded itself in a mud-bank, the concussion throwing half of us on the table, and the other half against the side of the cabin; while the cups, plates, &c., "mashed beautifully." We all ran for the deck, but before we reached it we heard the crack of a rifle, and imagine the turn given to our alarm, when we beheld C. D., rifle in hand, pointing to the shore, where a dead wild turkey lay, he observing, "that he saw the bird, and forgot the helm in the excitement of cracking it over." Fortunately the accident was soon remedied, and it was immediately resolved to have officers appointed who would be responsible, otherwise the Nimrod would soon be what the wood-chopper prophesied, "a bust-up, sure."

Night found us safely moored inside one of those beautiful little lakes that empty themselves into Red river. The engine stopped, and active preparations were made for the sports of the following day. The horses were taken on shore, and placed in a rude stable; they seemed to be in fine spirits, and fairly danced when their feet touched the soft earth. A wood-chopping hunter, one of those nondescripts that are to be met with along the Mississippi river, and at the mouths of its tributaries, attracted by our fires, came to us, and when he found out our objects and pursuits, reported an abundance of game, and our expectations were raised to the highest pitch. "Deer," he said, "you could stumble over anywhere; bar warn't scace, and turkies were sprinkled about amazin'." This information put us all in the best possible humor, and we determined to make him so. A bottle of *ancient* whiskey was accordingly set before him, and he took it up like a sponge. "'Pon my word, strangers, this is *leetle* the best 'biled corn' I have tasted since the overflow in '28," he coolly remarked, as he drank off the sixth "stiff horn." His reserve gradually wore away, and from a very modest man he became quite at his ease. The age of the liquor had given it a "riliness" that deceived him as to its strength, and he was soon pretty drunk. His eyes sparkled and looked dull by turns; his tongue broke loose, and among other edifying remarks, he said "he was glad to find so many congenial spirits;" one congenial spirit, at least, he certainly had found, and after bragging of his exploits, as no one but a western hunter can brag, he concluded by informing all present that he was the smartest fellow that ever lived, and that he had a bunch of brains in his head bigger than his fist that he never yet had occasion to use. With other equally extraordinary exhibitions of novelty, he sank into a profound slumber, his head gently resting on a boot-jack, while his feet reposed on the top of a champagne basket.

The company of the Nimrod soon followed the chopper's example, so far as sleeping was concerned, determining to greet the morning sun laden with the successful hunter's spoils. I was determined to immortalize myself. The spirit of the enthusiastic sportsman had seized me—I could see nothing but falling bucks, dead turkies, and wounded bear. My gun I was determined should never miss—such a time as I would have of it would cause a general excitement in the sporting world—immortalize the actor, and render the company of the Nimrod only less celebrated than the *menage* that went into the ark. Yes, said I, vauntingly, with this trusty weapon I'll work miracles. The suns of Davy Crockett and Daniel Boone henceforth set in obscurity. I will— "Fall off your chair, master."—As the sound greeted my ear, I woke from a long troubled sleep, induced by the warm sun of a Southern August. The "Spirit" was tightly grasped in my hand, the last thing that I had read, having been the "editorial" at the head of this article.

A PIANO IN ARKANSAS

We shall never forget the excitement which seized upon the inhabitants of the little village of Hardscrabble, as the report spread through the community that a real Piano had actually arrived within its precincts. Speculation was afloat as to its appearance and its use. The name was familiar with every body, but what it precisely meant, none could tell. That it had legs was certain, for a stray volume of Capt. Marryat's "Diary," was one of the most conspicuous works in the *floating* library of Hardscrabble. And Capt. Marryat stated that he saw a Piano, somewhere in New England, with pantalettes on. An old and foreign paper was brought forward, in which there was an advertisement headed "Soiree," which informed the "citizens generally," that Mr. Bobolink, "would preside at the Piano." This was presumed to mean, by several wiseacres, who had been to a menagerie, that Mr. Bobolink stirred the piano up with a long pole, in the same way the show-man did the lions, and rhi-no-ce-rus. So public opinion was in favor of its being an animal, though a harmless one, for there had been a land speculator through the village a few weeks before, who distributed circulars of a Female Academy for the accomplishment of young ladies. These circulars distinctly stated "the use of the Piano to be one dollar a month." One knowing old chap said, that if they would tell him what so-i-ree meant, he would tell them what a Piano was, and no mistake.

The owner of this strange instrument was no less than a very quiet, and very respectable, late resident in a little town somewhere "down east," who having "failed" at home, had emigrated into the new country of Arkansas, for the purpose of bettering his fortune, and escaping the heartless sympathy of his more lucky neighbors, who seemed to consider him an indifferent and degraded man because he had become honestly poor.

The new comers were strangers of course. The house in which they were setting up their furniture, was too little arranged "to admit of calls," and as they seemed little disposed to court society, all prospect of immediately solving the mystery that hung about the Piano, seemed hopeless. In the meantime public opinion was "rife"—the depository of this strange thing was looked upon by passers-by with undefinable awe—and as noises, unfamiliar, sometimes reached the street, it was presumed this was the Piano, and the excitement rose higher than ever. One or two old ladies, presuming on their age and respectability, called upon the strangers and enquired after their healths, and offered their services, and friendship. In the meantime they eyed every thing in the house with intensity, but seeing nothing strange, they hinted about the Piano. One of the new family observed carelessly, "that it had been much injured in bringing it out, that the damp had affected its tones, and that one of its legs was so injured that it would not stand up, and that for the present, it would not ornament the parlor."

Here was an explanation indeed—injured in bringing out—damp affecting its tones—leg broken—"poor thing," ejaculated the old ladies, as they proceeded to their homes, "travelling has evidently fatigued it, the Mass-sis-sip fogs has given it a cold, poor thing," and they all wanted to see it with increased curiosity. "The Village" agreed that if Moses Mercer, familiarly called Mo Mercer, was in town, they would soon have a description of the Piano, and the uses to which it was put, and fortunately, in the midst of the excitement, "Mo," who had been off on a hunting expedition, arrived in town.

Moses Mercer was the son of "Old Mercer," who was, and had been, in the State Senate, ever since Arkansas was admitted into the "Union." "Mo," from this fact, received great glory of course; his father's greatness would have been glory enough, but his having been twice to the "Capitol," when the legislature was in session, stamped his claims to pre-eminence over all competitors, and Mo Mercer was the oracle of the village. "Mo" knew every thing; he had all the consequence and complacency of a man who had never seen his equal and never expected to. "Mo" bragged extensively on his having been to the "Capitol" twice,—of his there having been in the most fashionable society,— of having seen the world. His return to town was received with a shout. The arrival of the Piano was announced to him, and he *alone*, of all the community, was not astonished at the news. His insensibility was wonderful; he treated the thing as a matter that he was used to, and went on to say he had seen more Pianos in the "Capitol" than he had ever seen woodchucks,—that it was not an animal, but a musical instrument, played upon by the ladies, and he wound up his description by saying, "that the way the dear creeters could pull the music out of it, was a caution to screech owls."

141

This new turn given to the Piano excitement in Hardscrabble, by Mo Mercer, was like pouring oil on fire to extinguish it, for it blazed out with more vigor than ever. That it was a musical instrument, made it a rarer thing than if it had been an animal, in that wild country, and people of all sizes, colors, and degrees, were dying to see and hear it.

Jim Cash was Mo Mercer's right hand man—in the language of refined society, he was "Mo's toady,"—in the language of Hard-scrabble, he was "Mo's wheel-horse." Cash believed in Mo Mercer with a faith that no Catholic believes in the Pope. Now Cash was dying to see the piano, and the first opportunity he had alone with his "Quixotte," he expressed the desire that was consuming his vitals.

"We'll go at once, and see it," said Mercer.

"Strangers," echoed the frightened Cash.

"Humbug,—do you think I have visited the "Capitol" twice, and don't know how to treat fashionable society? Come along, Cash, at once," said Mercer.

Off the pair started, Mercer all confidence, and Cash all fears as to the propriety of the visit. These fears Cash frankly expressed, but Mercer repeated for the thousandth time, his visit to the "Capitol," his familiarity with fashionable society and Pianos, which, Mercer observed, "was synonymous." And he finally told Cash, however abashed or ashamed he might be in the presence of the ladies, "that he needn't fear of sticking, for he would put him through."

A few minutes' walk brought the parties on the broad galleries of the house that contained the object of so much curiosity. The doors and windows were closed, and a suspicious look was on every thing.

"Do they always keep a house closed up this way that has a Piano in it?" asked Cash.

"Certainly," replied Mercer, "the damp would destroy its tones."

Repeated knocks at the doors, and finally at the windows, satisfied both Cash and Mercer that no body was at home. In the midst of this disappointment, Cash discovered a singular machine at the end of the gallery, crossed by bars, rollers, and surmounted with an enormous crank. Cash approached it on tip toe; he had a presentiment that this was the object of his curiosity, and as its intricate character unfolded itself, he gazed with distended eyes, and asked Mercer with breathless anxiety *"what that was?"* Mercer turned to the thing as coolly as a toper would to a glass of brandy and water, and said "that was *it.*" "That IT!!" exclaimed Cash, opening his eyes still wider, and then wished to see the "tones." Mercer pointed to the cross-bars and rollers.

With trembling hands, and a resolution that would enable a man to be scalped without winking, Cash reached out his hand, and seized the handle of the crank (Cash was at heart a brave and fearless man), he gave it a turn, the machinery grated harshly, and seemed to clamor for something to be put in its maw.

"What delicious sounds," said Cash.

"Beautiful," observed the complacent Mercer, at the same time seizing Cash's arm, and asking him to desist for fear of breaking the instrument, or getting it out of tune. The simple caution was sufficient, and Cash in the joy of his discovery, at what he had seen, and done, for a moment looked as conceited as Mo Mercer himself. Busy indeed, was Cash, from this time forward, to explain to gaping crowds the exact appearance of the Piano, how he had actually taken hold of it, and as his friend Mo Mercer observed, "pulled music out of it." The curiosity of the village was thus allayed, and it died comparatively away; Cash however, having risen to almost as much importance as Mo Mercer, for his having seen and handled the thing.

Our New England family knew little or nothing of all this excitement; they received the visits and congratulations of the hospitable villagers, and resolved to give a grand party to return some of the kindnesses they had received, and the Piano was for the first time moved into the parlor. No invitations on this occasion were neglected; early at the post was every visitor, for it was rumored that Miss Patience Doolittle would, in the course of the evening, perform on the Piano—The excitement was immense; the supper was passed over with a contempt that rivals that cast upon an excellent farce, played preparatory to a dull tragedy in which the *star* is to appear. The furniture was all critically examined, but nothing could be discovered answering to Cash's description. An enormously *thick table*, with a spread on it, attracted little attention, for *timber is cheap* in a new country, and so every body expected soon to see the Piano "brought in."

Mercer, of course, was the hero of the evening; he talked loud and long. Cash, as well as several young ladies, went into hysterics at his wit. Mercer grew more familiar as the evening wore away; he asserted that the company present reminded him of his two visits to the "Capitol," and other associations equally exclusive and peculiar. "Hope deferred maketh the heart sick," and the Piano, and the music had been deferred so long, that several old ladies and some young ones (who shrunk instinctively from showing any curiosity or desire), insisted upon Mercer's asking Miss Patience to favor the company with a little

143

music on the Piano. "Certainly," said Mercer, and with the grace of a city dandy, he called upon the lady to gratify all present with a little music, prefacing his request with the remark that if she was fatigued his friend Cash would give the instrument *a turn*. Miss Patience smiled, and looked at Cash,—his knees trembled; all eyes in the room turned upon him, and he sweat all over. Miss Patience was gratified to hear that *Mr.* Cash was a musician; she admired people with a musical taste. Cash fell into a chair, as he afterwards stated, "chawed up." Oh, that Beau Brummell, or any of his admirers, could have seen Mo Mercer all this while! Calm as a summer morning, and as complacent as a newly-painted sign; he smiled, and patronised, and was the only unexcited person in the room.—Miss Patience rose; a sigh escaped from all present—the Piano was to be brought in evidently—she approached the thick-leafed table, and removed the spread, throwing it carelessly, and gracefully aside,—opened it, presenting the beautiful arrangement of the dark and white keys.—Mo Mercer, at this, for the first time in his life, looked confused; he was Cash's authority in his descriptions of a Piano—while Cash himself began to recover the moment he ceased to be the object of attraction. Many a whisper ran through the crowd as to the tones, and more particularly the *crank*, none could see it. Miss Patience took her seat, ran her fingers over the octaves, and, if Moses in Egypt was not *executed*, "Moses" in Hard-scrabble was. "Miss," said Cash, the moment he could express himself, so entranced was he, and overcome with astonishment—"Miss Doolittle, what was that instrument that Mo Mercer showed me last Wednesday evening on your gallery, that went with a crank, and had bars and rollers in it?" It was now the turn for Miss Patience to blush, and away went the blood to her eye-brows; she hesitated only a moment, and said, "if he *must* know, that it was a—a—YANKEE WASHING MACHINE!" The name grated on Mo Mercer's ears, as if rusty spikes had been thrust in them; his knees trembled.—The sweat started on his brow, as he heard the taunting whispers of visiting the "Capitol" twice, and "seeing Pianos as plenty as woodchucks." The seeds of envy, and maliciousness of fashion were at that moment sown in the village of Hard-scrabble, and Mo Mercer, the great and invulnerable, surprising as it may seem, was the first victim sacrificed at its shrine.

Time wore on, and Pianos became common, and Mo Mercer less popular, and he finally disappeared entirely on the evening of the day, when a Yankee pedlar of notions, sold to the highest bidders, six "Patent and highly concentrated" "Mo Mercer's Pianos."

OPOSSUMS AND 'POSSUM HUNTING

Reader, if you never saw an opossum, you never saw a natural *lusus naturæ*, for they are certainly the most singular, inexplicable little animals that live.—Dame Nature seems to have become eccentric in their formation, and like her sex generally, shown a willingness to be ridiculous, if necessary, to introduce a *new fashion*. We will not, however, go into some particulars, for if we did we might infringe upon Mr. Walker's exclusive province of "breeding," and thereby "o'er step the modesty of nature."

The habits of the opossum resemble generally those of the "coon" and fox, though they are less intelligent in defending themselves against an attack of an enemy. Knock an opossum on the head, or any part of the body, with a weapon of any kind, small or great, and if he makes any resistance at all, he will endeavor to bite the weapon that hits him instead of the agent using it. The opossum seems willing to treat the world, as the Frenchman promised the bull dog. "If you will let me alone, I won't trouble you." Put the animal in a critical situation, and he will resort to stratagem instead of force to elude his pursuers; for if he finds escape impossible he will feign himself dead in advance of your own charitable intentions towards him, and when you think you have given him his quietus and secured him, he will unexpectedly wake up and be off. This trick of the little animal has given rise to a proverb of much meaning among those acquainted with his habits, of "playing 'possum," and probably it is as good an illustration of certain deceptive actions in life as can be imagined. Take an opossum in good health, corner him up until escape is impossible, give him a gentle tap that would hardly crush a mosquito, and he will straighten out as beautiful "a body" as you will ever see. In this situation you may thump him, cut his flesh, and half skin him; not a muscle will move; his eyes are glazed, and covered with dust, for he has no eyelids to close over them. You may even worry him with a dog and satisfy yourself that he is really dead, then leave him quiet a moment, and he will draw a thin film off of his eyes, and if not interfered with, be among the missing.

An Irishman meeting with one of these little animals in a public road, was thrown into admiration at its appearance, and on being asked why he did not bring the "thing" home with him? said he, "On sight, I popped him with my shillelah, he died off immediately, and I thrust the spalpeen into my coat pocket; thar's a dinner ony how, I said, to myself, and scarcely had I made the observation, than he commenced devouring one, biting through my breeches, the Lord presarve me. I took him out of my pocket, and gave him another tap on the head, that would have kilt an Orange man at Donnybrook fair—take that for a finis, you decateful crater, said I, slinging him on my back. Well, murther, if he did not have me by the sate of honor in no time. Och ye 'Merica cat ye, I'll bate the sivin lives out of ye; and at him I wint 'till the bones of his body cracked, *and he was clean kilt*. Then catching him by the tail, for fear of accidents, if he did not turn round and give my thumb a pinch, I'm no Irishman. 'Off wid ye!' I hallooed with a shout, 'for some ill-mannered ghost of the devil, with a rat's tail; and if I throubles the likes of ye again, may I ride backwards at my own funeral!'"

There is one other striking characteristic about the opossum, which, we presume, Shakespeare had a prophetic vision of, when he wrote that celebrated sentence, "Thereby hangs a tail;" for this important appendage, next to its "playing 'possum," is extraordinary. This tail is long, black, and destitute of hair, and although it will not enable its possessor, like the kangaroos, in the language of the show-man, "to jump fifteen feet upwards and forty downwards," still it is of great importance in climbing trees, and supporting the animal when watching for its prey. By this tail the 'possum suspends itself for hours to a swinging limb of a tree, either for amusement or for the purpose of sleeping, which last he will do while thus "hung up," as soundly as if slipping his hold did not depend upon his own will. This "tail hold" is so firm, that shooting the animal will not cause him to let go, even if you blow his head off; on the contrary, he will remain hung up until the birds of prey and the elements have scattered his carcass to the winds; and yet the tail will remain an object of unconquered attachment to its last object of circumlocuting embrace.

An old backwoods "Boanerges," of our acquaintance, who occasionally threw down his lap-stone and awl, and went through the country to stir up the people—to look after the "consarns of their latter end," enforced the necessity of perseverance in good works, by comparing a true Christian to an opossum up a tall sapling, in a strong wind. Said he, "My bretheren, that's your situation exactly; the world,

146

the flesh, and the devil compose the wind that is trying to blow you off
the gospel tree. But don't let go of it, hold on to it as a 'possum would
in a hurricane. If the fore legs of your passions get loose, hold on by
your hind legs of conscientiousness; and if they let go, hold on eter-
nally by your tail, which is the promise, that the saints shall persevere
unto the end."

As an animal of sport, the opossum is of course of an inferior character; the negroes, however, look upon the animal as the most perfect
of game, and are much astonished that the fox and deer should be
preferred; and the hilarity with which they pursue the sport of 'possum
hunting, far excels the enthusiasm of the most inveterate follower after
nobler game. Fine moonlight nights are generally chosen on such occasions, three or four negroes, armed with a couple of axes and accompanied by a cur dog, who understands his business, will sally out
for 'possum hunting, and nothing can be more joyous than their loud
laugh and coarse joke on these midnight hunts. The dog scents the
animal, for they are numerous, and "barks up the right tree." A torch
made of light wood or pitch pine, is soon diffusing a brilliant light, and
the axe is struck into the tree that contains the game, let it be a big
tree or a small one, it matters not; the growth of a century and of a few
years yields to the "forerunner of civilization," and comes to the
ground. While this is going on the dog keeps his eye on the 'possum,
barking all the while with the greatest animation. In the meantime the
negroes, as they relieve each other at the work of chopping, make
night vocal with laughter and songs, and on such occasions particularly you will hear "Sittin' on a Rail," cavatina fashion, from voices that
would command ten thousand a year from any opera manager on the
Continent. The tree begins to totter, the motion is new to the 'possum,
and as it descends to the ground the little animal instinctively climbs
to the highest limb. Crash, and off he goes to the ground, and not
unfrequently into the very jaws of the dog; if this is not the case, a
short steeple chase on foot ensues; 'possum finds escape impossible,
feigns himself dead, falls into the wrong hands, and is at once really
killed. Such is opossum hunting among the negroes, a sport in which
more hard labor is got through with in a few hours than will be performed by the same individuals through the whole of the next day.
Sometimes two or three opossums are killed, and if a negro is proud
of a yellow vest, a sky-blue stock, and red inexpressibles, with a dead
opossum in his possession, he is sublimated.

Among gentlemen, we have seen one occasionally who amuses

147

himself with bringing down an opossum with a rifle, and one we have met who has given the hunt a character, and really reduced it to a science. We were expressing some surprise at the kind manner with which our friend spoke of opossum hunting, and we were disposed to laugh at his taste; we were told very gravely that we were in the presence of a proficient in 'possum hunting, and if we desired we should have a specimen at sun-down, and by the dignity of the hunt we would be compelled to admit, that there were a great many ways to do the same thing. The proposition came from our host, and we at once consented. The night was *dark*, and I noticed this and spoke of it, and the reply was, that such a night only would answer the purpose. An half hour's ride brought us into the depths of the forest, and in the extra darkness of its deep recesses we were piloted by a stout negro bearing a torch. Our dogs—for there were two of them—soon gave notice that we were in the vicinity of an opossum, and finally directed by their noses—for eyes were of no use—they opened loud and strong, and satisfied us that an opossum was over our heads. At this moment I was completely puzzled to know how we were to get at the animal I must confess; we had no axe, and a mill-stone intervening between the opossum and our eyes, could not have shut it out of sight more effectually than did the surrounding darkness, which seemed to be growing "thicker" every moment, by contrast with the glaring torch. The negro who accompanied us without ceremony kindled a large fire, about twenty feet from the base of the tree in which our game was lodged, and as soon as it was well kindled and burning merrily, my companion seated himself about forty feet from the base of the tree, bringing the trunk of it directly between himself and the fire. I took a seat by his side by request, and waited patiently to see what would come next. The fire continued to burn each moment more brightly, and the tree that intervened between us and it became more prominent, and its dark outline became more and more distinct, until the most minute branch and leaf was perfectly visible. "Now," said mine host, "we will have the opossum. Do you see that large knotty looking substance on that big limb to the right? It looks suspicious; we will speak to it." The sharp report of the rifle followed, and the negro that accompanied us picked up a large piece of bark that fell rattling to the ground. The rifle was re-loaded, and another suspicious looking bunch was fired at, and another knot was shattered. Again was the rifle re-loaded, and the tree more carefully examined. Hardly had its shrill report awakened the echoes of the forest for the third time, before a grunt that would have done honor to a stuck pig was heard, and the solid fat body of the 'possum fell at out feet. The negro picked it up, relit his torch, and we proceeded homeward. When re-seated by a comfortable fire, we were asked our opinion by our host of "a white man's 'possum hunt;" we expressed our unqualified approbation of the whole affair, although we thought at first that any improvement on the negro's mode of doing the business would be "painting the lily!"

As an article of food the opossum is considered by many a very great luxury, the flesh, it is said, tastes not unlike roast pig. We should have liked very much to have heard "Elia's" description of a dish of it; he found sentiment and poetry in pig, where would he have soared to over a dish of 'possum? In cooking the "varmint," the Indians suspend it on a stick by its tail, and in this position they let it roast before the fire; this mode does not destroy a sort of oiliness, which makes it to a cultivated taste coarse and unpalatable. The negroes, on the contrary—and, by the way, they are all amateurs in the cooking art—when cooking for themselves do much better. They bury the body up with sweet potatoes, and as the meat roasts thus confined, the succulent vegetable draws out all objectionable tastes, and renders the opossum "one of the greatest delicacies in the world." At least so say a crowd of respectable witnesses. We profess to have no experience in the matter, not yet having learned to sing with enthusiasm the common negro song of

"'Possum fat and 'tater."

A GRIZZLY BEAR HUNT

The every-day sports of the wild woods include many feats of daring that never find a pen of record. Constantly in the haunts of the savage are enacting scenes of thrilling interest, the very details of which would make the denizen of enlightened life turn away with instinctive dread. Every Indian tribe has its heroes, celebrated respectively for their courage in different ways exhibited—some for their acuteness in pursuing the enemy on the war-path, and others for the destruction they have accomplished among the wild beasts of the forest. A great hunter among the Indians is a marked personage. It is a title that distinguishes its possessor among his people as a prince, while the exploits in which he has been engaged hang about his person as brilliantly as the decorations of so many orders. The country in which the Osage finds a home possesses abundantly the Grizzly Bear, an animal formidable beyond any other inhabitant of the North American forests—an animal seemingly insensible to pain, uncertain in its habits, and by its mighty strength able to overcome any living obstacle that comes within its reach as an enemy. The Indian warrior, of any tribe, among the haunts of the grizzly bear finds no necklace so honorable to be worn as the claws of this gigantic animal, if he falls by his own prowess; and if he can add an eagle's plume to his scalp lock, plucked from a bird shot while on the wing, he is honorable indeed. The Indian's "smoke," like the fireside of the white man, is often the place where groups of people assemble to relate whatever may most pleasantly wile away the hours of a long evening, or destroy the monotony of a dull and idle day. On such occasions the old "brave" will sometimes relax from his natural gravity, and grow loquacious over his chequered life. But no recital commands such undivided attention as the adventures with the grizzly bear;—and the death of an enemy on the war path hardly vies with it in interest.

We have listened to these soul stirring adventures over the urn, or while lounging on the sofa, and the recital of the risks run—the hardships endured—have made us think them almost impossible, when compared with the conventional self-indulgences of enlightened life. But they were the tales of a truthful man—a hunter—who had strayed away from the scenes once necessary for his life, and who loved, like the worn-out soldier, to "fight his battles over," in which he was once engaged. It may be, and is, the province of the sportsman to exaggerate, but the "hunter," surrounded by the magnificence and sublimity of an American forest, earning his bread by the hardy adventures of the chase, meets with too much reality to find room for coloring, too much of the sublime and terrible in the scenes with which he is associated to be boastful of himself. Apart from the favorable effects of civilization, he is also separated from its contaminations, *and boasting and exaggeration, are settlement weaknesses*, and not the products of the wild woods.

The hunter, whether Indian or white, presents one of the most extraordinary exhibitions of the singular capacity of the human senses to be improved by cultivation. The unfortunate deaf, dumb, and blind girl, in one of our public institutions,* selects her food, her clothing, and her friends, by the touch alone, so delicate has it become from the mind's being directed to that sense alone. The forest hunter uses the *sight* most extraordinarily well, and experience at last renders it so keen, that the slightest touch of a passing object on the leaves, trees, or earth, seems to leave deep and visible impresses, that to the common eye are as unseen as the path of the bird through the air. This knowledge governs the chase and the war path; this knowledge is what, when excelled in, makes the master spirit among the rude inhabitants of the woods, and that man is the greatest chief who follows the coldest trail, and leaves none behind by his own footsteps. The hunter in pursuit of the grizzly bear is governed by this *instinct of sight*—it directs him with more certainty than the hound is directed by his nose. The impresses of the bear's footsteps upon the leaves, its marks on the trees, its resting places, are all known long before the bear is really seen; and the hunter, while thus following "the trail," calculates the very sex, weight, and age with certainty. Thus it is that he will neglect or choose a trail, one because it's poor, another because it's small, another because it's with cubs, another because it's fat, identifying the very trail as the bear itself; and herein, perhaps, lies the distinction between the sportsman and huntsman. The hunter fol-

*Hartford Asylum for the Deaf and Dumb.

lows his object by his own knowledge and instinct, while the sportsman employs the instinct of domesticated animals to assist him in his
pursuits.

The different methods to destroy the grizzly bear by those who hunt
them, are as numerous almost as the bear that are killed. They are not
an animal that permits of a system in hunting them, and it is for this
reason that they are so dangerous and difficult to destroy. The experience of one hunt may cost a limb or a life in the next one, if used as a
criterion; and fatal, indeed, is the mistake if it comes to grappling with
an animal whose gigantic strength enables him to lift a horse in his
huge arms, and bear it away as a prize. There is one terrible exception
to this rule; one habit of the animal may be certainly calculated on,
but a daring heart only can take advantage of it.

The grizzly bear, like the tiger and lion, have their caves in which
they live, but they use them principally as a safe lodging place, when
the cold of winter renders them torpid and disposed to sleep. To these
caves they retire late in the fall, and they seldom venture out until the
warmth of spring. Sometimes two occupy one cave, but this is not
often the case, as the unsociability of the animal is proverbial, they
preferring to be solitary and alone. A knowledge of the forests, and an
occasional trailing for bear, inform the hunter of these caves, and the
only habit of the grizzly bear that can with certainty be taken advantage
of is the one of his being in his cave alive, if at the proper season. And
the hunter has the terrible liberty of entering his cave single-handed
and there destroying him. Of this only method of hunting the grizzly
bear we would attempt a description.

The thought of entering a cave inhabited by one of the most powerful beasts of prey, is one calculated to try the strength of the best
nerves; and when it is considered that the least trepidation, the
slightest mistake, may cause, and probably will result to the hunter in
instant death, it certainly exhibits the highest demonstration of physical courage to pursue such a method of hunting. Yet there are many
persons in the forests of North America who engage in such perilous
adventures with no other object in view *than the sport!* or a hearty
meal. The hunter's preparations to "beard the lion in his den" commence with examining the mouth of the cave he is about to enter.
Upon the signs there exhibited, he decides whether the bear is alone;
for if there are two the cave is never entered. The size of the bear is
also thus known, and the time since he was last in search of food. The
way this knowledge is obtained, from indications so slight, or unseen

152

to an ordinary eye, is one of the greatest mysteries of the woods. Placing ourselves at the mouth of the cave containing a grizzly bear, to our untutored senses there would be nothing to distinguish it from one that was empty; but if some Diana of the forest would touch our eyes, and give us the *instinct of sight* possessed by the hunter, we would argue this wise. "From all the marks about the mouth of this cave, the occupant has not been out for a great length of time, for the grass and earth have not lately been disturbed. The bear is in the cave, for the last tracks made are with the toe marks towards the cave. There is but one bear, because the tracks are regular and of the same size. He is a large bear, the length of the step and the size of the paw indicate this, and he is a fat one, because his *hind feet do not step in the impressions made by the fore ones*, as is always the case with a lean bear." Such are the signs and arguments that present themselves to the hunter, and mysterious as they seem when not understood, when explained they strike the imagination at once as being founded on the unerring simplicity and truthfulness of nature itself. It may be asked, how is it that the grizzly bear is so formidable to numbers when met in the forest, and when in a cave can be assailed successfully by a single man? In answer to this, we must recollect that the bear is only attacked in his cave when he is in total darkness, and suffering from surprise and the torpidity of the season. These three things are in this method of hunting taken advantage of, and but for these advantages no quickness of eye, no steadiness of nerve, or forest experience, would protect for an instant the intruder to the cave of the grizzly bear. The hunter having satisfied himself about the cave, prepares a candle, which he makes out of the wax taken from the comb of wild bees, softened by the grease of the bear. This candle has a large wick, and emits brilliant flame. Nothing else is needed but the rifle; the knife and the belt are useless, for if a struggle should ensue, that would make it available, the foe is too powerful to mind its thrusts before the hand using it would be dead. Bearing the candle before him, with the rifle in a convenient position, the hunter fearlessly enters the cave, he is soon surrounded by darkness, and is totally unconscious where his enemy will reveal himself. Having fixed the candle on the ground in a firm position, with an apparatus provided, he lights it, and its brilliant flame soon penetrates into the recesses of the cavern, its size of course rendering the illumination more or less complete. The hunter now places himself on his belly, having the candle between the back part of the cave, where the bear is, and himself; in this position, with the

153

muzzle of the rifle protruding out in front of him, he patiently waits for his victim. A short time only elapses before bruin is aroused by the light, the noise made by his starting from sleep attracts the hunter, and he soon distinguishes the black mass, moving, stretching, and yawning, like a person awakened from a deep sleep. The hunter moves not, but prepares his rifle; the bear, finally roused, turns his head towards the candle, and with slow and waddling steps approaches it. Now is the time that tries the nerves of the hunter; too late to retreat, his life hangs upon his certain aim and the goodness of his powder. The slightest variation in the bullet, or a flashing pan, and he is a doomed man. So tenacious of life is the common black bear, that it is frequently wounded in its most vital parts, and still will escape, or give terrible battle. But the grizzly bear seems protected by an infinitely greater tenacity of life; his skin, covered by matted hair, and the huge bones of his body, protect the heart, as if encased in a wall, while the brain is buried in a skull, compared to which adamant is not harder. A bullet striking the bear's forehead would flatten if it struck squarely on the solid bone, as if fired against a rock, and dangerous indeed would it be to take the chances of reaching the animal's heart. With these fearful odds against the hunter, the bear approaches the candle, growing every moment more sensible of some uncommon intrusion, he reaches the blaze, and either raises his paw to strike it, or lifts his nose to scent it, either of which will extinguish it, and leave the hunter and the bear in total darkness. This dreadful moment is taken advantage of—the loud report of the rifle fills the cave with stunning noise, and as the light disappears, the ball, if successfully fired, penetrates the eye of the huge animal, the only place where it would find a passage to the brain; and this not only gives the death wound, but instantly paralyzes, that no temporary resistance may be made. On such chances the American hunter perils his life, and often thoughtlessly courts the danger.

A STORM SCENE ON THE MISSISSIPPI

In the year 18— we found ourselves travelling "low down on the Mississippi." The weather was intensely hot, and as we threaded our way through the forests, and swamps, through which the river flows, there seemed to be a stifled atmosphere, and a silent one, such as required little wisdom to predict as the forerunner of a storm. The insects of the woods were more than usually troublesome, and venomous. The locust, would occasionally make its shrill sounds as on a merry day, then suddenly stop, give a disquiet chirp or two, and relapse into silence. The venomous musquito, revelled in the dampness of the air, and suspending its clamor of distant trumpets, seemed only intent to bite. The crows scolded like unquiet housewives, high in the air, while higher still, wheeled in graceful, but narrowed circles, the buzzard. The dried twigs in our path bent, instead of snapping, as the weight of our horses' hoofs pressed upon them, while the animals themselves, would put forward their ears, as if expecting soon to be very much alarmed, and lastly, to make all these signs certain, the rheumatic limbs of an old Indian guide, who accompanied us, suddenly grew lame, for he went limping upon his delicately formed feet, and occasionally looking aloft with suspicious eyes, he would proclaim, that there would be "storm too much!"

A storm in the forest is no trifling affair, the tree under which you shelter yourself, may draw the lightning upon your head, or its ponderous limbs, pressed upon by the wind, may drag the heavy trunk to the earth, crushing you with itself, in its fall; or some dead branch, that has for years protruded from among the green foliage, may on the very occasion of your presence, fall to the ground, and destroy you. The rain too, which in the forest, finds difficulty in soaking into the earth, will in a few hours, fill-up the ravines, and water courses, wash away the trail you may be following, or destroy the road over which you journey. All these things, we were from experience aware of, and as we were some distance from our journey's end, and also from any "settlement," we passed forward to a "clearing" which was in our path, as a temporary stopping place, until the coming storm should have passed away.

Our resting place for the night, was on the banks of the Mississippi; it consisted of a rude cabin in the centre of a small garden spot, and field, and had been the residence of a squatter; now deserted, for causes unknown to us, it was most pleasantly situated, and commanded a fine view of the river, both up and down its channel. We reached this rude dwelling just as the sun was setting, and his disappearance behind the low lands of the Mississippi, was indeed glorious. Refracted by the humidity of the atmosphere into a vast globe of fire, it seemed to be kindling up the Cypress trees, that stretched out before us, into a light blaze, while the gathering clouds extended the conflagration far north and south, and carried it upwards far into the heavens. Indeed, so glorious for a moment was the sight, that we almost fancied that another Phæton was driving the chariot of the Sun, and that, in its ungoverned course, its wheels were fired; and the illusion was quite complete, when we heard the distant thunder, echoing from those brilliant clouds, and saw the lightning, like silver arrows, flashing across the crimson heavens. A moment more, and the sun seemed extinguished in the waters, all light disappeared, and the sudden darkness that follows sun set as you approach the tropics surrounded us.

With the delightful consciousness of having already escaped the storm, we gathered round a pleasant blaze, formed of some dried twigs, kindled by flashing powder in the pan of an old fashioned gun. In the mean time the thunder was growing more and more distinct, the lightning flashed more brightly, and an occasional gust of wind, accompanied by sleet, would penetrate between the logs that composed our shelter. An old wood-chopper, who made one of our party, grew loquacious, as he became rested and comfortable, and he detailed with great effect, the woeful scenes he had been in at different times of his life, the most awful of which had been preceded by just such signs of weather, as were then exhibiting themselves. Among other adventures, he had been wrecked, while acting as a "hand" on a flat boat, navigating the Mississippi. He said, he had come all the way from Pittsburg, at the head of the Ohio, to within two or three hundred miles of Orleans, without meeting with any other accident, than that of getting out of whiskey twice. But one night, the captain of the flat-boat said the weather was "crafty," a thing he thought himself, as it was most too quiet to last so, long. After detailing several other particulars he finished his story by being wrecked, as follows: "After the quiet

156

weather I spoke of lasted a little, all of a sudden it changed, the river grew as rough as an alligator's back, thar was the tallest kind of a noise over head, and the fire flew up thar, like fur in a cat fight. 'We'll put in shore,' said the captain, and we tried to do it, that's sartain, but the way we always walked off from a tree, whar we might have tied up, was a caution to steamboats. 'Keep the current,' said the captain, 'and let us sweat it out.' We went on this way some time, when I told the captain, said I, 'captain, I have never been in these diggins 'afore, but if I havn't seen the same landscape three times, then I am a liar.' At this, the captain looked hard, and swore we were in an eddy, and doing nothing but whirling round. The lightning just at this time was very accommodating, and showed us a big tree in the river, that had stuck fast, and was bowing up and down, ready to receive us, and we found ourselves rushing straight on to it. The owner of the bakon was on board, and when he saw the 'sawyer,' he eyed it as hard as a small thief would a constable; says he, 'captain, if that ar fellow at the sweep,' (oar) 'fellow' meant me, said he, 'captain, if that ar fellow at the sweep, don't bear on it like ———, and keep us off that tree, I am a busted up pork merchant.' I did bear on it as hard as he suggested, but the current was too strong, and we went on the 'sawyer' all standing. The boat broke up, like a dried leaf would have done, pork and plunder scattered, and I swum half soaked to death, ashore. I lost in the whole operation just two shirts, eighteen dollars in wages, and half a box of Kentucky tobacker, beside two game cocks; I tell you what, a storm on that ar Mississippi, ain't to be sneezed at."

The wood-chopper's story, when concluded, would have occasioned a general laugh, had there not been outside our cabin, at this moment, a portentous silence, which alarmed us all. The storm had been upon us in its full fury, we thought, but we now felt that more was to come; in the midst of this expectation, a stream of fire rushed from the horizon upwards; when high over head, could be seen its zig-zag course, then rushing downwards almost at our very feet, a few hundred yards from us, a tall oak dropped some of its gigantic limbs, and flashed into a light blaze. The rain however powerful previously, now descended in one continued sheet. The roof of our shelter seemed to gather rain rather than to protect us from it; little rivulets dashed across the floor, and then widening into streams, we were soon literally afloat. The descending floods, sounded about us like the roll-call of a muffled drum, the noise sometimes almost deafening us, then dying off in the distance, as the sweeping gusts of wind drove the clouds before them. The burning forest hissed and cracked and rolled up great columns of steam. The muddy water of the Mississippi in all this war of the elements, rushed on, save where it touched its banks, with a smooth, but mysterious looking surface, that resembled in the glare of the lightning, a mirror of bronze. And to heighten this almost unearthly effect, the forest trees that lined its shores, rose up like dark mountains, impenetrable darkness, against clouds burning with fire. The thunder cracked and echoed through the heavens, and the half-starved wolf, nearly dead with fear, mingled his cries of distress with the noises without, startling us with the full conviction that we heard the voices of men dying in the storm. Hours passed away, and the elements spent their fury; and although the rain continued falling in torrents, it was finally unaccompanied by lightning. So sudden indeed were the extremes, that with your eyes dilating with the glare of the heavens, you found yourself surrounded by the most perfect darkness. Confused, bewildered, and soaking wet, we followed the stoical example of our Indian guide, and settling down in a crouching attitude, waited most impatiently for the light of the morning. The rain continued to descend, and the same deep darkness was upon us; my companions soon fell sleep, and snored as soundly as if they were at home; the long drawn respirations added to my misery. Wound up to the highest pitch of impatience, I was about starting to my feet, to utter some angry complaint, when the Indian, who I thought was asleep, touched me on the arm, and with a peculiar sound, signified that I must listen. This I did do, but I heard nothing but the dull clattering of the rain, and after a while I said so. For some time the Indian made no reply, although I was conscious that he was intensely listening. Suddenly he sprang upon his feet, gave a loud grunt, and groped to the door. This intrusive noise awoke the wood-chopper, who instantly seizing his rifle, sang out, "Halloo, what's the matter, you red varmint, snorting in a man's face like a scared buffalo bull, what's the matter?"

"*River too near,*" was the slow reply of the Indian.

"He's right, so help me ———," shouted the wood-chopper, "the banks of the Mississippi are caving in," and then with a spring he leaped through the door, and bid us follow. His advice was quickly obeyed. The Indian was the last to leave the cabin, and as he left its threshold, *the weighty unhewn logs, that composed it, crumbled, along with the rich soil, into the swift rushing current of the Mississippi.*

This narrow escape made our fortunes somewhat bearable, and we waited with some little patience for day. At the proper time the sun rose gloriously bright, as if its smiling face was never obscured by a cloud. The little birds of the woods sang merrily, there was the greenness, and freshness, of a new creation on every thing; and the landscape of the previous night, was indeed altered. The long jutting point where stood the squatter's hut and "clearing," had disappeared, house, garden spot, fields, and fences, were gone; the water-washed banks lined with the ancient forest. The stranger would never have dreamed that the axe, and the plough, had been in the vicinity. The caving banks had obliterated all signs of humanity, and left every thing about in a wild, and primitive solitude.

NOTE.—The banks of the Mississippi are evidently formed of alluvial deposit from the river; we presume geologists would find the sub-stratum of these banks in all cases, sand, the swift current sometimes undermining hundreds of acres of bank which falls into the river. Plantations are in this way often ruined, and lives sometimes lost.

ROMANCE OF THE WOODS. THE WILD HORSES OF THE WESTERN PRAIRIES

The head waters of the Arkansas and Black rivers flow through a country abounding in singular variety, with high and broken land and level prairie. Many of these abrupt eminences spring up from the plain, run along for a few miles, and again disappear in broken ridges. Standing upon one of these abrupt eminences, if it is a favorable season of the year, the eye is greeted with a sight of life, in the spring time of its existence, as beautiful and glorious as the age and decay of the old world is desolate and heart-breaking. There is a freshness in the whole scene, as vast as it is, that rests upon the new blown rose. The sun here sends its morning rays, through an atmosphere so dewy and soft, that it seems to kiss the prairie flowers gently, only meeting the sides of the abrupt hills with its noon-day heats. Among the prairie and broken land lives every species of game, the Antelope, the Deer, the Turkey, the Bear, and the Buffalo,—these are all found in abundance, but the most prominently attractive object is the Wild Horse. Here the noble animal has roamed untrammelled until every trace of subjection, which marked his progenitors, has disappeared. They are now children of the wind, and only need but one more touch of freedom to mount the air. The high mettled racer, wrought up to the perfection of civilized beauty, as he steps upon the turf causes indescribable emotions of pleasure. But the animal falls incomparably behind the wild horse of the prairie, in every point where mere beauty is concerned. There is a subjection in the gait and in the eye of the "blood" that tells of slavery, while the wild horse is the very personification of the freedom of his life, and proudly and nobly indeed does he wear his honors. To stand upon the high hills that rise up from the plains in this rich country of their home, and mark the wild horses as they exhibit their character, is one of the most interesting sights in nature. At one time, browsing with all quietness and repose, cropping the grass and herbs daintily, anon starting up as if in battle array, with fierce aspect, and terrible demonstrations of war. Changing in the instant, they will trot off with coquettish airs, that would, for affectation, do honor to a favorite troupe of ballet girls; then as the thought of their power comes over them, they will with lightning swiftness dash in straight lines across the plains, mingling into one mass, so obscure will they be by their flight. Changing still again, they will sweep round in graceful curves, rivalling the sportive flight of the eagle, then breaking into confusion, pursue a pell-mell course for a few moments, until suddenly some leader will strike out from the crowd, and lead off single file, thus stringing out over the plain in lines, looking in the distance like the current of some swift-running river. Approach them nearer, and see what beauty, as well as power. That stallion, whose mane floats almost down to his knees, shakes it as a warrior of the crusades would have done his plumes; he springs upon the turf as if his feet were dainty of the ground; and how that mare leaps, and paws, and springs into the air; she would teach her colt to fly, one would think,—and then, as the sun shines obliquely on the crowd, their skins betray the well-formed muscle, and darken and glisten like silver and gold. The groom of the stable labors in vain for such glossiness—it is the result of health—it's nature.

The wild Indian loves the horse, herein showing his humanity, and his soul. He has his traditions, that his ancestors were once without them, and the Great Spirit is daily thanked that he now possesses the treasure. The "happy hunting grounds" are filled with the noble animals, and the warrior, if he reposes in peace, is beside his steed, which sacrificed on his grave, follows him in spirit to the land of the Indian's fathers. In the Indian horseman the centaur of the ancients may be said to still exist, for as he dashes across his native wilds he forms almost really part of the animal on which he rides; without saddle or bridle, if he chooses, he will spring upon the bare back, and be off with the wind. The loose parts of his dress streaming out, and mingling with the flowing mane and tail of his charger so perfectly, that they seem literally and positively one being. Taming the wild horse forms, as may be imagined, one of the great characteristics of the distinguished Indian. Horsemanship being considered, as among enlightened nations, not only useful, but one of the splendid accomplishments. The noisy pride of exultation never rings louder in the forest than when the spirit of the untamed steed is first conquered, and his fiery impatience submits to the will of a rider.

On the banks of the "shining river" was encamped a successful war party of the Osages. They had stolen into their enemies' country when a majority of their men were off on a hunting expedition, and with their customary warfare they had butchered every living being they had met with. The scalps taken were numerous, and many were the "braves" who, for the first time, bravadoed over the bloody trophy, although it might once have graced the head of a young girl or infant. Songs, dances, and exultations were rife, old men forgot their dignity, and grew gay and jocular. The women sang songs of victory, and the children emulated their sires in mimic warfare, and in the imaginary shedding of blood. It was a jubilee, and the spirit of all was for excitement. As the sun set on this animated scene, a hundred fires curled up into the air, and with their forked tongues lighted up the rude buffalo-skin tent and its swarthy inhabitants, and showed off by the indistinct light the forest trees, as mysterious traceries of tremendous limbs, suspended as if by magic in the surrounding gloom.

The bustle and confusion was beyond description, but of all the sports exhibited on this occasion, none were so prominent, as feats of horsemanship. Gradually as the evening wore away, every thing centred in this chivalrous amusement, and the whole scene became more than ever striking and peculiar. The animals, alarmed by the glare of torches, and the shouts of the crowd, seemed crazed and confused, at one time they trembled at the voices of their masters, at other times, starting off in the swiftest speed, as if endeavoring to escape; all these caprices were taken advantage of by the riders, to display their skill, for at one time, they would bound upon the horses' backs, like panthers, and dash off into the woods, or, if the steeds were quietly disposed, mount their backs, and shame the Ducrows, and Norths, by their evolutions. Occasionally a horse would dash by us, apparently without a rider—when suddenly, there would rise up from the side opposite to the spectators, the form of an Indian, who had sustained himself by the slightest pressure of the foot on the horse's back and a hold in the mane. Another would follow at full speed, when the rider, as if suddenly paralyzed, would disappear, and as you involuntarily looked on the ground for his place of fall, you would hear his shrill cry ringing in the distance, as he was borne off on his steed. These feats involved some of the stratagems used in war, for the Indian cavalry, as they bear down upon their enemies, will pass them at full speed without a rider being seen; while the fatal arrow, or lead, will fly from under the horse's neck.

In the midst of these amusements, a strong, muscular Osage came into the camp, leading by a halter one of the largest black stallions ever seen among the tribe; he was powerfully built, his mane almost touched his knees, and his tail trailed upon the ground; his nostrils were distended to the largest diameter, and his eyes contracted and dilated like flames of fire. A more beautiful creature could not be imagined, and as he stared and snorted at the crowd, he seemed to say that the halter around his neck only confined his body, and that his spirit was still free. There were marks of the rope upon his sides and legs that showed a fierce contest had ensued, before he was thrown, so as to saddle him,—and for all this severe treatment, it only rendered him patient in following his captor at the full end of his rope; for if any nearer approaches were attempted, he resented them by the most powerful displays of anger. As the Indian led this noble animal up and down before the assembled multitude, for the double purpose of showing his beauty, and his own prowess in catching him, the cry became universal for the owner to mount him, and there was no bound to the wonder that ensued, when the most celebrated horseman of the tribe acknowledged himself incapable of "backing" the animal before them. Twenty living men, with forms of Apollo's, and the activity of the deer, offered eagerly to do it; and one more eager than the rest, at once approached the noble prisoner. We felt for the steed, and sympathised with the spirit that resented the mounting on his back. Held as he was, that the rider might mount him, he snorted, pawed the ground, rose into the air, and fairly yelled with rage; and if any one really succeeded in getting into the saddle, no sooner was the rider left to his own resources, than he was thrown, or dismounted by the animal's trying to crush him by rolling on the ground. This long continued opposition, surprising to all, by its success and endurance, heightened the wish to conquer him, and we waited with breathless impatience for the swarthy Alexander that was to conquer this modern Bucephalus. The continued trials satisfied me that the Indians were all astonished at the long resistance the horse made, for the sarcastic tone of voice ceased, as one "brave" after another, relinquished the task, and fell back into the crowd; and finally, as the last effort was made to ride the noble animal, and the usual want of success followed it, a general shout of good-natured exultation followed it, and the horse remained quietly, a prisoner unconquered among his captors.

Had it now been in our power, we would have been proud at this moment to have stepped forward and released the noble captive; we would have been delighted to have seen his heels as he bounded off among his fellows over the wild prairie; we would have exulted in his freedom, and prayed that he might never wear the badge of laborious submission. But this pleasure was denied us.

Among those associated with the Osages, was a white hunter, who from his prowess, had gained the name of the "horse tamer." The Indians had often spoken to me about him, and as he presented himself before the camp, at this particular time, his welcome was boisterous. The unsuccessful efforts to ride the horse before him were soon detailed, and he was challenged to make a trial himself. The hunter on this occasion was evidently fatigued,—the pack of fresh skins he brought into the camp on his shoulders, was a mule's burthen; the torn moccasins and leggings, as well as the slow walk, all denoted a long and laborious chase. Still, the hunter did not refuse the task; he bantered awhile with words, to see how much honor there would be in riding the horse, and when he once discovered that there was so much to be gained, his pride prompted him to accept the task.

It was with no common interest that we watched the proceedings of the "horse tamer." The Indians, who had given up the trial in despair, which the jaded hunter before me so confidently accepted, were men of powerful strength, of the most astonishing activity, and the best equestrians I ever saw, or imagined, and that they could be beaten, seemed no less than a miracle. The "horse tamer" approached the stallion, and examined the girth of plaited hair that held the rude trapping attached to it in its place. He took hold of the pommel, which rose like a goose-neck from the saddle, to see if it was firm; then, with cautious and critical care, he drew gently upon the bridle-reins to see if the slip nooses at the ends which encircled the horse's snout would readily tighten, for the Osage bridle has no bit. All these things being to his satisfaction, he next proceeded to roll up an Indian blanket into a hard body, which he fastened to the long pommel of the saddle in such a way that the ends of it would firmly bind upon his thighs, if once mounted; then, with a small deer-skin thong, he tied the wooden stirrups underneath the horse, so that they could not fly above the level of the animal's belly. All preparations being ended, the tamer proceeded to mount. Four of the most powerful Indians, seized hold of the animal's bridle, and pulling his head down, held the poor stallion so firmly that he could only use his heels; but in spite of their flying about, the "horse tamer" gained his seat, and sang out, "let him go."

The order was accompanied by a shout, that made the welkin ring. The stallion more than ever alarmed, gave one of his most furious efforts to throw off his burthen, but this had been anticipated, for as he threw himself into the air, the blanket bound the rider to his

164

seat—the second effort, that of rolling on the ground, also failed, for as the horse threw himself on his side, the tamer landed gracefully on his foot, the deer skin thong, kept the stirrups in their places, and at the next instant, as the "galled jade" sprang to his feet, the rider went up with him. A long, hearty, and prolonged shout followed the inimitable exhibition. The wild horse, for the first time felt the possibility of defeat, his proud bearing was already half gone, for all his succeeding efforts were those of despair. Vain indeed were his displays of power; the tiger with his deadly hold upon the haunch of the buffalo, could not be more securely fastened to his victim, than was the tamer to his. The rearing, pitching, shying, plunging, running and suddenly stopping, seemed all known before hand, and met with a perfect guard, that displayed the most consummate judgment, and skill, in horsemanship. At last, the "tamer" seemed tired of the cruel sport, and taking advantage of his infuriated victim, as he threw his fore feet in the air, he slipped off quietly behind him, and with a slight jerk, careened the horse over on his back, driving his head deeply into the soft turf. Stunned and confounded, the poor animal rolled upon his side, and the "tamer" threw his bridle over his neck and left him. The poor creature was completely conquered; trembling from head to foot, and half drowned, with the profuse sweat that rolled from his sides like foam, he cast a look of imploring despair at the crowd, and the big tear rolled down his cheeks. His spirit was completely broken.

A little coaxing brought him on his feet, the saddle was removed from his back, and the bridle from his head, and he walked slowly off, to be found, by a singular law of his nature, *associated with the pack horses of the tribe*, and waiting for the burthens of his master.

THE AMERICAN WILD CAT

In the southern portions of the United States, but especially in Louisiana, the wild cat is found in abundance. The dense swamps that border on the Mississippi, protect this vicious species of game from extermination, and foster their increase; and, although every year vast numbers are killed, they remain seemingly as plentiful as they ever were "in the memory of the oldest inhabitant." The wild cat seeks the most solitary retreats, in which to rear its young, where in some natural hole in the ground, or some hollow tree, it finds protection for itself and its kittens, from the destructive hand of man. At night, or at early morn, it comes abroad, stealing over the dried leaves, in search of prey, as quietly as a zephyr, or ascending the forest tree with almost the ease of a bird. The nest on the tree, and the burrow in the ground, are alike invaded; while the poultry yard of the farmer, and his sheep fold, are drawn liberally upon to supply the cat with food. It hunts down the rabbit, coon, and possum, springing from some elevated bough, upon the bird perched beneath, catching in its mouth its victim, and doing this while descending like an arrow in speed, and with the softness of a feather to the ground. Nothing can exceed its beauty of motion when in pursuit of game, or sporting in play. No leap seems too formidable, no attitude is ungraceful. It runs, flies, leaps, skips, and is at ease in an instant of time; every hair of its body seems redolent with life. Its disposition is untameable, it seems insensible to kindness, a mere mass of ill nature, having no sympathies with any, not even of its own kind. It is for this reason no doubt, that it is so recklessly pursued, its paw being, like the Ishmaelite's against every man: and it most indubitably follows, that every man's dogs, sticks, and guns, are against it. The hounds themselves, that hunt equally well the cat and fox, pursue the former with a clamourous joy, and kill it with a zest, that they do not display when finishing off a fine run after Reynard. In fact, as an animal of sport, the cat in many respects is preferable to the fox, its trail is always warmer, and it shows more sagacity in eluding its enemies.

In Louisiana, the sportsman starts out in the morning professedly for a fox chase, and it turns "cat," and often both cat and fox are killed, after a short but hard morning's work. The chase is varied, and is often full of amusing incident, for the cat, as might be expected, takes often to the "tree" to avoid pursuit, and this habit of the animal allows the sportsman to meet it on quite familiar terms; if the tree is a tall one, the excitable creature manages to have its face obscured by the distance, but if it takes to a dead limbless trunk, where the height will permit its head to be fairly seen, as it looks down upon the pack that are yelling at its feet, with such open mouths, that they
"Fetch shrill echoes from the hollow earth."
You will see a rare exhibition of rage and fury, eyes that seem living balls of fire, poisonous claws that clutch the insensible wood with deep indentations,—the foam trembles on its jaws, hair standing up like porcupine quills, ears pressed down to the head, forming as perfect a picture of vicious, ungovernable destructiveness as can be imagined. A charge of mustard seed shot, or a poke with a stick when at bay, will cause it to desert its airy abode, when it no sooner touches the ground, than it breaks off at a killing pace, the pack like mad fiends on its trail.

Beside "treeing," the cat will take advantage of some hole in the ground, and disappear when it meets with these hiding places, as suddenly as ghosts at cock crowing. The hounds come up to the hiding place, and a fight ensues. The first head intruded into the cat's hole is sure to meet with a warm reception, claws and teeth do their work, still the staunch hound heeds it not, and either he gets a hold himself, or acts as a bait to draw the cat from his burrow, thus fastened, the dog, being the most powerful in strength, backs out, dragging his enemy along with him, and no sooner is the cat's head seen by the rest of the pack, than they pounce upon him, and in a few moments the "nine lives" of the "varmint" are literally chawed up. At one of these burrowings, a huge cat intruded into a hold so small, that an ordinarily large hound could not follow. A little stunted but excellent hound, rejoicing in the name of Ringwood, from his diminutiveness, succeeded in forcing his way in the hole after the cat, in an instant a faint scream was heard, and the little fellow showed symptoms of having caught a tartar. One of the party present, stooped down, and running his arm under the dog's body, pressed it forward, until he could feel that the cat had the dog firmly clawed by each shoulder, with its nose in the cat's mouth, in this situation, by pressing the dog firmly under the chest, the two were drawn from the hole. The cat hung on until he discovered that his victim was surrounded by numerous friends, when he let go his cruel hold; the more vigorously to defend himself. Ringwood, though covered with jetting blood, jumped upon the cat and shook away as if unharmed in the contest.

Sportsmen in hunting the cat, provide themselves generally with pistols, not for the purpose of killing the cat, but to annoy it, so that it will desert from the tree, when it has taken to one, sometimes these infantile shooting irons are left at home, and the cat gets safely lodged out of the reach of sticks, or whatever other missile may be convenient. This is a most provoking affair, dogs and sportsmen lose all patience, and as no expedient suggests itself, the cat escapes for the time. I once knew of a cat thus perched out of reach, that was brought to terms in a very singular manner. The tree on which the animal was lodged being a very high one, secure from interruption it looked down upon its pursuers with the most provoking complacency, every effort to dislodge it had failed, and the hunt was about to be abandoned in despair, when one of the sportsmen discovered a grape vine that passed directly over the cat's body, and by running his eye along its circumvolutions, traced it down to the ground, a judicious jerk at the vine touched the cat on the rump, this was most unexpected, and it instantly leaped to the ground, from a height of over forty feet, striking on its fore paws, throwing a sort of rough somerset, and then starting off as sound in limb and wind as if he had leaped off of a "huckleberry" bush.

The hunter of the wild turkey, while "calling," in imitation of the hen, to allure the gobbler within reach of the rifle, will sometimes be annoyed by the appearance of the wild cat, stealing up to the place from whence the sounds proceed. The greatest caution on such occasions is visible, the cat advancing by the slowest possible movements, stealing along like a serpent. The hunter knows that the intruder has spoiled his turkey sport for the morning, and his only revenge is to wait patiently and give the cat the contents of his gun, then, minus all game, he goes home, anathematizing the whole race of cats, for thus interfering with his sport, and his dinner.

Of all the peculiarities of the cat, its untameable and quarrelsome disposition is its most marked characteristic. The western hunter, when he wishes to cap the climax of braggadocio with respect to his own prowess, says, "he can whip his own weight in wild cats." This is saying all that can be said, for it would seem, considering its size, that the cat in a fight can bite fiercer, scratch harder, and live longer, than any other animal whatever. "I am a roaring earthquake in a fight," sang out one of the half-horse and half-alligator species of fellows, "a real snorter of the universe, I can strike as hard as fourth proof lightning, and keep it up rough, and tumble as long as a wild cat." These high encomiums on the character of the pugnacity of the cat are beyond question. "A singed cat," is an excellent proverb illustrating that a person may be smarter than he looks. *A singed wild cat*, as such an illustration, would be sublime. There is no half way mark, no exception, no occasional moment of good nature; starvation and a surfeit, blows and kind words, kicks, cuffs, and fresh meat, reach not the sympathies of the wild cat. He has the greediness of the pawn-broker, the ill nature of an old usurer, the meanness of a pettifogging lawyer, the blind rage of the hog, and the apparent insensibility to pain of the turtle; like a woman, the wild cat is incomparable with any thing but itself. In expression of face, the wild cat singularly resembles the rattle snake. The skulls of these two "varmints" have the same venomous expression, the same demonstration of fangs, and probably no two creatures living attack each other with more deadly ferocity and hate. They will stare at each other with eyes filled with defiance, and burning with fire; one hissing and the other snarling, presenting a most terrible picture of the malevolence of passion. The serpent in its attitudes is all grace, the cat all activity; the serpent moves with the quickness of lightning, while making the attack, the cat defends itself with motions equally quick, bounding from side to side, striking with its paws, both are often victors, for they seldom separate until death blows have been inflicted on either side. The Indians, who, in their notions and traditions, are always picturesque and beautiful, imagine that the rattle snake, to live, must breathe the poisonous air of the swamps, and the exhalations of decayed animal matter, while the cat has the attribute of gloating over the meaner displays of evil passions of a quarrelsome person, or speaking of a quarrelsome family, they say, "the lodge containing them *fattens the wild cat*."

THE DISGRACED SCALP LOCK, OR INCIDENTS ON THE WESTERN WATERS

Occasionally may be seen on the Ohio and Mississippi rivers singularly hearty looking men, that puzzle a stranger as to their history and age. Their forms always exhibit a powerful development of muscle and bone; their cheeks are prominent, and you would pronounce them men, enjoying perfect health, in middle life, were it not for their heads, which, if not bald, will be sparsely covered with grey hair. Another peculiarity about these people is, that they have a singular knowledge of all the places on the river, every bar and bend is spoken of with precision and familiarity—every town is recollected before it was half as large as the present, or no town at all. Innumerable places are marked out, where once was an Indian fight, or a rendezvous of robbers. The manner, the language, and the dress of these individuals are all characteristic of sterling common sense; the manner modest, yet full of self reliance, the language strong and forcible, from superiority of mind rather than from education, the dress studied for comfort rather than fashion; on the whole, you insensibly become attached to them, and court their society. The good humor, the frankness, the practical sense, the reminiscences, the powerful frame, all indicate a character at the present day extinct and anomalous; and such indeed is the case, for your acquaintance will be one of the few remaining people now spoken of as the "last of the flat-boatmen."

Thirty years ago the navigation of the Western waters was confined to this class of men; the obstacles presented to the pursuit in those swift running and wayward waters had to be overcome by physical force alone; the navigator's arm grew strong as he guided his rude craft past the "snag" and "sawyer," or kept off the no less dreaded bar. Besides all this, the deep forests that covered the river banks concealed the wily Indian, who gloated over the shedding of blood. The qualities of the frontier warrior associated themselves with the boatman, while he would, when at home, drop both these characters in the cultivator of the soil. It is no wonder, then, that they were brave, hardy, and open-handed men; their whole lives were a round of manly excitement, they were hyperbolical in thought and in deed, when most natural, compared with any other class of men. Their bravery and chivalrous deeds were performed without a herald to proclaim them to the world—they were the mere incidents of a border life, considered too common to outlive the time of a passing wonder. Obscurity has obliterated nearly the actions and the men—a few of the latter still exist, as if to justify their wonderful exploits, which now live almost exclusively as traditions.

Among the flat-boatmen, there were none that gained the notoriety of Mike Fink: his name is still remembered along the whole of the Ohio as a man who excelled his fellows in everything, particularly in his rifle shot, which was acknowledged to be unsurpassed. Probably no man ever lived who could compete with Mike Fink in the latter accomplishment; strong as Hercules, free from all nervous excitement, possessed of perfect health, and familiar with his weapon from childhood, he raised the rifle to his eye, and having once taken sight, it was as firmly fixed as if buried in a rock. It was Mike's pride, and he rejoiced on all occasions where he could bring it into use, whether it was turned against the beast of prey, or the more savage Indian, and in his day these last named were the common foe with which Mike and his associates had to contend. On the occasion that we would particularly introduce Mike to the reader, he had bound himself for a while to the pursuits of trade, until a voyage from the head waters of the Ohio, and down the Mississippi, could be completed; heretofore he had kept himself exclusively to the Ohio, but a liberal reward, and some curiosity, prompted him to extend his business character beyond his ordinary habits and inclinations. In accomplishment of this object, he was lolling carelessly over the big "sweep" that guided the "flat" on which he officiated; the current of the river bore the boat swiftly along, and made his labor light; his eye glanced around him, and he broke forth in ecstasies at what he saw and felt. If there is a river in the world that merits the name of beautiful, it is the Ohio, when its channel is

"Without o'erflowing, full."

The scenery is everywhere soft—there are no jutting rocks, no steep banks, no high hills, but the clear and swift current laves beautiful and undulating shores, that descend gradually to the water's edge. The foliage is rich and luxuriant, and its outlines in the water are no less distinct than when it is relieved against the sky. Interspersed along its route are islands, as beautiful as ever figured in poetry as the land of fairies; enchanted spots indeed, that seem to sit so lightly on the water, that you almost expect them as you approach to vanish into dreams.

So late as when Mike Fink disturbed the solitudes of the Ohio with his rifle, the canoe of the Indian was hidden in the little recesses along the shore; they moved about in their frail barks like spirits, and clung, in spite of the constant encroachments of civilization, to the places which tradition had designated as the happy places of a favored people.

Wild and uncultivated as Mike appeared, he loved nature, and had a soul that sometimes felt, while admiring it, an exalted enthusiasm. The Ohio was his favorite stream; from where it runs no stronger than a gentle rivulet, to where it mixes with the muddy Mississippi, Mike was as familiar as a child could be with the meanderings of a flower garden. He could not help noticing with sorrow the desecrating hand of improvement as he passed along, and half soliloquizing, and half addressing his companions, he broke forth,—"I knew these parts afore a squatter's axe had blazed a tree; 'twas'nt then pulling a ——— sweep to get a living, but pulling the trigger done the business. Those were times, to see; a man might call himself lucky. What's the use of improvements? When did cutting down trees make deer more plenty? Who ever cotched a bar by building a log cabin, or twenty on 'em? Who ever found wild buffalo, or a brave Indian in a city? Where's the fun, the frolicking, the fighting? Gone! gone! The rifle won't make a man a living now—he must turn nigger and work. If forests continue to be used up, I may yet be smothered in a settlement. Boys, this 'ere life won't do,—I'll stick to the broad horn 'cordin' to contract, but once done with it, I'm off for a frolic. If the Choctas, or Cherokees, on the Massassip don't give us a brush as we pass along, I shall grow as poor as a starved wolf in a pit-fall. I must, to live peaceably, point my rifle at something more dangerous than varmint. Six months, and no Indian fight, would spile me worse than a dead horse on a prairie." Mike ceased speaking; the then beautiful village of Louisville appeared in sight; the labor of landing the boat occupied his attention—the bustle and confusion that in those days followed such an incident ensued, and Mike was his own master by law until his employers ceased trafficking, and again required his services.

At the time we write of, there were a great many renegade Indians who lived about the settlements, and which is still the case in the extreme South-west. These Indians generally are the most degraded of the tribe, outcasts, who, for crime or dissipation, are no longer allowed to associate with their people; they live by hunting or stealing, and spend their precarious gains in intoxication. Among the throng that crowded on the flat-boat on its arrival, were a number of these unfortunate beings; they were influenced by no other motive than that of loitering round, in idle speculation at what was going on. Mike was attracted towards them at sight, and as he too was in the situation that is deemed most favorable to mischief, it struck him that it was a good opportunity to have a little sport at the Indians' expense. Without ceremony, he gave a terrific war-whoop, and then mixing the language of the aborigines and his own together, he went on in savage fashion, and bragged of his triumphs and victories on the war path, with all the seeming earnestness of a real "brave." Nor were taunting words spared to exasperate the poor creatures, who, perfectly helpless, listened to the tales of their own greatness, and their own shame, until wound up to the highest pitch of impotent exasperation. Mike's companions joined in, thoughtless boys caught the spirit of the affair, and the Indians were goaded until they in turn made battle with their tongues. Then commenced a system of running against them, pulling off their blankets, together with a thousand other indignities; finally they made a precipitate retreat ashore, amidst the hooting and jeering of an unfeeling crowd, who considered them poor devils, destitute of feeling and humanity. Among this crowd of outcasts was a Cherokee, who bore the name of Proud Joe; what his real cognomen was no one knew, for he was taciturn, haughty, and in spite of his poverty, and his manner of life, won the name we have mentioned. His face was expressive of talent, but it was furrowed by the most terrible habits of drunkenness; that he was a superior Indian was admitted, and it was also understood that he was banished from his mountainous home, his tribe being then numerous and powerful, for some great crime. He was always looked up to by his companions, and managed, however intoxicated he might be, to sustain a singularly proud bearing, which did not even depart from him while prostrated on the ground. Joe was filthy in his person and habits; in these respects he was behind his fellows; but one ornament of his person was attended to with a care which would have done honor to him if surrounded by his people, and in his native woods. Joe still wore with Indian dignity his scalp lock; he ornamented it with taste, and cherished it, as report said, that some Indian messenger of vengeance might tear it from his head, as expiatory of his numerous crimes. Mike noticed this peculiarity, and reaching out his hand, plucked from it a hawk's feather, which was attached to the scalp lock. The Indian glared horribly on Mike as he consummated the insult, snatched the feather from his hand, then shaking his

173

clenched fist in the air, as if calling on heaven for revenge, retreated with his friends. Mike saw that he had roused the savage's soul, and he marvelled wonderfully that so much resentment should be exhibited, and as an earnest to Proud Joe that the wrong he had done him should not rest unrevenged, he swore he would cut the scalp lock off close to his head the first convenient opportunity he got, and then he thought no more of the matter.

The morning following the arrival of the boat at Louisville was occupied in making preparations to pursue the voyage down the river; nearly everything was completed, and Mike had taken his favorite place at the sweep, when looking up the river bank, he beheld at some distance Joe and his companions, and from their gesticulations, they were making him the subject of conversation. Mike thought instantly of several ways in which he could show them all together a fair fight, and then whip them with ease; he also reflected with what extreme satisfaction he would enter into the spirit of the arrangement, and other matters to him equally pleasing, when all the Indians disappeared, save Joe himself, who stood at times viewing him in moody silence, and then staring round at passing objects. From the peculiarity of Joe's position to Mike, who was below him, his head and upper part of his body relieved boldly against the sky, and in one of his movements he brought his profile face to view; the prominent scalp lock and its adornments seemed to be more striking than ever, and it again roused the pugnacity of Mike Fink; in an instant he raised his rifle, always loaded and at command, brought it to his eye, and before he could be prevented, drew sight upon Proud Joe and fired. The rifle ball whistled loud and shrill, and Joe, springing his whole length into the air, fell upon the ground. The cold blooded murder was noticed by fifty persons at least, and there arose from the crowd an universal cry of horror and indignation at the bloody deed. Mike himself seemed to be much astonished, and in an instant reloaded his rifle, and as a number of white persons rushed towards the boat, Mike threw aside his coat, and taking his powder horn between his teeth, leaped, rifle in hand, into the Ohio, and commenced swimming for the opposite shore. Some bold spirits present determined Mike should not so easily escape, and jumping into the only skiff at command, pulled swiftly after him. Mike watched their movements until they came within a hundred yards of him, then turning in the water, he supported himself by his feet alone, and raised his deadly rifle to his eye; its muzzle, if it spoke hostilely, was as certain to send a messenger of death through

174

one or more of his pursuers as if it were the lightning, and they knew it; dropping their oars, and turning pale, they bid Mike not to fire. Mike waved his hand towards the little village of Louisville, and again pursued his way to the opposite shore.

The time consumed by the firing of Mike's rifle, the pursuit, and the abandonment of it, required less time than we have taken to give the details, and in that time to the astonishment of the gaping crowd around Joe, they saw him rising with a bewildered air; a moment more and he recovered his senses, and stood up—*at his feet lay his scalp lock!* The ball had cut it clear from his head; the cord around the root of it, in which were placed feathers and other ornaments, held it together; the concussion had merely stunned its owner; farther he had escaped all bodily harm! A cry of exultation rose at this last evidence of the skill of Mike Fink; the exhibition of a shot that established his claim, indisputably, to the eminence he ever afterwards held; the unrivalled marksman of all the flat-boatmen of the Western waters. Proud Joe had received many insults; he looked upon himself as a degraded, worthless being, and the ignominy heaped upon him, he never, except by reply, resented; but this last insult, was like seizing the lion by the mane, or a Roman senator by the beard—it roused the slumbering demon within, and made him again thirst to resent his wrongs, with an intensity of emotion that can only be felt by an Indian. His eye glared upon the jeering crowd around; like a fiend, his chest swelled and heaved, until it seemed that he must suffocate. No one noticed this emotion, all were intent upon the exploit that had so singularly deprived Joe of his war lock; and smothering his wrath he retreated to his associates, with a consuming fire at his vitals; he was a different man from an hour before, and with that desperate resolution on which a man stakes his all, he swore by the Great Spirit of his forefathers that he would be revenged.

An hour after the disappearance of Joe, both he and Mike Fink were forgotten. The flat-boat, which the latter had deserted, was got under way, and dashing through the rapids in the river opposite Louisville, wended on its course. As is customary when night sets in, the boat was securely fastened in some little bend or bay in the shore, where it remained until early morn. Long before the sun had fairly risen, the boat was pushed again into the stream, and it passed through a valley presenting the greatest possible beauty and freshness of landscape, the mind can conceive. It was Spring, and a thousand tints of green developed themselves in the half formed foliage and bursting buds.

The beautiful mallard skimmed across the water, ignorant of the danger of the white man's approach; the splendid spoonbill decked the shallow places near the shore, while myriads of singing birds filled the air with their unwritten songs. In the far reaches down the river, there occasionally might be seen a bear, stepping along the ground as if dainty of its feet, and snuffing the intruder on his wild home, he would retreat into the woods. To enliven all this, and give the picture the look of humanity, there might also be seen, struggling with the floating mists, a column of blue smoke, that came from a fire built on a projecting point of land, around which the current swept rapidly, and carried every thing that floated on the river. The eye of a boatman saw the advantage of the situation which the place rendered to those on shore, to annoy and attack, and as wandering Indians, in those days, did not hesitate to rob, there was much speculation as to what reception the boat would receive from the builders of the fire. The rifles were all loaded, to be prepared for the worst, and the loss of Mike Fink lamented, as a prospect of a fight presented itself, where he could use his terrible rifle. The boat in the mean time, swept round the point, but instead of an enemy, there lay in a profound sleep, Mike Fink with his feet toasting at the fire, his pillow was a huge bear, that had been shot on the day previous, while at his sides, and scattered in profusion around him, were several deer and wild turkeys. Mike had not been idle; after picking out a place most eligible to notice the passing boat, he had spent his time in hunting, and he was surrounded by trophies of his prowess. The scene that he presented, was worthy of the time and the man, and would have thrown Landseer into a delirium of joy, could he have witnessed it. The boat, owing to the swiftness of the current, passed Mike's resting place, although it was pulled strongly to the shore. As Mike's companions came opposite to him, they raised such a shout, half in exultation of meeting him, and half to alarm him with the idea that Joe's friends were upon him. Mike, at the sound sprang to his feet, rifle in hand, and as he looked around, he raised it to his eyes, and by the time he discovered the boat, he was ready to fire. "Down with your shooting iron, you wild critter," shouted one of the boatmen. Mike dropped the piece, and gave a loud halloo, that echoed among the solitudes like a piece of artillery. The meeting between Mike and his fellows was characteristic. They joked, and jibed him, with their rough wit, and he parried it off, with a most creditable ingenuity. Mike soon learned the extent of his rifle shot—he seemed perfectly indifferent to the fact that Proud Joe was not dead. The only sentiment he uttered, was regret that he did not fire at the vagabond's head, and if he hadn't hit it, why he made the first bad shot in twenty years. The dead game was carried on board of the boat, the adventure was forgotten, and everything resumed the monotony of floating in a flat-boat down the Ohio.

A month or more elapsed, and Mike had progressed several hundred miles down the Mississippi; his journey had been remarkably free from incident; morning, noon, and night, presented the same banks, the same muddy water, and he sighed to see some broken land, some high hills, and he railed, and swore, that he should have been such a fool as to desert his favorite Ohio for a river that produced nothing but alligators, and was never at best half-finished. Occasionally, the plentifulness of game put him in spirits, but it did not last long, he wanted more lasting excitement, and declared himself as perfectly miserable, and helpless, as a wild cat without teeth or claws.

In the vicinity of Natchez, rise a few, abrupt hills, which tower above the surrounding lowlands of the Mississippi like monuments; they are not high, but from their loneliness, and rarity, they create sensations of pleasure and awe. Under the shadow of one of these bluffs, Mike and his associates made the customary preparations to pass the night. Mike's enthusiasm knew no bounds at the sight of land again; he said it was as pleasant as "cold water to a fresh wound;" and, as his spirits rose, he went on making the region round about, according to his notions, an agreeable residence. "The Choctas live in these diggins," said Mike, "and a cursed time they must have of it. Now, if I lived in these parts, I'd declare war on 'em, just to have something to keep me from growing dull; without some such business, I'd be as musty as an old swamp moccasin. I could build a cabin on that ar hill yonder, that could from its location, with my rifle repulse a whole tribe, if they came after me. What a beautiful time I'd have of it. I never was particular, about what's called a fair fight, I just ask a half a chance, and the odds against me; and if I then don't keep clear of snags and sawyers, let me spring a leak, and go to the bottom. It's natur that the big fish should eat the little ones. I've seen trout swallow a perch, and a cat would come along and swallow the trout, and prehaps on the Massissip, the alligators use up the cat, so on until the end of the row. Well, I walk tall into varmint and Indian, it's a way I've got, and it comes as natural as grinning to a hyena. I'm a regular tornado, tough as a hickory withe, long-winded as a nor'-wester. I can strike a blow like a falling tree, and every lick makes a gap in the crowd that lets in an acre of sunshine. Whew, boys," shouted Mike, twirling his rifle, like a walking stick around his head, at the ideas suggested in his mind. "Whew, boys! if the Chocta devils in them ar woods, thar, would give us a brush, just as I feel now, I'd call them gentlemen. I must fight something, or I'll catch the dry rot, burnt brandy won't save me." Such were some of the expressions which Mike gave utterance to, and in which his companions heartily joined; but they never presumed to be quite equal to Mike, for his bodily prowess, as well as his rifle were acknowledged to be unsurpassed. These displays of animal spirits generally ended in boxing, and wrestling matches, in which falls were received, and blows struck without being noticed, that would have destroyed common men. Occasionally angry words and blows were exchanged; but like the summer storm, the cloud that emitted the lightning purified the air, and when the commotion ceased, the combatants, immediately made friends, and became more attached to each other than before the cause that interrupted the good feelings occurred. Such were the conversation and amusements of the evening, when the boat was moored under one of the bluffs we have alluded to; as night wore on, one by one of the hardy boat men fell asleep, some in its confined interior, and others protected by a light covering in the open air. The moon rose in beautiful majesty, her silver light behind the high lands, gave them a powerful and theatrical effect, as it ascended, and as its silver rays grew perpendicular, they finally kissed gently the summit of the hills, and poured down their full light upon the boat, with almost noonday brilliancy. The silence, with which the beautiful changes of darkness and light were produced, made it mysterious. It seemed as if some creative power was at work, bringing form, and life out of darkness. In the midst of the witchery of this quiet scene, there sounded forth the terrible rifle, and the more terrible warwhoop of the Indian. One of the flat boat men, asleep on the deck, gave a stifled groan, turned upon his face, and with a quivering motion ceased to live. Not so with his companions—they in an instant, as men accustomed to danger and sudden attacks, sprang ready armed to their feet; but before they could discover their foes, seven sleek, and horribly painted savages, leaped from the hill into the boat. The firing of the rifle was useless, and each man singled out a foe, and met him with the drawn knife. The struggle was quick and fearful, and deadly blows were given, screams and imprecations rent the air. Yet the voice of Mike Fink could be heard in encouraging shouts above the clamor, "Give it to them, boys," he cried, "cut their hearts out, choke the dogs, here's hell afire, and the river rising!" Then clenching with the most powerful of the assailants, he rolled with him upon the deck of the boat. Powerful as Mike was, the Indian seemed nearly a match for him; the two twisted, and writhed like serpents, now one seeming to have the advantage and then the other. In all this confusion there might occasionally be seen glancing in the moonlight the blade of a knife, but at whom the thrusts were made, or who wielded it, could not be discovered.

The general fight lasted less time than we have taken to describe it. The white men gained the advantage, two of the Indians lay dead upon the boat, and the living, escaping from their antagonists leaped ashore, and before the rifle could be brought to bear, they were out of its reach. While Mike was yet struggling with his antagonist, one of his companions cut the boat loose from the shore, and with powerful exertion, managed to get its bows so far into the current, that it swung round and floated, but before this was accomplished, and before any one interfered with Mike, he was on his feet, covered with blood, and blowing like a porpoise; by the time he could get his breath, he commenced talking. "Ain't been so busy in a long time," said he, turning over his victim with his foot, "that fellow fou't beautiful; if he's a specimen of the Choctas, that live in these parts, they are screamers, the infernal sarpents, the d——d possums." Talking in this way, he with others took a general survey of the killed and wounded. Mike himself was a good deal cut up with the Indian's knife, but he called his wounds mere blackberry scratches; one of Mike's associates, was severely hurt, the rest escaped comparatively harmless. The sacrifice was made at the first fire, for beside the dead Indians, there lay one of the boat's crew, cold and dead, his body perforated with four different balls; that he was the chief object of attack seemed evident, yet no one of his associates knew of his having a single fight with Indians. The soul of Mike was affected, and taking the hand of his deceased friend between his own, he raised his bloody knife towards the bright moon, and swore, that he would desolate "the nation," that claimed the Indians who had made war upon them that night, and turning to his stiffened victim, that, dead as it was, retained the expression of implacable hatred and defiance, he gave it a smile of grim satisfaction, and then joined in the general conversation, which the occurrences of the night would naturally suggest. The master of the "broad horn" was a business man, and had often been down the Mississippi; this was the first attack he had received, or knew to have been made, from the shores inhabited by the Choctas, except by the white man, and he, among other things, suggested the keeping of the dead Indians, until daylight, that they might have an opportunity to examine their dress and features, and see with certainty who were to blame for the occurrences of the night. The dead boatman was removed with care to a respectful distance, and the living, except the person at the sweep of the boat, were soon buried in profound slumber. Not until after the rude breakfast was partaken of, and the funeral rites of the dead boatman were solemnly performed, did Mike and his companions disturb the corses of the red men. When both these things had been leisurely, and gently got through with, there was a different spirit among the men. Mike was astir, and went about his business with alacrity; he stripped the bloody blanket from the corpse of the Indian he had killed, as if it enveloped something disgusting, and required no respect; he examined carefully the moccasins on the Indian's feet, pronouncing them at one time Chickasas, at another time Shawnese; he stared at the livid face, but could not recognize the style of paint that covered it. That the Indians were not strictly national in their adornments was certain, for they were examined by practised eyes, that could have told the nation of the dead, if such had been the case, as readily as a sailor could distinguish a ship by its flag. Mike was evidently puzzled, and as he was about giving up his task as hopeless, the dead body he was examining, from some cause turned on its side, Mike's eyes distended, as some of his companions observed, "like a choked cat," and became riveted; he drew himself up in a half serious, and half comic expression, and pointing at the back of the dead Indian's head, there was exhibited a dead warrior in his paint, destitute of his scalp lock, the small stump which was only left, being stiffened with *red paint;* those who could read Indian symbols, learned a volume of deadly resolve, in what they saw. The body of Proud Joe was stiff and cold before them.

The last and best shot of Mike Fink, cost a brave man his life; the corpse so lately interred, was evidently taken in the moon-light by Proud Joe and his party, as that of Mike's, and they had resigned their lives, one and all, that he might with certainty be sacrificed. Nearly a thousand miles of swamps had been threaded, large and swift running rivers had been crossed, hostile tribes passed through by Joe, and his friends, that they might revenge the fearful insult, of destroying, *without the life*, the sacred scalp-lock.

THE DEVIL'S SUMMER RETREAT, IN ARKANSAW

It is not expected that a faithful description of the Devil's Summer Retreat, in Arkansas, will turn the current of fashion of two worlds, from Brighton and Bath, or from Ballston, or Saratoga, although the residents in the neighborhood of that delightful place, profess to have ocular demonstration, as well as popular opinion, that his Satanic Majesty, in warm weather, regularly retires to the "retreat," and "there reclines in the cool." The solemn grandeur that surrounds this distinguished resort, is worthy of the hero, as represented by Milton; its characteristics are darkness, gloom, and mystery; it is composed of the unrivalled vegetation and forest, of the Mississippi Valley. View it when you will, whether decked out in all the luxuriance of a Southern summer, or stripped of its foliage, by the winter's blasts; it matters not, its grandeur is always sombre. The huge trees seem immortal, their roots look as if they struck to the centre of the earth, while the gnarled limbs, reached out to the clouds. Here and there may be seen one of these lordly specimens of vegetation, furrowed by the lightning; from its top to the base you can trace the subtle fluid in its descent, and see where it shattered off the limb, larger than your body, or turned aside from some slight inequality in the bark. These stricken trees, no longer able to repel the numerous parasites that surround them, soon become festooned with wreaths and flowers, while the damp airs engender on living tree and dead, like funeral drapery, the pendant moss, that waves in every breeze and seems to cover the whole scene with the gloom of the grave. Rising out of this forest for ten square miles, is the dense cane brake that bears the name of the "Devil's Summer Retreat;" it is formed by a space of ground, which seemingly, from its superiority of soil, more delicate vegetation than surrounds it, has usurped its empire. Here the reed, that the disciple of Izaak Walton plays over the Northern streams like a wind, grows into a delicate mast, springing from the rich alluvium that gives it sustenance with the prodigality of grass, and tapering from its roots to the height of twenty or thirty feet, there mingling in compact and luxuriant confusion, its long leaves. A portion of this brake is interwoven with vines of all descriptions, which makes it so thick that it seems to be impenetrable as a mountain. Here in this solitude, where the noon-day sun never penetrates, ten thousand birds, with the instinct of safety, roost at night, and at the dawn of day, for a while, darken the air as they seek their haunts, their manure deadening, for acres round, the vegetation, like a fire, so long have they possessed the solitude. Around this mass of cane and vine, the black bear retire for winter quarters, where they pass the season, if not disturbed, in the insensibility of sleep, and yet come out in the spring as fat as when they commenced their long nap. The forest, the waste, and the dangers of the cane brake, add to the excitement of the Arkansas hunter; he conquers them all, and makes them subservient to his pursuits. Associated with these scenes, they to him possess no sentiment; he builds his log cabin in a clearing made by his own hands, amid the surrounding grandeur, and it looks like a gipsey hut among the ruins of a Gothic cathedral. The noblest trees are only valuable for fence rails, and the cane brake is "an infernal dark hole," where you can "see sights," "catch bear," and "get a fish-pole, ranging in size from a penny whistle, to that of a young stove-pipe."

The undoubted hero of the Devil's Summer Retreat, is old Bob Herring; he has a character that would puzzle three hundred metaphysicians consecutively. He is as bold as a lion, and as superstitious as an Indian. The exact place of his birth he cannot tell, as he says his parents "travelled" as long as he can remember them. He "squatted" on the Mississippi, at its nearest point to the Retreat, and there erecting a rude cabin commenced hunting for a living, having no prospect ahead but selling out his "pre-emption right" and improvements, and again squatting somewhere else. Unfortunately the extent of Arkansas, and the swamp that surrounded Bob's location, kept it out of market, until, to use his own language, he "became the ancientest inhabitant in the hull of Arkansaw." And having in spite of himself, gradually formed acquaintances with the few residents in this vicinity, and grown into importance from his knowledge of the country and his hunting exploits, he has established himself for life, at what he calls the "Wasps' diggins," made a potato patch, which he has never had time to fence in, talked largely of a corn field, and hung his cabin round with rifle pouches, gourds, red-peppers, and flaming advertisements with rampant horses and pedigrees; these latter ornaments he looks upon as rather sentimental, but he excuses himself on the ground that they look "hoss," and he considers such an expression as considerably resembling himself. We have stated that Bob's mind would puzzle three hundred metaphysicians consecutively, and we as boldly assert, that an equal number of physiologists would be brought to a stand by his personal appearance. The left side of his face is good looking, but the right side seems to be under the influence of an invisible air pump; it looks sucked out of shape; his perpendicular height is six feet one inch, but that gives the same idea of his length, that the diameter gives of the circumference; how long Bob Herring would be if he was drawn out, is impossible to tell. Bob himself says, that he was made on too tall a scale for this world, and that he was shoved in, like the joints of a telescope. Poor in flesh, his enormous bones and joints rattle when he moves, and they would no doubt have long since fallen apart, but for the enormous tendons that bind them together as visibly as a good sized hawser would. Such is Bob Herring, who on a Bear Hunt will do more hard work, crack more jokes, and be more active than any man living, sustaining the whole with unflinching good humor, never getting angry except when he breaks his whiskey bottle, or has a favorite dog open on the wrong trail.

My first visit to the Devil's Summer Retreat was propitious, my companions were all choice spirits, the weather was fine, and Bob Herring inimitable. The bustling scene that prefaced the "striking the camp" for night lodgings, was picturesque and animated; a long ride brought us to our halting place, and there was great relief in again stepping on the ground. Having hobbled our horses, we next proceeded to build a fire, which was facilitated by taking advantage of a dead tree for a back-log; our saddles, guns, and other necessaries were brought within the circle of its light, and lolling upon the ground we partook of a frugal supper, the better to be prepared for our morrow's exertions, and our anticipated breakfast. Beds were next made up, and few can be better than a good supply of cane tops, covered with a blanket, with a saddle for a pillow; upon such a rude couch, the hunter sleeps more soundly than the effeminate citizen on his down. The crescent moon, with her attendant stars, studded the canopy under which we slept, and the blazing fire completely destroyed the chilliness of a Southern December night.

The old adage of "early to bed and early to rise," was intended to be acted upon, that we might salute the tardy sun with the heat of our sport, and probably we would have carried out our intentions had not Bob Herring very coolly asked if any of us snored "unkimmonly loud," for he said his old shooting iron would go off at a good imitation of a bear's breathing. This sally from Bob brought us all upright, and then there commenced a series of jibes, jokes, and stories, that no one can hear, or witness, except on an Arkansas hunt with "old coons." Bob, like the immortal Jack, was witty himself, and the cause of wit in others, but he sustained himself against all competition, and gave in his notions and experience with an unrivalled humor and simplicity. He found in me an attentive listener, and went into details, until he talked every one but myself asleep. From general remarks, he changed to addressing me personally, and as I had everything to learn, he went from the elementary to the most complex experience. "You are green in bar hunting," said he to me, in a commiserating tone, and with a toss of the head that would have done honor to Mr. Brummell in his glory; "green as a jinson weed—but don't get short-winded 'bout it, case it's a thing like readin', to be larnt;—a man don't come it parfectly at once, like a dog does; and as for that, they larn a heap in time;—thar is a greater difference 'tween a pup and an old dog on a bar hunt than thar is 'tween a malitia man and a rigler. I remember when I couldn't bar hunt, though the thing seems onpossible now; it only requires time, a true eye, and steady hand, though I did know a fellow that called himself a doctor, that said you couldn't do it if you was narvious. I asked him if he meant by that agee and fever? He said it was the agee without the fever. Thar may be such a thing as narvious, stranger, but nothin' but a yarthquake, or the agee, can shake me; and still bar hunting ain't as easy as scearing a wild turkey, by a long shot. The varmint ain't a hog, to run with a w–h–e–w; just corner one—cotch its cub, or cripple it, and if you don't have to fight, or get out of the way, then thar ain't no cat-fish in the Mississip. I larnt that, nigh twenty year ago, and prehaps you would like to know about it." Signifying my assent, Bob Herring got up in his bed, for as it was the bare ground he could not well get off of it, and approaching the fire, he threw about a cord of wood on it, in the form of a few huge logs; as they struck the blazing heap the sparks flew upwards in the clear cold air, like a jet of stars; then fixing himself comfortably he detailed what follows:—

"I had a knowing old sow at that time that would have made a better hunter than any dog ever heer'd on; she had such a nose,—talk 'bout a dog following a cold trail, she'd track a bar through running water. Well, you see, afor' I know'd her vartu', she came rushing into my cabin, bristles up, and fell on the floor, from what I now believe to

184

have been regular sceare. I thought she'd seen bar, for nothing else could make her run; and taking down my rifle, I went out sort a carelessly, with only two dogs at my heels. Hadn't gone far 'fore I saw a bar, sure enough, very quietly standing beside a small branch—it was an old *He*, and no mistake. I crawled up to him on my hands and knees, and raised my rifle, but if I had fired I must have hit him so far in front, that the ball would have ranged back, and not cut his mortals. I waited, and he turned tail towards me, and started across the branch; afeer'd I'd lose him, I blazed away, and sort a cut him slantindicularly through his hams, and brought him down; thar he sat, looking like a sick nigger with the dropsy, or a black bale of cotton turned up on eend. 'Twas not a judgematical shot, and Smith thar" (pointing at one of the sleeping hunters) "would say so." Hereupon Bob Herring, without ceremony, seized a long stick, and thrust it into Smith's short ribs, who thus suddenly awakened from a sound sleep, seized his knife, and looking about him, asked, rather confusedly, what was the matter? "Would you," inquired Bob, very leisurely, "would you, under any circumstances, shoot an old *He* in the hams?" Smith very peremptorily told his questioner to go where the occupier of the Retreat in Summer is supposed to reside through the winter months, and went instantly to sleep again. Bob continued.—"Stranger, the bar, as I have said, was on his hams, and thar he sot, waiting to whip somebody and not knowing whar to begin, when the two dogs that followed me came up, and pitched into him like a caving bank. I knowed the result afor the fight began; Brusher had his whole scalp, ears and all, hanging over his nose in a minute, and Tig was laying some distance from the bar on his back, breathing like a horse with the thumps; he wiped them both out with one stroke of his left paw, and thar he sot, knowing as well as I did that he was not obliged to the dogs for the hole in his carcass, and thar I stood, like a fool, rifle in hand, watching him, instead of giving him another ball. All of a sudden he caught a glimpse of my hunting shirt, and the way he walked at me with his two fore legs was a caution to slow dogs. I instantly fired, and stepped round behind the trunk of a large tree; my second shot confused the bar, and he was hunting about for me, when just as I was patching my ball, he again saw me, and with his ears nailed back to his head, he gave the d——t w–h–e–w I ever heerd, and made straight at me; I leaped up a bank near by, and as I gained the top my foot touched the eend of his nose. If I ever had the 'narvious' that was the time, for the skin on my face seemed an inch thick, and my eyes had more rings in them than a mad wild-cat's. At this moment several of my dogs, that war out on an expedition of their own, came up, and immediately made battle with the bar, who shook off the dogs in a flash, and made at me agin; the thing was done so quick, that, as I raised my rifle, I stepped back and fell over, and thinking my time was come, wished I had been born to be hung, and not chaw'd up; but the bar didn't cotch me: his hind quarters, as he came at me, fell into a hole about a root, and caught. I was on my feet and out of his reach in a wink, but as quick as I did this he had cut through a green root the size of my leg: he did it in about two snaps, but weakened by the exertion, the dogs got hold of him, and held on while I blowed his heart out. Ever since that time I have been wide awake with a wounded bar—*cartainty, or stand off*, being my motto. I shall dream of that bar to-night," concluded Bob, fixing his blanket over him; and a few moments only elapsed before he was in danger of his life, if his rifle would go off at a good imitation of a bear's breathing.

Fortunately for me, the sun on the following morn was fairly above the horizon, before our little party was ready for the start, while breakfast was being prepared, the rifles were minutely examined, some were taken apart, and every precaution used, to ensure a quick, and certain fire. A rude breakfast having been despatched, lots were drawn, who should go into the *drive* with the dogs, as this task in the Devil's Summer Retreat, is anything but a pleasant one, being obliged at one time to walk on the bending cane—it is so thick for hundreds of yards that you cannot touch or see the ground—then crawling on your hands and knees, between its roots, sometimes brought to a complete halt, and obliged to cut your way through with your knife. While this is going on, the hunters are at *the stands*, places their judgments dictate as most likely to be passed by the bear, when roused by the dogs. Two miles might on this occasion have been passed over by those in the drive, in the course of three hours, and yet, although "signs were plenty as leaves," not a bear was started. Hard swearing was heard, and as the vines encircled the feet, or caught one under the nose, it was increased. In the midst of this ill humor, a solitary bark was heard; some one exclaimed, that was Bose! another shrill yelp, that sounded like Music's; breathing was almost suspended in the excitement of the moment; presently another, and another bark, was heard in quick succession; in a minute more, *the whole pack, of thirty-five staunch dogs, opened!* The change from silence to so much noise, made it almost deafening. No idea but personal demonstration, can be had of the effect upon the mind, of such a pack, baying a bear in a cane-brake. Before me were old hunters, they had been moving along, as if destitute of energy or feeling, but now their eyes flashed, their lips were compressed, and their cheeks flushed; they seemed incapable of fatigue. As for myself, my feelings almost overcame me, I felt a cold sweat stealing down my back, my breath was thick and hot, and as I suspended it, to hear more distinctly the fight, for by this time the dogs had evidently come up with the bear, I could hear the pulsation of my heart. One minute more to listen, to learn which direction the war was raging, and then our party, unanimously sent forth a yell that would have frightened a nation of Indians. The bear was in his bed when the dogs first came up with him, and he did not leave it until the pack surrounded him; then finding things rather too warm, he broke off with a "whew," that was awful to hear. His course was towards us on the left, and as he went by the cane cracked and smashed, as if rode over by an insane locomotive. Bob Herring gave the dogs a salute as they passed, close at the bear's heels, and the noise increased, until he said "it sounded as if all h——l was pounding bark." The bear was commented on as he rushed by, one said he was "a buster." "A regular built eight year old," said another. "Fat as a candle," shouted a third. "He's the beauty of the Devil's Summer Retreat, with a band of angels after him," sang out Bob Herring. On the bear plunged, so swiftly that our greatest exertions scarcely enabled us to keep within hearing distance; his course carried him towards those at the stands, but getting wind of them, he turned, and exactly retraced his course, but not with the same speed; want of breath had already brought him several times to a stand, and a fight with the dogs. He passed us the second time within two hundred yards, and coming against a fallen tree, backed up against it, and showed a determination if necessary, there to die. We made our way towards the spot, as fast as the obstacles in our way would let us, the hunters anxious to despatch him, that as few dogs as possible might be sacrificed. The few minutes to accomplish this, seemed months, the fight all the time sounding terrible, for every now and then, the bear evidently made a rush at the dogs, as they narrowed their circle, or came individually too near his person. Crawling through and over the cane-brake, was a new thing to me, and in the prevailing excitement, my feet seemed tied together, and there *was always a vine directly under my chin*, to cripple my exertions. While thus struggling, I heard a suspicious cracking in my rear, and looking round, I saw Bob Herring, a foot taller than common, stalking over the cane, like a colossus; he very much facilitated my progress, by a shove in the rear, "Come along, stranger," he shouted, his voice as clear as a bell, "Come along, the bar and the dogs are going it, like a high pressure nigger camp meeting, and I must be thar, to put a word in sartin." Fortunately for my wind, I was nearer the contest than I imagined, for Bob Herring stopped just ahead of me, examined his rifle, with two or three other hunters, just arrived from the stands, and by peeping through the undergrowth, we discovered within thirty yards of us, the fierce raging fight. Nothing distinctly however was seen; a confused mass of legs, heads, and backs of dogs, flying about as if attached to a ball, was all we could make out. A still nearer approach, and the confusion would clear off for a moment, and the head of the bear could be seen, with his tongue covered with dust, and hanging a foot from his mouth; his jaws were covered with foam and blood, his eyes almost protruding from their sockets, while his ears were so closely pressed to the back of his head, that he seemed destitute of those appendages; the whole, indicative of unbounded rage and terror. These glimpses of the bear were only momentary, his persecutors rested but for a breath, and then closed in, regardless of their own lives, for you could discover, mingled with the sharp bark of defiance, the yell that told of death. It was only while the bear was crushing some luckless dog, that they could cover his back, and lacerate it, with their teeth. One of the hunters in spite of the danger, headed by Bob Herring, crept upon his knees, so near, that it seemed as if another foot advanced would bring them within the circle of the fight. Bob Herring was first within safe shooting distance to save the dogs, and waving his hand to those behind him, he raised his rifle and sighted, but his favorite dog impatient for the report, anticipated it by jumping on the bear, who throwing up his head at the same instant, the bear received the ball in his nose; at the crack of the rifle, the well-trained dogs thinking less caution than otherwise necessary, jumped pell mell on the bear's back, and the hardest fight ever witnessed in the Devil's Summer Retreat, ensued; the hunter with Bob placed his gun almost against the bear's side, and the cap snapped; no one else was near enough to fire without hitting the dogs.—"Give him the knife!" cried those at a distance. Bob Herring's long blade was already flashing in his hand, but sticking a living bear, is not child's play; he was standing undecided, when he saw the hind legs of Bose upwards; thrusting aside one or two of the dogs with his hand, he made a pass at the bear's throat, but the animal was so quick, that he struck the knife with his fore paw, and sent it whirling into the distant cane; another was instantly handed him, which he thrust at the bear, but the point was so blunt that it would not penetrate the skin. Foiled a third time, with a tremendous oath on himself, and the owner of the knife, "that wouldn't stick a cabbage," he threw it indignantly from him, and seizing unceremoniously a rifle, just then brought up by one of the party, heretofore in the rear, he, regardless of his own legs, thrust it against the side of the bear with considerable force, and blowed him through; the bear struggled but for a moment, and fell dead; "I saw snakes last night in my dreams," said Bob, handing back the rifle to its owner, "and I never had any good luck the next day, arter sich a sarcumstance; I call this hull hunt, about as mean an affair as damp powder; that bar thar," pointing to the carcase, "that bar thar, ought to have been killed, afor he maimed a dog." Then speaking energetically, he said "Boys, never shoot at a bar's head, even if your iron is in his ear, its unsartin; look how I missed the brain, and only tore the smellers; with fewer dogs, and sich a shot, a fellow would be ripped open in a powder flash; and I say, cuss caps, and head shooting; they would have cost two lives to-day, but for them ar dogs, God bless 'em."

With such remarks, Bob Herring beguiled away the time, while he with others, skinned the bear. His huge carcass when dressed, though not over fat, looking like a young steer's. The dogs as they recovered breath, partook of the refuse with relish; the nearest possible route out of the Devil's Retreat was selected, and two horse loads took the meat into the open woods, where it was divided out in such a manner, that it could be taken home. Bob Herring, while the dressing of the bear was going on, took the skin, and on its inside surface, which glistened like satin, he carefully deposited the caul fat, that looked like drifted snow, and beside it, the liver; the choice parts of the bear, according to the gourmand notions of the frontier, were in Bob's possession; and many years' experience had made him so expert in cooking it, that he was locally famed for this matter above all competitors. It would be as impossible to give the recipe for this dish, so that it might be followed by the gastronomes of cities, as it would to have the articles composing it exposed for sale in the markets. Bob Herring managed as follows; he took a long wooden skewer, and having thrust its point through a small piece of bear fat, he then followed it by a small piece of the liver, then the fat, then the liver, and so on, until his most important material was consumed; when this was done, he opened the "bear's handkerchief," or caul, and wrapped it round the whole, and

189

thus roasted it before the fire. Like all the secrets in cookery, this dish depends for its flavor and richness, upon exactly giving the proper quantities, as a superabundance of one or the other, would completely spoil the dish. "I was always unlucky, boys," said Bob, throwing the bear skin and its contents over his shoulder, "but I've had my fill often, of caul fat and liver; many a man, who thinks he's *lucky*, lives and dies ignorant of its virtue, as a 'possum is of corn cake. If I ever look dead, don't bury me until you see I don't open my eyes when its ready for eating; if I don't move when you show me it, then I am a done goner, sure." Night closed in before we reached our homes, the excitement of the morning wore upon our spirits and energy, but the evening's meal of caul fat, and liver, and other similar "fixins," or Bob Herring's philosophical remarks, restored me to perfect health, and I shall recollect that supper, and its master of ceremonies, as harmonious with, and as extraordinary as is, the Devil's Summer Retreat.

PLACE
DE LA CROIX

There is much of beautiful romance in the whole history of the early settlements of Florida.* De Soto and Ponce de Leon have thrown around the records of their searches for gold and the waters of life a kind of dreamy character, that renders them more like traditions of a spiritual than of a real world. They and their followers were men of stern military discipline, who had won honors in their conquests over the Moors; and they came hither not as emigrants, seeking an asylum from oppression, but as proud nobles anxious to add to their numerous laurels by conquests in a new world. The startling discoveries, the fruits, the gold, and the natives that appeared with Columbus at the court of Isabella, gave to fancy an impetus and to enthusiasm a power that called forth the pomp of the 'Infallible Church' to mingle her sacred symbols with those of arms; and they went joined together through the wilds of America.

Among the beautiful and striking customs of those days was the erection of the cross at the mouths of rivers and prominent points of land that presented themselves to the discoverers. The sacred symbol thus reared in solitude seemed to shadow forth the future, when the dense forest would be filled with its followers instead of the wild savage; and it cheered the lonely pilgrim in his dangerous journeys, bringing to his mind all the cherished associations of this life, and directing his thoughts to another world. In the putting up of these crosses, as they bore the arms of the Sovereign whose subjects erected them, and as they were indicative of civil jurisdiction and empire, the most prominent and majestic locations were selected, where they could be seen for miles around, towering above every other object, speaking the advances of the European, and giving title to the lands over which they cast their shadows. Three hundred years ago the sign of the cross was first raised on the banks of the Mississippi. From one of the few bluffs or high points of land that border that swift-running river, De Soto,

*The name of 'Florida' was given originally to almost the whole of the southern portion of the continent east of the Mississippi.

guided by the aborigines of the country, was the first European that looked upon its turbid waters, soon to be his grave. On this high bluff, taking advantage of a lofty cotton-wood tree, he caused its majestic trunk to be shorn of its limbs; on this tall shaft was placed the beam that made the cross. This completed, the emblazoned banners of Spain and Aragon were unfurled to the breeze, and amid the strains of martial music and the firing of cannon, the steel-clad De Soto, assisted by the priests in his train, raised the host to Heaven, and declared the reign of Christianity commenced in the valley of the Mississippi.

The erection of this touching symbol in the great temple of nature was full of poetry. The forests, like the stars, declare the wonderful works of the Creator. In the silent grandeur of our primeval forests, in their avenues of columns, their canopies of leaves, their festoons of vines, the cross touched the heart, and spoke more fully its office than it ever will, glistening among the human greatness of a Milan cathedral, or the solemn splendor of a St. Peter's.

Two hundred years after Ponce de Leon mingled his dust with the sands of the peninsula of Florida, and De Soto reposed beneath the current of the Mississippi, the same spirit of religious and military enthusiasm pervaded the settlements made by both French and Spanish in this 'land of flowers.' Among the adventurers of that day were many who mingled the romantic ambition of the crusaders with the ascetic spirit of the monk, and who looked upon themselves as ambassadors of religion to new nations in a new world. Of such was Rousseau.

It requires little imagination to understand the disappointment that such a man would meet with in forest life, and as an instructer of the untractable red man. The exalted notions of Rousseau ended in despondency, away from the pomp and influence of his church. Having been nurtured in the 'Eternal City,' he had not the zeal and lacked the principle to become an humble teacher to humbler recipients of knowledge. Disregarding his priestly office, he finally mingled in the dissipations of society, and in the year 1736 he started off as a military companion to D'Artaguette in his expedition against the Chickasas. The death of D'Artaguette and his bravest troops, and the dispersion of his Indian allies, left Rousseau a wanderer, surrounded by implacable enemies, he being one of the few who escaped the fate of battle. Unaccustomed to forest life, more than a thousand miles from the Canadas, he became a prey of imaginary and real dangers; unprovided with arms, his food was of roots or herbs; at night the wild beast howled round his cold couch, and every stump in the day time seemed to conceal an Indian.

Now it was, that Rousseau reviewed the incidents of his past life with sorrow. He discovered when it was too late that he had lost his peace of mind and his hopes of a future existence for a momentary enjoyment. Wasting with watching and hunger, he prayed to the Virgin to save him, that he might by a long life of penance obliterate his sins. On the twelfth day of his wanderings he sank upon the earth to die, and casting his eyes upward in prayer, he saw far in the distance, towering above every object, the cross! It seemed a miracle, and inspired strength in his trembling limbs; and he pressed forward that he might breathe his last at its foot. As he reached it, a smile of triumph lighted up his way-worn features, and he fell insensible to the earth.

Never perhaps was this sacred emblem more beautifully decorated or touchingly displayed, than was the one that towered over Rousseau. From indications, some fifteen years might have elapsed since the European pilgrim had erected it. One of the largest forest trees had been chosen that stood upon the surrounding bluffs; the tall trunk tapered upward with the proportions of a Corinthian column, which, with the piece forming the cross, was covered with ten thousand evergreen vines, that spread such a charm over the southern landscape. It seemed as if Nature had paid tribute to the sacred symbol, and festooned it with a perfection and beauty worthy of her abundance. The honey-suckle and the ivy, the scarlet creeper and fragrant jasmine, the foliage enamelled with flowers, shed upon the repentant and insensible Rousseau a shower of fragrance.

Near where he lay, there was a narrow and amply-worn footpath; you could trace it from where it lost itself in the deep forests to where it wound round the steep washed bank until it touched the water's edge. At this point were to be seen the prints of footsteps; the traces of small fires were also visible, and one of them still sent up puffs of smoke. Here it was that the Choctaw maidens and old women performed their rude labor of washing. In the morning and evening sun a long line of the forest children might be seen with clay jars and skins filled with water, carrying them upon their heads, and stringing up, single file, the steep bank and losing themselves in the woods; with their half-clad and erect forms making a most picturesque display, not unlike the processions figured in the hieroglyphical paintings of Egypt.

Soon after Rousseau fell at the cross, there might have been seen emerging from the woods, and following the path we have described, a delicately-formed Indian girl. In her hand was a long reed and a basket, and she came with blithe steps toward the river. As she passed the cross, the form of Rousseau met her eyes. Stopping and examining him, with almost overpowering curiosity, she retreated with precipitation, but returned almost instantly. She approached nearer and nearer, until the wan and insensible face met hers. Strange as was his appearance and color, the chord of humanity was touched; the woman forgot both fear and curiosity, in her anxiety to allay visible suffering. A moment had hardly elapsed, before water was thrown over Rousseau, and held to his lips. The refreshing beverage brought him to consciousness. He stared wildly about him, and discovering the Indian form bending over him, he sunk again insensible to the earth. Like a young doe the girl bounded away and disappeared.

A half an hour might have elapsed when there issued out of the forest a long train of Indians. At their head was the young maiden surrounded by armed warriors; in the rear followed women and children. They approached Rousseau, whose recovery was but momentary, and who was now unconscious of what was passing around him. The crowd examined him first with caution, gradually with familiarity; their whispers became animated conversation, and finally blended in one noisy confusion. There were among those present many who had heard of the white man and of his powers, but none had ever seen one before. One Indian, more bold than the rest, stripped the remnant of a cloak from Rousseau's shoulder; another, emboldened by this act, caught rudely hold of his coat, and as he pulled it aside there fell from his breast a small gilt crucifix, held by a silken cord. Its brilliancy excited the cupidity of all, and many were the eager hands that pressed forward to obtain it. An old chief gained the prize, and fortunately for Rousseau, his prowess and influence left him in undisputed possession. As he examined the little trinket, the Indian girl we have spoken of, the only female near Rousseau, crossed her delicate fingers and pointed upward. The old chief instantly beheld the similarity between the large and small symbol of Christianity, and extending it aloft with all the dignity of a cardinal, the crowd shouted as they saw the resemblance, and a change came over them all. They associated at once the erection of the large cross with Rousseau, and as their shout had again called forth exhibitions of life from his insensible form, they threw his cloak over him, suspended the cross to his neck, brought in a moment green boughs with which a litter was made, and bore him with all respect toward their lodges. The excitement and exercise of removal did much to restore him to life; a dish of maize did more; and nothing could exceed his astonishment on his recovery, that he should be treated with such kindness; and as he witnessed the respect paid the cross, and was shown by rude gestures that he owed his life to its influence, he sank upon his knees, overwhelmed with its visible exhibition of power, and satisfied that his prayer for safety had been answered in the perfection of a miracle.

The Choctaws, into whose hands the unfortunate Rousseau had fallen, (although he was not aware of the difference,) were not the bloody-minded Cherokees, from whom he had so lately escaped. Years before, the inhabitants of the little village on their return from a hunting expedition discovered the cross we have described: its marks then were such as would be exhibited a few days after its erection. Footsteps were seen about its base, that from their variance with the mark left by the moccasin satisfied the Indians that it was not erected by any of their people. The huge limbs that had been shorn from the trunk bore fresh marks of terrible cuts, which the stone hatchet could not have made. As is natural to the Indian mind, on the display of power they cannot explain, they appropriately though accidentally associated the cross with a Great Spirit, and looked upon it with wonder and admiration. Beside the cross there was found an axe, left by those who had formed it. This was an object of the greatest curiosity to its finders. They stuck it into the trees, severed huge limbs, and performed other powerful feats with it, and yet fancied their own rude stone instruments failed to do the same execution from want of a governing spirit equal to that which they imagined presided over the axe, and not from difference of material. The cross and the axe were associated together in the Indians' minds, and the crucifix of Rousseau connected him with both. They treated him therefore with all the attention they would bestow upon a being who was master of a superior power.

The terrible and strange incidents that had formed the life of Rousseau, since the defeat of his military associate D'Artaguette, seemed to him, as he recalled them to his mind, an age. His dreams were filled with scenes of torment and death. He would start from his sleep with the idea that an arrow was penetrating his body, or that the bloody knife was at his heart. These were then changed into visions of starvation, or destruction by wild beasts. Recovering his senses, he would find himself in a comfortable lodge, reposing on a couch of soft skins, while the simple children of the woods, relieved of their terrors, were waiting to administer to his wants. The change from the extreme of suffering to that of comfort he could hardly realize. The cross in the wilderness, the respect they paid to the one on his breast, were alike inexplicable; and Rousseau, according to the spirit of his age, felt that a miracle had been wrought in his favor; and on his bended knees he renewed his ecclesiastical vows, and determined to devote his life to enlightening the people among whom Providence had placed him.

The Indian girl who first discovered Rousseau was the only child of a powerful chief. She was still a maiden, and the slavish labor of savage married life had consequently not been imposed upon her. Among her tribe she was universally considered beautiful, and her hand was sought by all the young 'braves' of her tribe. Wayward, or difficult to please, she had resolutely refused to occupy any lodge but her father's, however eligible and enviable the settlement might have appeared in the eyes of her associates. For an Indian girl she was remarkably gentle; and as Rousseau gradually recovered his strength, he had through her leisure more frequent intercourse with her than with any of the tribe. There was also a feeling in his bosom that she was, in the hands of an overruling Providence, the instrument used to preserve his life. Whatever might have been the speculations of the elders of the tribe, as day after day Rousseau courted her society and listened to the sounds of her voice, we do not know; but his attentions to her were indirectly encouraged, and the Indian girl was almost constantly at his side.

Rousseau's plans were formed. The painful experience he had encountered while following the ambition of worldly greatness had driven him back into the seclusion of the church, with a love only to end in this life by death. He determined to learn the dialect of the people in whose lot his life was cast, and form them into a nation of worthy recipients of the 'Holy Church;' and the gentle Indian girl was to him a preceptor, to teach him her language. With this high resolve, he repeated the sounds of her voice, imitated her gesticulations, and encouraged with marked preference her society. The few weeks that Rousseau passed among the Choctaws had made him one bitter, implacable enemy. Unable to explain his office or his intentions, his preference for Chechoula had been marked by the keen eye of a jealous and rejected lover.

Wah-a-ola was a young 'brave,' who had distinguished himself on the hunting and war-paths. Young as he was, he had won a name. Three times he had laid the trophies of his prowess at the feet of

Chechoula, and as often she had rejected his suit. Astonished at his want of success, he looked upon his mistress as laboring under some charm, for he could find no accepted rival for her hand. The presence of Rousseau, the marked preference which Chechoula exhibited for his society, settled in his own mind that the 'pale face' was the charmer.

With this conviction, he placed himself conveniently to meet his mistress, and once more pleaded his suit, before he exhibited the feelings of hatred which he felt toward Rousseau. The lodge of Chechoula's father was, from the dignity of the chief, at the head of the Indian village, and at some little distance. The impatient Wah-a-ola seated himself near its entrance, where from his concealment he could watch whoever entered its door. A short time only elapsed before he saw in the cold moon-light a group of Indian girls approaching the lodge, in busy conversation, and conspicuously among them all, Chechoula. Her companions separated from her, and as she entered her father's lodge, a rude buffalo-skin shut her in. Soon after her disappearance, the little groups about the Indian village gradually dispersed; the busy hum of conversation ceased; and when profound stillness reigned, a plaintive note of the whip-poor-will was heard; it grew louder and louder until it seemed as if the lone bird was perched on the top of the lodge that contained Chechoula. It attracted her ear; for she thrust aside the buffalo-skin, and listened with fixed attention. The bird screamed, and appeared to flutter as if wounded. Chechoula rushed toward the bushes that seemed to conceal so much distress, when Wah-a-ola sprang up and seized her wrist. The affrighted girl stared at her captor a moment, and then exclaimed: 'The snake should not sing like the birds!' Wah-a-ola relaxed not his hold; there was a volcano in his breast that seemed to overwhelm him as he glared upon Chechoula with blood-shot eyes. Struggling to conceal his emotion, he replied to her question by asking, 'if the wild flowers of the woods were known only by their thorns?' 'The water-lilies grow upon smooth stems,' said Chechoula, striving violently to retreat to her father's lodge. The love of Wah-a-ola was full of jealousy, and the salute and reply of his mistress converted it into hate. Dashing his hand across his brow, on which the savage workings of his passion were plainly visible, he asked, 'if a 'brave' was to whine for a woman, like a bear for its cubs? Go!' said he, flinging Chechoula's arm from him, 'go! The mistletoe grows not upon young trees, and the pale-face shall be a rabbit in the den of the wolf!'

197

From the time Rousseau was able to walk, he had made a daily pilgrimage to the cross, and there upon his bended knees greeted the morning sun. This habit was known to all the tribe. The morning following the love-scene between Wah-a-ola and Chechoula, he was found dead at the foot of the sacred tree. A poisoned arrow had been driven almost through his body. Great was the consternation of the whole tribe. It was considered a mysterious evidence of impending evil; while not a single person could divine who was the murderer. 'The mistletoe grows not upon young trees!' thought Chechoula; and for the first time she knew the full meaning of the words, as she bent over the body of Rousseau. She attended his obsequies with a sorrow less visible but more deeply felt than that of her people; although the whole tribe had, in the short residence of the departed, learned to respect him and to look upon him as a great 'Medicine.'

His grave was dug where he had so often prayed, and the same sod covered him that drank his heart's blood. According to Indian custom, all that he possessed, as well as those articles appropriated to his use, were buried with him in his grave. His little crucifix reposed upon his breast, and he was remembered as one who had mysteriously come and as mysteriously passed away.

A few years after the events we have detailed, a Jesuit missionary, who understood the Choctaw language, announced his mission to the tribe, and was by them kindly received. His presence revived the recollections of Rousseau, and the story of his being among them was told. The priest explained to them his office, and these gentle people in a short time erected over the remains of Rousseau a rude chapel; his spirit was called upon as their patron saint; and Chechoula was the first to renounce the superstitions of her tribe, and receive 'the holy sacrament of baptism.'

In the year 1829 a small brass cross was picked out of the banks of the Mississippi near Natchez, at the depth of several feet from the surface. The crucifix was in tolerable preservation, and was exposed by one of those cavings of the soil so peculiar to the Mississippi. The speculations which the finding of this cross called forth revived the almost forgotten traditions of the story of Rousseau, and of his death and burial at the PLACE DE LA CROIX.

A VISIT TO "CURNEL PARDON JONES"

We have always had a passion for great men; our feelings therefore can be "imagined better than described" as we went "up the coast" on a special visit to "Curnel Pardon Jones." The distinguished position he has occupied as a candidate for Congress, the enlarged views that govern his political sentiments, together with his military services, are claims upon his constituency not often found possessed by candidates; and his election will render the country essentially "safe." He therefore may be said to "fill the public eye;" a halo of glory is glittering in his path, and narrowing its circle to settle upon his capacious brow. When the war cry sounded upon every breeze that blew across the Atlantic, when the "Maine question," and "Creole case" seemed to be letting slip the terrible dogs of war, then, and then only, was the "Curnel" clamorous for his election. No sooner had Ashburton been favorably received on his mission of peace, and published to the world that "the United States agreed to the concessions made by England, and that the United States, with entire justice, granted all that England asked, which was nothing," than we see the "Curnel" quietly withdrawing from the field, hanging up his battered arms, and waiting the soul-stirring times which he long since anticipated would call him again into action.

With a sagacity unparalleled in the history of politics, the close observer will perceive that the "Curnel" has been aiming to be the nominee as fourth member of Congress. Diffusive, expanded, gigantic in his views, he has scorned the elections by districts, and appeals for support to a whole state! Thus anticipating by mere intellect alone the present time in the political history of Louisiana, when an extra member of Congress could be elected by a general ticket. The whole world will therefore understand, and Louisiana particularly notice, that the *flag is up*

FOR FOURTH MEMBER OF CONGRESS,

FOR LOUISIANA,

PARDON JONES.

Our visit to the distinguished "Curnel" was propitious. We entered our names on the steamboat book as bound "up the coast," and it soon became noised about among my fellow passengers that I was on a visit to *the Curnel*. I was treated with great consideration, one man going so far as to intimate that I was Shocco Jones coming on to get the "Curnel's" advice relative to the subject of removing the deposits generally, and of my own interests in particular. This same man asked me if Shocco and the "Curnel" were related, as their names were the same? The steward directed an extra fine "desart" for the *Curnel's friend*, and the captain waived his title to the head of the dinner table, and left me the honor of carving a tough Muscovy duck, with a dull knife.

On landing "up the Coast" I was particularly fortunate, for I saw the "Curnel" immediately on touching the levee, surrounded by his particular friends, as all great men always are. We knew *the Curnel* at sight, being as easily distinguished from the crowd in which he mingled as is a half eagle from a handful of dimes. He was dressed up in the true citizen military style, there *having been expected a parade* the very morning of my arrival. The "Curnel" on noticing me stepped out from his circle of friends, gave me a military salute from habit, and a warm shake of the hand from goodness of heart. I found myself at my ease, and retiring to the shade of a large pecan tree, we sat down upon a pile of shingles and talked over the important matters of the day. The "Curnel" was communicative and straight-forward: he said he had nothing to conceal in his political sentiments, he went emphatically for the people, the whole people, and for nothing but the people: and what the people wanted was the constitutional wants of the land. I asked him his frank and open opinion with regard to a United States Bank. The "Curnel" said he would speak plainly though it was a delicate subject; accordingly the "Curnel" said if there could be a Bank established without any influence, capable of relieving the distresses of individuals without using government funds, causing the exchanges to be always in favor of "Luzianna," reducing the tariff, and at the same time protecting manufactories, and if such a Bank met with the approbation of the executive and two-thirds of both houses of Congress, he would then go in for it heart and sword; but if otherwise, the thing was up, and stood no more chance than a "stumped tail bull in fly-time."

The "Curnel's" ideas of the land distribution bill, and on the subject of the tariff, were all spoken of in an equally clear and statesman like manner. In conclusion he said, "These, however, are not the important questions that will agitate the nation,"—and his face grew red, and he punched the heel of his boot fiercely into the ground, and fell into a reverie. I saw that he was agitated, and, afraid to disturb his cogitation, I handed my walking stick to Capt. Potter, and told him it was an ill-favored affair, but I treasured it on account of its being a relic of the "Santer Fee Expedition." Had I held the muzzle of an engine pipe in the "Curnel's" face, and drenched him with cold water, he could not have started up more suddenly or have been more excited. He seized hold of the scabbard of his sword, and rattled it in a most ominous manner; then, turning to me with a mild look, although the indignation of his soul was radiating from his face like heat from a pent up furnace, the "Curnel" insinuated that *it was fortunate* that he had never met with Gov. Armijo or Salezar of Mexico. "To punish such rascals, I wish to go to Congress: once let me be a chairman of a committee on military affairs, along with John Q. Adams, and you will see whereabouts Armijo and Salezar would come out at." I modestly hinted that probably the government at this time could not stand such an outlay of money as it would require to punish them. The "Curnel" replied, "Sacrez l'expence! as the French say;" and then he continued: "The next two years will be big with fate;—Gov. Dorr is not dead." At the mention of the governor's name the "Curnel" drew his sword and flourished it in the air, then bringing it down, shaving off the toe of his boot and burying the point deeply in the bunch of shingles on which he sat, intimately connected with him by the consanguinious ties of friendship; and wearing the sword that he *wanted* when he got his other one—"My advice will be needed at Washington, should there be any more difficulties in Rhode Island." But at the sound of the ominous word the "Curnel's" communicativeness drew in as suddenly as an alarmed terrapin draws in its head, repeating it the second time; but he concluded by saying, that the Watch-Tower of Patriotism would soon have in its ample columns his ideas in full on the subject, and he would cease invading the conventionality of private life by the conflicting ones of state.

Hereupon the conversation grew general in its character, and I took an opportunity in the midst of it to speak of the knowing way he had been for the last nine months aiming at being the candidate for the fourth member of Congress for Louisiana. The "Curnel" put his finger to his nose, and looked at the corner of his cocked hat with his left eye, as much to say, "I am deep, very deep."

My visit being finished, which on the whole was a pleasant one, I took an affectionate leave of the "Curnel," but not until he informed me that as he was regularly out as a fourth member, he should allay public excitement by coming out at once in the "Watch Tower of Patriotism" *and define his position*, and Capt. Potter took me aside and told me in strict confidence that the "Curnel" had written out a "thunderin tall speech, which the 'Curnel' was to deliver *extemporaneously*, and then have it out in print as having been taken down by one of the reporters of the Picayune; the 'Curnel,'" as the Captain remarked, "bein as thick as hasty puddin with the Pic family." As it will soon be fashionable to visit the "Curnel" at home, as I have done, I would recommend that visiters say as little as possible about the "Santer Fee Expedition" and Gov. Dorr, as the "Curnel" always shows great agitation at the mention of either of them, and can only be calmed by an appeal to the necessity at present of his "smothering his just indignation."

The "Curnel" said he expected the papers throughout the Union to come out in his favor, but he more particularly relied on the influence of Adjt. Haile, of the Plaquemine Gazette, and Maj. Kelly, of the Louisiana Chronicle, they being in office and thereby able to sympathize with his "military ardor." Col. Greene, of the Boston Post stands pledged to strain every muscle in the contest, so that there may be expected a regular campaign and no mistake.—We say "hoora" for "Curnel" Pardon Jones.

MY FIRST DINNER IN NEW ORLEANS

There ought to be nothing about a dinner to make it an era in one's history in any way, generally speaking. The power merely to gratify the appetite just sufficient to sustain life, is eating in poverty; the life spent merely in gratifying the appetite, is brutal. We like a good dinner, and we sit down at one with that complacency of feeling that denotes a thankfulness that may be called a silent blessing, yet we feel more pity for a man that recollects his bad dinners than we do for one who distinctly remembers his good ones. In every day life things commemorative often start from the table, "do you recollect," says Gustibus, "that so and so happened the day we eat the fresh salmon?" "I remember the event," replies Dulce, "from that exquisite bon mot uttered on the occasion." I remember my first dinner in New Orleans as distinctly as I remember my first love. I trust it was impressed upon my mind through the intellect as well as through the senses, or else I should be ashamed to remember it at all. As I journeyed on to the city for the first time, I naturally suggested to my travelling companion my desire to be most pleasantly provided for, and contrary to usual custom, my friend launched forth in eloquent declamations upon the table of his host, drew pictures of plenty which threw my most sanguine expectations and hopes into the shade, and caused me to look forward with a kind of strange interest at what I was about to see offered up to the palate. I landed at the levee fronting the city, in the middle of the morning; although it was early spring, a glorious sun, such as Pomona loves, was making everything look gay; the swollen Mississippi dashed a few waves over the artificial barrier that confined it to its channel, and as they coursed along in little rivulets they sparkled like molten silver and gold, indicative we thought of the wealth which was borne upon its waters, and which paid tribute to the city.

I need not say where I ate my first dinner in New Orleans, it was not at the St. Charles, for that building in the night following it looked, in the cold moonlight, like a magnificent ruin, so quiet, so grand withal. The clink of the money drawer, the noise of glasses, or the confused hum of the crowd had not yet usurped the place of the hammer and trowel. I forget about the St. Louis. However, the dining hall was a long one, and the dinners numerous. I made my entrance after the soup dishes had done their office, and consequently was a little late. It might have been the exercise, or the excitement, or a hasty breakfast, that made me feel uncommonly well to enjoy a dinner. I was unusually disposed that way, and looked down the long tables crowded to excess, with great concern for fear there was no room for me, until that melancholy time, when gravies grow into water and globules of fat, and meats are just as warm as when alive, the cruets half filled, and the cloth awry. I trembled at the prospect, when to my inexpressible relief, on my left, near the door at the head of the two long dining tables, was a small one, around which sat some six or eight gentlemen. The head of this table was unoccupied, and I without ceremony seated myself in the vacant chair. I never saw a man come in late to dinner who did not look around on the company present with a kind of expression of "who cares if I did come in late?" I looked that way on the gentlemen upon the right and left, and before me, and they all looked much as if they thought I was intruding a little upon their presence. I never knew any other expression to come from strangers at a public table, and not being in a bad humor I asked the waiter for soup if he had any hot, and having been accommodated in the twinkling of a spoon, I went to work lustily to lay the foundation of what my friend in the morning had promised, *a splendid dinner.*—Oysters and fish, as a first course, seem to be founded in nature, reason, and taste, and I made the remark to the gentleman on the right, he very politely assented to the proposition and ate sparingly, I pressed him, and suggested that he might be troubled with the dyspepsia, this sally was received by all the gentlemen at the table with what I thought an unnecessary quantity of laughter, particularly from the one at the foot of the table, but as I remarked this latter personage had a sparkling eye and a rubicund nose, I concluded he was easily pleased, and that the gentleman, on my right was bashful. Venison, all tumbling about in its dish, with its spirit lamp, and wine condiments, very beautiful indeed all this, but to me not so much of a rarity as it would have been had I not lived in the country where deer were plenty.—Determined to call out the bashful man on my right, I observed that if I had had the arrangement of the dinner I should have ordered roast beef as I understood New Orleans was famous for the dish. The bashful man smiled and the rest of the table were delighted, and agreed it was a most valuable suggestion. I then went on to inform them that the sweetest

204

venison I ever ate was while travelling on the frontier, and then it was not cooked like the dish present, but merely cut off of the quarter and roasted on hot coals, devoured with butter and salt. Hereupon the gentleman with the rubicund nose told the bashful man that this second suggestion of mine was invaluable, and another hearty laugh followed.—Prairie hens followed in some way, the venison, the meat was as delicate in its color as a white kid glove, and was really delicious, they came from Illinois some body said; this showed the enterprise of the landlord of the hotel, so I thought and remarked, and found my feelings in this matter entirely appreciated by the little group around me. The woodcock, or *becasse*, as I heard them called for the first time excited unbounded astonishment; there they were, in a large dish, packed side by side "like newly married couples," round as balls, and looking as inviting as ice in August. I took one on my plate, turned it over and discovered that the bird had probably committed suicide by running its own bill through its body; as I drew the bill out I exclaimed woodcocks as I live! Our bashful friend responded, "exactly." I helped him liberally, and every one else; the birds flew about under my administration like mad, and there was expressed the most astonishing good humor at my beneficent liberality.

In the meantime the two long tables of the hotel were deserted, the waiters at them were walking about maunching bits, and odd ends, piling up plates and "clearing off," but our little party grew more and more merry and happy; wine delicious and old, flowed freely, course after course followed, and then came the thousand varieties of the confectioner's skill. Toasts and sentiments really new, were engendered by the old wine, songs, sentimental and patriotic; bosom friends were all mingling together as sweetly and harmoniously as the waters in the vale of Avoca. I was particularly happy in my feelings, and in my remarks, whatever I said, was received with a roar; in fact I never met with the same number of gentlemen so congenial and so easily pleased. The sun gradually sunk in the West, and the proposition for candles seemed to be a signal for departure, one more drink around and a sentiment from myself was to finish. Certainly, said I, fill up, fill up, fill to the brim. I raised my glass high, and addressed my friends as follows:—"Gentlemen—I have heard much said of the fine table set in this hotel; of the great liberality and enterprise of its host. I have heard nothing equal to its merits in this respect, which is unsurpassed in my experience, except by the pleasant and sociable, literary and scientific gentlemen who assembled round its hospitable board. Gentlemen, I propose the host." This speech, or sentiment, was received with tremendous applause. Two of the gentlemen fell under the table, and three suspender buttons flew against the window opposite me. Shaking hands all round, I left the best dinner of my life—my first dinner in New Orleans, and the cleverest party assembled in my knowledge.

Somehow about one o'clock at night I met my friend whom I left in the morning. I found him in his room suffering with a severe attack of the cholic; I was very communicative about the events of the day, and thanked him warmly for introducing me to a hotel where they gave such fine dinners. "Fine dinners," he exclaimed, with a groan, "do I look as if I had had a fine dinner, nearly dead with eating from necessity cabbage and pork?" "Where did you dine?" I inquired with alarm. "Why in this hotel." I told him he was dreaming, and gave him a running commentary of my own dinner at the same time and place. The pains of the cholic could not completely destroy the twinkle of his eye, when he informed me that *the table* I sat down at was a *private table*, and a "game dinner," got up at a great deal of time and expense! The conceit of my ability to amuse a dinner party of strangers suddenly vanished! the wit of my jokes was revealed, and although I was fortunate in eating a good dinner, I was still more fortunate in meeting with a party of gentlemen who were so delicate as not to wound my feelings by an explanation of my innocent mistake.

THE LOUISIANA LAW OF COCK-FIGHTING

About one hundred and twenty miles from New Orleans reposes, in all rural happiness, one of the pleasantest little towns in the south, that reflects itself in the mysterious waters of the Mississippi. To the extreme right of the town, looking at it from the river, may be seen a comfortable looking little building, surrounded by China trees, just such a place as sentimental misses dream of when they have indistinct notions of "settling in the world." This little "burban bandbox," however, is not occupied by the airs of love, nor the airs of the lute, but by a strong limb of the law, a gnarled one too, who knuckles down to business, and digs out of the "uncertainties of his profession," decisions, and reasons, and causes, and effects, no where to be met with except in the science called, par excellence, the "perfection of human reason." Around the interior walls of this romantic looking place may be found an extensive library, where all the "statues," from Moses' time down to the present day, are ranged side by side; and in these musty books the owner revels day and night, digesting "digests," and growing the while sallow himself with indigestion. On the evening-time of a fine summer's day, the sage lawyer might have been seen walled in with books and manuscripts, his eye full of thought, and his bald high forehead sparkling with the rays of the setting sun, as if his genius was making itself visible to the senses; page after page he searched, musty parchments were scanned, the expression of care and anxiety indented itself in the stern features of his face, and with a sigh of despair he desisted from his labors, uttering aloud his feelings that he feared his case was a hopeless one. Then he renewed again his mental labor with tenfold vigor, making the very silence with which he pursued his thoughts ominous, as if a spirit were in his presence. The door of the lawyer's office opened, there pressed forward a tall, gaunt figure of a man, a perfect model of physical power and endurance, a western flatboatman. The lawyer heeded not his presence, and started as if from a dream, as the harsh tones of enquiry, "Does a 'Squire live here?" grated upon his ears. "They call me so," was the reply, as soon as the lawyer recovered from his astonishment.

"Well 'Squire," continued the intruder, "I have got a case for you, and I want jestess, if it costs the best load of produce that ever came from In-di-an'." The man of the law asked what was the difficulty. "It's this, 'Squire: I'm bound for Orleans, and put in here for coffee and other little fixins; a chap with a face whiskered up like a prairie dog, says, says he, 'stranger, I see you have cocks on board of your boat—bring one ashore, and I'll pit one against him that'll lick his legs off in less time than you could gaff him.' Well, 'Squire, *I never take a dar*. Says I, stranger, I'm thar at wunce, and in twenty minutes the cocks were on the levee, like parfect saints. We chucked them together, and my cock, 'Squire, now mind, my cock never struck a lick, not a single blow, but tuck to his heels and run, and by thunders, puked. The stakeholder gave up the money against me, and now I want jestess; as sure as fogs, my cock was physicked, or he'd stood up to his business like a wild cat."

The lawyer heard the story with patience, and flatly refused to have any thing to do with the matter. "Perhaps," said the boatman, drawing out a corpulent pocket book, "perhaps you think I can't pay—here's the money; help yourself—give me jestess, and draw like an ox team."

To the astonishment of the flatboatman, the lawyer still refused, but unlike many of his profession, gave his would-be client, without charge, some general advice about going on board his boat, shoving off for New Orleans, and abandoning the suit altogether. The flatboatman started with profound astonishment and asked the lawyer "if he was sure enough 'Squire." Receiving an affirmative reply, he pressed every argument he could use, to have him undertake his case and get him "jestess," but when he found his efforts were unavailing, he quietly seated himself for the first time, put his hat aside, crossed his legs, and looking up to the ceiling with the expression of great patience, requested the "'Squire to read him the Louisiana laws on cock-fighting." The lawyer said he did not know of a single statute in the state on the subject; the boatman started up as if he was shot, exclaiming, "No laws in the state on cock-fighting? No, no, 'Squire, you can't possum me; give us the law." The refusal again followed; the astonishment of the boatman increased, and throwing himself in a comico heroic attitude, he carried his long fingers round the sides of the room and asked "what all them thar books were about?" "All about the law." "Well then, 'Squire, am I to understand that not one of them thar books contain a single law on cock-fighting?"

"You are."

"And, 'Squire, am I to understand that thar ain't no laws in Louisiana on cock-fighting?"

"You are."

"And am I to understand that you call yourself a 'Squire, and that you don't know any thing about cock-fighting?"

"You are."

The astonishment off the boatman at this reply for a moment was unbounded, and then suddenly ceased; the awe with which he looked upon "the 'Squire" also ceased, and resuming his natural awkward and familiar carriage, he took up his hat, and walked to the door, and with a broad grin of supreme contempt in his face, he observed, "that a 'Squire that did not know the laws of cock-fighting, in his opinion, was distinctly a dam fool."

THE WATER CRAFT OF THE BACK WOODS

Starting among the volcanic precipices, eternal snows, and arid deserts of the Rocky Mountains, the Snake river winds its sinuous way towards the Pacific; at one time, rushing headlong, through deep gorges of the mountains, and at another, spreading itself out in still lakes, as it sluggishly advances through ever varying scenes of picturesque grandeur and of voluptuous softness. In all this variety, the picture only changes from the beautiful to the sublime; while the eye of the civilized intruder as it speculates on the future, can see on the Snake river, the city, the village, and the castle, in situations more interesting and romantic, than they have yet presented themselves to the world. The solitary trapper, and the wild Indian, are now the sole inhabitants of its beautiful shores; the wigwams of the aborigine, the temporary lodge of the hunter and the cunning beaver, rear themselves almost side by side, and nature reposes like a virgin bride in all her beauty and loveliness, soon to be stripped of her natural charms to fulfil new offices, with a new existence. On an abrupt bank of this beautiful stream, overlooking the surrounding landscape for miles—a spot of all others to be selected for a site of beauty and defence, might be seen a few lodges of the Wallawallah Indians. On the opposite shore stood a fine young warrior, decked in all the tinsel gewgaws his savage fancy suggested to catch the love of his mistress. With stealthy step he opened the confused undergrowth that lined the banks, taking therefrom a delicate paddle, he searched in vain, until the truth flashed upon him that some rival had stolen his canoe.— Readily would he have dashed into the bosom of the swollen river, and as another Leander, sought another Hero, but his dress was not to be spoiled. Like a chafed lion, he walked along the shore, his bosom alternately torn by rage, love, and vanity, when far up the bank he saw a herd of buffalo slaking their thirst in the running stream. Seizing his bow and arrow, with noiseless step he stole upon his victim, and the unerring shaft soon brought it to the earth, struggling with the agonies of death. It was only the work of an adept to strip off the skin, and spread it on the ground. Upon it were soon laid the gaily wrought moccasins, leggings, and hunting shirt—the trophies of honorable warfare, and the skins of birds of beautiful plumage. The corners of the hide were then brought together, tied with thongs, the bundle was set afloat upon the stream, and its owner dashed on in its rear, guiding it to the opposite shore with its contents unharmed. Again decking himself, and bearing his wooing tokens before him, he leaped with the swiftness of a deer to the lodge that contained his mistress, leaving the *simplest of all the water craft* of the back woods to decay upon the ground.

The helplessness of age, the appealing eyes and hands of infancy, the gallantry of the lover, the hostile excursions of a tribe, are natural incentives to the savage mind to improve upon the mere bundle of inanimate things that could be safely floated upon the water. To enlarge this bundle, to build up its sides, would be his study and delight, and we have next in the list of back woods craft, what is styled by the white man, the *Buffalo skin boat.*—This craft is particularly the one of the prairie country, where the materials for its construction are always to be found, and where its builders are always expert. A party of Indians find themselves upon the banks of some swift and deep river— there is no timber to be seen for miles around, larger than a common walking stick; the Indians are loaded with plunder—for they have made a successful incursion into the territory of some neighboring tribe, and cannot trust their effects in the water; or they are perchance migrating to a favorite hunting ground, and have with them all their domestic utensils, their squaws and children. A boat is positively necessary, and it must be made of the materials at hand. A fire is kindled, and by it are laid a number of long slender poles, formed by trimming off the limbs of the saplings growing on the margin of the stream. While this is going on, some of the braves start in pursuit of buffalo; two of the stoutest bulls met with, are killed and stripped of their skins. These skins are then sewed together, the poles having been well heated, the longest is selected and bent into the proper form for a keel; the ribs are then formed and lashed transversely to it, making what would appear to be the skeleton of a large animal. This skeleton is then placed upon the hairy side of the buffalo skin, when it is drawn round the frame and secured by holes cut in the skin, and hitched on to the ribs; a little pounded slippery elm bark is used to caulk the seams, and small pieces of wood cut with a thread-like screw, are inserted in the arrow or bullet holes of the hide. Thus, in the course of two or three hours, a handsome and durable boat is completed, capable of carrying eight or ten men with comfort and safety.

Passing from the prairie we come to the thick forest, and there we find the most perfect of the water craft of the back woods—of the varieties of the canoe. The inhabitant of the woods never dreams of a boat made of skins; he looks to the timber for a conveyance. Skilled in the knowledge of plants, he knows the exact time when the bark of the tree will readily unwrap from its native trunk, and from this simple material he forms the most beautiful craft that sits upon the water. The rival clubs that sport their boats upon the Thames, or ply them in the harbor of Mannahatta, like things of life—formed as they are by the high scientific knowledge and perfect manual skill of the two greatest naval nations in the world, are thrown in the shade by the beautiful and simple bark canoe, made by the rude hatchet and knife of the red man.

The American forest is filled with trees, whose bark can be appropriated to the making of canoes; the pecan, all the hickories, with the birch, grow there in infinite profusion. A tree of one of these species, that presents a trunk clear of limbs for fifteen or twenty feet, is first selected; the artisan has nothing but a rude hunting knife and tomahawk for the instruments of his craft; with the latter he girdles the bark near the root of the tree—this done, he ascends to the proper height, and there makes another girdle; then taking his knife and cutting through the bark downwards, he separates it entirely from the trunk. Ascending the tree again, he inserts his knife blade under the bark, and turning it up, soon forces it with his hand until he can use more powerful levers; once well started, he will worm his body between the bark and the trunk, and thus tear it off, throwing it upon the ground, like an immense scroll. The *ross*, or outside of the bark, is scraped off until it is smooth, the scroll is then opened, and braces inserted to give the proper width to the gunnels of the canoe. Strong cords are then made from the bark of the linn tree or hickory, the open ends of the bark scroll are pressed together and fastened between clamps, the clamps secured by the cord. If the canoe be intended only for a temporary use, the clamps are left on. A preparation is then made of deer tallow and pounded charcoal, and used in the place of pitch to fill up the seams, and the boat is complete; but if time permit, and the canoe be wanted for ornament, as well as use, then the clamps are displaced by sewing together the ends of the bark. This simple process produces the most beautiful model of a boat that can be imagined; art cannot embellish the form, or improve upon the simple mechanism of the back woods. Every line in it is graceful, its sharp bows indeed seem almost designed to clear the air as well as water, so perfectly does it embrace every scientific requisite for overcoming the obstructions of the element in which it is destined to move. In these apparently frail machines, the red man, aided by a single paddle, will thread the quiet brook and deep running river, speed over the glassy lake like a swan, and shoot through the foaming rapids as sportively as the trout, and when the storm rages and throws the waves heavenward, and the lurid clouds seem filled with molten fire, you will see the Indian, like a spirit of the storm, at one time standing out in bold relief against the lightning-riven sky, and then disappearing in the watery gulf, rivalling the gull in the gracefulness of his movements, and rejoicing like the petrel in the confusion of the elements.

The articles used in savage life, like all the works of nature, are simple, and yet perfectly adapted to the purposes for which they are designed. The most ingenious and laborious workman, aided by the most perfect taste, cannot possibly form a vessel so general in its use, so excellent in its ends, as the calabash. The Indian finds it suspended in profusion in every glade of his forest home, spontaneous in its growth, and more effectually protected from destruction from animals, through a bitter taste, than by any artificial barrier whatever. So with all the rest of his appropriations from nature's hands. His mind scarcely ever makes an effort, and consequently seldom improves.

The simple buffalo skin, that forms a protection for the trifles of an Indian lover, when he would bear them safely across the swollen stream, compared with the gorgeous barge that conveyed Egypt's queen down the Nile to meet Antony, seems immeasurably inferior in skill and contrivance. Yet the galley of Cleopatra, with all its gay trappings, and its silken sails glittering in the sun, was as far inferior to a "ship of the line," as the Indian's rude bundle to the barge of Cleopatra. Imagination may go back to some early period, when the naked Phœnician sported upon a floating log; may mark his progress, as the inviting waters of the Mediterranean prompted him to more adventurous journeyings, and in time see him astonishing his little world, by fearlessly navigating about the bays, and coasting along the whole length of his native home. How many ages after this was it, that the invading fleets of classic Greece, proud fleets, indeed, in which the gods themselves were interested, were pulled ashore as now the fisherman secures his little skiff? Admire the proud battle ship, riding upon the waves, forming a safe home for thousands, now touching the clouds with its sky-reaching masts, and then descending safely into the deep.— With what power and majesty does it dash the intruding wave from its prow, and rush on in the very teeth of the winds! Admire it as the wonder of human skill, then go back through the long cycle of years, and see how many centuries have elapsed in thus perfecting it—then examine the most elaborate craft of our savage life, and the antiquity of their youth will be impressed upon you.

THE WAY AMERICANS GO DOWN HILL

"But who has not been both wearied and amused with the slow caution of the German drivers? At every little descent on the road, that it would almost require a spirit-level to discern that it is a descent, he dismounts, and puts on his drag. On a road of the gentlest undulations, where a heavy English coach would go at the rate of ten English miles an hour, without drag or pause, up hill or down, he is continually alighting and putting on one or both drags, alighting and ascending with a patience and perseverance that amazes you. Nay, in many states, this caution is evinced also by the government, and is forced on the driver, particularly in Bavaria, Wurtemberg and Austria, by a post by the way-side, standing at the top of every slope on the road, having painted on a board, a black and conspicuous drag, and announcing a fine, of commonly six florins (ten shillings) on any loaded carriage which shall descend without the drag on. In every thing they are continually guarding against those accidents which result from hurry, or slightness of construction."—*Howitt's Moral and Domestic Life in Germany.*

The stage in which we travelled across "the Alleganies," was one of the then called "Transit line." It was, as the driver termed it, a "rushing affair," and managed by a refined cruelty to dumb beasts, to keep a little ahead of the "Opposition," that seemed to come clattering in our rear, like some ill-timed spirit, never destined exactly to reach us. The drivers of our different "changes" all seemed to be made upon the go-ahead principle, and looked upon nothing as really disgraceful but being behind the stage that so perseveringly pursued us. Unfortunately, too, for our safety, we went in an "extra," and managed by a freak of fortune, to arrive at the different stations, when drivers and horses were changed just as the former had got comfortably to bed; and it was not the least interesting portion of my thoughts, that every one of these Jehus, made the most solemn protestations, that they would "upset us over some precipice, not less than three hundred and sixty-five feet high, and knock us into such a perfect nonentity, that it would save the coroner the trouble of calling a jury to sit upon our remains."

It is nine years since, and if the winter of that year is not set down as "remarkably cold" in the almanacs, it shows a want of care in those useful annuals. We say it was nine years since we crossed the Allegan-

215

ies. At the particular time we allude, the "oldest inhabitant" of the country, and we met him on the road side, informed us that he had no recollection of such a severe season. How we lived through it has puzzled us quite as much as it did Captain Ross, after he returned to England from his trip to the north pole. The fire in every house we passed smoked like a Pittsburg furnace, and around its genial warmth were crowded groups of men, women and children, that looked as if they might have been born in the workshop of Vulcan. The road over which we travelled, was McAdamized and then frozen; it was as hard as nature will permit, and the tramping of the horses' feet upon it, sounded in the frosty air as if they were rushing across a continuous bridge.

The inside of a stage coach is a wonder; it is a perfect denial to Newton's theory, that two things or twenty cannot occupy the same place at the same time. The one we travelled in was perfectly full of seats and their backs, straw, buffalo robes, hat boxes, rifles, flute cases, small parcels, and yet nine men, the very nine muses at times, (all the cider along the road was frozen and we drank the heart of it,) stowed themselves away within its bowels, but how, we leave to the inventor of exhausted air pumps and hydraulic presses. We all, of course, froze more or less, but it was in streaks: the curtains of the stage were fastened down, and made tight, and then like pigs we quarrelled ourselves into the snuggest possible position and place, it being considered fortunate to be most *in the middle*, as we then parted with the least heat, to satisfy the craving appetite of Jack frost, who penetrated every little hole and nook, and delighted himself in painting fantastic figures upon the different objects exposed to his influence, out of our misery and breath.

By one of those extraordinary phenomena exhibited in the climate of our favored country, we unexpectedly found ourselves travelling over a road that was covered with a frozen sleet; cold as was the season there was no snow, the horses' shoes had no corks on them worth noticing, and the iron bound wheels on this change in the surface of the earth, seemed to have so little hold upon the road, that we almost expected they would make an effort to leave it, and break our necks as a reward for their aspirations. On we went, however, and as night came on, the darkness enveloped us in a kind of cloud, the ice glazed surface of the ground reflecting a dull mysterious light upwards. Our whereabouts never troubled us, all places between the one we were anxious to reach and where we were, made no impression upon us, and perhaps we would never have known a single particular place, but for the incident we are about to detail.

I think that all my companions as well as myself were asleep, when I was awakened by that peculiar sawing motion a stage body makes upon its springs when suddenly stopped. "What's the matter now?" was the general exclamation of the "insides," to the driver, who was discovered through the glass window on the ground, beating his arms around his body with a vehemence that almost raised him into the air. "Matter," he exclaimed, sticking his nose above a woolen blanket that was tied around his face, which from the cold and his breath was frosted like a wedding cake, "Matter! matter enough, here we are on the top of 'Ball mountain,' the drag chain broken, and I am so infernal cold, I could not tie a knot in a rope if I had eighteen thousand hands."

It was a rueful situation truly. I jumped out of the stage, and contemplated the prospect near and at a distance with mixed feelings. So absorbed did I soon become, that I lost sight of the unpleasant situation in which we were placed, and regarded only the appearance of things about me disconnected with my personal happiness. There stood the stage upon the very apex of the mountain, the hot steaming breath of my half smothered travellers pouring out of its open door in puffs like the respirations of a mammoth. The driver, poor fellow, was limping about, more than half frozen, growling, swearing and threatening. The poor horses looked about twenty years older than when they started, their heads being whitened with the frost. They stamped with impatience on the "hard ribbed ice," the polished iron of their shoes looking as if it would penetrate their flesh with biting cold. But such a landscape of beauty, all shrouded in death, we never saw or conceived, and one like it is seldom presented to the eye. Down the mountain could be traced the broad road in serpentine windings, lessening in the distance until it appeared no wider than a foot path, obscured by the ravines and forest trees through which it ran. On either side were deep yawning chasms, at the bottom of which the hardy pines sprung upward a hundred and fifty feet, and yet they looked from where I stood like creeping plants. The very mountain tops spread out before me like pyramids. The moon shone upon this vast prospect, coming up from behind the distant horizon, bathing one elevation in light, and another in darkness, or reflecting her silvery rays across the frozen ground in sparkling gems, as if some eastern princess scattered diamonds upon a marble floor, then starting in bold relief the shaggy rock born hemlock and poison laurel, penetrating the deep solitudes,

217

and making "darkness visible" where all before had been deep obscurity. There too might be seen the heat driven from the earth in light fogs by the intense cold, floating upwards in fantastic forms, and spreading out in thin ether as they sought more elevated regions. As far in the distance in every direction as the eye could reach, were the valleys of Penn, all silent in the embrace of winter and night, calling up most vividly the emotions of the beautiful and the sublime.

"How are we to get down the outrageous hill, driver," bawled out a speculator in Western lands, that had amused us through the day passed, with nice calculations of how much he could have saved the government and himself, had he had the contract of making the "National road" over which we were travelling. The reply of the driver was exceedingly apt and characteristic.

"There is no difficulty in getting *down the hill*, but you well know there are a variety of ways in doing the same thing; the drag-chain would be of little use, as the wheel tire would make a runner of it. I think you had better all take your places inside, say your prayers, and let me put off, and if yonder grinning moon has a wish to see a race between a stage and four horses down 'Ball mountain,' she'll be gratified, and see sights that would make a locomotive blush."

The prospect was rather a doleful one; we had about ninety chances in a hundred that we would make a "smash of it," and we had the same number of chances of being frozen to death if we did not take the risk of being smashed, for the first tavern we could get to was at the foot of the mountain. The driver was a smart fellow, and had some hostage in the world worth living for, because he was but three days married—had he been six months we would not have trusted him. The vote was taken, and it was decided to "go ahead."

If I were to describe an unpleasant situation, I should say that it was to be in a stage, the door closed on you, with the probabilities that it will be opened by your head thrusting itself through its oak pannels, with the axle of the wheel at the same time falling across your breast. It seemed to me that I would be, with my companions, if I entered that stage, buried alive: so preferring to see the coming catastrophe, I mounted the driver's seat, with a degree of resolution that would have enabled me to walk under a falling house without winking.

At the crack of the whip, the horses impatient of delay, started with a bound, and ran on a short distance, the boot of the stage pointing to the earth; a sudden reverse of this position, and an inclination of our bodies forward, told too plainly that we were on the descent. Now commenced a race between gravitation and horseflesh, and odds would have been safely bet on the former. One time we swayed to and fro as if in a hammock; then we would travel a hundred yards sideways, the wheels on the ice sparkling with fire and electricity, and making a grating sound, as terrible to my nerves as the extracting of a tooth. The horses frightened at the terrible state of things in the rear, and the lashing of the whip, would pull us around for a moment, and away we would go again, sideways, bouncing, crashing about like mad. A quarter way down the mountain, and still perfectly sound; but by this time the momentum of our descending body was terrible, and the horses with reeking hot sides and distended nostrils, lay themselves down to their work, while the lashing whip cracked and goaded in the rear, to hasten their speed. The driver, with a coolness that never forsook him, guided his vehicle as much as possible in zig-zag lines across the road. Obstacles no larger than pebbles would project us into the air as if we had been an Indian rubber ball, and once as we fell into a rut, we escaped upsetting by a gentle tap from the stump of a cedar tree upon the hub of the wheel, that righted us with the swiftness of lightning. On we went, the blood starting in my chilled frame, diffusing over me a glowing heat, until I wiped huge drops of perspiration from my brow, and breathed in the cold air as if I were smothering. The dull stunning sound that now marked our progress was scarcely relieved by the clattering hoofs of the horses, and the motion became perfectly steady, except when a piece of ice would explode from under the wheel, as if burst with powder. Almost with the speed of thought we rushed on, and the critical moment of our safety came. The slightest obstacle, the stumbling of a horse, the breaking of a strap, a too strongly drawn breath almost, would have, with the speed we were making, projected us over the mountain side as if shot from a cannon, and buried us beneath the frozen ground and hard rocks beneath. The driver, with distended eyes and an expression of intellectual excitement, played his part well, and fortune favored us. As we made the last turn in the road the stage for an instant vibrated between safety and destruction—running for several yards upon one side, it exposed two wheels in the air, whirling with a swiftness that rendered them almost invisible. With a severe contusion it righted, the driver shouted, and we were rushing *up an ascent*. For a moment the stage and horses went on, and it was but for a moment; for the heavy body,

219

lately so full of life, settled back upon the traces a dead weight, dragging the poor animals in one confused heap downwards, until shaking violently upon its springs, it stood still.

"A pretty severe tug," said one of the insides to the driver as he stretched himself with a yawn. "Well, I rather think it was," said Jehu, with a smile of disdain.

"I've driv on this road fifteen years, but I never was so near ———— as to night. If I was on t'other side of 'Ball Mountain,' and my wife on this, (only three days married, recollect,) I would not drive that stage down 'Ball Mountain' as I have to-night to keep her from running away with a nigger!"

"Why, you don't think there was any real danger, do you?" inquired another "inside," thrusting his head into the cold air.

"I calculate I do; if the off fore leader, when I reached the 'devil's rut,' had fallen, as he intended, your body would now be as flat as either back seat cushion in that stage."

"Lord bless us, is it possible," sighed another "inside;" "but it is all very well, we have escaped, and one must run *a little risk* rather than to be delayed in a journey."

Appreciating the terrible ordeal through which I had passed better than my fellow travellers, I have often in my dreams, fancied myself on a stage coach, just tumbling down the ravines that yawn on the sides of "Ball Mountain;" and when I have started into wakefulness, I have speculated on that principle of the American character that is ever impelling it forward; but it never so forcibly struck me as a national peculiarity, until I read Howitt's journey down hill, among the sturdy Germans of the Old World.

THE LAST FROM "ARKANSAW"

Capt. Raft, of the steamer Hurricane, was one of those eccentric men that took a great deal of pleasure in running his boat where no one but himself would or could. In one of his eccentric humors, he run the Hurricane up Red River into Arkansas, as his pilot observed, about "a feet," which in the Southwest means several hundred miles. Among the patrons of the Hurricane was old Zeb Maiston, a regular out-and-outer frontiersman, who seemed to spend his whole life in settling out of the way places, and locating his family in sickly situations. Zeb was the first man that "blazed" a tree in Eagle Town, on the Mountain Fork, and he was the first man that ever choked an alligator to death with his hands, on the Big Cossitot. He knew every snag, sawyer, nook and corner of the Sabine, the Upper Red River, and their tributaries, and when "bar whar scace," he was wont to declare war on the Cumanches, for excitement, and "used them up terribly." But to our story. Zeb moved on Red River, settled in a low, swampy, terrible place, and he took it as a great honor that the Hurricane passed his cabin; and every trip the boat made there was tumbled out at Zeb's yard a barrel of new whiskey, (as regularly as she passed,) for which was paid the proper amount of cord wood. Now, Capt. Raft was a kind man, and felt disposed to oblige every resident that lived on his route of travel, but it was unprofitable to get every week to Zeb's out of the way place, and as he landed the fifteenth barrel, he expressed his surprise at the amount of whiskey consumed at his "settlement," and hinted it was rather an unprofitable business for the boat. Zeb, at this piece of information, "flared up," raised his mane, shut his "maulers," and told Capt. Raft he could whip him, the pilot, and deck hands, and if they would give him the "under grip," he would let the piston rod of the engine punch him in the side all the time the fight was going on. Raft, at this display of fury from Zeb, cooled down immediately, acknowledged himself "snagged," begged Zeb's pardon, and adjourned to the bar for a drink. One glass followed another, until the heroes got into the mellow mood, and Zeb on such occasions always "went in strong" for his family. After praising their beauty individually and collectively, he broke into the pathetic, and set the Captain crying, by the following heart-rending appeal:—"Raft, Raft, my dear fellow, you talk about the trouble of putting out a barrel of whiskey every week at my diggins, when I have got a sick wife, and five small children, and *no cow!*—whar's your heart?"

LETTERS
FROM
THE
FAR
WEST

Crow Indians; Philology; Difficulties of Traveling; Yellow Stone; Anecdotes; Scotch Fiddle; A Fight; Crow feet; False alarm; Resume our journey.

I take advantage of a "half-bried," who is about leaving for "the settlements," to send you a line, a thing you neglected in packing up my stores, that you may know how we are all getting on. The chances out here for literary pursuits are rather bad, and for a desk I am obliged to use Sir Wm. Stuart's best pistol case, giving it a sort of *slant* by resting one end on the skull of a late Buffalo bull, who, I am told by one of the old trappers that compose the vanguard of our party, killed three Sioux Indians before he was killed himself. I must acknowledge that this rude writing desk inspires me with a hunting ardor, and makes me sweat all over to be in the chase. Speaking of the chase, it is expected that the "Crow Indians," who are thus named, from the fact that they *eat green corn*, and make a noise like the fish-hawk, will give us a chase, which is said to be very unpleasant: so you perceive the chase has its dark sides as well as its bright ones.

We have had a great many difficulties so far: the "dry season" being a constantly rainy one, and the warm weather, instead of setting in, set out, and left us freezing to death, in the wrong time of the year. It is very unfortunate that the cold weather came on before we got our overcoats made; but we cannot get any cloth, until we skin some *varmints*. I shall introduce technical terms as much as possible, as it has great effect in such descriptions I intend to give. Sir William Stuart thinks if we had not started on our trip until next year, the *calves* would have been twelve months older, and, consequently, larger and more fit for game. I differed with him on the subject, but he said I was not hunter enough yet to know much about life on the frontiers. Our journey up the Yellow Stone was by water, but owing to the want of any water in the channel, we took it on foot, and left our boats at its mouth. This is a very beautiful stream, being composed, at this present writing, of sand-bars, interspersed with gullies and overhung with small trees, which trees, considering the time they have had to grow, are remarkably backward. The name "Yellow Stone," is a corruption of the Indian title "Yhalhoo Stunn," literally "the running water with green pebbles." I got this information from a trapper, who has resided several years above the Falls of St. Anthony, on the Upper Missouri.

I have a great deal of interesting matter, and many curious anecdotes to relate, two of which I will give here, and I would detail more, but I do not know whether this letter will ever reach you; if it don't, you will inform me the first opportunity. One night we were alarmed by a dreadful scuffle on the outside of the encampment: we all ran to see what was the matter, and found that one of the men, and one of Sir William Stuart's servants had got to quarreling; it seems that the difficulty rose from some remarks about a *Scotch fiddle*, which was in the possession of Sir William Stuart's servant; it would seem that "Scotch fiddle" is a term that has more meanings than one, but I did not enquire what they were.

"Mat Fields," as he is termed, is the "*sowl*" of the whole party: he has more anecdotes and drolleries than all the rest of the party besides. He says that Kendall, of the Picayune, got a white horse on the prairies in Mexico, eighteen hands high, and that he was mistaken in Vermont, where he is now visiting, for an old Naraganset pacer; but I don't believe it, as he is a quiz. "Mat" is a practical joker, but got it rather hard a few nights ago. It was unpleasant weather, and we sat around the camp-fire until late, telling stories. One of the hunters told a great many tales about Canibal Indians, particularly the "Black feet;" he said they were the most savage fellows in the world, and would roast a fellow, and devour him as quick as twenty-five hungry wolves would a buffalo. That night, about one hour before morning, "Mat" came into the encampment with eyes staring out of his head, walking like a robber on a theatrical stage; he said nothing at first, but got out his pistols, which he stuck in his belt, without loading; he, then, went and waked up Sir Wm. Stuart and Mr. Audibon, and whispered in their ears: Stuart said, "*hombog, mon*," and Audibon said, "there was no such a *bird* in a thousand miles." "Mat" insisted; we all got awake, an alarm was given, "*Black feet* in the camp;" we rushed to our rifles and followed "Mat." We shall never forget the laughter that followed. The "Black feet in the camp" turned out to be a nigger's who had stuck them under and outside the tent in which he was sleeping. "Mat" said it was all a joke, but I think not; however, we were all expecting that a fight would come off between us and the *varlets* (technical,) but there was no such fun. We whipped the nigger, though, for airing his shins in such a public way. Order was restored, and we found the sun up, and prepared for our day's journey.   P. O. F.

P. S. The Sioux Indians, which I said was killed by the buffalo, in the first part of my letter, should read, "three *Sioux Indian's dogs*."

[2]

Prospect of sport; Frontier Temperance Society; a real wild Indian; his natural eloquence and its power; meeting with Buffaloes; their peculiar behavior; my first hunt; head-work; a joke of misfortunes.

ABOVE THE YELLOW STONE, *June* 6, 1843.

In my last letter you could easily perceive that we were getting on the buffalo hunting grounds, in fact I thought for several days that I could hear the bulls bellowing in the night, but my companions told me it was only owing to my glowing imagination. The prospect of sport inspirited all of us, especially after the whiskey jug had been freely passed around, previous to the grand temperance society we shall form after we get out of liquor. We have had a great many savages with us one time and another, but most of them are more than half civilized, as they will get drunk and steal as quick as any white man I ever saw. Yesterday, however, we were blessed with the sight of a real wild chap, he came into the encampment looking like a corn field scare-crow, dressed up in a coat of feathers; a man with us from Arkansas, said it would improve his appearance very much in his estimation if the feathers had been stuck on with a coat of tar; Audubon said he put him in mind of a sick Pelican, in the moulting season. This Indian was a brave looking fellow, though, walked splendidly, evidently imitated Forrest the actor in Metamora, or a parrot, I don't know which. He was short thick set, and smelt strongly of rancid bear's oil, which he used as we do cologne; he is said to be the blackest Indian of his tribe; his name I learned, was Tar-pot-wan-ja, which means literally translated, *the tall white Crane*. I took to him naturally; there was something that pleased me in his eye, and the grateful expression of his face, as I gave him a drink out of my canteen; I asked him if he ever had been in war, at the question he started back, placed himself in a most elegant attitude, a perfect representation of a corpulent Apollo, then tracing the sun's course with his finger through the heavens, he turned his face full towards me, uttered a gutteral "ugh!" took a plug of tobacco out of my hand, stuck it in the folds of his blanket, and quietly walked out of the tent, to attend to the sale of some venison at a dime a hind quarter; I never saw a more noble, and beautiful exhibition of savage life. Yesterday was an era in our history, the first of our seeing Buffalo, which are now skirting along the horizon as if we were in a great farm yard of fine cattle. Its a mighty great idea that a fellow owns as many of these monsters as he can catch, though the latter is more difficult than you would at first imagine. I was determined to be at last, first, as I was always before behind in every thing, so I mounted my horse unbeknown to my companions and sallied out, pretty soon I got near the reptiles, and oh! thunder and turf, such looking beasts as they were, no more like decently behaved cattle than I am like a flat-head. There they were, bless their souls, looking at me through their sweet little eyes, and seeming as willing to tuck me up with their fine little horns, as if I had been a bundle of prairie grass. Buffalo indeed, they all looked like Aesop's donkey in the lion skin, they were so shaggy in front the villains, and so slick and smooth behind. My horse at first did not seem to mind them, but all of sudden he pricked up his ears; came to a stand still and snorted; as he did this, the buffaloes raised their elegant countenances, and stopped eating; the biggest ones sort of forming a half circle round me, and making obeisances by lowering their heads, and scraping their left fore feet in the ground. "Good manners to you," said I, taking off my hat, determined not to be out-done in politeness; as I did this, I thought I heard thunder; I just got a glimpse of some confused thing in a big dust, and here and there, a swab sticking in the air, that I now believe to be buffalo tails. My horse, all this time, was not idle; he took to his heels, started off, first spilling my gun, then my hat, bad luck to it, then me, and afterwards my saddle; I came to the ground under the impression I had been struck with lightning, but recovering myself I found that the top of my head had just come exactly on top of a buffalo skull, cracking it into three halves, and driving them into the ground. If you had seen me the next day, you would have thought I had painted myself in imitation of the savages; my face, particularly round my eyes, was of so many colors. It may be set down as a fact in natural history, that human heads are not generally as hard as a buffalo's. I gathered up my gun, hat and saddle, and walked towards the encampment. "Did you catch a buffalo bull," said one to me, as I presented myself, half dead with the fall, and the foot travel. "It was an Irish bull he was after," said Mat Field. "Out upon you, you unfeeling blackguard of a wit," said I, getting good humored in a minute. "It's Mat, is it, that cracks his wit, on my cracked head?" but I'll forgive him, hoping he may run his own against a live bull, that 'ill pay him for all his sins, bless his soul. Thus ended my first hunt, and as I shall go properly prepared to-morrow, I trust you will hear that I have done myself honor in bringing down as big a critter, as ever run over these big grass plots, called "prairies." P. O. F.

P. S.—I am happy to say, as this letter did not go on the day I sealed it up, that I have had a fair view of the far-famed *one horned* buffalo, that has kept undisturbed possession of this country and has never yet been killed. He is known from the mouth of the Yellow Stone to the tributaries of the Columbia, as the "one horned buffalo of the prairies." I shall take great pains to learn all the anecdotes respecting him, particularly how he lost his duplicate horn. Sir William Stuart has put us all under "martial law," and some of the "young uns" make wry faces at it; but he is an old campaigner, and I think knows as much about the ways of this heathen world, as any one about here. So I sing "Scots wa ha," and go ahead.

[3]

ABOVE THE YELLOW STONE, June 16, 1843.

Indian philosophy; start for another buffalo hunt; success; miraculous escape; troubles of frontier life; prophecy; a new bird; curiosities, &c.

In my last I gave you an account of a fall from my horse, and the ornamental effect it had about my eyes. As an Indian's face is the color of a smoked copper kettle, you may hit them in the face, or run their skulls against a post, and you don't see any black eyes as a consequence; but with me, it was different. The only person that I saw when I started on my hunt, was Tar-pot-wan-ja's squaw, and she met me soon after I returned after the accident. Her curiosity was very much excited to know how I had painted my eyes in such beautiful colors, and she took it for granted I was imitating her ugly looking husband. Not content with mere looking, she insisted upon rubbing her fingers across the colors, and when she found them under the skin, she looked upon the whole matter as the effect of the "medicine man" who is of our party. She told her husband that my eyes resembled "bright shells, surrounded by rainbows." The indian language is so figurative and beautiful, that I cannot resist the temptation of giving in full, their expressions whenever I hear them. As soon as I was able, I took advantage of the first hunting party which left our encampment, determined to redeem my lost reputation as a hunter, and distinguish myself, so as to put down some of my companions, who were continually crowing over me because they had killed buffalo. I mounted one of the baggage horses, that was said to understand his business, armed with two horse pistols, and decked out with a pair of old spanish spurs, of the same size as those worn by Mat. Field, though his are new, and of polished steel, and when he is dashing about in the sun, on his "mustang," you would think he had fire works tied on his heels; they are so beautiful. We only rode a few miles before we came in sight of a drove of the curly pated varments, a few hasty orders were given, the party separated with a "whoop" and dashed off, I after them. My horse got within about two hundred yards of the animals, and in spite of my spurs, took the back track, and never again came within a quarter of a mile of them. From this awkward situation, I was relieved accidentally by Audubon himself, who came up with me on his return to camp, having found a rare bird, and wishing immediately to preserve it, so we exchanged horses; and now mounted on a regular "hunter," I felt as proud as any beggar on horseback ever did. Off I went like a streak—the rattling of my spurs seem to alarm my steed, but when I stuck them in his flank, he seemed furious; it was only a few minutes before I was amongst a crowd of animals, who running and crowding together, striking their horns and snorting, made most dreadful noise. I might have been within a few feet of a fine bull, when I found that it was all I could do to keep my horse from running him down, and I could not get an opportunity to draw my pistols; in this situation I went a mile or two, and concluded *to quit*, when, to my astonishment, I discovered my horse was more willing to hunt than the others I had mounted were unwilling, and I expected very shortly not only to be between *the horns* of a dilemma, but to have both of them run into me. Another thing astonished me, my horse, who had every thing his own way, finally succeeded in separating the object of his special pursuit from the herd, and off we went together on a bit of a private hunt, sure enough; how long we run, I don't know; when, horrible to relate, the big monster, with his tail stuck up in the air, and his tongue hanging down on the ground, came to a stand-still, and so did my horse, but I did not; over I went on his neck, and would have next descended to the ground, had he not started forward to avoid a charge from the buffalo, that brought me way behind the crupper of the saddle. I rolled down the highest hill of Ireland, "Old Howth," but that was smooth riding, to bouncing about over a saddle, especially a Spanish one, that had a high goose-neck looking pommel that did dig into me awful. "Here is fun to travel after three thousand miles," thought I to myself, beginning to say my prayers, for, somehow, the bull's horns seemed to be growing larger and sharper every minute, and I had all kinds of queer feelings that were caused by the drafts of cold air, I thought would soon circulate through my body. Pop, pop, said a pistol, and over I went on the ground with a force that made the contact with the skull mere imagination. "Oh murther, murther!" I hollered; "killed with hard riding, and shot to death with a pistol." "Oot o' the wa' mon, or ye'l git an Irish hist," sang out Sir William Stuart, and I opened my eyes and saw the wounded bull, gathering himself up to charge at me, he having been shot twice in the side; before I could get out of the way, he made a dash; his horns struck about two inches from me, and he threw a complete somerset over my body, striking the earth with a force that made every thing shake again. This was considered the most miraculous escape ever known in the hunting grounds, the bull made no further efforts to make fight, but died off like a kitten.

It is a beautiful time I have of it, getting information for the Intelligencer. Here I was surrounded by about twenty hunters, all grinning at me like so many hyena's, and all congratulating me on my good fortune. All I have got to say is, that horses on the prairie are the worst broke animals I ever saw, except the buffalo bulls, the varmints.

I got home that night, and slept, by sitting up, and nursing my poor body, that was more broken up than a whiskey jug, under a load of brick. This frontier life, ain't what it is cracked up to be, and a great many persons in Sir William's party *will say so when they get home.*

P. S.—The new bird that Audubon caught, he has named the "Oxydendiaonicumtionsurtimonium," that being the classical name, he says, for a poor little feathered creature no bigger than the end of your thumb. Besides, I have got some prairie grass in my port-folio, and so has my horse in his, and they are both fatter for it. My next letter will be principally on scientific subjects, and a particular account of the first scientific society ever formed in this wild country.

[4]

ABOVE THE YELLOW STONE, June 29, 1843.

Face of the country; death of a buffalo; singular incidents in the history of a dead buffalo; the manner of an Indian's death; anecdotes; the best joke of the expedition.

Two buffalo hunts I have detailed, in which I was engaged, and both were very little to my notion—the first one having been a hunt too little, and the second one being a hunt too much. I have now a horse in training which is so gentle that I am certain will permit me to have my own way, and that I shall soon be able to write you something successful in which I was engaged. The country in which we are at present traveling, is one of the most extraordinary in the world, being decidedly the poorest, and yet producing the most. It is composed of broken land, high clay bluffs, that wash into all kinds of fantastic shapes, and look in the distance like old ruined Irish castles, and small parcels of prairie. The River Missouri about here, runs as fierce as a scared horse, tumbling about as if old Nick himself was underneath it, rollicking it about, and leaving it no more peace than a poor tenant has, that is in debt to a mean lanlord's deputy agent. Here it is that the buffaloes try to swim across the river, and get tripped up before they do it; in this way hundreds meet with a watery grave, being thrown high and dry on shore dead as hammers. It is a melancholy thing, to be sure, to see the big varment on its back, as helpless as a chicken in the yolk, just insulted by every wolf and buzzard that chooses to stick their ill–looking bills into its side. Only a few days since a gigantic bull that had struggled across the river like a big saw-mill, but so fatigued that he could scarcely crawl, just managed to get up the bank of the river, about ten feet high, where he lay down regardless of my presence, and with an eye as peaceably disposed as a fawn's, just breathed his last as quietly as a christain. In less than ten minutes, down wheeled a buzzard rattling about his ribs, with his beak and making a sound not unlike a bass drum. I moved a short distance off, when a couple of wolves pitched in, and tugged away at the animal's tongue. While watching these vultures, the body of the buffalo being almost poised on the edge of the bank, turned over, and rolled down hill—the wolves held on, and so did the buzzard. At first I thought the beast had been playing "possum," and had just laid down to make a *trap* of himself, but he was dead. I walked up to the carcass and found that both wolves had had a strong grip on the tongue, and as the body fell head first, and the wolves held on in the descent, the short horns of the buffalo were driven exactly through the wolves' backs, pinning them to the earth, and in their agony and fury, they got their heads together, and before they died, bit out each other's eyes, and nearly scalped themselves. The first turn over the bull made crushed the buzzard so flat between himself and the earth, that a gentle breeze blew his remains away, as if they had been an old mourning scarf, tipped on one end with a red ribbon.

I mentioned these singular circumstances when I got "to camp," and it called forth from an old hunter the following incident connected with the death of Tarpot-wan-ja's brother. He and his brother were out hunting buffaloes with the usual Indian weapon, the arrow; they both were pursuing the same animal—Tarpot-wan-ja shot an arrow, and by some bad management of his horse, hit the buffalo in the head, just between the horns: the pain to the animal was so exquisite for the moment, that, though under headway, it raised its hind foot instantaneously to the wounded spot, caught the fetlock in its horns and rolled over on the ground like a ball—the same instant Tarpot's brother shot the animal through the heart, and he lay on the ground dead. The brothers went on and killed several buffaloes; on their return they stopped at the body of the one we have particularly alluded to, to take out its hump and marrow bones, when, to their astonishment, they found the hind leg of the animal still behind the animal's horns. Tarpot seized hold of the animal's head to unloose the hoof, just as his brother stooped to take hold of the tail, the movement of the head unloosed the leg, it flew back, striking Tarpot's brother on top of his shaved head, impressed the cloven hoof in his skull, driving his scalp-lock out of his mouth, and killed him instantly. Since that time, from the peculiarity of the Indian notion of vengeance, he is constantly killing buffaloes to avenge his brother's death. From these anecdotes of the terrible destructiveness of the animal, when dead, you can form some idea of their power while living. This story was told me by a chap who has acquired among the Indians the names of Ahn-ahn-ni-as, or "the teller of truth," so I believe it. When Mat Field heard it, he put his thumb to his nose and shook his fingers at Sir William, who laughed heartily; they have already between them picked up many Indian signs which are not yet familiar to me. I will conclude this letter of anecdotes by saying that the scientific meeting did not come off, but will in due time. Audubon made a fine pun to-day, that pleased Sir William so much, that he treated all round with some choice "mountain dew," much to the great comfort of all of us. We were talking about buffaloes and their habits, particularly their fondness for water, in which they seem to live when near, when Audubon said that it had just struck him how the animal got its name, buf-fa-lo from the French "boeuf a l'eau." This was decidedly the best joke, so far, of the expedition—so I think, except the idea of coming *out here for sport.* P. O. F.

P. S.—The trouble of the Texans, and the Americans, and the Spaniards, relative to the Sante Fe expedition, has roused up the Indians, who, not understanding the difference among white men, are apt to treat all alike, and for fear we may be taken for Spaniards, whom the Texans have advised to destroy, we sleep with our eyes open, and in our own arms—that is the order of Sir William Stuart.

[5]

Above the Yellow Stone, Aug. 1, 1843.

Difficulties of communication; Singular rocks; Audubon's remarks thereat; my own; Singular chase; Dilemma; Escape; Burial of a horse; Perils of Far West sport.

The Post-office Department, in this heathen region, is very much neglected—the *runner* that will bring you this lettar, is so lame, that he will have to walk all the way. This tumbling over the prairies is a very flat piece of business, and a little diversity in the scenery was a great comfort to me. A few days since, the land became broken, and I determined to enjoy the novelty; I clambered up some queer looking rocks, and while thus seated, it slid off, and I rolled down about twenty feet into a sink hole. I scrambled out, when Audubon came along, and examining the rock carefully awhile, turned round to me and said, "these rocks are what a mineralogist would call a vertical dike of trap!" "They are that same," said I, "bad luck to their traps, and the dirty dikes at the bottom of them." "You are not afraid of bulls," said Audubon, laughing. "Bulls, indeed," said I, "is it the varments that must be continally pitched into my teeth, because I aint killed any." I was a little angry, and put off, determined to take the life of the first bull I met with, killed as I was with the sport of hunting them. An opportunity soon occurred; a night or two only passed when Tar-pot-wan-ja reported that buffaloes were in every direction round our camp; every one prepared himself for the morning hunt, and I among the number. Armed with great determination, and a good rifle, I thought I could not fail to do something; beside, I had at last got a good horse, one that had an eye like a fawn, and kept his ears and tail down, and would not budge if a buffalo gnat stung him in the nose. As was my custom, I avoided the hunting party, and went off by myself. I soon came up with the animals, and was very much surprised to find that while I was looking out for a big bull, a big bull was in my rear, looking out for me. Afraid he would begin the hunt, instead of myself, I gave a yell as much like an Indian as possible, and he turned on his heels, gave a fierce bellow, and started off with the herd. For a quarter of a mile, the run was beautiful, the prairies were covered with about two inches of water, and it made the animals in motion look like a mist, the water flew about so; on they went and I after them, until I was brought up short and immovable as if astride a log, by bogging down to my saddle girth in a swamp hole. The harder I thumped the beast, the more he stood still, and just went to eating the grass as quietly as if he was hoppled for the night. The morning was cold, and the fallen rain filled the air with mist, that blew over the prairies in scudding clouds, as the sun continued to rise. Here and there I could catch a glimpse of buffaloes on the edge of the horizon, and could sometimes see the horsemen dashing after them with a speed that seemed inconceivable, when I considered the situation of the horse I rode. About two hundred yards was the nearest point of hard land, and while contemplating what I should do, I was brought to a sudden resolution, by seeing approaching towards me the whole herd of buffaloes, presenting a front something like the inside of a half circle. My horse, alarmed, made a furious effort to extricate himself, turned over on his side, and me into the mire. I crawled out as a fly would from treakle, and made a push for the camp. The buffaloes, impelled on by the frightened, and pursued in the rear, were approaching me at a right angle with the direction I was running; it was a life matter entirely, and I just got beyond the extreme right of the wing, as it passed within twenty yards of me, clattering like a drunken hurricane. Confounded with my situation, the horrors of it was increased by the phenomenon, of what I thought to be the one horned buffalo, coming directly towards me, thus cutting off all chance of escape. Shutting up my eyes, I lay down, said my prayers, and determined to die like a man; a moment or two only

233

elapsed, before I was roughly stirred up by what I supposed to be a buffaloe's horn, but it turned out to be the muzzle of Sir William Stewart's gun, just thrust into my ribs to see if I was dead. "A gude mornin' to you, mon," said he, calling up Mat Field to poke his fun at me. "And you are not the one horned buffalo after all," said I, opening my eyes and breathing more freely. "Not a bit of it," said Mat, handing me Sir William's flask. "There *run one horn* into your own body, and commit suicide," he continued, like an angel, as he was; for the "Mountain dew;" had a very excellent effect on the prairie dew I had swallowed, I tell you. "I shall die between the jokes and St. Louis," said I to Sir William. "Pace to your sowl," said he, turning up the flask, but finding it empty, he finished his blessing with, "and purgatory to your bowels, you sponge." The buffalo in the mean time, had got nearly out of sight, and I observed, with consternation, that my horse had gone off with them. "Where did you leave him," cried several. I pointed in the direction, and we all started for the spot. Thunder and turf what did I see, the bog hole dry, and hollowed out like a bowl, at the bottom of which lay the *skin of my horse cut up into strips*. "Is that the burial that I would have got from the varments, if they had run over me?" said I, musing over the corpse. "The same," said every body. "Oh murther!" I exclaimed, "the idea of being killed and having nothing left of your body, but your coat and pantaloons!"   P. O. F.

P. S.—The necessity of sleeping in our arms has been removed, by the removing of the hostile Indians. We can now sleep in perfect peace, if the mosquitoes and gallinippers would not be continually eating us. This is a delightful country indeed, and if it was only situated somewhere nearer to a Christian land, would soon be filled up with decent people, like Tennessee, Kentucky, and other frontier States.

[6]

ABOVE THE YELLOW STONE, Aug. 17, 1843.

Far West comforts; Indian names; Discovery of a strange animal, with a description, &c.; Yankee enterprise; Flat heads and curiosities.

The last few days we have been traveling on what is known out here, as the "Kiln dried Forks," which are at this season of the year about three inches under water, much to our discomfort. Our party, however, has been enjoying itself very much; and I think, situated as we are, that we might *go farther and fare worse*, as I am informed that the whole country a few miles ahead, is entirely under water. The other night we sat out all night in the rain, as our baggage took the wrong fork, which is a greater mistake in the prairies, than taking the wrong tooth brush at a hotel. It would have done you good to see us enjoying ourselves out here, sitting Indian fashion, in a ring, soaked through, and smoking all over, like rotten straw stirred up in a cold morning. Sir William was terrible cross, particularly when the water gathered into small channels on his coon skin cap, and run off of his prominent nose in their course to the ground. Tar-pot-wan-ja, who is like all aborigines, very expressive in his names, calls Sir William, from this peculiarity of face, "*Ah-gno-knoose*," and by this cognoman he is known for the distance of "six moon's" travel. We have had in our possession now three days, a very strange animal, and as *I never saw one like it* before, I conclude it is a new discovery, and one that will add immortality to my name. It is curious every way, and has created great excitement among the scientific gentlemen attached to the party. Audubon says it is decidedly the greatest *bird* he ever saw, and he has been drawing it off with a chord, ever since it has been with us; he has proposed several times to *kill it*, so that it might be preserved. He describes it as follows, on a paper handed to me to copy. *Characteristics—Brownish above, feet and all beneath white; ears, large; tail, hairy, and longer than its body.* Description—*Head, rather large, with pointed muzzle*—this last means they pointed a muzzle of a rifle at it, when it gave up, for fear of being brought down; *rounded above, and membranious*; can't say that I see any of these peculiarities about it. *Whiskers, numerous*, exactly to the original—as numerous whiskers as you would see on Count D'Orsay, or any other fop. *Fore feet, four toed*; right, of course—the four toes must be on the fore feet, *with five tubercles*, like the membranious beyond my comprehension. The *thumb is rudimentary*—what in the name of turf does that mean? *Tail, hairy and slender*, as much like it as two peas, *and subquadrate*, out of my depth again—*Molars tubuculated*. There is a description of the monster, and it looks quite a heathen and outlandish on paper, as it does on land, the varment. This critter affords us a great deal of amusement, as it frightened one of the horses after we first got it, so badly, that he came near throwing his rider and breaking his neck. This animal jumps by the means of its tail, and Mat Field says, will jump lower than he will higher, owing to his peculiar formation. To give you some idea of its agility, I need only to say that it, at one bound, cleared a pack of twenty-eight buffaloes, without touching them, and might have done better, if occasion required it. About two months ago some Yankee speculators passed us, on their way to Missouri, with twenty young buffaloes; they told us that they intended to show them off in the northern states, and that was the reason they only got *calves*, as they would meet with more sympathy in that part of the country. The owner of these animals were very much alarmed at the way Tar-pot-wan-ja looked at the fattest one; but kept on with his amusement of throwing a loop in a long bed-cord, over a tent pin; and I have heard that he intended to *laso* buffaloes in the States. The speculation is a good one; out here he could not laso a dead buffalo, if he was full grown. While we were at our last rendez-vous, a party of strange Indians came into our camp, and exhibited some valuable gold and diamond trinkets, which, from their workmanship, were pronounced Spanish, and thought to have been lost by, or stolen from some rich Sante Fe trader. The Indians offered to exchange them for jack knives, which, from their ugly appearance, I thought they deserved. A bargain was soon made, and they marched off highly gratified, paying about fifteen hundred dollars for a few dimes' worth of knives. This strange conduct induced me to ask which tribe these Indians belonged to, when I was informed to the "Flat Head" tribe. Certainly they richly deserve the name, as the anecdote will show. I ought to mention that my cabinet of natural curiosities are daily increasing, and in spite of accidents continually occurring, I shall bring home with me some rare things. I have got a real Indian tomahawk, that has been much used, as its appearance indicates. The history of this weapon is singular, as it once belonged to an old hunter by the name of "Collins," who seems to have originally come from "Hartford, Ct.," as he has cut his name on the side. I also had a very fine "buffalo chip," which I had taken great care of, but having got my coat wet, it has injured it very much, and I shall have to look around for another specimen. In my next text I shall have passed above the Yellow forks, and get into a more interesting country, which will be a great relief to me—the great fault of the Far West being, that there is too much of it.   P. O. F.

P. S.—I should have said that the strange animal jumped, at one bound, over a "pack of twenty-eight buffalo skins"—the meat having been taken out of them some time previous.

[7]

ABOVE THE HEAD OF PLATTE, Aug. 21, 1843.

Interesting situation; Our appearance; Danger from the backwoods; Dresses; Singular appearance; Anecdotes; Reflections.

It is an elegant way of living we have in this far west. Here is Sir William, as rich as a Santa Fe nabob, traveling about, talking Indian, and looking like Robinson Crusoe; and here is myself, bad luck to my enterprise, out here too, dressed up in clothes made of skins, and looking like a scare-crow out of a corn-field. "It's sport we have," said Mat Field, with a big twine round his front tooth, trying to pull it out. "It's hu-wah-me-kas-haw," says Tar-pot-wan-ja, the villain, looking as comfortable as a setting hen. "It's all kind of scrapes that I am getting into continually," thought I, as I reflected on the elegant adventure of which I was the hero. You see it had rained some four weeks steadily, and my raw deer skin clothes, hair outside, were as loose and comfortable as an Ottomans. Six times since I wore them, have I been near being shot for an Elk, which makes my situation very pleasant indeed; but to the adventure. I was out on a hunting expedition, which took me a full days' journey from the camp, and was detained over night— sleeping on the ground in about two inches of water. In the morning I started for home, and to my great relief, the sun came out hot, and magnificent; if you could just have seen me traveling across the prairie, and drying slowly, and sending up steam like a locomotive. I ate dinner that day with great relish—the sun so inspired my appetite, and I indulged myself for the first time in some of Tar-pot-wan-ja's dishes, who was with me. It might have been three o'clock in the evening, when I felt a singular rush of blood to my head, a want of breath, and other unpleasant signs; presently my clothes seemed to grow *too small*, and kept tightening in an alarming manner. "How do people feel that are poisoned?" said I to Audubon. "Like a stuffed bird's skin," said he. "Then," said I, growing pale, "my mother's son will leave his bones among heathen." He enquired, with interest, what I ate for dinner, I told him some Indian dish; he rolled up his eyes with astonishment, and bid me hurry to the camp. I pushed on, all my alarming symptoms increasing with violence, until it seemed as if my legs and my head would burst. When I got to the camp, I was so stiff I had to be lifted off my horse, and laid upon my back. A consultation was held within sight, but not in hearing, in which Tar-pot-wan-ja, pulling out a sharp knife, and shaking it at me, took a very active part. My feelings were indescribable. How I had offended the Red man, I could not imagine, for it was now evident he had poisoned me, and wished to finish the job, by cutting my throat. Not a soul pitied me, but looked upon the whole affair as a pleasant joke. *"Soak it out of him,"* said Sir William finally; and to my horror, Tar-pot-wan-ja my enemy, and another Indian, took me up and laid me in a neighboring stream, just leaving my head out of the water. "They are all savages thought I," closing my eyes, and when I opened them the Indians were gone. "Is this the way to treat a sick man, pitch him into the river to die like a dog, for fear of a little trouble?" "Soak it out of him," indeed; its the breath they alluded to! Such were my thoughts, when, to my astonishment, I began to feel relieved—the blood seemed to leave my head, and limbs, and I began to have some power of locomotion—less than half an hour elapsed before I got up and walked as well as usual. I went to the camp, wet as I was, burning with vengeance; as I approached it, a general shout of laughter saluted me. "Oh you unchristian bastes that you are," said I, shaking my fist at the whole of them, "is it for you to leave a sick friend to die, you savages; but I've got well, and can whip the whole of ye." *"Not if you'r deer skin clothes dry up in the sun until you can't move,"* said somebody, when the truth flashed upon me, that Tar-pot-wan-ja wished to cut me out of them, instead of out of my breath, and not "soak me out," as proposed by Sir William. My feelings altered at once, and I joined in the laugh; it only being one of those pleasant jokes peculiar to the *sport* of this part of the world. I find upon inquiry into accidents resulting from a precipitate use of deer skin clothing, that the most dreadful things have happened. An old hunter informed me that a whole party of white men, who were thus dressed, were caught by a sudden coming out of a hot sun, while eating their dinner; they were rendered helpless, before they were conscious of the reason, and sat staring at each other, with a buffalo steak in each hand, until they starved to death, their clothes not permitting them to move; and what made it more awful, after they were dead, damp weather came on—they melted down on the ground, and remained prostrate until the next sun shine—they then, as their skin clothing contracted by the heat, came up right again, in all imaginable positions, exhibiting one of the most melancholy spectacles that ever greeted the eye of humanity. The escape I made was miraculous indeed, for which I cannot be too thankful. And here, permit me to say one word, as I feel in a moral mood about the fitness of nature, the

238

buffaloes it seems, from the inquiries I have made, are dressed in raw skins, as I was—hair outside—they are fond of water, and also fond of the sunshine. To avoid the fatal accidents that overtake the human species, they are provided over the shoulder with a *large hump*, containing nothing but fat. When indulging in the sun, this fat melts, runs over the skin, and keeps the water from penetrating the pores, so as to make the texture, when drying, susceptible to the sun's rays. Taking advantage of this beautiful law, I grease my clothes every morning with buffalo grease; and although they smell exceedingly rancid, and compel me to associate entirely with Tar-pot-wan-ja, still I had rather do this, than endanger my life, as I have already done.   P. O. F.

P. S.—The wild turkies of last year, were all killed by the rains, so that this season there are none to be met with; all sorts of game are very scarce. I bear up under my misfortunes, like a man, as I frequently hear the remark, I am *such game*.

[8]

ABOVE THE FORKS OF LAPLATTE, Sept. 3, 1843.

An encampment; sudden attack; its consequences; Far West dinner; Toasts, &c.; Storm; First trip in a canoe; Prospects.

After the incident detailed in my last letter, relative to the danger of precipitately wearing deer skin clothing, our party traveled several days across the country, faring badly. We had little or nothing to eat or drink, our mules were fagged out, and it was determined that when we arrived at a convenient halting place, that we would rest for some days. Coming to the banks of a running stream, which were about ten feet high, it was thought a favorable location for an encampment, and in a few hours we were fixed in a manner perfectly agreeable. We made out tents by driving long poles into the banks, and resting them on forked sticks, then covering this frame with buffalo skins. About midnight of the second day, we were aroused by a whoop and a volley of shot and arrows—the balls did no damage—but the arrows, as they came sticking half way through the skins, looked rather frightful. Sir William rushed out, and gave the enemy a broadside in Scotch; they retreated a few paces, and talked back in Indian. A parley ensued, when it was discovered that a roving party of Kansas had mistaken our tents for those of their enemies—the Crow Feet—as this latter tribe are called "Prairie Dogs," because they lie in the side hills. The mistake was very natural, but as the party was small, and as some one observed only Indians, they were severely thrashed, to learn them better in future. The Indians were very submissive and seemed sorry for what they had done—the night following this adventure, we lost three horses, a chain, and a pistol; no doubt that is the way they took satisfaction for the injuries they received from us.

It is needless for me to say that our party was pretty sick of the Far West *sport*. Audubon had already packed up to return to the civilized haunts of mankind; we knew this from the fact that every thing was secured with lock and key that could be, to keep them from being stolen—a precaution generally unnecessary in savage life. Taking advantage of our resting-place we resolved upon having a good dinner, and perhaps the dishes may not be uninteresting to your readers. We had the breast of the wild turkey boiled as dry as a chip, which we used as bread; buffalo marrow for butter; bar ribs for pork; and prairie grouse christened chicken. To give the thing more the air of civilization, we all sat up bold, and in unnatural positions, and to make it still more "white folks fashion," we did not grease our faces in eating above our nose, and only used one hand when it was possible. Toasts were drank—one or two which I have preserved. By ———, "*The Far West—great country—like small pox, it need only be gone* through once to *answer every useful purpose*"—drank in silence. By ———, "Our sport out here—*like interesting Indians*—all in my eye," also in silence. By an old hunter, "The great diggins between Yellow Stone and the mouth of the Columbia—*the only field* on which a smart white man can display his abilities." Great applause from Tar-pot-wan-ja. By myself, "The Indian hunting grounds—like the Indians themselves, more interesting in ladies' books, than any where else"—three brays from one of the waggon mules. By Sir William, "Oot here, as much ahead of fiction as a sterling pound is worth more than a Scotch." Old Lang Syne, whistled by the party. By Tar-pot-wan-ja,—"Hoke-poke-hum-bug-ocken-wocken-khantkumit ex sho," which literally translated means, "white man worth nothing after the whiskey is gone." The night following the dinner was exceedingly pleasant, until about midnight, when the wind rose and from a severe blow turned into a hurricane; for a while it passed over us, the bank of the stream keeping it off; but after a while it chopped round, and blew directly down the river—the rain also fell and put out our fires. The stream by which we were encamped, called by the Indians, "Shallahrille," from its great depth, rose rapidly; and lastly, to complete our difficulty, our tents blew over, our waggons were knocked down, our arms upset, sending the charge of two barrels of buck shot among us by exploding the caps. The morning dawned, and presented the worst looking set of fellows that ever appeared in these parts, and that is saying a great deal, when you reflect that the Indians live out here. After hunting about we found that we had saved most of our property, as nothing had floated off but a copper kettle and a box containing some old horse shoes, and a broken wagon tire. Sir William was anxious to obtain them, and commissioned Tar-pot-wan-ja and myself to take canoes and go after them.

To do any thing was a relief, so following the example of the Indian, I jumped into a canoe, took my seat in its bottom, and one stroke of my paddle sent me into the middle of the stream; the next instant I was balancing from side to side with a rapidity of motion that upset my stomach, and would have upset me had I not fallen into the bottom of the canoe. My gyrations afforded the spectators more amusement than it did me, and as I floated off they wished me a pleasant trip. I started up to reply, when I found to my horror that the least motion on my part destroyed the equilibrium of the canoe, and gave it a turn over motion truly alarming—in fact I had to keep my paddle perfectly erect like a mast, for fear it would tumble me over, and as I concluded I should be downed I thought it was a *jury mast* erected over my remains. Down the stream I went, my feet close together, hardly daring to wink, when an eddy drew in my frail bark—it was a bark canoe—into a sort of bay, striking it against a log and turning me into the water as if I had been so much lead. I rose to the surface and snorted like a porpoise, seized hold of the tree, and flattered myself with the hope that I was born to be hung. A little reflection on my part and exertion got me safe ashore, and found myself about half a mile below where we had encamped, and on the opposite side of the stream. I walked back and found Tar-pot-wan-ja had already returned; with great difficulty I got across the stream nearly drowned, and a good deal sick, concluding I was the most unfortunate man of the party. After a days hard work, we got things together, and took a trail leading towards the "cross timbers," where, it is said, if the Blackfeet Indians are not in possession of them, and the wild turkies don't taste too strong of turpentine, living on pine burrs, we shall have some rest and enjoyment.

P. O. F.

241

P. S.—It is possible Audubon may reach St. Louis before this letter reaches you; he is a great man, and one of the few white ones that ever made traveling in this part of the world advantageous to himself and his country.

[9]

ABOVE THE PLATTE, Sept. 23, 1843.

Hard traveling; significant sounds; novel ride; bear chase; bad fix; good shot; exciting sport; something new.

The morning after the storms detailed in my last letter, we were proceeding slowly down the "Shallahrill," amusing ourselves with catching terrapins, a few which were to be seen, and for which, as food, Sir William is passionately fond; when we most unexpectedly found ourselves in a soft, boggy soil, that gave way under our feet, and rendered our progress slow and painful. Here and there, were small clumps of stunted oak, and thick undergrowth, that seemed to spring up on the little ridges that presented themselves in this swampy land. About noon we halted at one of these little groves; clearing and cutting away a place sufficiently large for our use; we sat down and talked over the various adventures of the expedition, with such other associations as were called up. While thus pleasantly engaged, we heard a low whine, that altered finally into an immense yawn, that gave me an idea of the largest mouth I had ever conceived of; presently the mouth came together—the teeth rattling most ominously as they met. The old hunters sprang instinctively for their rifles, and in a moment afterwards the ball of one sped its lightning way into the thicket—the sharp ringing sound was answered by a fierce growl, and a huge bear rushed passed us. Unfortunately I was directly in his course, and stooping down at the time, to see if I could discover any thing between the openings in the undergrowth, the bear, blinded with rage, he rushed between my legs, and carried me backwards some ten paces or more, when I fell off, and rolling down a steep bank, planted myself immovably in the mud—the bear kept down the edge of the ravine. The members of our party, as they pursued him—Tar-pot-wan-ja among the number, hooting and yelling—were soon almost out of hearing, and I undertook to extricate myself from my unpleasant situation. It seems I had fallen into a puddle, made by the rain running down one of those narrow

242

foot-paths, known as the track made by the buffalo and wild horses. The more, however, I exerted myself to get out, the more I got in, and at last I resigned myself to fate, and the assistance of some of my friends. Presently I heard the shout of the hunters, and every instant it grew more and more distinct, and I was certain the bear had turned, and was coming towards me. Satisfied with having rode the animal, I was alarmed with the idea that if he should attempt to get on the high land, by running up the narrow foot-path, he might take the liberty of jumping *on me*. Dangers thickened—for, looking up, I just saw at the head of the foot-path, the hunting cap of Sir William, and the muzzle of his famous smooth-bore rifle called "Jeffries," that I knew was loaded with thirty buck shot, and *scattered like thunder*. Here was murther—buried alive to save the trouble of a funeral, but I had no time for reflection; the bear did come, and Tar-pot hallooing at his heels. He made a straight line for the foot-path, working his way through the mud like a turtle, his mouth open, it looking to me as large and fiery as a glass-house furnace. Sir William ran down the foot-path, and raised *Old Jeffries* to his eye and fired away. The shot, as they passed within a few inches of my head, made a noise like a flight of wild pigeons, but they caught the bear in the face and eyes, who, finding it all up with him, and seemingly determined to die game, rushed on me, seized hold of my deer-skin breeches, and shook them as clear of mud as if I had been laying on a feather bed; it need only be said, that to such attentions I was *insensible*. When I came to myself I was laid out on the grass, rather used up; but our party was in excellent *spirits*, a little of which being administered to me, I found I was more scared than hurt, and towards evening we were wending our way to the "Cross Timbers," so named, because when cut or blown down, they fall across one another.

My having rode the bear, which Tar-pot-wan-ja thinks was intentionally done, has raised me very much in his estimation, as there is a tradition in his family that his father jumped on a grizzly bear and never deserted him until he had given him a death stab behind his ear. We have a new-comer to our party—a sort of nondescript half breed, who has lived much of his life at Santa Fe, and a tremendous fellow with the lassoo; he calls himself *Don Desparato el Triumpho*, and to hear him rattle it off, with the gutteral sound of the Indian and Spanish mixed, would put you in mind of an expert fellow, calling the roll on the head of a base drum. He is expert in frontier life, and "jerked" the bear that so awfully *jerked* me, which he most ingeniously did, by cutting off the whole of the meat from the bones in one strip, and fixing it on the bushes to dry, very much as you would a bed cord.   P. O. F.

P. S.—I send you with this, a very faithful drawing, taken from the inside of Tar-pot-wan-ja's buffalo robe, in commemoration of his bold attempt, to shoot a buffalo at the distance of *three miles*, a feat, except by him, never before attempted.

[10]

CROSS TIMBERS, October 2, 1843.

Throwing the Laso; Unintelligible Jokes; Far West Fun; Singular Phenomenon; New way to catch Wild Game; Escape from Indians; Scientific failures; Prospects for immortality.

In my last, I mentioned the addition to our party of the famous laso thrower, *Don Desparato*; as a catcher of wild horses, and even deer, he has no equal. The day following my ride on the bear, we halted on our way to the "Cross Timbers," upon a very beautiful hillock that, but for its extent, might have been taken for an Indian mound. Desperato, who was idle, and vain of his accomplishment, amused himself by throwing his laso over "Spanish quarters," which he did with great precision at thirty yards, and in that way won a pocket full of silver coin. Sir William proposed for amusement to turn one of his saddle horses loose on the plain, and that Desparato should, at full gallop catch the horse with the laso by the hind foot. The thing was encouraged, and was soon ready for execution. The Spaniard mounted his "Indian poney," that, from its small size, compared with the big saddle on his back, looked at a distance as if it was standing under a shed, and gave the word. I let go Sir William's horse, and hit him a severe lick to send him ahead; but the animal, instead of running off, turned round, and walked back to the baggage wagons. We were not to be thus disappointed, and at the suggestion of several, I mounted the horse myself, and putting whip to his flanks, dashed off, down the hillock, but circling round the base, so as to give all the party at the top, a fair chance to see the Spaniard catch the horse by the *hind foot*. On he came, shouting like a Pawnee, and making the diameter of my circle, of course he soon came up, threw the laso, and missed. A shout of derision followed this failure, and as my blood was up, I laughed myself, and went on the harder. Now my horse had the heels, and I bothered him tremendously; I could hear him muttering big words, that I knew was Spanish, for swearing. Presently he came near me again and threw his laso; I felt a slight tap on the head, heard a great shout and laughter, then my respiration stopped, and I realized a shock over my whole system, that felt as if I had been caught under a falling tree. Respiration returned, and on opening my eyes, there sat Desparato on his poney, I on the ground, the laso round my neck, and he holding on the opposite end of it, grinning at me like an enraged monkey.

"Halloo!" said I.

"Senor Necio!" he growled.

"Let me up," cried I, with alarm, seizing hold of the laso. Hereupon he gave it a jerk that tightened it up, and I concluded the dog intended hanging me—the motion, however, exposed a piece of tobacco that was in my pocket—so, getting down, he very quietly took the quid, released my neck, and mounted his horse, and rode towards the party on the hillock. I was so bruised by the fall from my horse, and so sore about the neck, that I could with difficulty get up the hill. "Haw, haw, haw," uttered all the party when I got among them.

"Villians!" gnashed I, through my teeth.

"Don't get mad, that was a *Spanish joke*," said somebody.

"And he don't understand the language well enough to enjoy the wit of it," said every body.

For the fifteenth time since I have been out here, I saw there was no use at being offended at merely being killed, if it was done in fun, so I joined in the laugh, but in my heart execrated Spanish jokes and lasos'.

As was anticipated by some of our old hunters, the "mast," which means the fruit of the forest trees, is very scarce, and we find ourselves, since our arrival here at the "Cross Timbers," nearly starved. Nothing is found in the woods but the Pine burr—the tree which bears it, flourishing here in its most magnificent grandeur. As we relied principally, upon the wild turky for food, and they having been compelled, from necessity, to eat these pine burrs for food for a long time, they become so impregnated with turpentine, that they caught fire whenever we attempted to roast them, and burnt up. I really believe we should have starved to death but for the ingenuity of an old fellow with us, who said he was originally from Bunkum, North Carolina. He took some dozen turkies, well cleaned, covered them with about six inches of dirt, and then built a large fire over the pile. In the course of the day, small streams of clear tar were seen running out of the heap, and when evening came, the turkies, shrunk up to the size of chickens, were taken from "the kiln," and eaten—tolerably fair food, but, as might be imagined, *very dry*.

This singular impregnation of wild game, with the article of food on which it exists, has been strangely overlooked by naturalists. I would in this connection, relate a singular escape made by a party of hunters connected with these "turpentine birds." It seems that while they were out hunting they were attacked by a large number of Soshonees, and surrounded. Protected by a small skirt of woods, they entrenched themselves for the night, expecting in the morning to have their scalps hung on long poles, and dried in the smoke like Dutch herring—an idea, by the way, that makes my head ache—just to think of. Well, in the night there came up a terrible storm, in the midst of which, the lightning struck a tree near the white hunter's camp, on which were roosting several of these pine burr fed turkies. The birds, as the light-ning descended, were instantly on fire, and flying towards the Indians, fell blazing, and hissing among them, such an exhibition struck them with consternation, and supposing the white men had the means of destruction they were not acquainted with, the Indians fled, and left the hunters in peaceable possession of the country, and, I am sorry to add, they were found afterwards starved to death, from the great in-clemency of the season.

As may be imagined, a person of my enquiring mind and aptness to learn, would pick up many many useful hints in this wild country. I have among other things, as leisure permitted, practised much to get the art of preserving birds and animals. Now Audubon will take either, and in an incredible short space of time, make the expressionless mass of skin, teem with life, as if the bird or beast had been suddenly petrified in some graceful action. But, some how, I cannot get the hang of it—my quadrupeds look like sausages, and my birds like a roll of dough. I have got a crane with a neck as big as his body, and a wild cat that resembles a gigantic weasel.

Sir William says he would not trust me to stuff a pillow. I intend to keep my "specimens" as works of art, if not of nature, and when I get home, if they are mistaken by some natural history society for *new species*, of course I shall be mum, and they will receive unpronounce-able names, and my memory will be handed down to posterity, pre-served in a dead language.   P. O. F.

P. S.—Tar-pot-wan-ja is very anxious for me to stuff for him a buffalo skin; he says if I will do it, it will be "Knochanee-shokbou-nahoola," which literally translated, signifies buffalo made ugly will be handsome "heap."

[11]

CROSS TIMBERS, October 23, 1843.

Alarming Pantomine; Its consequences; The result; Hunt for a Bear; Incidents; Getting up a tree; Keeping a promise.

In my last I wrote particularly about scarcity of food, and the singular manner we kept from starving. We might have been encamped two weeks at the "Cross Timbers," and thus faring badly, when, one night as we lay grouped round the camp fire, thinking of our distant friends, and the comforts of civilized life, Tar-pot-wan-ja, who, as is usual with him, sat resting his chin on his knees, and thinking of nothing; suddenly threw up his head, leered round with his eyes, and distending his nostrils like the ends of two speaking trumpets, snuffed up the cold air, and uttered a most significant *ugh!* Now it so happened that nobody was at the fire but fellows from the settlements, as *green as myself*; and knowing something was wrong, I, by signs, asked him what was the matter? Tar-pot. replied, with a most agreeable smile, by going through the motions of shooting a rifle, *cutting his own throat*, and then *pulling off something*, which we presumed to be a scalp. "It is all up with us," was the general exclamation, particularly as our Indian friend shut up his eyes and seemed to resign himself to his fate. The effect of all this on "Mat" was truly awful; his hair fairly crawled about his head, while mine rose like the quills on the fretful porcupine. "Good by, Woeful," said Mat to me, without winking, for his hair just at that moment had retreated to the back of his head, and drawn the skin on his forehead so tight he could not.

"Good by; I ain't used to scalping, and I expect it will strike in and kill me; it is worse acclimating than yellow fever; ain't it Woeful?"

I acknowledged the impeachment, and told him I had been killed so often *in fun*, since I had been out in the "Far West," that I thought to have it done seriously would be quite a relief.

"I think," said "Mat," philosophizing, "that people have lived after being scalped."

"They do that thing in Texas," I replied, for I recollected of hearing

247

such cases in that country; "And if we live through it," I suggested, "we will have our bumps mapped off, and labeled, and make a fortune by illustrating the science of phrenology."

"I think," said Mat, moralizing, "scalping is nothing; it is merely the knife of the savage, anticipating for a few days, the scythe of time."

"That is all," I groaned, putting my hands on the top of my head.

"Quien sirve nos libre, San Carlos," shouted Don Desparato to his horse.

"Them's my sentiments," said Mat, musing. "That was a cruel allusion to *St. Charles* just at this time, Woeful, wasn't it?" he continued, as if his feelings were wandering back to temporal things.

"It is just the time to call on the Saints, when you expect to be scalped," said I.

"Well," said Mat, in desparation, "I don't know any, but St. Charles, and St. Louis, and I have called on them *so often* they have got used to it."

While this conversation was going on, Tar-pot-wan-ja had stealthily and Indian-like left us, gun in hand, and when our expectations of the coming foray were at the highest pitch, we heard Sir William's yager, "Old Jefferys," and immediately a shout from Tar-pot., and a second and third discharge of fire arms. A long, low groan, and a struggle among the bushes followed, and every thing was silent; presently in came our faithful Indian draging a dead body, and throwing it down beside the fire, we heard him sharpen his knife on his gun barrel. Mat and I both opened our eyes at the same time to see the scalp taken, when, lo and behold, a half grown bear cub, lay before us, and the mysterious signs of Tar-pot., that alarmed us so, merely alluded to his smelling the scent of a bear, and the shooting it, cutting its throat and skinning it. As the truth flashed upon our minds, Mat and I breathed as simultaneously as the puff of a double engine.

"Did you ever, Woeful," said Mat, "see a man before that could *voluntarily* move his hair about his head as I can?"

"Or make it *stand up* as I can?" I suggested.

"We showed great presence of mind, Woeful, did'nt we?" said Mat, looking very comical.

"Certainly," said I; "we would have been killed if the Indians had really come, as dignifiedly as the Roman Senators."

The following morning we breakfasted upon bear meat; and as the animal was small, "Mat's" share and mine, lay between a small piece of the neck, and two paws; we took them and ate away voraciously,

Mat tearing the meat between his teeth, as they do flax through a hatchel. I insinuated that the meat was tough; Mat. acquiesced, suddenly stopping, his eye lit up in fine phrenzy, and twinkled with humor, when he uttered the following impressively:

"Woeful, its a piece of *grizzly bear*."

"I think it is, as the French say, a "*fore paw*," holding up my particular piece.

Hereupon we both lay down on the prairie and laughed and kicked our heels into the earth, until we raised a dust like a herd of running buffaloes.

After our breakfast, an old hunter suggested that whenever there was a young bear killed, a cub or two more, and the old one were about; and it was suggested that we set out in pursuit of them, to the great edification of Tar-pot., who had been anxious to be at the work at the early dawn of day. The sun shone out beautifully, and a more merry party than we were, never buckled a horse-hair girth. Guns were loaded with care, and, unlike good bear-hunters, we started off with a shout. We had no dogs, and depended entirely upon the "signs." Tar-pot. and the old hunters would see marks and tracks, where I could see nothing; however, we came on the bears—an old one with one cub;—they were hidden away in the hollow of a pine tree; a smoke was soon raised and applied to the hole, and as we had smooth ground, Sir William said the bear must not be murdered, but *run down*. Very soon the old bear broke out, and rushing past us with a growl, set off at a killing pace. We all followed her in the rear, shouting and yelling; she was very fat and soon tired, and entrenching herself in a small skirt of wood, backed up against a large tree, and squared off as if for a boxing match, in the most scientific manner. We all dismounted, hitched our horses, and determined to make the best fight we could without powder and ball. It would be impossible to describe the feats of valor, and agility that followed; but the bear, in the contest, got the worst of it, and got wounded, and then got desperate, and pitched into us regardless of danger or death. Now Mat. and I were unconsciously merely looking on, and standing some distance from the thick fight, when the infuriated animal, with a hog-like *wugh*, broke after us. "Take to a tree," shouted a dozen voices, as we broke for some stunted pines, up which we sprang, and climbed into the branches in an instant. Here we clung with a hug for dear life, shutting our eyes to the danger about us. An hour might have thus passed, which seemed an age, when I heard Mat. say "Woeful, what an escape;

249

suppose these pines had not been at hand to have got into?" I opened my eyes, and discovered Mat. few yards of me, and both of us with our toes within an *inch of the ground*—the young pines had insensibly bent towards the earth by our weight. It was a most ridiculous figure we cut, and both of us promised never to say any thing about it.

P. O. F.

[12]

BEYOND THE CROSS TIMBERS, Oct., 1843.

An amiable mule; Tar-pot-wan-ja's astonishment; Transmigration; New troubles; Fun alive; A fix peculiar; A dream; End of the days' work.

Our party hailed with pleasure the announcement that we were to leave the "cross timbers," and take up our line of march towards the fine country lying beyond them. We packed up with alacrity, and as the bright morning sun in long reaching rays, lit up the prairie, we were in motion. Every thing went ahead, but a long eared mule in one of the baggage waggons—a stubborn representative, that did honor in this respect to his respectable progenitor, whoever he was. Don Desparato pounded him on one side, and Tar-pot-wan-ja, voluntarily, for an Indian never works by compulsion, labored on the other.

"Fire-consume-your-heart," said Desparato in Spanish, hitting the brute across the head.

"Ah-whooh-hah!" grunted Tar-pot., as he followed the example; here the mule laid down, and turning his head over his harness collar, and eying his tormenters very cooly, gave a loud bray, extended himself at full length on the ground, and seemed inclined to go to sleep under the hands of his tormenters, as a Turk will while under the process of shampooing. All this seemed to amuse the red man highly; between every blow, he would place his extended hands over his ears, and flap them, as if in imitation of wings; then laugh heartily, and hit the mule again. Desparato in the mean time, gathered some light wood, kindled a fire around and near the beast's body, and as the curling flame increased in force, and the rough hair began to singe, and smoke, while the animal paid no attention to it, Tar-pot's. enthusiasm extended into admiration; his vivid imagination pictured the animal possessed of a soul of some Indian warrior, who defied blows and the faggot— kicking the fire about the prairie, he rushed forward and embraced the animal; muley not understanding the nature of the hug, got upon his feet and commenced kicking in a most violent manner. Tar-pot. sprang out of the way of the dangerous heels, fully convinced that a mule and an Indian were of the same identical breed.

In time we fairly got under way, and the horsemen, including myself, instead of following the wagon trail, took a short cut through some low, swampy land, covered by what is known out here as the "scrub-oaks;" they are the same kind of trees I mentioned as peculiar to the "yallah stun" in one of my first letters. When we got fairly among them, we noticed them covered with little balls of earth, as we thought; but upon close examination they proved to be hornet's nests, which, disturbed by our intrusion, commenced issuing out in formidable numbers. Now a hornet is decidedly a very passionate yellow coated insect, and pitching into us with a vehemence truly commendable, attacked us in the front and rear. A general *scrub race* commenced— the horses flew through the low growth of brush, the tallest of which only came up to their breasts, as if they were pursued by torches of fire. Sir William Stewart's grey horse, which was the most powerful animal, snorted like a hurricane; while Desparato, swearing in Indian and Spanish, threw his arms about like a wind-mill. Tar-pot-wan-ja, Indian like, took it more coolly—he and his horse seemed above complaining, except as evinced by the poor animal's tail, that kept whirling around like a piece of fire works. On we went, knocking at every step, the little mud balls on the ground, as rapidly as if we were dropping potatoes from a cart, while the inhabitants, first astonished, would for a moment confusedly crawl about, and then with unerring instinct make a straight line for the luckless invaders of their homes. My horse, not at any time one of the best, coming to a hole in the earth, caught his foot and fell to the ground; before I could recover myself, my companions were some distance ahead of me, and the hornets, to my horror, instead of pursuing on, turned back and made a general attack on me. My horse, infuriated by the hornets, would keep running around me, kicking and snorting, and raising up new enemies every instant; I finally mounted and pushed on, enveloped in a cloud of burning stings. Whatever might have been my troubles in my search of sport out in the Far West, this excelled every thing in my unfortunate experience. I fought and knocked about, expecting every moment to fall from mere pain, when my horse again stumbled, and threw me in a hole about five feet deep,—the hornets buzzed above me for a moment like a thin mist, and then, as if afraid to descend, where I lay,

251

separated to their dilapidated nests. Bruised and poisoned, I felt some relief from the absence of the hornets; no part of my body, but my face and hands, was much stung. Presently my face began to swell, my eyes closed up, and I was left in total darkness. In this situation, covered head, neck and heels with mud, for the hole into which I had fallen, was, at its bottom, composed of it, exhausted with pain, and sightless, from the swollen state of my face, I gradually swooned away and lost myself. While thus, I dreamed that the learned members of the Royal Society, London, had issued a circular, offering a thousand pounds reward for a "perpetual motion," and a display of the most foolish thing in the world; and I dreamed that I gave to the society a journal of my adventures "Out West," and proved that I went out there for the purpose of "sport," and the society unanimously awarded to me the thousand pounds. Taking the money, I awoke with joy, and discovered that my eyes would open—that I was much relieved of the pain in my face, and that the sun was just setting. Crawling out of the hole, as the chilly air of the night came on, I found the hornets benumbed with cold; I lit a fire by flashing powder in the pan of my pistol, and sat down beside it, and from the fix I was in when thoroughly warmed, I resembled a huge hornets nest, from my close resemblance to a ball of mud. About midnight, I discovered the camp fire of my fellow travellers, about two miles off, and made towards it, the most miserable dog that ever went sport-seeking in the Far West.　　　　　P. O. F.

THE LITTLE STEAMBOATS OF THE MISSISSIPPI

The steamboats of the Mississippi are as remarkable for size and form as is the river itself. Gigantic specimens of art, that go bellowing over the swift and muddy current like restless monsters, breathing like the whisperings of the hurricane, clanking and groaning as if an earthquake was preparing to astonish the world, obscuring in clouds of smoke the sun in the day time, or rolling over the darkness of night a volume of flame, as if the volcano had burst from the bosom of the deep. Who sees them for the first time, without wondering, as they rush along, filled with the ever busy throng of travellers, and loaded with boundless wealth, that teems from the rich soil, as the reward of the slight labor of the American husbandman. The Mississippi is also remarkable for little steamboats, small specimens of water craft, that are famous for their ambitious puffings, noisy Captains, gigantic placards, boats that "run up" little streams that empty into bayous, that empty into rivers, that empty into the Mississippi—boats that go beyond places ever dreamed of in geography, ever visited by travellers, or even marked down in the scrutinizing book of the tax collector. The first time I found myself on one of these boats I looked about me as did Gulliver when he got in Lilliput. It seemed as if I had got larger, and more magnificent than an animated colossal. When I walked on board of the boat, I found my feet on the lower deck and my head up stairs; the "after" cabin was so disposed of, that you could set inside of it and yet be near the "bows." The ladies' cabin had but one berth in it, and that was only as wide as a shelf. The machinery was tremendous, two large kettles firmly set in brick, attached to a complicated looking coffee mill, two little steam pipes, and one big one. And then, the way the big steam pipe would smoke, and the little ones let off steam was singular. Then the puffing of the little coffee mill! why, it worked as spiteful as a tom cat with his tail caught in the crack of a door. Then the engineer, to see him open "the furnace" doors and pitch in wood, and open the little stop cocks to see if the steam was not too high, all so much like a big boat. Then the name of the boat, "THE U. S. MAIL, EMPEROR," the letters covering over the

whole side of the boat, so that it looked like a locomotive advertisement. Then the "U. S. Mail" deposited in one corner of the cabin, and
two rifles standing near it, as if to guard it, said mail being in a bag
that looked like a gigantic shot pouch, fastened to a padlock, and said
pouch filled with three political speeches, franked by M. C.'s, one letter
to a man that did not live at the place of its destination, and a bundle
of post-office documents put in by mistake.

The bell that rung for this boat's departure, was a tremendous bell;
it swung to and fro awfully; it was big enough for a Cathedral, and as
it rung for the twentieth last time, one passenger came on board
weighing about three hundred, and the boat got under weigh. "Let go
that hawser," shouted the Captain, in a voice of thunder. Pe, wee, wee,
pish-h-h, went the little steam pipe, and we were off. Our track lay for
a time down the Mississippi, and we went ahead furiously, overhauled
two rafts and a flat-boat within two hours, and resented the appearance
of a real big steamer most valiantly, by nearly shaking to pieces in its
waves. Being light myself I got along very well, but whenever the fat
passenger got off of a line with the centre of the cabin, the pilot would
give the bell *one tap*, and the Captain would bawl out "trim the boat."
Dinner came on, and the table was covered with the biggest roast beef,
the biggest potatoes, and the biggest carving knife and fork that ever
floated, and the steward rung the biggest bell for dinner, and longer
than any other steward, and the Captain talked about the immense
extent of the Mississippi, the contemplated canal through the isthmus
of Darien, and the ability of steam war ships; he said that in the contemplation of the subject "his feelings were propelled by five hundred
horse power, that the bows of his imagination cut through the muddy
waters of reality, that the practicability of his notions were as certain
as a rudder in giving the proper direction, that his judgment, like a
safety valve to his mind, would always keep him from advocating any
thing that would ever burst up, and that it was unfortunate that Robert
Fulton had not lived to be president of the United States." With such
enlarged ideas he wiled away the hour of dinner; arrived at the mouth
of "dry outlet," (a little gutter, that draws off some of the water of the
Mississippi when very high) turned the bows of the "Emperor" into its
mouth, and shot down it along with an empty flour barrel, with an
alacrity that sent the bows of the boat high and dry on the land, the
first bend it came to. A great deal of hard work "got us off," and away
we went again, at one time sideways, at another every way, hitting
against the soft alluvial banks, or brushing our pipes among the

branches of overhanging trees. Finally the current got too strong, and carried us ahead with alarming velocity; the bows of the boat were turned in the opposite direction from what we were going, and thus managed to keep an onward progress compatible with our safety. The banks of the "dry outlet," were very low, very swampy, and were disfigured occasionally with wretched cabins, in which lived human beings, who, the captain of the "Emperor" informed me, lived, as far as he could judge, by sitting on the heads of barrels and looking out on the landscape, and at his boat as it passed; from the fact that they had no cultivatable land, and looked like creatures fed on unhealthy air, we presume that was their only occupation.

In time we arrived at the "small village," the destination of the "mail pouch," and landing, visited the town. It was one of the ruins of a great city, conceived of by land speculators in "glory times." Several splendid mansions were decaying about, in the half finished frames that were strewn upon the ground. A barrel of whiskey was rolled ashore, the mail delivered, the fat man got out, and we departed. The "dry outlet" merged itself into a broad inland lake, that itself, as a peculiarity of the tributaries of the Mississippi emptied into that river. Our little boat plunged on, keeping up with untiring consistency all its original pretension and puffing, and the same clanking of tiny machinery, scaring the wild ducks and geese, and scattering the white cranes over our heads, and making the cormorant screech with astonishment in hoarser tones than the engine itself. Occasionally we would land at "a squatter's settlement," turn round and come up to the banks with grandeur, astonishing the squatter's children and two very invalid hens that lived in the front yard. The captain would pay up the bill for wood, and off he would go again as "big as all out doors," and a great deal more natural. Thus we struggled on, until sailing up a stream with incessant labor such as went down when we commenced our sketch, we merged into the world of water that flows in the Mississippi. Down the rapid current we gracefully went, the very astonishment of the regular inhabitants on its banks.

Again for the "innumerable time," the "furnaces" consumed the wood, and as it had to be replenished, we ran alongside one of those immense wood yards, so peculiar to the Mississippi, where lay in one continuous pile thousands of cords of wood. The captain of the "Emperor," as he stopped his boat before it, hallowed out from his "upper deck," in a voice of the loudest kind—

"Got any wood here?"

Now the owner, who was a very rich man, and a very surly one, looked on the "heap," and said "he thought it possible."

"Then" said the captain, "how do you sell it a cord?"

The wood-man eyed the boat, and its crew, and its passengers, and then said "he would not sell *the boat* any wood, but that the crew might come ashore, and get their hats full of chips for nothing."

Hereupon the five hundred horse power of the captain's feelings, the rudder and the safety-valves of his well-regulated mind became surcharged with wrath, and he vented forth abuse on the wood-yard and its owner, that was expressive of "thoughts that breathe, and words that burn." A distant large boat, breasting the current like a thing of life, gave me a hint, and rushing ashore amid the shot, we bid the "Emperor" and its enlarged captain a hearty and great good-bye, and in a few moments more we dwindled into mere insects on board of the magnificent ———— the pride and wonder of the western waters.

BROKER VS. BANKER. SCENE IN A NEW ORLEANS COURT

In 1843 the Legislature of our State passed a law imposing a fine of two hundred and fifty dollars on "Exchange Brokers," which was considered by that class of our fellow citizens unjust and oppressive. In many instances the Brokers resisted the payment of the tax. As a matter of course, the eagle eye of the law peeped into various places of mammon, where we see daily exposed the glittering and *uncounted* stores of wealth that so eminently distinguishes these shops in these hard times, and without regard to persons, brought them into court to answer for the dreadful offence of trying to get an honest living, without paying two hundred and fifty dollars for the attempt.

A day or two since, some score of these victims to oppressive legislation were in court—the State was represented by the proper authority, and the defendants by their chosen counsel. Now, as the law is framed that the tax was only laid on "Exchange Brokers," the brokers were at once prompted to turn into something else, and slip through the uncertainties of the law. We were in court when the first case was called, and were somewhat amused with the Sam Weller sort of evidence elicited by the State, in the prosecution. It ran as follows:

Do you know the defendant in the suit?

Yes!

What is his profession?

Banker!

Pray how much capital does it require to be a banker?

That depends altogether on circumstances—it being expected, however, that a private banker in liquidation will pay more than some of our incorporated banks.

Does the defendant make any purchases?

He sometimes buys uncurrent money.

What does he do with that uncurrent money?

Sells it, when he can get a profit on it.

Did you ever see any thing but uncurrent money in his establishment?

Yes! heaps of gold.

257

Did you ever hear him say he was a broker?

No! but have heard him say he would scorn to be a broker.

Have you ever known him to buy bills of exchange?

Yes.

When this answer was made, the prosecuting attorney brightened up and concluded he had caught the witness napping, as it was only necessary for the developement to be made that the defendant *sold* these bills of exchange, to prove him a broker, and subject to the fine—the question followed—

What did the defendant do with these bills of exchange?

Presume he remitted them to his correspondents.

This answer threw the whole examination off again, when the prosecution determined to follow up the scent closely, asked:

Have you an intimate knowledge of the defendant's business?

No! he is too smart to permit any one to know his business.

Have you ever had any transactions with him?

I have had the honor to have been his partner.

Did you never know him to buy or sell Texas money on commission?

The defendant don't call Texas scrip money, and when he operates in that article he does it exclusively for his own benefit.

You have said the defendant was a *banker*—explain how it differs from a broker?

A broker bears the same relation to a banker, that a blank check does to one filled up.

Does the defendant receive deposits?

Don't know that he does, but feel safe in saying he would if any offered.

Do you know any broker in the city?

Yes, ship brokers, cotton brokers, tobacco brokers, and other brokers.

Don't you know of any money brokers in New Orleans?

Never met with one, since the law was passed imposing a tax of two hundred and fifty dollars on them.

Here the witness took his seat, having thrown about as much light on the subject of brokers as a turnip would in a dark cellar.

258

TRAITS
OF
THE
PRAIRIES

We have wandered over the Louisiana prairies, our little pony, like an adventurous bark, seemingly trusting itself imprudently beyond the headlands, a mere speck, moving among the luxuriant islands of live oak that here and there sit so quietly upon the rolling waves of vegetation. Myriads of wild geese would often rise upon our intrusion, helping out the fancy of being at sea; but the bounding deer, or wild cattle, that occasionally resented our presence and rattled off at breakneck pace, kept us firmly on the land. In the spring seasons, the prairies are covered with the choicest flowers, that mix with the young grass in such profusion as to carpet them more delicately, and more richly, than in the seraglio of a sultan. Upon this vegetation innumerable cattle feed and fatten, until they look pampered, and their skins glisten like silk in the sun. Apparently wild as the buffalo, they are all marked and numbered, and in them consist the wealth of the inhabitant of the prairie. It is easy to imagine that herdsmen of such immense fields live a wild and free life; ever on horseback, like the Arabs, they have no fear save when out of the saddle, and nature has kindly provided a "steed" that boasts of no particular blood, that may be called the "yankee" of his kind, because it never tires, never loses its energy, and makes a living and grows fat, where all else of its species would starve.

The mustang pony, the invariable companion of the inhabitant of the prairie, whether he is rich or poor, is a little creature, apparently narrow-chested, and small across the loins. Its head is not finely formed or well set upon a straight neck. There is a want of compactness about the figure, and a looseness about the muscles. The hind legs are long, and form, from the hip to the hoof, a bend as regular as a bow. It is not handsome, but it gives a spring when under the saddle most delightful. The mustang is not subject to the ordinary evils of horseflesh. Sparing in diet, a stranger to grain, easily satisfied, whether on growing or dead grass, it seems to be stubbed and twisted, tough and everlasting, never poor or markedly fat; under all weathers and seasons, it does an amount of work, with ease, that would turn all other horses, if they lived through it, into broken down drudges. The eyes of the mustang pony, however, tell you a tale; they are of a witching hazel, of curiously crimson-speckled blue, deep and beautiful as a precious stone, and lighted up by a bit of mischief that betrays the lurking devil within. Such is the mustang pony, adapted to the prairie as perfectly as its sunshine and flowers. Their riders cherish the trappings for them that betray old Spain; the saddle with its high pummel and crupper; dangling on either side are the enormous wooden stirrups, looking like a huge pair of mallets; the whole so disproportioned to the horse, that they appear to be an overload of themselves. The bridle envelopes the head as complicatedly as the bandages on a broken arm, crossing and recrossing, filled with side latches and throat latches, and holding a bit that might be mistaken for some ancient machine of torture; attached to which are levers so powerful, that a slight jerk would snap off any thing in the world but the under jaw of a mustang pony. Mounted by a rider that is as much a part of him as his hide, he goes rollicking ahead, with the "eternal lope," such as an amorous deer assumes when it moves beside its half galloping mate, a mixture of two or three gaits, as easy as the motions of a cradle, and in which may be traced some little of the stately tramp of the Moorish Arabian, exhibited centuries since upon the plains of the Alhambra, and pricked by enormous spurs, that rattle with a tingling sound, of which the mustang's sides, so far from resenting the operation, seem to enjoy it as a taste dulled by luxuries requires mustard and cayenne.

The origin of the cattle of the prairies is lost in obscurity; but the wide-spreading horn, the heavy leg, and predominance of black and white, carries the mind back to the times when old Spain sent her colonies, with their rich possessions, under Pizarro and Cortez, into the western world. Their ancestors, in the troublesome times of early conquest, breaking away from the restraint of their owners, in course of centuries have multiplied and spread from the Californias to the Gulf of Mexico. The wide savannas, with their elevated boundaries of rich dividing country of two great oceans, warmed by a tropical sun, and cooled by the mountain breeze, and covered by never-failing vegetation, have multiplied the cattle as the sands of the sea. Among the *vacheries* of New Spain, they are killed for their skins alone, their fat carcasses being left a prey to the vulture and the wolf. Those that inhabit the prairies of Attakappas and Opelousas are less wastefully disposed of, as their bodies find a quick sale, to sustain the constantly increasing population that concentrates at the mouth of the great valley of the Mississippi.

In the warm month of June, commences the annual herding of the cattle. At a place fixed upon as the herding ground, a few horsemen will drive together fifty thousand head; and when once grouped together in a solid mass, from a peculiar instinct, a whole troop of cavalry could not again scatter them over the plain. It may readily be imagined that this work is not accomplished without incidents and accidents. In the excitement of the *drive*, horses fall, or run headlong over slow-footed cows, bulls stop to joust, enraged mothers plunge madly with their horns, in pursuit of their calves. A sulky ox refuses to move in the proper direction; off starts a rider, who catching the stubborn animal by the tail, it at once becomes frightened into a lope; advantage is taken of the unwieldy body, as it rests upon the fore feet, to jerk it to the ground; before the ox has recovered from its astonishment, a hair rope has been passed through his nose, secured to the mustang pony's tail, and it is led along subdued by pain. A stampede sometimes seizes the herd, and then, with upturned heads and glaring eyes, the animals rush along, making the earth tremble beneath their feet. Then it is that feats of horsemanship are performed that would delight Bedouin Arabs. The *vacher*, armed with an ash stick, some seven feet in length, pointed at the end by a small three-cornered file, scours ahead of the flying cattle, thrusting his rude weapon against their rumps, rolling them over as suddenly on the prairie as if they were shot. Or with a whip, with a handle of a few inches long, and a heavy raw-hide thong of eight feet, will he lash their reeking sides, drawing blood from the flesh as with a knife. Should the drove however move kindly, as they start in the morning so they remain until night, the same plodders in the rear, the same lordly Andalusian in the van. After the cattle have been at the herding ground two or three days, their respective owners separate them and drive them off to brand. Upon the hind quarter is pressed the hot iron that marks ownership and servility. This is known and numbered as the wealth of the stock-raisers of the prairies. The dowry of many a fair bride is in cattle; the announcement of the birth of a son or daughter gives rise to a gift, from some kind uncle or doating aunt, to the new-comer, of perhaps a single white heifer. When the little one is grown up, it finds in the sacredly-kept increase a fair start in the world, from which may result a fortune. Through the prairies meander no running streams, yet the cattle have beautiful reservoirs of water to slake their impatient thirst. The ponds of the prairies call forth the admiration, their beauty being even excelled by the simple and perfect contrivance for their formation. The low and marshy spots of the prairie offer to the heated hoofs of the herd a cooling place for their feet; crowded in dense masses upon these places, their continual stepping indents the turf. The rains, attracted by the predisposition to moisture, accumulate in these "standing places," mix with the earth, which is wrought into well tempered clay, and is in this form borne off upon the hoofs of the cattle. As time rolls on, this constant loss displays itself in the incipient basin: deepening by degrees, its bottom finally grows impervious and a pond is made, and thus they are multiplied indefinitely as demanded. Perfectly round and shelving gently to the centre, they soon become skirted with richer and more varied foliage than is elsewhere to be met with. The nelumbium rests its huge leaves for a shade upon the surface of the water, and rears its beautiful flowers in the air as an ornament. The smaller water lilies spring up upon the margins of the ponds; even the wild violet is hidden away among the rank grass. Here resort the plover, the wild goose, and duck, and the delicately plumed flamingo, that seems to have stolen from the opening rose-bud its colour. The fruit of the nelumbium fattens the feathered vagrants, and the clear field that surrounds these choice feeding places protects them from the wiles of the sportsman. In the depths of these ponds, among the tangled roots and grasses, sports the gormandizing trout, the beautiful perch, and soft-shell terrapin, as innocent of snares as if there were no anglers or aldermen in the world.

But the greatest pride of the Louisiana prairie is the live oak. In these beautiful wastes, the little acorn, that vies with the thimble of the fair hand in size, swells into a vast world of itself. It would seem incredible, but from the knowledge of experience, that in so small a germ so much beauty and strength could originate. The little rivulet that gurgles down some gentle declivity, and is obstructed by the rolling stone, or falling limb of the overhanging tree, turning into the proud swelling river, bearing upon its surface the wealth of commerce, and the rage of the driving storm, resembles the oak, that from almost nothing becomes stately in grandeur, and, unaffected, meets the rattling hail of the cannon's mouth, and frowns defiance in the glare of the lightning and the blasts of the hurricane. The live oaks of the Louisiana prairie compare with none but their own kindred which adorn the plains that stretch away towards the tropics. In "merry old England," where the titled of the land, with a reverence that smacks of the superstitions of the Druid priests, look upon their gnarled oaks as their antiquities, and trace back their history with the same pride they do their own exalted race, they would almost fall down and worship, could they see these wonders of the new world, that overtop their favourites as the Jura does the Alps. Among them, there are none touched with age, or promising in youth; they all seem to be rejoicing in their prime, and to stand forth terrible in their strength; yet their waving branches rustle as delicately as the brachen, and the evergreen leaves glisten in the sun, and at a distance from their delicacy appear like silken fringe. Stand beside the mighty trunks!—behold the huge columns of iron gray, how hard they look, and well adapted to sustain the huge forest above them in the air!—the gigantic limbs aspire to reach the horizon!—how they have gracefully bent and bowed in their onward course, and tapered off, almost imperceptibly, to little stems! In those limbs we see the broad swell of the seventy-four, and the ribs for her sides.

What a world is above you in the noble confusion! what a rich mellowed light plays in the vernal shades! The lively squirrel has found a speck in the bark wherein to make its nest; and the delicate twig way yonder, which bears that cluster of leaves, so far in the clouds, hides beneath its quiverings the nest of the little bird that will teach its happy young to try their ambitious wings to fly through the broad world within the body of the tree, resting their tiny pinions by the way, as eagles do, when they soar among the clouds and stoop upon the precipice. Here, when the summer sun radiates from the heated plain, and the dust flies from every step upon the parched soil, come the cattle by thousands to cool their burning sides in the never-failing shade, and, in quiet repose, pass the noon of day. Nature, beautiful in her economy, thus erects her sacred temples, for the benefit of her creatures. Centuries before the cattle that now rest so quietly beneath these oaks came to our continent, the wild buffalo took their place, and the wilder Indian was the keeper of the *vacheries*. By whom and when was planted the acorn? How came the magic seed so mysteriously scattered over the vast field? What drew them to the moist places, and buried them beside the water-courses? and in the old times of their youth, who were the dryads to preserve the tender plant from the cud, or heavy crushing foot? Easy indeed is it, in looking upon these wonderful exhibitions of nature, reared up in so lovely places, open ever to the sunshine and the storm, with no shade but from the clouds, no ambitious rivals to retard their growth, to imagine, in their first bud-

263

ding, they were the care of fairy hands, and protected by guardian spirits, until they grew into temples, whose foundations reach deep into the earth, and whose canopy catches the first rays of the morning sun.

Ho! for the prairies! those broad fields in the arcana of nature, where the grasses and ground-flowers revel, and their interlaced roots usurp the soil, broad rolling waves of green earth that glisten in the setting sun, as if they would turn a sparkling ripple from their tops, and then settle down into quiet inland seas. Rich wastes, whereon the deer roam as in a boundless park, and where the cattle herd in stately pride swelling their sleek sides with never-failing herbage,—where the horizon plays before you in deceptive circles, seeming to sink from your wearied footsteps as you move towards it;—grand trysting-places of magnificent sport, where man and beast, free from the crowded mart or thick-set forest trees, perform their different parts on nature's grandest stage, exulting in freedom.

PISCATORY ARCHERY*

In treating of the most beautiful and novel sport of arrow-fishing, its incidents are so interwoven with ten thousand accessories, that we scarce know how to separate our web without breaking it, or destroying a world of interest hidden among the wilds of the American forest. The lakes over which the arrow-fisher twangs his bow, in the pleasant spring-time, have disappeared long before the sere and yellow leaf of autumn appears, and the huntsman's horn and the loud-mouthed pack clamour melodiously after the scared deer upon their bottoms. To explain this phenomenon, the lover of nature must follow us until we exhibit some of the vagaries of the great Mississippi; and, having fairly got our "flood and field" before us, we will engage heartily in the sport.

If you will descend with me from slightly broken ground through which we have been riding, covered with forest trees singularly choked

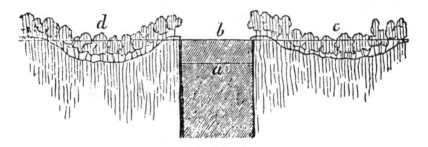

a, The level of the Mississippi, at its ordinary stage of water. *b*, The height of the spring rise. *c,d,* The "dry lakes." By examination of the above drawing, an idea may be formed of the manner of the rises of the Mississippi. The observer will notice that when the water is at *a*, the lakes *c* and *d* will be *dry*, affording a fine hunting-ground for deer, &c. When the water is at *b*, the lakes are formed, and arrow-fishing is pursued. (See description.) A correct idea may also be formed by what is meant by a *water-line* on the trees, indicating the last rise; the water-line will be formed of the sediment settling on the trees at the line *b*, marked above.

*The writer would mention, as a preliminary, thát in speaking of fishes, no scientific names are used; he refers to some that are familiar, the carp, for instance, of others that he believes are not yet classified by naturalists. As far as possible, the technical names peculiar to the sport described are used, as they are always more characteristic than any other.

up with undergrowth, to an expanse of country beautifully open between the trees, the limbs of which start out from the trunk, some thirty
feet above the ground, you will find at your feet an herbage that is luxuriant, but scanty; high over your head, upon the trees, you will perceive
a line marking what has evidently been an overflow of water; you can
trace the beautiful level upon the trees as far as the eye can reach. It is
in the fall of the year, and a squirrel drops an acorn upon your shoulder, and about your feet are the sharp-cut tracks of the nimble deer.
You are standing in the centre of what is called, by hunters, a "dry
lake." As the warm air of April favours the opening flowers of spring,
the waters of the Mississippi, increased by the melting snows of the
north, swell within its low banks, and rush in a thousand streams back
into the swamps and lowlands that lie upon its borders; the torrent
sweeps along into the very reservoir in which we stand, and the waters
swell upwards until they find a level with the fountain itself. Thus is
formed the arrow-fisher's lake. The brawny oak, the graceful pecan,
the tall poplar, and delicate beech spring from its surface in a thousand tangled limbs, looking more beautiful, yet most unnatural, as the
water reflects them downwards, hiding completely away their sub-
merged trunks. The arrow-fisher now peeps in the nest of the wild bird
from his little boat, and runs its prow plump into the hollow that marks
the doorway of some cunning squirrel. In fact, he navigates for a while,
his bark where, in the fall of the year, the gay-plumed songster and the
hungry hawk plunge midair, and float not more swiftly nor gayly, on
light pinioned wings, than he in his swift canoe.

A chapter from nature: and who unfolds the great book so under-
standingly, and learns so truly from its wisdom, as the piscator? The
rippling brook as it dances along in the sunshine bears with it the
knowledge, there is truthfulness in water, though it be not in a well.
We can find something, if we will, to love and admire under every
wave; and the noises of every tiny brook are tongues that speak elo-
quently to nature's true priests.

We have marked that, with the rise of the waters the fish grow gre-
garious, and that they rush along in schools *with the waters that flow
inland* from the river, that they thus choose these temporary sylvan
lakes as depositories of their spawn; thus wittingly providing against
that destruction which would await their young in the highways of their
journeyings. It is a sight to wonder at in the wilds of the primitive
forest, to see the fish rushing along the narrow inlets, with the current,

in numbers incredible to the imagination, leaping over the fallen tree that is only half buried in the surface of the stream, or stayed a moment in their course by the meshes of the strong net, either bursting it by force of numbers, or granting its wasteful demands by thousands, without seemingly to diminish the multitude more than a single leaf would, taken from its foliage. We have marked, too, that these fish would besport themselves in their new homes, secluding themselves in the shadows of the trees and banks; and, as the summer heats come on, they would grow unquiet; the outlets leading to the great river they had left would be thronged by what seemed to be busy couriers; and when the news finally spread of *falling water*, one night would suffice to make the lake, before so thronged with finny life, deserted; and a few nights, perhaps, will only pass, when the narrow bar will obtrude itself between the inland lake and the river that supplied it with water. Such was the fish's wisdom, seen and felt, where man, with his learning and his nicely wrought mechanisms, would watch in vain the air, the clouds, and see "no signs" of falling water.*

Among arrow-fishermen there are technicalities, an understanding of which will give a more ready idea of the sport. The surfaces of these inland lakes are unruffled by the winds or storms; the heats of the sun seem to rest upon them; they are constantly sending into the upper regions warm mists. Their surfaces, however, are covered with innumerable bubbles, either floating about, or breaking into little circling ripples. To the superficial observer these air-bubbles mean little or nothing; to the arrow-fisherman, they are the very *language of his art*; visible writing upon the unstable water, unfolding the secrets of the depths below, and guiding him, with unerring certainty, in his pursuits.

Seat yourself quietly in this little skiff, and while I paddle quietly out into the lake, I will translate to you these apparent wonders, and give you a lesson in the simple language of nature. "An air-bubble is an air-bubble," you say, and "your fine distinctions must be in the imagination." Well! then mark how stately ascends that large globule of air; if

---

*It may not be uninteresting to naturalists to be informed, that these fish run into the inland lakes to spawn, and they do it with the rise of the water of course. These overflows are annual. A few years since the season was very singular, and there were *three* distinct rises and falls of water, and at each rise the fish followed the water inland, and spawned: a remarkable example where the usual order of nature was reversed in one instance, and yet continuing blindly consistent in another. It is also very remarkable that the young fish, native of the lakes, are as interested to mark the indications of falling water as those that come into them; and in a long series of years of observation, but one fall was ever known where the fish were in the lakes.

you will time each succeeding one by your watch, you will find that while they appear, it is at regular intervals, and when they burst upon the surface of the water, there is the least spray in the world for an instant sparkling in the sun. Now, yonder, if you will observe, are very minute bubbles that seem to *simmer* towards the surface. Could you catch the air of the first bubble we noticed, and give it to an ingenious chemist, he would tell you that it was a light gas, that exhaled from decaying vegetable matter. The arrow-fisherman will tell you they come from an old stump, and are denominated *dead bubbles*. That "simmering" was made by some comfortable turtle, as he gaps open his mouth and gives his breath to the surrounding element.

Look ahead of you: when did you ever see an Archimedean screw more beautifully marked out than by that group of bubbles? They are very light, indeed, and seem thus gracefully to struggle into the upper world; they denote the eager workings of some terrapin in the soft mud at the bottom of the lake. In the shade of yonder lusty oak you will perceive what arrow-fishermen call a "feed;" you see the bubbles are entirely unlike any we have noticed; they come rushing upwards swiftly, like handfuls of silver shot. They are lively and animated to look at, and are caused by the fish below, as they, around the root of that very oak, search for insects for food. To those bubbles the arrow-fisherman hastens for game: they are made by the fish he calls legitimate for his sport.

In early spring the fish are discovered, not only by the bubbles they make, but by various sounds uttered while searching for food. These sounds are familiarized, and betray the kind of fish that make them. In late spring, from the middle of May to June, the fish come near the surface of the water and expose their mouths to the air, keeping up, at the same time, a constant motion with it, called "piping." Fish thus exposed are in groups, and are called a "float." The cause of this phenomenon is hard to explain, all reasons given being unsatisfactory. As it is only exhibited in the hottest of weather, it may be best accounted for in the old verse:

> "The sun, from its perpendicular height,
> Illumed the depths of the sea;
> The fishes, beginning to sweat,
> Cry, 'Dang it, how hot we shall be!'"

There are several kinds of fish that attract the attention of the arrow-fishermen. Two kinds only are professedly pursued, the "carp" and the "buffalo." Several others, however, are attacked for the mere purpose of amusement, among which we may mention a species of perch, and the most extraordinary of all fish, the "gar."

The carp is a fish known to all anglers. Its habits must strike every one familiar with them, as being eminently in harmony with the retreats we have described. In these lakes they vary in weight from five to thirty pounds, and are preferred by arrow-fishermen to all other fish. The "buffalo," a sort of fresh-water sheep's-head, is held next in estimation. A species of perch is also destroyed, that vary from three to ten pounds; but as they are full of bones and coarse in flesh, they are killed simply to test the skill of the arrow-fisherman.*

The incredible increase of fishes has been a matter of immemorial observation. In the retired lakes and streams we speak of, but for a wise arrangement of Providence, it seems not improbable that they would outgrow the very space occupied by the element in which they exist. To prevent this consummation, there are fresh-water fiends, more terrible than the wolves and tigers of the land, that prowl on the finny tribe with an appetite commensurate with their plentifulness, destroying millions in a day, yet leaving, from their abundance, untold numbers to follow their habits and the cycle of their existence undisturbed. These terrible destroyers have no true representatives in the sea; they seem to be peculiar to waters tributary to the Mississippi. There are two kinds of them, alike in office, but distinct in species; they are known by those who fish in the streams they inhabit as the "gar." They are, when grown to their full size, twelve or fifteen feet in length, voracious monsters to look at, so well made for strength, so perfectly protected from assault, so capable of inflicting injury. The smaller kind, growing not larger than six feet, have a body that somewhat resembles in form the pike, covered by what look more like large flat heads of wrought iron, than scales, which it is impossible to re-

---

*The carp to which we allude is so accurately described in its habits in "Blane's Encyclopedia of Rural Sports," when speaking of the European carp, that we are tempted to make one or two extracts, that are remarkable for their truthfulness as applied to the section of the United States where arrow-fishing is a sport. In the work we allude to we have the following:

"The usual length of the carp in our own country (England) is from about twelve to fifteen or sixteen inches; but *in warm climates*, it often arrives at the length of two, three, or four feet, and to the weight of twenty, thirty, or even forty pounds." Par. 3448. Again, "The haunts of the carp of stagnant water are, during the spring and autumn months, in the deepest parts, particularly near the flood-gates by which water *is received and let off*. In the summer months they frequent the weed beds, and *come near to the surface*, and particularly are fond of aquatic plants, which spring from the bottom and rise to the top." Par. 3453. We find the fish retains the same distinctive habits in both hemispheres, altering only from the peculiarities of the country.

move without cutting them out, they are so deeply imbedded in the flesh. The jaws of this monster form about one-fourth of its whole length; they are shaped like the bill of a goose, armed in the interior with triple rows of teeth, as sharp and well set as those of a saw. But *the terror* is the "alligator gar," a monster that seems to combine all the most destructive powers of the shark and the reptile. The alligator gar grows to the enormous length of fifteen feet; its head resembles the alligator's; within its wide-extended jaws glisten innumerable rows of teeth, running down into its very throat in solid columns. Blind in its instinct to destroy, and singularly tenacious of life, it seems to prey with untiring energy, and with an appetite that is increased by gratification. Such are the fish that are made victims of the mere sport of the arrow-fisherman.

The implements of the arrow-fisherman are a strong bow, five or six feet long, made of black locust or of cedar, (the latter being preferred.) An arrow of ash, three feet long, pointed with an iron spear of peculiar construction. The spear is eight inches long, one end has a socket, in which is fitted *loosely* the wooden shaft; the other end is a flattened point; back of this point there is inserted the barb, which shuts into the iron as it enters an object, but will open if attempted to be drawn out. The whole of this iron-work weighs three ounces. A cord is attached to the spear, fifteen or twenty feet long, about the size of a crow quill, by which is held the fish when struck.

Of the water-craft used in arrow-fishing, much might be said, as it introduces the common Indian canoe, or as it is familiarly termed, the "dug out," which is nothing more than a trunk of a tree, shaped according to the humour or taste of its artificer, and hollowed out. We have seen some of these rude barks that claimed but one degree of beauty or utility beyond the common log, and we have seen others as gracefully turned as was ever the bosom of the loving swan, and that would, as gracefully as Leda's bird, spring through the rippling waves. To the uninitiated, the guidance of a canoe is a mystery. The grown-up man, who first attempts to move on skates over the glassy ice, has a command of his limbs, and a power of locomotion, that the novice in canoe navigation has not. Never at rest, it seems to rush from under his feet; overbalanced by an overdrawn breath, it precipitates its victim into the water. Every effort renders it more and more unmanageable, until it is condemned as worthless. But let a person accustomed to its movements take it in charge, and it gayly launches into the stream; whether standing or sitting, the master has it entirely under his control, moving any way with a quickness, a pliability, quite wonderful, forward, sideways, backwards; starting off in an instant, or while at the greatest speed, instantly stopping still, and doing all this more perfectly than any other water-craft of the world. The arrow-fisher prefers a canoe with very little rake, quite flat on the bottom, and not more than fifteen feet long, so as to be turned quick. Place in this simple craft the simpler paddle, lay beside it the arrow, the bow, the cord, and you have the whole outfit of the arrow-fisherman.

In arrow-fishing, two persons only are employed; each one has his work designated—"the paddler" and "bowman." Before the start is made, a perfect understanding is had, so that their movements are governed by signs. The delicate canoe is pushed into the lake, its occupants scarcely breathe to get it balanced, the paddler is seated in its bottom, near its centre, where he remains, governing the canoe in all its motions, without *ever taking the paddle from the water*. The fisherman stands at the bow; around the wrist of his left hand is fastened, by a loose loop, the cord attached to the arrow, which cord is wound around the forefinger of the same hand, so that when paying off, it will do so easily. In the same hand is, of course, held the bow. In the right, is carried the arrow, and by its significant pointing, the paddler gives directions for the movements of the canoe. The craft glides along, scarcely making a ripple; a "feed" is discovered, over which the canoe stops; the bowman draws his arrow to the head; the game, disturbed, is seen in the clear water rising slowly and perpendicularly, but otherwise perfectly motionless; the arrow speeds its way; in an instant the shaft shoots into the air, and floats quietly away, while the wounded fish, carrying the spear in its body, endeavours to escape. The "pull" is managed so as to come directly from the bow of the canoe; it lasts but for a moment before the transfixed fish is seen, fins playing, and full of agonizing life, dancing on the top of the water, and in another instant more lies dead at the bottom of the canoe. The shaft is then gone after, picked up, and thrust into the spear; the cord is again adjusted, and the canoe moves towards the merry makers of those swift ascending bubbles, so brightly displaying themselves on the edge of that deep shade, cast by yonder ever-green oak.

There is much in the associations of arrow-fishing that gratifies taste, and makes it partake of a refined and intellectual character. Besides the knowledge it gives of the character of fishes, it practises one in the curious refractions of water. Thus will the arrow-fisherman, from long experience, drive his pointed shaft a fathom deep for game, when

271

it would seem, to the novice, a few inches would be more than sufficient. Again, the waters that supply the arrow-fisherman with game,
afford subsistence to innumerable birds, and he has exhibited before
him the most beautiful displays of their devices to catch the finny tribe.
The kingfisher may be seen the livelong day, acting a prominent part,
bolstering up its fantastic topknot, as if to apologize for a manifest
want of neck; you can hear it always scolding and clamorous among
the low brush, and overhanging limits of trees, eyeing the minnows as
they glance along the shore, and making vain essays to fasten them in
his bill. The hawk, too, often swoops down from the clouds, swift as
the bolt of Jove; the cleft air whistles in the flight; the sporting fish
playing in the sunlight is snatched up in the rude talons, and borne
aloft, the reeking water from its scaly sides falling in soft spray upon
the upturned eye that traces its daring course. But we treat of fish, and
not of birds.

Yonder is our canoe; the paddle has stopped it short, just where you
see those faint bubbles; the water is very deep beneath them, and
reflects the frail bark and its occupants, as clearly as if they were floating in mid-air. The bowman looks into the water—the fish are out of
sight, and not disturbed by the intrusion above them. They are eating
busily, judging from the ascending bubbles. The bowman lets fall the
"heel" of his arrow on the bottom of the canoe, and the bubbles instantly cease. The slight tap has made a great deal of noise in the
water, though scarcely heard out of it. There can be seen rising to the
surface a tremendous carp. How quietly it comes upwards, its pectoral
fins playing like the wings of the sportive butterfly. Another moment,
and the cold iron is in its body. Paralyzed for an instant, the fish rises
to the surface as if dead, then, recovering itself, it rushes downwards,
until the cord that holds it prisoner tightens, and makes the canoe
tremble; the effort has destroyed it, and without another struggle it is
secured.

When the fish first come into the lakes, they move in pairs on the
surface of the water, and while so doing they are shot, as it is called,
"flying." In early spring fifteen or twenty fish are secured in an hour.
As the season advances, three or four taken in the same length of time
is considered quite good success. To stand upon the shore, and see
the arrow-fisherman busily employed, is a very interesting exhibition
of skill, and of the picturesque. The little "dug out" seems animate
with intelligence; the bowman draws his long shaft, you see it enter

272

the water, and then follows the glowing sight of the fine fish sparkling in the sun, as if sprinkled with diamonds. At times, too, when legitimate sport tires, some ravenous gar that heaves in sight is made a victim; aim is taken just ahead of his dorsal fin; secured, he flounders a while, and then drags off the canoe as if in harness, skimming it almost out of the water with his speed. Fatigued, finally, with his useless endeavours to escape, he will rise to the surface, open his huge mouth, and gasp for air. The water that streams from his jaws will be coloured with blood from the impaled fish that still struggle in the terrors of his barbed teeth. Rushing ahead again, he will, by eccentric movements, try the best skill of the paddler to keep his canoe from overturning into the lake, a consummation not always unattained. The gar finally dies, and is dragged ashore; the buzzard revels on his carcass, and every piscator contemplates, with disgust, the great enemy to his game, the terrible monarch of the fresh-water seas.

The crumbling character of the alluvial banks that line our southern streams, the quantity of fallen timber, the amount of "snags" and "sawyers," and the great plentifulness of game, make the beautiful art of angling, as pursued in England, impossible. The veriest tyro, who finds a delicate reed in every nook that casts a shadow on the water, with his rough line, and coarser hook, *can catch fish*. The greedy perch, in all its beautiful varieties, swim eagerly and quickly around the snare, and swallow it, without suspicion that a worm is not a worm, or that appearances are ever deceitful. The jointed rod, the scientific reel, cannot be used; the thick hanging bough, the rank grass, the sunken log, the far reaching *nelumbium*, the ever still water, make these delicate appliances useless. Arrow-fishing only, of all the angling in the interior streams of the southwest, comparatively speaking, claims the title of *an art*, as it is pursued with a skill and a thorough knowledge that tell only with the experienced, and to the novice is an impossibility.

The originators of arrow-fishing deserve the credit of striking out a rare and beautiful amusement, when the difficulties of securing their game did not require it, showing that it resulted in the spirit of true sport alone.

The origin of arrow-fishing we know not; the country where it is pursued is comparatively of recent settlement; scarce three generations have passed away within its boundaries. We asked the oldest piscator that lived in the vicinity of these "dry lakes" for information, and he told us that it was "old Uncle Zac," and gave us his history in a brief and pathetic manner, concluding his reminiscences of the great departed as follows:

"Uncle Zac never know'd nothing 'bout flies, or tickling trout, but it took him to tell the differance 'twixt a yarth-worm, a grub, or the young of a wasp's nest; in fact, he know'd fishes amazin', and bein' natur-ally a hunter, he went to shooten 'em with a bow and arrer, to keep up yearly times in his history, when he tuck inguns, and yerther varmints in the same way."

WIT OF THE WOODS

Originally the wild turkey was found scattered throughout the whole of our continent, its habits only differing, where the peculiarity of the seasons compelled it to provide against excessive cold or heat. In the "clearing," it only lives in its excellent and degenerated descendant of the farm-yard. In the vast prairies and forests of the "far west," this bird is still abundant, and makes an important addition to the fare of wild life. It is comparatively common on the "frontiers;" but every passing year lessens its numbers, and as their disappearance always denotes their death, their extermination is progressive and certain. In Louisiana, Alabama, South Carolina, and the southern states, there are fastnesses, in which they will find support and protection for a long time to come. The swamps and lowland that offer no present inducement to "the settler," will shelter them from the rifle; and in the rich productions of the soil they will find a superabundance of food. The same obscurity, however, that protects them, leaves the hole of the wildcat in peace; and this bitter enemy of the turkey wars upon it, and makes its life one of cunning and care. Nor is its finely flavoured meat unappreciated by other destroyers, as the fox and weasel select the young for an evening repast, according to their strength. The nest, too, may be made, even the young bird in peace may have broken its shell, and frightened at its own piping note, hid instinctively away, when the Mississippi will rise, bearing upon its surface the waters of a thousand floods, swell within its narrow banks, and overflow the lowlands. The young bird, unable to fly, and too delicate to resist the influence of the wet, sickens and dies. Upon the *dryness* of the season the turkey-hunter builds his hopes of the plentifulness of the game.

The wild turkey-hunter is distinct and peculiar. The eccentric habits of the bird, its exceeding wildness is sympathized with, and enjoyed only by a class of persons, who are themselves different from the ordinary hunter. As a general thing, turkey-hunters, if they are of literary habits, read Izaak Walton, and Burton's "Anatomy of Melancholy," and all, learned or unlearned, are enthusiastic disciples of the rod and line.

The piscator can be an enthusiastic admirer of the opera, the wild turkey-hunter could not be, for his taste never carries him beyond the simple range of natural notes. Here he excels. Place him in the forest with his pipe, and no rough Pan ever piped more wilily, or more in harmony with the scenes around him. The same tube modulates the note of alarm, and the dulcet sound of love; it plays plaintively the complaining of the female, and, in sweet chirps, calls forth the lover from his hiding-place; it carols among the low whisperings of the fledgling, and expresses the mimic sounds of joy at the treasure of food that is discovered under the fallen leaf, or hidden away in the decayed wood. And all this is done so craftily, that ears, on which nature has set her stamp of peculiar delicacy, and the instinct, true almost as the shadow to the sunlight, are both deceived.

It is unnecessary to describe the bird, though we never see it fairly represented except in the forest. The high mettled racer that appears upon the course is no more superior to the well fed cart-horse than is the wild turkey to the tame; in fact nothing living shows more points of health and purity of blood than this noble bird. Its game head and clear hazle eye, the clean firm step, the great breadth of shoulder, and deep chest, strike the most superficial observer. Then there is an absolute commanding beauty about them, when they are alarmed or curious, when they elevate themselves to their full height, bringing their head perpendicular with their feet, and gaze about, every feather in its place, the foot upraised ready at an instant, to strike off at a speed, that, as has been said of the ostrich, "scorneth the horse and his rider."

The wild turkey-hunter is a being of solitude. There is no noise or boisterous mirth in his pursuit. Even the dead leaf, as it sails in circuitous motion to the earth, intrudes upon his caution, and alarms the wary game, which, in its care of preservation, flies as swiftly before the imaginary, as before the real danger. Often, indeed, is the morning's work destroyed by the cracking of a decayed limb under the nimble spring of the squirrel. The deer and timid antelope will stop to gratify curiosity, the hare scents the air for an instant, when alarmed, before it dashes off; but the turkey never speculates, never wonders; suspicion of danger prompts it to immediate flight, as quickly as a reality.

The implements of the turkey-hunter are few and simple; the "call," generally made of the large bone of the turkey's wing, and a sure rifle complete the list. The double-barrel fowling-piece is used when the game is plentiful, and requires little or no science to hunt them, aim being taken at the head. A turkey, wounded elsewhere than in the brain, although a rifle ball may have passed through its body, seems to retain the power of locomotion in the most remarkable manner, and will, when thus crippled, run long enough, unless pursued by a dog, to be lost to the hunter.

Where turkeys are plentiful and but little hunted, indifferent persons succeed in killing them; of such hunters we shall not speak. The bird changes its habits somewhat with its haunts, growing wilder as it is most pursued; it may therefore be said to be the wildest of game. Gaining in wisdom according to the necessity, it is a different bird where it is constantly sought for as game, from where it securely lives in the untrodden solitude. The turkey will therefore succeed at times in finding a home in places comparatively "thickly settled," and be so seldom seen, that they are generally supposed to be extinct. Under such circumstances, they fall victims only to the very few hunters who may be said to make a science of their pursuit. "I rather think," said a turkey-hunter, "if you want to find a thing *very cunning*, you need not go to the fox or such varmints; take a gobbler. I once hunted regular after the same one for three years, and never saw him twice. I knew the critter's 'yelp' as well as I know Music's, my old deer dog; and his track was as plain to me as the trail of a log hauled through a dusty road. I hunted the gobbler always in the same 'range,' and about the same 'scratchins,' and he got so, at last, that when I 'called,' he would run from me, *taking the opposite direction to my own foot-tracks*. Now the old rascal kept a great deal on a ridge, at the end of which, where it lost itself in the swamp, was a hollow cypress tree. Determined to outwit him, I put on my shoes *heels foremost*, walked leisurely down the ridge, and got into the hollow tree, and gave a 'call,' and boys," said the speaker exultingly, "it would have done you good to have seen that turkey coming towards me on a trot, the fool looking at my tracks, and thinking I had *gone the other way*."

Of all turkey-hunters, our friend W—— is the most experienced; he is a bachelor, lives upon his own plantation, studies, philosophizes, makes fishing tackle, and kills turkeys. With him it is a science reduced to certainty. Place him in the woods where turkeys are, and he is as certain of their bodies as if they were already in his possession. He understands the habits of the bird so well, that he will, on his first essay, on a new hunting-ground, give the exact character of the hunters the turkeys have been accustomed to deal with. The most crafty turkeys are those which W—— seeks, hemmed in by plantations, inhabiting uncultivatable land, and always in more or less danger of pursuit and discovery, they become, under such circumstances, beyond any game whatever wild. They seem incapable of being deceived, and taking every thing strange, as possessed to them of danger, whether a moth out of season, or a veteran hunter, they appear to common, and even to uncommon observers, annihilated from the country, were it not for their footprints occasionally to be seen in the soft soil beside the running stream, or in the light dust in the beaten road.

A veteran gobbler, used to all the tricks of the hunter's art, one who has had his wattles cut with shot, against whose well-defended breast has struck the spent ball of the rifle, one, who, although most starved, would walk by the treasures of grain in the "trap" and "pen," a gobbler who will listen to the plaintive note of the female until he has tried its quavers, its length, its repetitions, by every rule nature has given him, and then perhaps not answer, except in a smothered voice for fear of being deceived. Such a turkey will W—— select to break a lance with, and, in spite of the chances against him, win. We, then, here have the best specimen of wild turkey-hunting, an exhibition of skill between the perfection of animal instinct, and the superior intellect of man.

The turkey-hunter, armed with his "call," starts into the forest, he bears upon his shoulder, the trusty rifle. He is either informed of the presence of turkeys, and has a particular place or bird in view, or he makes his way cautiously along the banks of some running stream; his progress is slow and silent; it may be that he unexpectedly hears a noise, sounding like distant thunder; he then knows that he is in close proximity of the game, and that he has disturbed it to flight. When such is the case his work is comparatively done.

We will, for illustration, select a more difficult hunt. The day wears towards noon, and the patient hunter has met with no "sign," when suddenly a slight noise is heard, not unlike, to unpractised ears, a thousand other woodland sounds; the hunter listens, again the sound is heard, as if a pebble was dropped into the bosom of a little lake. It may be that woodpecker, who, desisting from his labours, has opened his bill to yawn—or, perchance, yonder little bird so industriously scratching among the dead leaves of that young holly. Again, precisely the same sound is heard; yonder, high in the heavens, is a solitary hawk, winging its way over the forests, its rude scream etherealized, might come down to our ears in just such a sound as made the turkey-hunter listen; again the same note, now more distinct. The quick ear of the hunter is satisfied; stealthily he entrenches himself behind a fallen tree, a few green twigs are placed before him, from among which protrudes the muzzle of his rifle. Thus prepared, he takes his "call," and gives one solitary *cluck*, so exquisitely, that it chimes in with the running brook and the rustling leaf.

It may be, that a half a mile off, if the place is favourable to convey sound, is feeding a "gobbler;" prompted by his nature, as he quietly scratches up the herbage that conceals his food, he gives utterance to the sounds that first attracted the hunter's attention. Poor bird! he is bent on filling his crop; his feelings are listless, common place; his wings are awry; his plumage on his breast seems soiled with rain, his wattles are contracted and pale,—look, he starts, every feather is instantly in its place, he raises his delicate game-looking head full four feet from the ground, and listens; what an eye, what a stride is suggested by that lifted foot! gradually the head sinks; again the bright plumage grows dim, and with a low *cluck*, he resumes his search for food. The treasures of the American forest are before him; the choice pecan-nut is neglected for that immense "grub-worm" that rolls down the decayed stump, too large to crawl,—now that grasshopper is nabbed, presently a hill of ants presents itself, and the bird leans over it, peering down the tiny hole of its entrance, out of which are issuing the industrious insects, with wondering curiosity. Again that *cluck* greets his ear, up rises the head with lightning swiftness, the bird starts forward a pace or two, looks around in wonder, and answers back. No sound is heard but the falling acorn, and it fairly echoes, as it rattles from limb to limb, and dashes off to the ground. The bird is uneasy, he picks pettishly, smooths down his feathers, elevates his head slowly, and then brings it to the earth; raises his wings as if for flight, jumps upon the limb of a fallen tree, looks about, settles down finally into a brown study, and evidently commences thinking. An hour may elapse, and he has resolved the matter over; his imagination has become inflamed, he has heard just enough to *wish to hear more*; he is satisfied that no turkey-hunter uttered the sounds that reached his ear, for they were *too few, and far between*, and there rises up in his mind some disconsolate mistress, and he gallantly flies down from his low perch, gives his body a swaggering motion, and utters a distinct and prolonged *cluck*, significant of both surprise and joy. On the instant the dead twigs near by crack beneath a heavy tread, and he starts off under the impression he is caught; but the meanderings of some poor cow inform him of his mistake. Composing himself, he listens, ten minutes since he challenged, when a low cluck in the distance reaches his ears.

Now, our gobbler is an old bird, and has escaped with his life by a miracle several times. He has grown very cunning, indeed. He don't roost two successive nights on the same tree, so that daylight never exposes him to the hunter, who has hidden himself away in the night, to catch him in the morning's dawn. He never gobbles without running a short distance at least, as if alarmed at his own noise. He presumes every thing suspicious, and dangerous naturally, and his experience has heightened the instinct. Twice, when young, was he coaxed within gunshot, but got clear by some fault of the percussion caps. After that, was he fooled by an idle school-boy, who was a kind of ventriloquist, and would have been killed, had not the urchin's gun been over-loaded. Three times did he only escape death by heedlessly wandering with his thoughtless fellows. Once was he caught in a "pen," and got out by an overlooked hole in its top. Three feathers of his last year's tail, decayed under the weight of a spring-trap. He is, in fact, a very "deep" bird, and will sit and plume himself, when common hunters are about, tooting away, but never so wisely as to deceive him twice. They all reveal themselves by overstepping the modesty of nature, and *woo him too much:* his loves are more coy, far less intrusive. Poor bird! he does not know that W—— is spreading his snare for him, and is even then so sure of his victim, as to be revolving in his mind whether his goodly carcass should be a present to a married friend, or be served up in savoury fumes from his own bachelor, but hospi-table board.

The last *cluck* heard by the gobbler fairly roused him, and he presses forward; at one time he runs with speed, then stops as if not yet quite satisfied; something turns him back; still he lingers only for a moment in his course, until coming to a running stream, where he will have to fly; the exertion seems too much for him. Stately parading in the full sunshine, he walks along the margin of the clear stream, admiring his fine person as it is reflected in the sylvan mirror, and then, like some vain lover, tosses his head, as if to say, "let them come to me." The listless gait is resumed, expressive that the chase is given up. Gaining the ascent of a low bank, that lines the stream he has just deserted, he stops at the foot of a young beech; in the green moss that fills the interstices of the otherwise smooth bark is hid away a cricket; the turkey picks at it, without catching it; something annoys him. Like the slipper of Cinderella, to the imagination of the young prince, or the glimpses of a waving ringlet, or a jewelled hand to the glowing passions of the young heart, is the remembrance of that sound, that now full two hours since was first heard by our hero, and has been, in that long time, but *twice* repeated. He speculates that in the shady woods that surround him, there must wander a mate; solitary she plucks her food, and calls for me; the monster man, impatient of his prey, doles not out his music so softly or so daintily. I am not deceived, and by my ungallant fears, she will be won by another. *Cluck.* How well-timed the call. The gobbler entirely off his guard, contracts himself, opens wide his mouth, and rolls forth, fearlessly, a volume of sound for his answer. The stream is crossed in a flutter, the toes scarce indent themselves in the soft ground over which they pass. On, on they plunge, until their owner's caution again brings them to a halt. We could almost wish that so fine a bird might escape, that there might be given one "call" too much, one that grated unnaturally on the poor bird's ear; but not so; they lead him to his doom, filling his mind with hope and love.

To the bird there is one strange incongruity in the "call," never before has he gone so far with so little success; but the note is perfect, the time most nicely given. Again he rolls forth a loud response, and listens, yet no answer, his progress is slow. The *cluck* again greets his ear; there was a slight quaver attached to it this time, like the forming of a second note; he is nearing his object of pursuit, and, with an energetic "call;" he rushes forward, his long neck stretched, and his head moving inquiringly from side to side. No longer going round the various obstacles he meets with in his path, but flying over them, as if impatiently, he comes to open ground, and stops.

Some six hundred yards from where he stands may be seen a fallen tree, you can observe some green brush that looks as if it grew out of the very decayed wood; in this "brush" is hidden away the deadly rifle, and its muzzle is protruding towards the open ground. Behind it is the hunter, flat upon the ground, yet so placed that the weapon is at his shoulder. He seems to be as dead as the tree in front of him. Could you watch him closely, you would perceive he scarcely winks for fear of alarming his game. The turkey, still in his exposed situation, gobbles on the instant the hunter raises his "call" to his lips, and gives a prolonged *cluck*, loud and shrill, the first that could really be construed by the turkey into a direct answer. The noble bird, now certain of success, fairly dances with delight; he starts forward, his feathers and neck amorously playing as he advances; now he commences his "strut;" his slender body swells, the beautiful plumage of his breast unfolds itself, his neck curves, drawing the head downward, the wattles grow scarlet, while the skin that covers the head changes like rainbow tints. The long feathers of the wings brush the ground, the tail rises and opens into a semi-circle, the gorgeously coloured head becomes beautifully relieved in its centre. On he comes, with a hitching gait, glowing in the sunshine in purple and gold. The siren *cluck* is twice repeated; he contracts his form to the smallest dimensions; upwards rises the head to the highest point; he stands upon his very toes, and looks suspiciously around; fifty yards of distance protects him from the rifle: he even condescends to pick about. What a trial for the expecting hunter! how does he recollect that one breath too much has spoiled a morning's work! The minutes wear on, and the bird again becomes the *caller;* he gobbles, opens his form, and when fully bloomed out, the enchanting *cluck* greets his ear; on he comes, like the gay horse, towards the inspiring music of the drum, or like a gallant bark beating against the wind, gallantly but slowly.

The dark cold barrel of the rifle is now not more silent than is its owner; the game is playing just outside the very edge of its deadly reach; the least mistake and it is gone. One gentle zephyr, one falling twig, might break the charm, and make nature revolt at the coyness apparent in the supposed mistress, and the lover would wing his way full of life to the woods. But on he comes, so still is every thing that you can hear his wings as they brush the ground, singularly plain, while the sun plays in conflicting rays and coloured lights about his gaudily bronzed plumage.

The woods ring in echoing circles back upon you, the sharp report of the rifle is heard; out starts, alarmed by the noise, a blue jay, who squalls as he passes in waving lines before you, so suddenly wakened was he from his sleep. But our rare and beautiful bird, our gallant and noble bird, our cunning and game bird, where is he? The glittering plumage, the gay step, the bright eye, all are gone, without a movement of the muscles, he has fallen a headless body to the earth.

PICTURES OF BUFFALO HUNTING

The buffalo is decidedly one of the noblest victims that is sacrificed to the ardour of the sportsman. There is a massiveness about his form, and a magnificence associated with his home, that give him a peculiar interest. No part of North America was originally unoccupied by the buffalo. Where are now cities and towns, is remembered as their haunts; but they have kept with melancholy strides before the "march of civilization," and now find a home, daily more exposed and invaded, only on that division of our continent west of the Mississippi. In the immense wilds that give birth to the waters of the Missouri, on the vast prairies that stretch out like inland seas between the "great lakes" and the Pacific, and extend towards the tropics until they touch the foot of the Cordilleras, the buffalo roams still wild and free. Yet the day of his glory is past. The Anglo-Saxon, more wanton of place than the savage himself, possessed of invincible courage and unlimited resources, and feeling adventure a part of life itself, has already penetrated the remotest fastnesses, and wandered over the most extended plains. Where the live lightning leaps from rock to rock, opening yawning caverns to the dilating eye, or spends its fury upon the desert, making it a sheet of fire, there have been his footsteps, and there has the buffalo smarted beneath his prowess, and kissed the earth.

The child of fortune from the "old world," the favourite of courts, has abandoned his home and affections, and sought, among these western wilds, the enjoyment of nature in her own loveliness. The American hunter frolics over them as a boy enjoying his Saturday sport. The Indian, like his fathers, never idle, scours the mountain and the plain; and men of whatever condition here meet *equal, as sportsmen*, and their great feats of honour and of arms are at the sacrifice of the buffalo.

In their appearance, the buffalos present a singular mixture of the ferocious and comical. At a first glance they excite mirth; they appear to be the sleek-blooded kine, so familiar to the farm-yard, muffled about the shoulders in a coarse shawl, and wearing a mask and beard, as if in some outlandish disguise. Their motions, too, are novel. They dash off, tail up, shaking their great woolly heads, and planting their feet under them, with a swinging gait and grotesque precision, that suggests the notion, that they are a jolly set of dare-devils, fond of fun and extravagances, and disposed to have their jokes at the expense of all dignity of carriage, and the good opinion of the grave portion of the world. Upon nearer examination, you quail before the deep destructive instinct expressed in the eye; the shaggy mane distends, and shows the working of muscles fairly radiant with power; the fore-foot dashes into the hard turf, and furrows it, as if yielding water; the tail waves in angry curves; the eyeballs fill with blood, and with bellowing noise that echoes like the thunder, the white foam covers the shaggy jaws. Then the huge form grows before you into a mountain, then is animal sublimity before you, a world of appetite without thought, and force without reason.

Standing on one of the immense prairies of the "south-west," you look out upon what seems to be the green waving swell of the sea, suddenly congealed, and it requires but little fancy to imagine, when the storm-cloud sweeps over it, and the rain dashes in torrents against it, and the fierce winds bear down upon it, that the magic that holds it immovable may be broken, and leave you helpless on the billowy wave. On such an expanse, sublime from its immensity, roams the buffalo, in numbers commensurate with the extent, not unfrequently covering the landscape, until their diminishing forms mingle in the opposite horizons, like mocking spectres. Such is the arena of sport, and such in quantity is the game.

To the wild Indian the buffalo hunt awakens the soul as absorbingly as the defying yell on the war-path. With inflated nostril and distended eye, he dashes after his victim, revelling in the fruition of all the best hopes of his existence, and growing in his conceits of his favour with the "Great Spirit." To the rude white hunter, less imaginative than the savage, the buffalo hunt is the high consummation of his habit and power to destroy. It gratifies his ambition, and feasts his appetite; his work is tangible; he feels, hears, tastes, and sees it; it is the very unloosing of all the rough passions of our nature, with the conscience entirely at rest. To the "sportsman," who is matured in the constraint of cities and in the artificial modes of enlightened society, and who retains within his bosom the leaven of our coarser nature, the buffalo hunt stirs up the latent fires repressed by a whole life; they break out with an ardour, and he enters into the chase with an abandonment, that, while it gratifies every animal sense possessed by the savage and hunter, opens a thousand other avenues of high enjoyment known only to the cultivated and refined mind.

INDIAN BUFFALO HUNTERS.

Among the Indians there are but few ways to kill the buffalo; yet there are tribes who display more skill than others, and seem to bring more intellect to bear in the sport. The Cumanches in the south, and the Sioux in the north, are, from their numbers, warlike character, and wealth, among the aborigines, *the buffalo hunters*. The Cumanches in winter inhabit one of the loveliest countries in the world. While their summer haunts are covered with snow, and desolated with storm, they are travelling over the loveliest herbage, variegated with a thousand perfumed flowers, that yield fragrance under the crush of the foot. The wide savannas, that are washed by the Trinity and Brasos rivers, are everywhere variegated with clumps of live oak trees, among which you involuntarily look for the mansion of some feudal lord. Here are realized almost the wildest dreams of the future to the red man; and here the Cumanches, strong in numbers, and rich in the spontaneous productions of their native land, walk proud masters, and exhibit savage life in some of the illusive charms we throw around it while bringing a refined imagination to view such life in the distance. Thousands of this tribe of Indians will sometimes be engaged at one time in a buffalo hunt. In their wanderings about the prairies, they will leave trails, worn like a long-travelled road. Following the "scouts," until the vicinity of the animal is proclaimed, and then selecting a halting place, favourable for fuel and water, the ceremonies preparatory to a hunt take place. Then are commenced, with due solemnity, the prayers of the priests. The death-defying warrior, who curls his finger in his scalp-lock in derision before his enemies, bows in submission to the Invisible presence that bestows on the red man the great game he is about to destroy. The fastings, prayers, and self-sacrifices being finished, the lively excitement of the chase commences.

The morning sun greets the hunter divested of all unnecessary clothing, *his arrows numbered*, his harness in order; a plume floats from his crown, his long hair streams down his back, his well-trained horse, as wild as himself, anticipates the sport, and paws with impatience the ground. Far, far in the horizon are moving about, in black masses, the game; and with an exulting whoop, a party start off *with the wind*, dash across the prairie, and are soon out of sight.

285

The buffalo is a wary animal; unwieldy as he appears, he has a quick motion, and he takes the alarm, and at the approach of a human being, instinctively flies. An hour or two may elapse, when the distant masses of buffalo begin to move. There is evident alarm spreading through the ranks. Suddenly they fly! Then it is that thousands of fleet and impatient horsemen, like messengers of the wind, dash off *and meet the herds*. The party first sent out are pressing them in the rear; confusion seizes upon the alarmed animals, and they scatter in every direction over the plain. Now the hunters select their victims, and the blood is up. On speed the Indian and his horse. The long mane mingles with the light garments of the rider, and both seem instigated by the same instinct and spirit. On plunges the unwieldy object of pursuit, shaking his shaggy head, as if in despair of his safety. The speed of the horse soon overtakes the buffalo. The rider, dropping his rein, plucks an arrow from his quiver, presses his knees to the horse's sides, draws his bow, and with unerring aim, drives the delicate shaft into the vitals of the huge animal, who rushes on a few yards, curls his tail upwards, falters, falls on his face, and dies. An exulting shout announces the success, and the warrior starts off after another; and if he has performed his task well, *every bow that has twanged* marks the ownership of a huge carcass upon the sea of the prairie, as sacredly as the waiffe of the whaleman his victim on the sea itself. Thus, when the day's sport is over, every arrow is returned to its owner. If two have been used to kill the same animal, or any are wanting, having been carried away in mere flesh wounds, the want of skill is upbraided, and the unfortunate hunter shrinks from the sarcasms and observation of the successful with shame.

Following the hunter are the women, the labourers of the tribe. To them is allotted the task of tearing off the skin, selecting the choice pieces of flesh, and preserving what is not immediately consumed. Then follows the great feast. The Indian gluts himself with marrow and fatness, his eyes so bright with the fire of sport are glazed with bestiality, and he spends days and nights in wasteful extravagance, trusting to the abundance of nature to take care of the future. Such are the general characteristics of the buffalo hunt; and the view applies with equal truth to all the different tribes who pursue, as a distinct and powerful people, this noble game.

An Indian armed for the buffalo hunt, and his horse, form two of the most romantic and picturesque of beings. The little dress he wears is beautifully arranged about his person, disclosing the muscles of the

286

shoulder and chest. Across his back is slung his quiver of arrows, made from the skin of some wild animal; his long bow, slightly arched by the sinewy string, is used gracefully as a rest to his extended arm. The horse, with a fiery eye, a mane that waves over his front like drapery and falls in rakish masses across his wide forehead, a sweeping tail ornamented with the brilliant plumage of tropical birds, champs on his rude bit, and arches his neck with impatience, as the scent of the game reaches his senses. Frequently will the two pass along, the rider's body thrown back, and the horse bounding gracefully along, as if in emulation of the equestrians portrayed upon the Elgin marbles. Then they may be seen dashing off with incredible swiftness, a living representation of the centaur; and as one of these wild horses and wilder men, viewed from below, stand in broad relief against the clear sky, you see a living statue that art has not accomplished. The exultation of such a warrior, in the excitement of a buffalo hunt, rings in silvery tones across the plain, as if in his lungs was the music of a "well-chosen pack;" the huge victims of pursuit, as they hear it, impel on their bodies with redoubled speed, as if they knew there was a hurricane of death in the cry.

A HUNTING-PARTY.

Take a hunting-party of fifty "warriors," starting on a buffalo hunt. Imagine a splendid fall morning in the southern part of the buffalo "grounds." The sun rises over the prairie, like a huge illuminated ball; it struggles on through the mists, growing gradually brighter in its ascent, breaking its way into the clear atmosphere in long reaching rays, dispelling the mists in wreathing columns, and starting up currents of air to move them sportively about; slowly they ascend and are lost in the ether above. You discover before you, and under you, a rich and beautifully variegated carpet, crowded with and enamelled by a thousand flowers, glistening with the pearly drops of dew, as the horizontal rays of the sun reach them. Here and there are plants of higher growth, as if some choice garden had been stripped of its enclosures: shrubbery waves the pendant blossom, and wastes a world of sweetness on the desert air. Among these flowery coverts will be seen browsing the graceful deer and antelope. Far before you are the long dark lines of the buffalo. In the centre of the group feed the cows and calves. Upon the outside are the sturdy bulls: some, with their mouths to the ground, are making it shake with their rough roar; others sportively tear up the turf with their horns; others, not less playful, are rushing upon each other's horns with a force that sends them reeling to the ground. Animal enjoyment seems rife, as they turn their nostrils upwards and snuff in the balmy air and greet the warm sun, little dreaming that around them are circling the sleek Indian, wilder, more savage, and more wary than themselves.

Fancy these Indians, prompted by all the habits and feelings of the hunter and warrior, mingling in the sport the desire to distinguish themselves, as on a field of honour, little less only in importance than the war-path. With characters of high repute to sustain, or injured reputations to build up, of victory for the ear of love, of jealousy, of base passions, and a thirst of blood, and you will have some idea of the promptings of the hearts of those about to engage in the chase.

The time arrives. The parties already out are driving the herd towards the starting-place of the warriors. They have sent up their war-cry in one united whoop, that has startled the feeding monsters, as if the lightning had fallen among them. With a fearful response, they shake their heads, and simultaneously start off. The fearful whoop meets them at every point. Confusion seizes upon the herd. The sport has begun. In every direction you see the unequal chase; the Indians seem multiplied into hundreds; the plain becomes dotted over with the dying animals, and the whoop rings in continuous shouts upon the air, as if the fiends themselves were loose.

Now you see a single warrior: before him is rushing a buffalo which shows, from his immense size, that he was one of the masters of the herd: his pursuer is a veteran hunter, known far and near for his prowess. Yonder go some twenty buffalos of every size, pursued by three or four tyros, yet who know not the art of separating their victim from the herd. Yonder goes a bull, twice shot at, yet only wounded in the flesh: some one will have to gather wood with the women for his want of skill. There goes an old chief: his leggins are trimmed with the hair of twenty scalps, taken from the heads of the very Indians on whose grounds he was hunting buffalo: he is a great warrior; he sings that his bow unbent is a great tree that he alone can bend. See the naked arm, and the rigid muscles, as he draws the arrow to the *very head:* the bull vomits blood, and falls: beyond him, on the grass, is the arrow; it passed through where a rifle bail would have stopped and flattened, ere it had made half the journey. Here are two buffalo bulls side by side; they make the earth tremble by their measured tread; their sides are reeking with sweat. Already have they been singled out. Approaching them are two horsemen; upon the head of one glistens the silvery hair of age; the small leggins also betray the old man: the other is just entering the prime of life; every thing about him is sound, full, and sleek. The eyes of one dance with excitement, the blood flows quickly through the dark skin, and gives a feverish look to the lip and cheek. The other, the old man, has his mouth compressed into a mere line; the eye is open and steady as a basilisk, the skin inanimate. What a tale is told in these differences of look! how one seems reaching into the future, and the other going back to the past! He of the flushed cheek touches his quiver, the bow is bent, the arrow speeds its way and penetrates its victim. The old man, he too takes an arrow, slowly he places it across his bow, then bending it as if to make its ends meet, he leans forward—sends the arrow home—the bull falls, while the first wounded one pursues his way. The old man gives a taunting shout, as the token of his success. The young warrior, confused by his want of skill, and alarmed lest his aged rival should complete the work he so bunglingly began, unguardedly presses too near the bull, who, smarting with his wound, turns upon his heels, and, with one mad plunge, tears out the bowels of the steed, and rolls him and rider on the ground. He next rushes at the rider. The Indian, as wary as the panther, springs aside, and the bull falls headlong on the ground. Ere he recovers himself the bow is again bent, the flint-headed arrow strikes the hard rib, splits it asunder, and enters the heart. The old warrior has looked on with glazed eye and expressionless face. The young man feels that he has added no laurels to his brow, for an arrow has been spent in vain, and his steed killed under him.

There goes a "brave" with a bow by his side, and his right hand unoccupied. He presses his horse against the very sides of the animal which he is pursuing. Now he leans forward until he seems hidden between the buffalo and his horse. He rises; a gory arrow is in his hand; he has plucked it from a "flesh wound" at full speed, and while in luck has, with better aim, brought his victim to the earth. The sun is now fairly in its zenith: the buffalos that have escaped are hurrying away, with a speed that will carry them miles beyond the hunter's pursuit. The Indians are coming in from the field. The horses breathe hard, and are covered with foam. The faces of the Indians are still lit up with excitement, that soon will pass away, and leave them cold and expressionless. The successful hunters spare not the gibe and joke at the expense of the unfortunate. Slowly they wend their way back to "the encampment;" their work is done.

The squaws, who, like vultures, have been following in the rear, have already commenced their disgusting work. The maiden is not among them; slavery commences only with married life; but the old, the wrinkled, the viragoes and vixens, are tearing off the skins, jerking the meat, gathering together the marrow-bones, and the humps, the tongues, and the pouch; and before the sun has fairly set, they are in the camp with the rewards of the day's hunt.

The plain, so beautiful in the morning, is scattered over with bodies already offensive with decay; the grass is torn up, the flowers destroyed, and the wolf and buzzard and the carrion-crow are disputing for the loathsome meal, while their already gorged appetites seem bursting with repletion.

OUR FIRST BUFFALO STEAK.

On the confines of the buffalo hunting-grounds, migrated a family, consisting of a strange mixture of enterprise and idleness, of ragged-looking men and homely women. They seemed to have all the bad habits of the Indians, with none of their redeeming qualities. They were willing to live without labour, and subsist upon the bounties of nature. Located in the fine climate of Northern Texas, the whole year was to them little else than a continued spring, and the abundance of game with which they were surrounded afforded what seemed to them all the comforts of life. The men never exerted themselves except when hunger prompted, or a spent magazine made the acquisition of "pelt-ries" necessary to barter for powder and ball. A more lazy, contempt-ible set of creatures never existed, and we would long since have forgotten them, had not our introduction to them associated itself with *our first buffalo steak*.

It was a matter of gratulation to my companions as well as myself, that, after sleeping on the open prairies, over which we had been travelling for many days, we discovered ahead of us what evinced the location of a "squatter." A thousand recollections of the comforts of civilized life pressed upon us before we reached the abode. We speculated upon the rich treat of delicacies which we should enjoy. A near inspection at once dispelled our illusions. A large rudely-constructed shed, boarded up on the northern side, was all we found. Upon nearer examination, it appeared that this "shed" was the common dwelling-place of the people described above, with the addition of two cows, several goats, poultry, and, as we soon after discovered, three horses. Immediately around the caravansera the prairie grass struggled for a sickly growth. As you entered it, you found yourself growing deeper and deeper in a fine dust, that had been in the course of time worked out of the soil. Some coarse blankets were suspended through the enclosure, as retiring rooms for the women. On the ground were strewn buffalo skins, from which the animal inhabitants kept aloof. We entered without seeing a human being. After some delay, however, a little nondescript, with a white sunburnt head, thrust aside the blankets, and hallooed out, "They ain't injuns." The mother then showed herself. She was as far removed from feminine as possible, and appeared as unmoved at our presence as the post that sustained the roof of her house. We asked for lodging and food; she nodded a cold assent and disappeared. Not disposed to be fastidious, we endeavoured to make ourselves as comfortable as possible, and wait for the developement of coming events. In the course of an hour a woman younger than the first made her appearance, somewhat attractive because younger. On hearing the detail of our wants, she wrinkled her soiled visage into a distorted smile, and told us that the "men" would soon be home with "buffalo meat," and then our wants should be attended to.

Whatever might have been our disappointment at what we saw around us, the name of buffalo meat dispelled it all. The great era in our frontier wanderings was about to commence, and with smiles from our party that for expression would have done credit to rival belles, we lounged upon the skins upon the ground. It is needless for us to say what were our ideas of the "men," soon to make their appearance. Buffalo hunters were, of course, tall, fine-looking fellows, active as cats, mounted upon wild steeds, armed with terrible rifles, and all the paraphernalia of the hunter's art. The Dutch angels, that figure so conspicuously on many a gem of art in the "Lowlands," are certainly not farther removed from the beautiful creations of Milton, than were the buffalo hunters that we saw from the standard our imagination and reading had conjured up.

Two short, ill-formed men, with bow-legs, long bodies, and formidable shocks of red hair, destitute of intelligence, clothed in skins, and moving with shuffling gaits, were the realities of our conceptions. Whatever might have been the charms of their faces, our admiration was absorbed in viewing their nether garments. They were made of undressed deer-skin, the hair worn outside. When first made, they were of the length of pantaloons, but the drying qualities of the sun had, in course of time, no doubt imperceptibly to the wearers, shortened them into the dignity of breeches. To see these worthies standing up was beyond comparison ridiculous. They seemed to have had immense pummels fastened to their knees and seats. Under other circumstances, the tailor craft of the frontier would have elicited great merriment; but a starving stomach destroys jokes. Courtesies suitable were exchanged, and the preliminaries for a hearty meal agreed upon, the basis of which was to be *buffalo steaks*.

A real buffalo steak! eaten in the very grounds which the animal inhabits! What romance! what a diploma of a sportsman's enterprise! Whatever might have been my disappointment in the hunters, I knew that meat was meat, and that the immutable laws of nature would not fail, though my notions of the romantic in men were entirely disappointed. A promise that our wants should soon be supplied brought us to that unpleasant time, in every-day life, that prefaces an expected and wished-for meal. Seated, like barbarians, upon the floor, myself and companions had the pleasing mental operation of calculating how little the frontier family we were visiting were worth for any moral quality, and the physical exercise of keeping off, as much as possible, thousands of fleas and other noxious insects that composed part of the dust in which we sat. While thus disposed of, the "hunters" were busy in various ways about the premises, and received from us the elegant names of "Bags" and "Breeches," from some fancied or real difference in their inexpressibles. "Breeches," who was evidently the business man, came near where we were sitting, and threw down upon the ground, what appeared, at a superficial glance, to be an enormous pair of saddle-bags. He then asked his companion in arms for a knife, to cut off the strangers some buffalo steaks. Now if the nondescript before me had as coolly proposed to cut steaks off an ill-natured cur that was wistfully eyeing the saddle-bags, no more surprise could have been exhibited by my companions than was, when they heard the suggestion.

The knife was brought, and "Breeches" made an essay at cutting up the saddle-bags, which gave him, dressed as he was in skins, the appearance of a wild robber just about to search the effects of some murdered traveller. The work progressed bravely, and, to our surprise, soon were exhibited crude slices of meat. What we saw were the fleshy parts of a buffalo's hams, ingeniously connected together by the skin that passed over the back of the animal, and so dissected from the huge frame as to enable it easily to be brought "into camp." As the sounds that accompany the frying of meat saluted our ears, we moved into the open air, to avoid the certain knowledge that we were about to complete the eating of the peck of dirt, said to be necessary before we die. Before the door were the two horses belonging to our hosts, just as they returned from the hunt, and upon one still reposed the huge pieces of meat, thus simply, and frontier-like, held together for transportation.

Our first buffalo steak disappointed us. The romance of months and of years was sadly broken in upon. The squalid wretchedness of those who administered to our wants made rebellious even our hungry stomachs, and we spent our first night of real disappointment on the great prairies, under circumstances which we thought, before our sad experience, would have afforded us all the substantial food for body and mind that we could have desired.

OUR FIRST BUFFALO HUNT.

The morning following the adventure with the steak found our little party, rifles in hand, and bent upon a buffalo hunt. The animals, it would seem, for the especial benefit of "Breeches" and "Bags," had come "lower down" than usual, and we were among the animals much sooner than we expected to be. So far fortune favoured us; and a gayer party never set out on a frolic than followed the deer-skin inexpressibles on the fine December morning to which we allude. As we jaunted along, crushing a thousand wild flowers under our horses' feet, the deer would bound like visions of grace and beauty from our presence; but we essayed not such small game. Our ideas and nostrils expanded, and we laughed so loud at the merry conceit of a man drawing a deadly weapon on a helpless thing as small as a woodcock, that the wild half devil and half Indian horses on which we were mounted pricked up their ears and tails, as if they expected the next salute would be the war-whoop and a fight. Ahead of us we beheld the buzzard circling in groups, whirling down in aerial flights to the earth, as if busy with their prey. We passed them at their gross repast over a mountain of meat that had, the day before, been full of life and fire, but had fallen under the visitation of our guides and scarecrows, and provided the very steaks that had met with so little affection from our appetites. Soon we discovered signs of immediate vicinity of the buffalo, and on a little examination from the top of a "swell of land," we saw them feeding off towards the horizon, like vast herds of cattle, quietly grazing within the enclosure of the farm-yard. As far off as they were, our hearts throbbed violently as we contemplated the sanguinary warfare we were about to engage in, and the waste of life that would ensue. Still we were impelled on by an irresistible and overpowering instinct to begin the hunt.

Breeches and Bags carried, over their shoulders, poles about six feet long; but as they were destitute of any spear, we looked upon them as inoffensive weapons, and concluded they had come out just to act as guides. In fact we could not imagine that such beastly-looking fellows, so badly mounted, could hunt any thing. For ourselves, we were armed with the terrible rifle, and so satisfied were we of its prowess, that we thought the very appearance of its muzzle more deadly than the rude implement of warfare used by the Indians.

Keeping to the windward of the buffalo, we skirted round until we got them between us and the shed wherein we passed the night. Then the signal was given, and in a pellmell manner we charged on, every man for himself. We approached within a quarter of a mile before the herd took the alarm. Then, smelling us on the air, they turned their noses towards the zenith, gave a sort of rough snort, and broke simultaneously off at a full gallop. As soon as this noise was heard by our horses, they increased their speed, and entered into the sport as ardently as their riders. The rough beasts rode by Bags and Breeches did wonders, and seemed really to fly, while their riders poised themselves gallantly, carrying their long poles in front of them with a grace that would have done honour to a Cossack bearing his spear.

The buffalo, with their tails high in the air, ran close together, rattling their horns singularly loud; while the horses, used to the chase, endeavoured to separate a single object for pursuit. This once accomplished, it was easy to range alongside, and in this situation the members of our party severally found themselves, and drawing deadly aim, as they supposed, the crack of the sharp rifle was heard over the prairies, and yet nothing was brought to the ground. Contrary to all this, a noble bull lay helpless in the very track I took, the fruit of Breeches' skill, and from the energetic manner he pressed on, we became satisfied that there was a magic in those sticks we had not dreamed of. Our curiosity excited, we ran across the diameter of a circle he was forming and came by his side. Soon he overtook his object of pursuit, and thrusting forward his pole, we saw glittering, for the first time, on its end a short blade; a successful thrust *severed the hamstring*, and a mountain of flesh and life fell helpless on the prairie. The thing was done so suddenly, that some moments elapsed before we could overcome our astonishment. My horse approached the animal and thrusting forward his head and ears muted in his face, and then commenced quietly cropping the grass. It would be impossible for me to describe my emotions as I, dismounting, examined the gigantic and wounded bull before me. There he lay, an animal, that from his singular expression of face and general appearance, joined with his immense size, looked like some animated specimen of the monsters of the antediluvian world. Rising on his fore legs, with his hind ones under him, he shook his mane and beard in defiance, and flashed from his eyes an unconquerable determination that was terrible to behold. His small delicate hoofs were associated in our minds with the farm-yard and the innocent pleasures of rural life. Gazing upwards, we beheld, fearfully caricatured, the shaggy trappings of the lion, and the wild fierceness of a perfect savage, the whole rising above us in huge unwieldy proportions. Making no demonstration of attack, the expression of defiance altered into that of seeming regret and heartsick pain; his small bright eye appeared to roam over the beautiful prairie, and to watch the retreating herds of his fellows, as would an old patriarch when about to bid adieu to the world; and as he looked on, the tear struggled in his eye, rolled over the rough sunburnt hair of his face, dashed like a bright jewel upon his knotted beard, and fell to the ground. This exhibition of suffering nature cooled the warm blood of the hunt within me; the instinct of destruction was for the time overpowered by that of better feelings, and could we have restored to health the wounded animal, it would have given us a thrill of real pleasure to have seen him bounding over the plain, again free. Instead of this, we took from our belt a pistol, called upon mercy to sanction our deed, and sent the cold lead through the thoughtful eye into the brain: the body sank upon its knees, in ready acknowledgment of the power of man; the heavy head plunged awkwardly to the ground; a tremulous motion passed through the frame—and it was dead.

The momentary seriousness of my own feelings, occasioned by the incidents above related, was broken in upon by a loud exulting whoop, prolonged into a quavering sound, such as will sometimes follow a loud blast of a trumpet at the mouth of an expert player. It was a joyous whoop, and vibrated through our hearts; we looked up, and saw just before us a young Indian warrior, mounted upon a splendid charger, rushing across the plain, evidently in pursuit of the retreating buffalo. As he swept by, he threw himself forward in his saddle, placed his right hand over his eyes, as if to shade them from the sun, making a picture of the most graceful and eager interest. His horse's head was low down, running like a rabbit, while the long flowing mane waved in the wind like silk. Horse and rider were almost equally undressed; both wiry; and every muscle, as it came into action, gave evidence of youth and power. Over the horse's head, and inwrought in the hair of the tail, streamed plumes plucked from the flamingo. Every thing was life—moving, dashing life—gay as the sunshine that glistens on the rippling wave where the falcon wets his wing. This soul-stirring exhibition warmed us into action, and, mounting our horses, we dashed after the red man. Our direction soon brought us in sight of the retreating buffalo; and, with the Indian and myself, dashed on a third person, the valiant "Breeches." I followed as a spectator, and, keeping close to both, was enabled to watch two beings so widely different in form, looks, and action, while bent on the same exciting pursuit.

Fortunately, two buffaloes, of large size, cut off from the main body, were being driven towards us by some one of our party; a distant report of a rifle, and the sudden stopping of one of the animals told its own tale. The remaining bull, alarmed by the report of the rifle, rushed madly on with enemies in front and rear. Discovering its new danger, it wheeled almost on its heels, and ran for life. Whatever might have been our most vivid imaginings of the excitement of a buffalo chase, we now felt the fruition beyond our sanguine hopes. Before us ran the buffalo, then followed the Indian, and beside him "Breeches," so closely that you would have thought a dark Apollo on a mettled charger by some necromancy casting the shadow of a cornfield scarecrow. We soon gained on the buffalo, rapidly as he moved his feet under him. "Breeches" poised his rude instrument to make the fearful cut at the hamstrings, when the Indian, plucking an arrow from his quiver, bent his bow, and pointing it at "Breeches's" side, as we thought, let it fly. The stick held by "Breeches" leaped from his grasp as if it had been struck by a club; another instant, and again the bow was bent; guiding his horse with his feet, he came alongside of the buffalo, and drove the arrow to the feather into his side. A chuckling guttural laugh followed this brilliant exploit, and as the animal after a few desperate leaps fell forward and vomited blood, again was repeated the same joyous whoop that roused our stagnant blood at the beginning of the chase.

The instant that "Breeches" dropped his stick, his horse, probably from habit, stopped, and the one I rode followed the example. The Indian dismounted and stood beside the buffalo the instant he fell. There was a simplicity and beautiful wildness about the group that would have struck the eye of the most insensible. The shaggy and rough appearance of the dead animal, the healthy-looking and un-groomed horse with his roving eye and long mane, and the Indian himself, contemplating his work like some bronze statue of antique art. "Breeches," alike insensible to the charms of the tailor's art, and the picturesque, handed the Indian his first fired arrow, and then stooping down, with a gentle pressure, thrust the head of the one in the buffalo's body through the opposite side, from which it entered, and handed it to its owner, with disgust marked upon his face, that displayed no great pleasure at his appearance and company.

Among the Indian tribes, there are certain styles of doing things which are as essential to command the attention and win the favour of a real hunter as there are peculiar manners and modes commended, and only acknowledged by sportsmen. A poor despicable tribe, bearing the name of Ta-wa-ki-na, inhabiting the plains of Texas, kill the buffalo by hamstringing them, and are, therefore, despised and driven out from among "Indian men." A young Cumanche chief, fond of adventure, and friendly with "Breeches," had gone out of his way to join in our sport; and having shown to the white man his skill, and for Breeches his contempt for his imitations of a despised tribe, he passed on in pursuit of his own business, either of war or of pleasure.

HAMSTRINGING THE BUFFALO.

The experience of our first buffalo-hunt satisfied us that the rifle was not the most effective instrument in destroying the animal. The time consumed in loading the rifle is sufficient for an Indian to shoot several arrows, while the arrow more quickly kills than the bullet. As the little party to which I was attached had more notions of fun than any particular method of hunting, a day was set apart for a buffalo hunt, "Ta-wa-ki-na fashion," and for this purpose rifles were laid aside, and poles about seven feet long, with razor blades fastened on them a few inches from the end, so as to form a fork, were taken in their place. Arriving in the vicinity of the buffalo, those who were disposed entered into the sport pellmell. Like a faithful squire I kept close at the heels of "Breeches," who soon brought a fine young heifer bellowing to the ground. As the animal uttered sounds of pain, one or two fierce-looking bulls that gallantly followed in the rear, exposing themselves to attack to preserve the weaker members of the herd, stopped short for an instant, and eyed us with most unpleasant curiosity. This roused the knight of the deer skin, Breeches, and brandishing his stick over his head with a remarkable degree of dexterity, he dashed off as if determined to slay both at once. My two companions who started out, Ta-wa-ki-nas, had done but little execution, not understanding their work, or alarmed at so near an approach of the animals they wounded, without bringing them to the earth. As "Breeches" dashed on after the bulls, he severally crossed the route of all who were on the chase; and as he was unquestionably the hero of the day, all followed in his train, determined to see hamstringing done scientifically.

It is a singular fact in the formation of the buffalo, and the familiar cattle of the farm-yard, that, although so much alike in general appearance, the domesticated animals will, after being hamstrung, run long distances. The buffalo, on the contrary, the moment the tendon is severed, falls to the ground entirely helpless, and perfectly harmless beyond the reach of its horns. A very short chase in company with "Breeches" brought us up to one of the bulls; he poised his stick, thrust it forward, and the *tendo Achillis*, full of life and full of action, was touched by the sharp blade; its tension, as it sustained the immense bull in his upward leaps, made it, when severed, spring back as will the breaking string of the harp; and the helpless beast, writhing in pain, came to the ground. One of our party witnessing this exhibition, gave an exulting shout, and declared he would bring a buffalo down, or break his neck; he soon came beside a venerable bull, and as he made repeated thrusts, a thousand directions were given as to the manner of proceeding. The race was a well-contested one, the heels of the pursued animal were strangely accelerated by the thrusts made at him in his rear. A lunge was finally accomplished by the "Ta-wa-ki-na," that almost threw him from his horse; the fearful cut brought the huge bull directly under the rider's feet; the next instant the noble steed was impaled upon the buffalo's horns, and the unfortunate rider lay insensible on the ground. The wrong hamstring, in the excitement, had been cut, the animal *always falling on the wounded side*. We hastened to our unfortunate companion, chafed his temples, and brought him to his senses. The first question he asked was, "whereabouts the buffalo struck him." Happily, save the loss of a generous steed, no great damage was done. The "Ta-wa-ki-na" acknowledged hamstringing buffalo was as contemptible as it was thought to be by the Cumanche chief. Thus ended this novel and barbarian hunt, that afforded incidents for many rough jokes, and amusing reflections on hamstringing buffaloes.

As a reward for these frontier sports, it is but just to say that we feasted plentifully upon buffalo steaks, marrow bones, humps, and tongues, yet we were not satisfied. There was a waste of life and of food accompanying the hunting of the animal, that, like an ever-present spirit of evil, took away from our enjoyment that zest which is necessary to make it a favourite sport.

ALLIGATOR KILLING

In the dark recesses of the loneliest swamps, in those dismal abodes where decay and production seem to run riot; where the serpent crawls from his den among the tangled ferns and luxuriant grass, and hisses forth its propensities to destroy unmolested; where the toad and lizard spend the livelong day in their melancholy chirpings; where the stagnant pool festers and ferments, and bubbles up its foul miasma; where the fungi seem to grow beneath your gaze; where the unclean birds retire after their repast, and sit and stare with dull eyes in vacancy for hours and days together; there, originates the alligator; there, if happy in his history, he lives and dies. The pioneer of the forest invades his home; the axe lets in the sunshine upon his hiding-places: he frequently finds himself, like the Indian, surrounded by the encroachments of civilization, a mere intruder in his original domain, and under such circumstances only does he become an object of rough sport, the incidents of which deserve a passing notice.

The extreme southern portions of the United States are exceedingly favourable to the growth of the alligator: in the swamps that stretch over a vast extent of country, inaccessible almost to man, they increase in numbers and size, live undisputed monarchs of their abodes, exhibiting but little more intelligence, or exerting but little more volition than the decayed trunk of the tree, for which they are not unfrequently taken. In these swampy regions, however, are frequently found high ridges of land inviting cultivation. The log cabin takes the place of the rank vegetation; the evidences of thrift appear; and as the running streams display themselves, and are cleared for navigation, the old settler, the alligator, becomes exposed, and daily falls a victim to the rapacity of man. Thus hunted, like creatures of higher organization, he grows more intelligent, from the dangers of his situation; his taste grows more delicate, and he wars in turn upon his only enemy; soon acquires a civilized taste for pork and poultry, and acquires also a very uncivilized one for dogs.

An alligator in the truly savage state is a very happy reptile: encased in an armour as impenetrable as that of Ajax, he moves about unharmed by surrounding circumstances. The fangs of the rattlesnake grate over his scales as they would over a file; the constrictor finds nothing about him to crush; the poisonous moccasin bites at him in vain; and the greatest pest of all, the musquitto, that fills the air of his abode with a million stings, that burn the flesh like sparks of fire, buzz out their fury upon his carcass in vain. To say that he enjoys not these advantages, that he crawls not forth as a proud knight in his armour, that he treads not upon the land as a master, and moves in the water the same, would be doing injustice to his actions, and his habits, and the philosophical example of independence which he sets to the trembling victims that are daily sacrificed to his wants.

The character of an alligator's face is far from being a flattering letter of recommendation. It suggests a rude shovel; the mouth extends from the extreme tip of the nose backwards until it passes the ears; indeed, about one-third of the whole animal is mouth, with the exact expression of a tailor's shears; and this mouth being ornamented with a superabundance of rows of white teeth, gives the same hope of getting out of it, sound in body and mind, if once in, as does the hopper of a bark-mill. Its body is short and round not unlike that of a horse; its tail is very long and flattened at the end like an oar. It has the most dexterous use of this appendage, propelling along, swiftly, and on land it answers the purpose of a weapon of defence.

The traveller through the lonely swamp at nightfall often finds himself surrounded by these singular creatures, and if he is unaccustomed to their presence and habits, they cause great alarm. Scattered about in every direction, yet hidden by the darkness, he hears their huge jaws open and shut with a force that makes a noise, when numbers are congregated, like echoing thunder. Again, in the glare of the campfire, will sometimes be seen the huge alligator crawling within the lighted circle, attracted by the smell of food—perchance you have *squatted* upon a nest of eggs, encased with great judgment in the centre of some high ground you yourself have chosen to pass the night upon. Many there are, who go unconcernedly to sleep with such intruders in their immediate vicinity; but a rifle-ball, effectively fired, will most certainly leave you unmolested, and the dying alligator, no doubt, comforts itself that the sun will not neglect its maternal charge, but raise up its numerous young as hideous and destructive as itself.

The alligator is a luxurious animal, fond of all the comforts of life, which are, according to its habits, plentifully scattered around it. We have watched them, enjoying their evening nap in the shades of

301

tangled vines, and in the hollow trunk of the cypress, or floating like a log on the top of some sluggish pool. We have seen them sporting in the green slime, and catching, like a dainty gourmand, the fattest frogs, and longest snakes; but they are in the height of their glory, stretched out upon the sand-bar, in the meridian sun, when the summer heats pour down and radiate back from the parched sand, as tangibly as they would from red hot iron. In such places will they bask and blow off, with a loud noise, the inflated air and water, that would seem to expand within them as if confined in an iron pipe, occasionally rolling about their swinish eyes with a slowness of motion, that, while it expresses the most perfect satisfaction, is in no way calculated to agitate their nerves, or discompose them by too suddenly taking the impression of outward objects. While thus disposed of, and after the first nap is taken, they amuse themselves with opening their huge jaws to their widest extent, upon the inside of which, instinctively settle, thousands of musquittoes and other noxious insects that infest the abode of the alligator. When the inside of the mouth is thus covered, the reptile brings his jaws together with inconceivable velocity, gives a gulp or two, and again sets his formidable trap for this small game.

Some years since, a gentleman in the southern part of Louisiana, "opening a plantation," found, after most of the forest had been cleared off, that in the centre of his land was a boggy piece of low soil covering nearly twenty acres. This place was singularly infested with alligators. Among the first victims that fell a prey to their rapacity, were a number of hogs and fine poultry; next followed most of a pack of fine deer hounds. It may be easily imagined that the last outrage was not passed over with indifference. The leisure time of every day was devoted to their extermination, until the cold of winter rendered them torpid and buried them up in the mud. The following summer, as is naturally the case, the swamp, from the heat of the sun, contracted in its dimensions; a number of artificial ditches drained off the water, and left the alligators little else to live in than mud, about the consistency of good mortar: still the alligators clung, with singular tenacity, to their native homesteads as if perfectly conscious that the coming fall would bring them rain. While thus exposed, a general attack was planned, carried into execution, and nearly every alligator of any size was destroyed. It was a fearful and disgusting sight to see them rolling about in the thick mud, striking their immense jaws together in the agony of death. Dreadful to relate, the stench of those decaying bodies in the hot sun produced an unthought-of evil. Teams of oxen were used in vain to haul them away; the progress of corruption under the sun of a tropical climate made the attempt fruitless. On the very edge of the swamp, with nothing exposed but the head, lay a huge monster, evidently sixteen or eighteen feet long; he had been wounded in the melee, and made incapable of moving, and the heat had actually baked the earth around his body as firmly as if imbedded in cement. It was a cruel and singular exhibition, to see so much power and destruction so helpless. We amused ourselves in throwing things into his great cavernous mouth, which he would grind up between his teeth. Seizing a large oak rail, we attempted to run it down his throat, but it was impossible; for he held it for a moment as firmly as if it had been the bow of a ship, then with his jaws crushed and ground it to fine splinters. The old fellow, however, had his revenge; the dead alligators were found more destructive than the living ones, and the plantation for a season had to be abandoned.

In shooting the alligator, the bullet must hit just in front of the fore legs, where the skin is most vulnerable; it seldom penetrates in other parts of the body. Certainty of aim, therefore, tells, in alligator shooting, as it does in every thing else connected with sporting. Generally, the alligator, when wounded, retreats to some obscure place; but if wounded in a *bayou*, where the banks are steep, and not affording any hiding-places, he makes considerable amusement in his convolutions in the water, and in his efforts to avoid the pain of his smarting wounds. In shooting, the instant you fire, the reptile disappears, and you are for a few moments unable to learn the extent of injury you have inflicted. An excellent shot, that sent the load with almost unerring certainty through the eye, was made at a huge alligator, and, as usual, he disappeared, but almost instantly rose again, spouting water from his nose, not unlike a whale. A second ball, shot in his tail, sent him down again, but he instantly rose and spouted: this singular conduct prompted a bit of provocation, in the way of a plentiful sprinkling of bits of wood, rattled against his hide. The alligator lashed himself into a fury; the blood started from his mouth; he beat the water with his tail until he covered himself with spray, but never sunk without instantly rising again. In the course of the day he died and floated ashore; and, on examination, it was found that the little valve nature has provided the reptile with, to close over its nostrils when under water, had been cut off by the first shot, and thus compelled him to stay on the top of the water to keep from being drowned. We have heard of many since who have tried thus to wound them, and although they have been hit in the nose, yet they have been so crippled as to sink and die.

The alligator is particularly destructive on pigs and dogs, when they inhabit places near plantations; and if you wish to shoot them, you can never fail to draw them on the surface of the water, if you will make a dog yell, or pig squeal; and that too, in places where you may have been fishing all day, without suspecting their presence. Herodotus mentions the catching of crocodiles in the Nile, by baiting a hook with flesh, and then attracting the reptile towards it by making a hog squeal. The ancient Egyptian manner of killing the crocodile is different from that of the present day, as powder and ball have changed the manner of destruction; but the fondness for pigs in the crocodile and alligator, after more than two thousand years, remains the same.

CONCORDIA LAKE*

Opposite the high bluffs of "the Natchez" lies the beautiful country of Concordia, level as the surface of water, and rich in its soil as it is possible for earth to be. At present a few large plantations occupy much of its space, laid off in enormous fields, where the plough sometimes progresses a mile without turning in the furrow. In old times the Mississippi ran through the lower part of Concordia, making one of those sudden bends where it comes back almost to the very point of diverging. In one of its capricious moods, it cut through this thusformed isthmus, and ran more directly to the sea, leaving a kind of horse-shoe furrow to mark the old bed of

*A DIAGRAM ILLUSTRATING THE FORMATION OF INLAND LAKES, NEAR THE BANKS OF THE MISSISSIPPI.

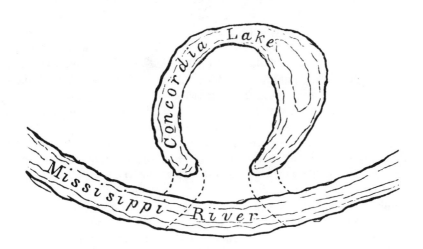

A "Cut-off."

In the above diagram by the dotted lines the original course of the Mississippi may be seen. At some time the river *cut off* its circular route and pursued its way straight ahead, leaving an inland lake of horse-shoe form. By a reference to any correct map, these lakes will all be found of the same general character and appearance. Many of the finest and largest known have thus been formed within the memory of inhabitants living on the river or the lakes.

the river. The high waters of the spring, bearing within their bosom the sediment of almost unlimited caving shores, deposited in time at the mouth of the "cut off" the solid earth, and thus formed, as has been done a hundred times before and is constantly doing now, the bed of an inland lake, bordering the shores of the Mississippi. Thus originated the beautiful lake of Concordia, upon the shores of which, we can imagine, in years not far hence, the continuous line of semi-palaces and the crowded mart; and resting upon its waters the gay pleasure-boat, and the cumbrous one of commerce, together with all the associations of a country long settled and full of wealth. At present, however, a different scene is presented; comparatively all is wild; the residences that reflect in its clear waters are like angels' visits, few and far between, while the fairy island, that is set like a gem in its centre, still remains in its primeval wilderness.

Along the shores of Concordia Lake is heard the oft-repeated echo of the sharp rifle and the ringing melody of the hound. In the luxuriant foliage of "the island" the beautiful deer graze plentifully and almost undisturbed. The wild turkey "clucks" to daylight almost as securely as its representative in the farm-yard. The hunter, starting his game on the mainland, expects that it will plunge into the lake to avoid the ruthless hound: and often, indeed, is the angler startled from his quiet by the deep-mouthed bay of the hard-pressing pack while in the still dark water, where he expected to deceive the trout, and to which he stole so stealthily, there will plunge the swelled-neck buck, bearing his proud antlers aloft, and, breasting the waves nobly, labouring for life. The light canoe or the rude skiff is pressed into service, by some "volunteer of the hunt," and pushed across to "the island." The buck, thus pressed on all sides, and perhaps met with a salute as he touches the shore from a murderous fowling-piece, plunges again into the lake. Every thing seems full of animation: you hear the shout of the hunters encouraging the dogs; amidst the music, trumpet-tongued, the breezes seem to spring up and shake the pendant foliage from sympathy. At break-neck pace, the well-trained horse, with distended eyes, leaps over the ravine and fallen tree, the happiest being in the chase, then checks his swift speed at command, and as steady as a rock awaits the shot from off his back; then again bounds forward to mark the work of death. The poor buck, pressed on all sides, and at every movement of his muscles parting, through his wounds, with his life's blood, turns upon his enemies, rears, plunges and strikes with his fore-feet; but he is dragged down and slain, his hair turned forward as roughly as the

306

quills of the porcupine, his eye mysteriously green from rage, and un-flinching in its defiance to the last. The excitement passes away. The horn rings merrily as a token of triumph, and silence again reigns. The angler resumes his sport, and the flocks of white crane settle down in the shallows. The waves, caused by the last throes of the dying deer, spend themselves in light shore-reaching circles until they are lost in the mirrored surface, and the last token of the presence of the most beautiful inhabitant of the forest is obliterated as if it had not been.

The angling of Lake Concordia is one of its distinctive features: if you will go to the favourite places, you can, at any time, overload yourself with fish. In the centre of the lake is its outlet; the Cocodra, a narrow and deep stream, bears off its waters towards the great Missis-sippi; a few miles run, it widens into "Turtle Lake," with bolder, and therefore, seemingly wilder scenery than is often to be met with in the alluvial. Turtle is a beautiful name; it suggests pleasant pictures. Upon the shores of Turtle Lake is heard the cooing of many doves; but it is Turtle Lake from its abundance of "green, amphibious soft-shells" that cover the fallen timber when the sun shines hot, and drop into the water at your near approach

"As easy as falling off a log."

In the immediate influence of the Cocodra, you can catch an abun-dance of trout or perch without much skill or trouble; but as you ap-proach the extreme ends or heads of the lake, more art and patience are required. It has been convenient for us to throw the line just where least reward might be expected, yet we have always been paid for our labour, and served our purpose well. We are great anglers, though we seldom catch fish. There is a spirit in the still waters or running brook that laves the soul, but we cannot communicate with it, unless it comes to us along the rod and line; herein, if naught else, would be our reward.

The winds, and the sky, and the tide, and the bait, and the tackle, affect catching fish; but they affect not thought. We sit down under the shade of the favourite tree, or the shelving bank, and cast our snare, and philosophize. We have often let the naked hook play the scare-crow among the game, while we have watched the mischievous black-bird shoot along the margin of the water, dabbling for minnows. There were a pair of eagles when we first knew Lake Concordia, that in the morning light rose up over the lowlands, as if they would peep down into the east, and surprise the sun at its getting up. There were no towering Himmalahs to rest their wings midway, and when they had

307

gilded their pinions with the coming glory, thus hailing the birth of another day, then they would shoot down to earth as if with glad tidings, and soar joyously over their wild home, fanning the still air into zephyrs, and sending the fearful waterfowl in confused groups from their presence. A tall cypress that peered over its fellows, held among its dead limbs at the top, a black confused mass that was known as "the eagle's nest;" it was entrenched by matted foliage that revels in the southern swamps, hiding away the alligator and other reptiles: it was beyond the reach of the rifle; the tallest and safest eyry for miles about. A hurricane may have prostrated it, or the thunderbolt shattered it—the eagles and their nest have disappeared.

A rough Virginia fence, over which the Cherokee rose had entwined itself, as if in mercy to its jagged appearance, made a good shade and a deep shadow at some hours of the day, and from its prodigal wealth in little buds, enlivened dull fishing. A little wren we remember in particular, who had built its nest in the hollow of the unsightly skull of an ox, suspended on an upright post of the fence. It was a little fellow, and busy beyond description; a perfect hen hussy; there was always a stray horsehair, or bit of moss in the wrong place, or too much down protruded from the eyeless sockets. We have watched the bird as we sat lazily waiting our fortune, and thought nature would thus pleasantly teach us a lesson of industry, and also one of gratitude. We have seen its little throat palpitate and swell with song until it seemed almost to despair of wringing out its music. It would throw its head upon its downy breast, and then raise it with each ascending note until it fairly screamed on its tiptoes, then tripping into its nest, a new thought would suggest itself, and again the air would be laden with sweet sounds, uttered, but never written, inspired by Him who created the harmony which met the ear when "the stars sang together for joy." A tap from our rod, but gently though, as if from a beauty's fan, and we turn to our occupation—struggling upon our line is a black perch; and now that we remember it, the float was out of sight when that bit of sweet sounds done up in feathers commenced pouring out its little heart to the spring and the sunshine.

Our early friend Elliott is a devoted angler; he has an interminable quantity of trappings; and when we first looked into his collection of rods, reels, hooks and swivels, we told him we feared they were like the rules of logic, more for show than use. He replied, we might make the same remark of the marriage ceremony, and think so too, if we put no value upon legitimacy. We saw there was something deeper than our philosophy in his answer, and have believed in costly tackling ever since. We found Elliott once fishing at a spot that commanded a fine view of the lake; just beyond him, there ran out into the water a sharp point graced with live oak trees covered with moss; behind the deep foliage, the sun was sinking, throwing dark shadows, while a stray pencil of light would here and there glance through the trees and kiss the water with almost blinding brilliancy. His thoughts were dissipated, for he was speculating upon the landscape, then listlessly looking at his success of the evening as an angler. He held up his "string" to our gaze; upon it was a beautiful fish burnished with silver; he was attractive indeed, to look at, but one acquainted with its merits knew too well of the infinite bones that spread under his gay exterior as confusedly as the stems of a brier-patch. This fish was kept merely for show. The next, and only one, was a juvenile perch; the poor innocent had scarcely got clear of the spawn, and become able to flourish in water fairly over its head, when his want of experience had placed him at the tender mercies of the hook and line. We pitied him as he occasionally whipped his tail about, and then worked his jaws upon the string that held him fast as if it were a cud of bitterness. Such had been Elliott's fortune. With slowly decreasing interest had he watched his float as it sat daintily on the water, and wished it to disappear.

"I love to see it tremble," said Elliott, pointing to it, speaking in a softened voice, "tremble as if it had a pulse ere it darts so swiftly from the sight. What expectations it gives rise to! It moves a little; some gigantic fish has just brushed against the bait and is now preparing to gulp it down. Again it trembles"—Elliott struck, and drew into the air a "little one," playing its fins like a humming bird, and as transparent as if it were made of amber. How astonished and disappointed were the beating hearts at both ends of the line. Elliott took the incipient off carefully, and let it roll down towards the water through a little dry earth. How the prismatic scales grow dim with the contact, but for its moving about, it might be taken for a chip. A dash in the water—it's off—cleaned of dust, its yellow sides turn downwards, and the little black line of its back passes away like thought.

A juvenile toad that was playing "leap-frog" for the sake of exercising his developing body, chanced, as his bad luck would have it, to pass our way. A little exertion secured the creature, and with as much delicacy as a groomsman would place a ring upon the finger of his beloved bride, Elliott secured the toad on his hook, and committed it to the lake. The little unfortunate toad struck out for dear life, and swam boyfully; but his time had come; the very ripple his little arms made in the water had caught the never-closed eye of a lazy trout. The fish came to the surface, and eyed the bait as a gourmand will the dishes of an arranging dessert, rolled over its spotted sides sportively, and disappeared. An instant elapsed, when the trout appeared coming up vertically, its fine head glistened in the sun a moment, then, as quick as thought, again it disappeared; it then rose, floated nearer the bait, "mouthing at it" most provokingly. We were all excitement; Elliott, on the contrary, performed his office as silently and immovedly as a statue. In fact his rod lay carelessly across his knee as if he never expected to use it; but his eye the while was upon his game; he knew its humours perfectly, and was contentedly indulging its capriciousness. Presently the trout turned and swam towards the centre of the lake—we thought it lost. Elliott raised his delicate rod, and, for the first time, moved it slowly, skimming his bait along the surface of the water in little leaps—a ripple—a rushing noise—a tail quivering in the air, and our poor frog was in the trout's maw. The fish had turned from its course to gather one more dainty mouthful ere it buried itself in the deep water. The capture was gracefully made, and the fish was game to the last. The noble fellow pressed back his gills, distended his mouth, until you could put in it your hand to disengage the hook, then, laid upon some wet moss, with a few convulsive struggles, he died—a trophy of the angler's skill.

Among the fastnesses that border on Concordia Lake still linger some few renegade Indians, who make a precarious living in the barter of game; disappearing sometimes for months, then presenting themselves with illy-prepared peltries, a dead deer or turkey—the sale of which procures their few necessaries—and again they will wander off, as wild and heedless as the passing winds. These "red children" complete the picturesque. Gypsy-like, they choose the happiest locations for their "smokes," the men with the ingenuity of cats finding a soft and fitting place for comfortable sleep, while the women always sit by watching. An old oak, at whose foot centuries since the earth-dissolving waters of the Mississippi boiled, robbing the roots of its soil, until they protruded like the writhing forms of a hundred serpents, seeking nourishment deeper in the bosom of the earth for their attempted exhumation. An old oak, whose largest limbs are dead, yet, like proud age, affects youth by false appointments; of wigs, of vanilla-scented muscadines; of rouge, of the deep-red foliage of a hundred flowering vines; of props, of the quick growing cotton-wood that shoots aloft amid its vines; of stays, the convolving grape, binding together its wind-whistled ribs. Under this old oak we have "frequent met" a family of the once powerful Choctaws. From where they dozed away the noontide heats, but for a narrow belt of intervening forest, could be seen the Natchez bluffs, and on them, breaking darkly against the sky, the ruins of old Fort Rosalie.

Four generations since, and the ancestors of this Indian family, "seven hundred strong," fell upon the Natchez, while exulting over the massacre of the French at the fort of Rosalie, stormed their villages, liberated their prisoners, and, without loss, exulted in the possession of three-score scalps. Ten days after, the French from New Orleans completed the victory, and thus destroyed the most singular nation of all our aborigines; scattering them among the Chicasas and Musco-gees; and seizing their great seer and two hundred prisoners as slaves. The flying remnant of the tribe crossed the Mississippi, swept by the old oak we have described in their flight, coursed along the margin of Concordia Lake, reflected fleetingly in the Cocodra and Turtle lakes, and entrenched themselves for deathly siege, in ancient mounds, a day's travel from their native homes, over which the white man now incuriously wanders, ignorant alike of their associations or purposes, and known but to the few who cherish the traditions and antiquities of our western home.

Such are a few of the incidents and associations of Concordia Lake.

THE CHASE

The people of the South are extravagantly fond of the excitement of the Chase. The planters of the country are men who can at the proper season of the year, command their time, and from their youth up they are practiced in "the field." A sufficient number of them to form a "pleasant hunting party," promiscuously brought together, have only to *will*, and a hunting party is formed, all good shots, and all eminently possessed of the qualifications for refined pleasure. Accidental meetings of friends in the evening, frequently result in arrangements for the Chase in the morning; and, as the party in the gray dawn, scour through the country, the cheerful cry of the hounds, and the music of the mellow horn, will be answered by *volunteers*, who will thus at a moment's warning, mount their chargers, and dash off with the crowd, as well prepared for the fun, as if they had had a month's warning. In this respect the Southern States excel all other parts of the Union, and were never equalled, except in the "Old Dominion" in those ancient days, when the chivalrous Knights of the Golden Horse Shoe, under the guidance of Gov. Spottswood, made the Blue Ridge ring with their sports.

The fair South has its Die Vernon too, as lovely as she, and if possible as daring, who will salute the rising sun with cheers, more delicately tinged with red, than even the other, that surrounds the rising King of day. We have seen them often, dashing across the broken land, mingling their merry laugh with the distant mellowed horn, as fearless of danger in their seat, as the noble steeds that bore them. The training from childhood, to ride upon the "school pony," the wild dashing, and independent life of the planter makes them witch the world with their noble horsemanship. We have wondered and admired, as stray "cit" would find himself in the country, "gallanting the ladies to ride," mounted on some well broken horse, yet swaying from side to side, often breathless with alarm, as he, for the honor of his sex would leap some gully or fallen tree, over which his fair tormentors would spring, as nimbly as birds, and thus spending a morning's ride, mischievously

teaching a specimen of the "lords of creation" a lesson for their imprudent assumption of superiority.

When the cotton hangs pendant from the boll, which the cold frosts
of November and December wither to nought, then is the time that the
fox is started from his hole, and made to pay for his robberies of the
poultry yard. Poor Reynard is wakened from his torpidity by the yelping
of the loud mouthed hound. He rises, yawns, stretches himself and
listens, he discovers that the "Philistines are upon him." With nose
low to the earth, and with high heels, he starts for his life. But his
pursuers are true as the needle to the pole upon his track. He casts
behind him the furtive glance, his eye becomes worried, and his
tongue lolls from his feverish mouth. It is in vain that he "doubles"
upon his path, he leaps and springs from stump to stump, and conceals his footsteps in the running stream, yet the hounds are coming
more and more near, and by their sharp yelps betray their impatience
to snap him behind the ears.—Tired out, and completely exhausted,
he buries himself in some hollow stump or deserted burrow, rears
himself upon his quarters and waits his death. Reynard makes but little
resistance, "Leader" or "Music" are shaking him already as if they were
misers, and thought his poor carcase contained hidden gold, a throw
or two and the cunning fox is a stiffened inanimate thing, the merry
horn sounds an appropriate requiem for death, and his tail is elevated
as a trophy to the daring rider, and the fastest horse.

Did you ever, gentle reader, see a "pack" and their riders dash
through a cotton field, rich for picking? If not, you have lost an imitation of a snow storm, and been saved the hearing of much growling
from the victimized planter.

We knew an old gentleman, whilom, who hated fox-hunting because it wasted his "staple," and broke down his fences. He had forgotten what a hard rider he was in his youth, and had little mercy upon
the follies peculiar to that age. One frosty morning he was riding down
his mile-square field, when there came along the road that bounded
it, a pack of hounds in "full cry." Insensibly to himself he urged his
surprised horse into a gallop, and soon began to halloo as loudly "as
the best," the hounds came suddenly at fault, the fox leaped the fence
and took straight *across the field*. The old man was in ecstasies, the
hunters came up, he was the first to point out the direction taken by
the fox, and the first to pull down the rails to let the hunters "come
in," a moment only elapsed, when away went the hounds and hunters,

across and through the cotton, throwing it in clouds into the air, the old gentleman with the "hunt," encouraging on the chase. In the midst of the field his slow-paced horse fell behind, the old gentleman reined up and looked.

"There goes," said he, musingly, "a dozen bales of cotton at least, all for a fox's tail not worth a tooth-pick. I'll make these young folks pay for this."

Unfortunately, just as he made the threat, the fox doubling on its track, came past him, away went the old hunter again, cheering and hallooing, and he came out ahead at "the death." From that time ever afterwards not a complaint was heard because the young folks chased the fox through his well cultivated fields. He had had a lesson "of his own feelings in his youth, and he forgave the boys."

The deer hunt is less exciting than that of the fox, and the chase is more general. Deer are common to every part of the South, but foxes are never found *west* of the Mississippi. The reason why is perhaps to be explained in the want of high and broken land to shelter them. It is sometimes dull work to sit hours at a *stand*, yet, however tedious it may become, the bounding buck as he flies past you, with the eager pack at his heels, forms a picture of such interest, as will justify the loss of much time for the pleasure of feeling the momentary enjoyment, and no wonder is it, that the tyro in the sport often gazes on in a transport of admiration, and thinks not of his gun, until his "intended victim" is beyond his reach.

It is the manly sports of the South, encouraged in the Chase, that make its denizens noble in their dispositions, and open in their carriage with the rest of the world. It polishes, and encourages the chivalrous sentiments of the soul, that are so apt to be deadened by the artificialities of "city life." It encourages health, and the possession of that greatest of all blessings, prepares the heart and the mind for the full and perfect enjoyment of all the innocent pleasures of life.

ENEMY IN FRONT AND REAR, OR— A BEAR AND SNAKE STORY

Having been an interloper in the hunt, we did not know who our companions were until the excitement of the day was ended, and we were called into the "camping ground" by the repeated firing of guns, and the blasts of the huntsman's horn. For our own part, we were delighted that the day had drawn to a close; the "sport" had been nothing, and the "stand" where we were posted, seemed to be in the entire possession of that race of immense gallinippers that make their appearance only in the fall, and, in the sunshine of the day, bite through your thick coat and shoes. Our trouble in this matter was that of others, and one young man, recently from New England, seemed to have been particularly afflicted, for, judging from his face, a doctor would have said he had a bad attack of the small pox, so full was it of blotches and marks. The cold atmosphere of the approaching fall chilled these stinging pests, and left the night, the starlight and a generous fire to be enjoyed in peace. We never cared much about the "excitement of the chase," and although we never refused a chance to "get a shot," still we never jumped "impassable ravines," "broke our neck" and killed our horse, to head a deer, or get a scare from an old "he bar." The camp fire is our delight—there, with an immense quantity of venison, cold ham, biscuit, some claret stowed away under our jacket, and a woolen blanket carefully tucked around the outside of it, we love to lie upon the lap of earth, and with our eyes dreamily viewing the firmament, and with our ears wide open, listen to the hunters' tales, who generally keep Truth on a full gallop to be any where in sight of their *facts*, or having distanced her entirely at the outset, cause her to abandon them for the evening.

Among the group before us, on the occasion we speak of, was a wiry looking personage, with a complexion of a young man inconsistantly disfigured with crow feet marks, peculiar to age, while his hair seemed prematurely gray, and showed that disregard of mixing black and white, that would have done honor to an amalgamation meeting, assembled under the most amiable auspices. To learn the cause of this phenomenon, became a matter of interest to us, and after consid-

315

erable beating round the bush, one of our companions told the following story, the hero sitting by, to put in the corrections:

"You see," said our informant, pointing at the prematurely gray hunter, "that Hopgood was remarkable all his life, up to a certain day, for his coal black hair, his head rivalled a bar's back in the fat season, for glossiness and stiffness."

"Not stiffness," said Hopgood, running his fingers through his long, and rather silky head covering.

"Yes, stiffness, Hopgood, genuine stiffness, real bristle stiffness, but don't interrupt me, Hopgood. Well, you see his black, stiff har was his pride, and when he went a courting, he used to bow at the girls so as to bring his shoe brush direct in their faces, to impress them with its beauty."

"Pooh!" said Hopgood, throwing a big log on the camp fire, to interrupt the story teller.

"You may 'pooh,' as much as you please," said the story teller, "you know your har was your pride, and that it was a sort of mysterious providence, as parson Angel said, that took away its beauty from you, so that you could set your affections on something better."

Hopgood, by this time, was asleep, and the story teller continued.

Hopgood is a young man about four and twenty, and he had the worst scare that a man ever had on a first bear hunt. He never lived in woods where the varmints were to be met with, until he opened his place upon this pre-emption, although he was a good deer hunter, and considerable at treeing a cat. Well, you see, Hopgood one day went out, back of his location, with his double barrel on his shoulder, looking for trees to split rails from. He took his gun, naturally, for a deer is often to be caught napping.—While trailing about, he came near the decayed stump of a butternut wood tree, at the foot of which were playing in all the innocence of nine days' childhood, two bear cubs. There they were, as black as charcoal, biting and hugging each other, and rolling about among the dead leaves, as perfectly unsuspecting of harm as Hopgood himself, who rushed forward and seized one of the cubs in his hand. Such a squalling and squealing was never before heard. Hopgood was delighted—he held on to the varmint, and rather encouraged its cries, when he was suddenly impressed with the idea that an earthquake was coming up in his rear. He turned and looked, and there was a she-bear rushing upon him as black as its cub, and to Hopgood looking like a railroad engine with its furnace door open.

Hopgood dropped his prize, and fairly flew towards a fallen tree, up which he ran with commendable precipitancy. The bear followed— another horror met Hopgood's vision—on the highest part of the trunk of the fallen tree, sat in battle array, an immense rattle snake. It raised its head, and gave the note of alarm. Its skin glistened, and changed color rapidly, showing that the muscles underneath were preparing for a spring. Hopgood stopped and turned on the bear; she was now within ten feet of him, her mouth open so wide that Hopgood said he saw room enough down her throat to be buried in. Taking deliberate aim, he fired his double barrel, one load after the other. The bear brushed his leg with her fore paw, and rolled heavily off the tree, fairly shaking the earth when she struck the ground. A moment more, Hopgood was out of reach of the serpent. He had saved his life, but his hair had, from very fear, in the meantime, wilted down, and became motley grey.

"That is very strange," said we, with unaffected astonishment.

"Not at all," said Hopgood with animation, apparently waking out of a sound sleep, "it seems to me that I was in that tree one thousand years between those two varmints, and that is time enough to whiten any body's head." There was a general assent, that a thousand years would whiten any body's head, and one story teller, after observing that Hopgood was one thousand and twenty-four years old, soon fell asleep, and left us to speculate on the strange effects of sudden terror, that in an instant impressed upon youth all the physical signs of age.

Of all our Indian tribes, none were more interesting or more rudely destroyed than the Natchez. What is remembered of them, is calculated to make a deep impression upon the imagination, and cause regret, that some historian had not preserved a truthful history of this singular people. In the early traditions of the Mexicans, preserved to us in their hieroglyphical paintings, there is presented the wonderful spectacle of families and nations, from innate impulses, moving from "the north," and ever restless, wandering over the unoccupied continent in search of homes. It is evident that the same wisdom, that confounded the primitive language at Babel, and scattered the swarming millions of Asia, impelled the early occupants of our continent, to move onward like advancing waves of the sea.

In these strange migrations, some chief must have separated from the parent multitude, and turned his face with his followers towards the west, and finally reaching the delectable lands of all the valley of the lower Mississippi, there established what was afterwards known as the tribe of the Natchez.

The country selected is of surpassing loveliness, for, from the precipitous bluff that so unexpectedly frowns down upon the Mississippi, inland to where the nation erected its great mound, is one continuous undulation of picturesque scenery, originally enriched with groves of live oaks, and magnolias—it was really a fairy land, and enough of the primitive forest still remains, to give the sanction of truth to the most florid description of it preserved in legendary lore.

There cannot be a doubt, that at the time these nomadics took possession of their adopted homes, that the surrounding country was without inhabitants, for the savage and warlike nations which lived in the neighborhood, never would have permitted the Natchez when in their infancy to take possession of their lands, which afterwards even they defended more by moral than by physical force.

As fire worshipers, the Natchez displayed their Oriental origin, and they were more sincere in this most poetic of all idolatries than the magi of the East. They possessed a tradition, which unlike all other nations, gallantly ascribed the salvation of their race to a woman; it was, that after the destruction of all the inhabitants of the earth save a single family, which family was about to die because of the continued darkness of the heavens, a young girl inspired with the wish to save her race, threw herself into the fire which was used as a light, and that no sooner was her body consumed, than she arose in the East, surrounded with such surpassing glory, that her form could not be looked upon, and thus enshrined, she became the chief, her nearest female relation being elected her successor. Hence was established the worship of the sun, and the living sacrifice of the sacred fire, together with the belief, that so long as it blazed upon their altars, the Natchez would be powerful and happy.

The sun, a female sovereign, was absolute in power. The rewards of the chase, and of the cultivation of the soil were placed under her charge, implying that they were the results of her genial rays, and through her, as if direct from the hands of Providence, they were distributed among the people.

The Natchez must have rapidly increased after their establishment on the banks of the Mississippi, for their tradition was, that in the first century of their settlement they erected those monuments of industry, so much admired to this day, on which to bury their dead and erect their temples. Their great work was built upon a hill, where they believed fire fell from the sun, indicating that their wanderings were at an end. This series of mounds, the most remarkable in the valley of the Mississippi, have been almost entirely overlooked, by the curious in such relics of ancient days.

A natural hillock was leveled upon the top, and used as the foundations, the only example known. Upon a base thus prepared was raised the grand elevation for the great temple of the Sun, and the inferior works, used for defence, and the graves of the nobles. In examining these singular ruins, now covered with trees a century's growth, it is not difficult to conceive them rising in their perfection from the open plain, smoking at their tops with sacrificial fires and covered with priests and people. It was only on this mound, and at the festival of fruits that the Sun showed herself to the multitude. Attired in robes of white cotton, adorned with feathers, and her breast glistening with various brilliant stones, she assisted in the early greeting of her supposed ancestor, and as the God of day ascended in the East, and shot her bright rays across the landscape, they first of all greeted

319

the sacred priestess, and were reflected back in ten thousand rays, which were taken by the worshipers as a recognition of sympathy and acknowledged relationship.

According to the belief of the Natchez, the extinction of the fires of the temple, would be the signal for their destruction, thus having it would seem, with some other nations mentioned in history a foreboding of their extermination. A brief period before the French invaded their homes, by some accident this fearful catastrophe happened, and the nation was consequently suffering from superstitious depression, it was therefore that they fell a comparatively easy prey to the superior arms and discipline of the European invader.

In their struggle for existence, after an obstinate defence they were first driven from the banks of the river, and again rallying they then gathered for their final struggle at the base of the great mound. As soon as the tribe thought themselves sufficiently prepared, they provoked attack, and their last great battle took place. The Sun Chief was killed in the struggle, and the survivors believing that the dark prophecy that rested upon the Natchez had been fulfilled, as a crowd of flying fugitives retreated west of the Mississippi, and after various misfortunes, were lost, or became absorbed among the Oumas, the Tensas and other friendly tribes.

The enlightened mind, in speaking of Natchez explains their destruction upon philosophical reasons, it was the weak giving away to the strong, but their fate appealed to more sympathising, and more imaginative hearts, who have softened the story of their ruin, stripped it of its harsher features, and left it so interwoven with golden light, that we learn the unwelcome truth, and think hopefully of the departed. The southern Indians of our day when sitting beside their "council fires," and speak of the times that are past, of the Natchez, tell us—

That a young Natchez chief, famed for his virtue and bravery, became enamored of a beautiful maiden, and that his passion was returned. His interviews were stolen ones, and these were few and far between. On one occasion, when the young chief was keeping his night watch over the sacred fire of the temple, he heard the plaintive song of a day bird, and flying to the neighboring groves, there met his mistress, and exchanged the solemn vows of eternal love. Returning to the altar, the young chief, to his horror, discovered, that the flame had expired in his to him unconsciously long absence, and all that was left upon the altar, were cold ashes where there should have been living fire.

Alarm filled the young warrior's breast, despair was impressed upon his features, and as the Sun illumed the hills and made the homes of the Natchez glisten in its refreshing and to them sacred radiance, there was no response of ascending sacrifice, and the priests rushed with precipitation to the temple, to learn the cause.

Terrible indeed were the wailings that ascended from the soul stricken worshipers; it was deemed, that a curse had fallen upon the nation, that its speedy extinction was shadowed forth, and amidst the excitement, by order of the great Sun, the young maiden was sacrificed, not only as a propitiation, but that her surpassing beauty, should no longer tempt the guardians of the sacred altars to neglect their vigils.

The young chief was doomed to make expiation, in fastings and prayers, and after due ceremonies, he was imprisoned in the center of the great mound, there to remain until he wooed back the lost fire from heaven. It was in vain that he essayed the comparatively easy task of lighting the proper combustibles by rapid friction. Overwhelmed by religious fear, his strength of arm appeared to have departed, and even when from long and patient labor, the fire was about to descend, a tear of regret for the memory of his mistress, would fall upon the just igniting wood, and leave his interminable task to be again renewed.

Although years, yea centuries have passed away, although the entrance to the great mound has crumbled undistinguishable into the surrounding mass, and huge trees have usurped the places of the ascents, and the altars, yet the old Indians in their day dreams, visit the young chief who is still in the center of the mound perseveringly engaged in his labor, and assert, that when he recovers the sacred fire, he will appear at the altar, and that the Natchez, in all their former glory will again take possession of their abandoned homes.

321

PART THREE

Textual
Apparatus

TEXTUAL NOTES

These notes record the first available appearance of each sketch and its succeeding publications by Thorpe. The reprintings by William T. Porter are also included because they helped to establish Thorpe's reputation and because in several instances Thorpe adopted the variants in them in later versions. The notes clarify the transmission of a text where necessary, comment on Thorpe's selection of copy-text when he reprinted a sketch that had appeared in several publications, and briefly describe the revisions in those passages that became part of other sketches after originally appearing elsewhere.

TOM OWEN, THE BEE-HUNTER

83.1 This sketch appeared in the *Spirit of the Times*, IX (July 27, 1839), 247, in *The Mysteries of the Backwoods* (1846), 185–90, and in *The Hive of "The Bee-Hunter"* (1854), 47–53.

WILD TURKEY SHOOTING

87.1 This sketch appeared in the *Spirit*, X (August 1, 1840), 253. Thorpe extensively reworked it for *Mysteries* and changed the title to "Wit of the Woods."

91.10 The copy-text lacks the final "s" in "companions," but the word is at the end of a line where a space exists for the necessary letter.

PRIMITIVE FORESTS OF THE MISSISSIPPI

92.1 This sketch appeared in the *Spirit*, X (October 3, 1840), 361. A revised version of the last half of the third paragraph, from 94.30 to 95.26, is in the *Hive* text of "The Mississippi." The sentences in the revised version are more concise and direct. Thorpe changed first-person wordings to second-person and rewrote most of the section in the present tense instead of the past, revisions not recorded in the list of substantive variants that follows.

A FRONTIER INCIDENT

97.1   This sketch appeared in the *Spirit*, X (October 31, 1840), 409, and in *Mysteries*, 164–69.

THE MISSISSIPPI

101.1   This sketch appeared in the *Knickerbocker Magazine*, XVI (December, 1840), 461–64, in *Mysteries*, 170–77, and in *Hive*, 94–104. After its publication in *Mysteries*, Porter reprinted it in the *Spirit*, XV (January 31, 1846), 576–77.

103.30   In *Hive* a revised section from "Primitive Forests of the Mississippi" follows this paragraph.

SPORTING IN LOUISIANA

106.1   This sketch appeared in the *Spirit*, X (January 30, 1841), 571. Thorpe revised the first paragraph to serve as the introduction for "The Chase," which appeared six years later.

THE BIG BEAR OF ARKANSAS

112.1   This sketch appeared in the *Spirit*, XI (March 27, 1841), 43–44. Porter reprinted it in the *American Turf Register*, XII (May, 1841), 274–80, and in his anthology *The Big Bear of Arkansas* (1845), 13–31. Thorpe included it in *Hive*, 72–93. Collation indicates that Porter used the *Spirit* text, rather than the one in the *American Turf Register*, as copy-text for his *Big Bear* anthology. Thorpe, in turn, used the *Big Bear* anthology when preparing the sketch for *Hive*. Doggett's comments about mosquitoes, from 114.17–38, appeared in the *Concordia Intelligencer*, March 15, 1845. The corruptions in that text suggest Thorpe simply reprinted an excerpt being carried in other newspapers. Since none of those variants appears in the *Hive* text, they are not listed here.

WOODCOCK FIRE HUNTING

123.1   This sketch appeared in the *Spirit*, XI (May 1, 1841), 103. Porter reprinted it in the *American Turf Register*, XII (November, 1841), 633–35, and in his edition of Peter Hawker's *Instructions to Young Sportsmen* (1846), 241–44. Thorpe included it in *Hive*, 225–31.

AN EXTRA DEER HUNT IN LOUISIANA

127.1   This sketch appeared in the *Spirit*, XI (July 10, 1841), 223.

SCENES ON THE MISSISSIPPI

129.1   This sketch appeared in the *Spirit*, XI (September 4, 1841), 319–20, and in *Mysteries*, 108–17. Thorpe changed the title to "Familiar Scenes on the Mississippi" in *Hive*, 114–25.

134.15   The *Hive* spelling of *strangers* has been preferred over the copy-text reading in this case. The *Spirit* spells the word with a double *g*, but the compositor divided the word after the *g* at the end of a line. Thus the doubling may well represent his own error rather than Thorpe's spelling in the manuscript.

THE FIRST HUNTING TRIP OF THE STEAMER "NIMROD," OF "BARROW SETTLEMENT," LOUISIANA

135.1   This sketch appeared in the *Spirit*, XI (September 11, 1841), 331.

A PIANO IN ARKANSAS

140.1   This sketch appeared in the *Spirit*, XI (October 30, 1841), 409–10, in *Mysteries*, 21–29, and in *Hive*, 145–54. In *Mysteries*, Thorpe changed the spelling in the title to "A Piano in 'Arkansaw.'"

141.36   In neither *Mysteries* nor *Hive* does "pianos" appear as a possessive. This edition similarly corrects that error and uses a capital "P" as in the first printing.

OPOSSUMS AND 'POSSUM HUNTING

145.1   This sketch appeared in the *Spirit*, XI (December 4, 1841), 469. Porter reprinted it under the title "Opossum Hunting" in his edition of Hawker's *Instructions*, 313–18. Thorpe also chose that title in *Hive*, 255–65, and used the *Instructions* printing as copy-text.

A GRIZZLY BEAR HUNT

150.1   This sketch appeared in the *Spirit*, XI (December 18, 1841), 499–500, and in *Mysteries*, 145–52. Porter changed the title to "Grizzly Bear Hunting" when he published it in his edition of Hawker's *Instructions*, 368–73, and Thorpe retained that title in *Hive*, 135–44.

A STORM SCENE ON THE MISSISSIPPI

155.1   This sketch appeared in the *Spirit*, XII (March 26, 1842), 43–44, and in *Hive*, 126–34.

ROMANCE OF THE WOODS. THE WILD HORSES OF THE WESTERN PRAIRIES

160.1   This sketch appeared in the *Spirit*, XII (April 9, 1842), 61.

THE AMERICAN WILD CAT

166.1   This sketch appeared in the London *New Sporting Magazine*, n.s. IV (July, 1842), 58–61. Porter reprinted it in the *American Turf Register*, XIII (September, 1842), 518–21, and as "The Wild Cat" in his edition of Hawker's *Instructions*, 246–50. Thorpe used the original title in *Mysteries*, 178–84, and "Wild-Cat Hunting" in *Hive*, 155–62. Collation indicates that the *American Turf Register* printing served as copy-text for both *Mysteries* and *Instructions*. Probably coincidentally, two substantive variants in the *Instructions* text appear in *Hive* (both are shown in the list of variants below).

169.11–29   In *Hive* the section from "There is" through "on either side." follows the sentence which ends at 163.38.

THE DISGRACED SCALP LOCK, OR INCIDENTS
ON THE WESTERN WATERS

170.1 This sketch appeared in the *Spirit*, XII (July 16, 1842), 229–30, and in *Mysteries*, 118–36. Thorpe changed the title to "Mike Fink, the Keel-Boatman" in *Hive*, 163–83.

THE DEVIL'S SUMMER RETREAT, IN ARKANSAW

181.1 This sketch appeared in the *Spirit*, XII (August 20, 1842), 295–96. Porter included it in his collection *A Quarter Race in Kentucky* (1846), 130–45, under the title "Bob Herring, the Arkansas Bear Hunter," and in his edition of Hawker's *Instructions*, 339–50, under the title "Bear Hunting in Arkansas." Thorpe entitled it "Summer Retreat in Arkansas" in *Hive*, 28–46. Collation indicates that the *Spirit* printing served as copy-text for each of the later appearances.

PLACE DE LA CROIX

191.1 This story appeared in the *Knickerbocker*, XX (October, 1842), 364–70. Thorpe subtitled it "A Romance of the West" in *Mysteries*, 46–58, and in *Hive*, 240–54.

A VISIT TO "CURNEL PARDON JONES"

199.1 This article appeared in the New Orleans *Daily Picayune*, November 30, 1842.

MY FIRST DINNER IN NEW ORLEANS

203.1 According to the earliest known reprinting, this sketch first appeared in the New Orleans *Tropic*. Because the issue of the *Tropic* carrying it is apparently not extant, the copy-text for this edition is the reprinting in the Baton Rouge *Gazette*, February 18, 1843. Thorpe printed the piece in the *Intelligencer*, February 1, 1845, and later reworked it for *Hive*, 271–79, where it is entitled "Major Gasden's Story." A major change is the addition of a frame which introduces the story as one told by the major.

THE LOUISIANA LAW OF COCK-FIGHTING

207.1   Both the *Spirit*, XIII (March 4, 1843), 3, and the Baton Rouge *Gazette* of the same day reprinted this piece from an issue of the New Orleans *Tropic* that is apparently not extant. The sketch is entitled "A 'Hoosier' in Search of Justice" in *Hive*, 266–70. The *Spirit* reprinting serves as copy-text here, and the list of variants records the seven substantive differences between it and the *Gazette* reprinting.

207.13   The meaning of "burban" remains elusive. In reprinting this sketch in *With the Bark On*, John Q. Anderson silently emended the spelling to "urban" even though Thorpe did not revise the word in the *Hive* reprinting.

THE WATER CRAFT OF THE BACK WOODS

210.1   This sketch appeared in the *Southern Sportsman*, March 18, 1843. Thorpe reprinted it in the *Intelligencer*, August 3, 1844; in *Mysteries*, 73–79; and in *Hive*, 232–39. Collation indicates that he used the *Southern Sportsman* printing as copy-text for *Mysteries*, and the *Intelligencer* printing for *Hive*.

THE WAY AMERICANS GO DOWN HILL

215.1   This sketch appeared in the *Southern Sportsman*, April 17, 1843, in the *Intelligencer*, December 30, 1843, and in the *Spirit*, XIII (January 20, 1844), 560–61. Collation indicates that Thorpe used the *Southern Sportsman* version as copy-text for the reprinting in *Hive*, 302–12.

THE LAST FROM "ARKANSAW"

221.1   This anecdote appeared in the *Southern Sportsman*, May 1, 1843. Thorpe later incorporated it into the *Hive* version of "The Little Steamboats of the Mississippi," where Zeb's last name is Marston and the boat is the *Emperor*.

LETTERS FROM THE FAR WEST

223.1   The first letter appeared in the *Intelligencer*, August 5, 1843, and in the *Spirit*, XIII (August 26, 1843), 303.

225.8   The second letter appeared in the *Intelligencer*, August 12, 1843, and in the *Spirit*, XIII (September 9, 1843), 333.

227.21   The third letter appeared in the *Intelligencer*, August 19, 1843, and in the *Spirit*, XIII (September 9, 1843), 333.

230.1   The fourth letter appeared in the *Intelligencer*, September 2, 1843, and in the *Spirit*, XIII (September 23, 1843), 356.

232.14   The fifth letter appeared in the *Intelligencer*, September 23, 1843, and in the *Spirit*, XIII (October 14, 1843), 392.

234.29   The sixth letter appeared in the *Intelligencer*, September 30, 1843, and in the *Spirit*, XIII (October 21, 1843), 405.

237.1   The seventh letter appeared in the *Intelligencer*, October 14, 1843, and in the *Spirit*, XIII (November 4, 1843), 421.

239.16   The eighth letter appeared in the *Intelligencer*, November 4, 1843, and in the *Spirit*, XIII (November 18, 1843), 445.

242.5   The ninth letter appeared in the *Intelligencer*, November 25, 1843, and in the *Spirit*, XIII (December 16, 1843), 497.

244.7   The tenth letter appeared in the *Intelligencer*, December 16, 1843, and in the *Spirit*, XIII (January 27, 1844), 569.

247.4   The eleventh letter appeared in the *Intelligencer*, December 30, 1843, and in the *Spirit*, XIII (January 20, 1844), 557.

250.7   The twelfth letter appeared in the *Intelligencer*, February 10, 1844, and in the *Spirit*, XIV (March 16, 1844), 33.

THE LITTLE STEAMBOATS OF THE MISSISSIPPI

253.1   This sketch appeared in the *Spirit*, XIV (March 9, 1844), 19, and in the *Intelligencer*, March 30, 1844. In *Hive*, 105–13, Thorpe entitled it "Large and Small Steamers of the Mississippi" and recast in present tense the passages describing the steamer, changes not recorded in the list of significant variants that follows.

254.19   In *Hive* a revised form of the anecdote "The Last from 'Arkansaw' " follows this line.

BROKER VS. BANKER. SCENE IN A NEW ORLEANS COURT

257.1   This piece appeared in the *Intelligencer*, December 14, 1844, and in the *Spirit*, XIV (January 4, 1845), 531.

TRAITS OF THE PRAIRIES

259.1   This sketch appeared in *Mysteries*, 11–20.

PISCATORY ARCHERY

265.1   This sketch appeared in *Mysteries*, 30–45, and under the title "Arrow-Fishing" in *Hive*, 54–71.

271.4   In *Hive* the two sentences beginning at this line appear after the sentence ending at 270.31.

WIT OF THE WOODS

275.1   This sketch appeared in *Mysteries*, 59–72, and under the title "Wild Turkey Hunting" in *Hive*, 9–27. It is an extensive reworking of "Wild Turkey Shooting."

275.34   In *Hive* a lengthy revised section from "Wild Turkey Shooting" follows this paragraph.

276.14   In *Hive* the paragraph beginning at this line appears immediately before the sentence starting at 275.38.

PICTURES OF BUFFALO HUNTING

283.1   This sketch appeared in *Mysteries*, 80–107. Thorpe divided it into two sketches for *Hive* so that the first four sections compose "Buffalo Hunting," 193–212, and the last two compose "Scenes in Buffalo Hunting," 213–24.

290.27   In *Hive* the four sentences beginning at this line appear immediately before the sentence starting at 290.13.

ALLIGATOR KILLING

300.1   This sketch appeared in *Mysteries*, 137–44, and in *Hive*, 184–92.

CONCORDIA LAKE

305.1 This sketch appeared in *Mysteries*, 153–63.

THE CHASE

312.1 This sketch appeared in the *Spirit*, XVI (January 9, 1847), 548. Porter reprinted it from Thorpe's *Louisiana Conservator* (Baton Rouge), no issues of which are apparently extant. The opening paragraph is a revision of the introduction to "Sporting in Louisiana," which serves as the authority to emend typographer's errors in that section.

ENEMY IN FRONT AND REAR, OR— A BEAR AND SNAKE STORY

315.1 ˙ This sketch appeared in the New Orleans *Daily National*, October 6, 1847, and in the *Spirit*, XVII (October 23, 1847), 407.

A TRADITION OF THE NATCHEZ

318.1 This sketch, apparently the only one for which Thorpe's manuscript survives, appeared in *The Knickerbocker Gallery* (1855), 375–79, under the title "Traditions of the Natchez."

EMENDATIONS

This list records all emendations in the copy-texts, both accidental and substantive, except for the infrequent silent insertion of a missing letter for which the printed word has a blank space and also the insertion of a necessary semicolon or period that did not print on the page of the copy-text as intended. The reading of this edition is to the left of the bracket, to the right of which is a symbol indicating the text or texts that are the authority for the reading. To the right of the semicolon is the reading of the copy-text and those texts agreeing with it. The text cited following *omit* does not contain the reading to the left of the bracket. The curved dash ~ used in recording punctuation variants represents the same word that appears to the left of the bracket, and the caret ˄ indicates the omission of a punctuation mark. If an asterisk precedes the page and line numbers, the reading is discussed in Textual Notes.

These abbreviations identify the manuscript and the publications which contain the sketches in this edition:

ATR	*American Turf Register*
BB	*The Big Bear of Arkansas* (1845)
CE	Critical edition
CI	Vidalia, La., *Concordia Intelligencer*
DN	New Orleans *Daily National*
G	Baton Rouge *Gazette*
H	*The Hive of "The Bee-Hunter"* (1854)
IYS	*Instructions to Young Sportsmen* (1846)
K	*Knickerbocker Magazine*
KG	*The Knickerbocker Gallery* (1855)
M	*The Mysteries of the Backwoods* (1846)
MS	Author's signed manuscript of "A Tradition of the Natchez"
NSM	London *New Sporting Magazine*
P	New Orleans *Daily Picayune*

S   New York *Spirit of the Times*
SS   New Orleans *Southern Sportsman*

TOM OWEN, THE BEE-HUNTER

83.14   antedeluvians] M, H; antideluvians S
85.32   was full] M, H; full S

WILD TURKEY SHOOTING

88.13   Buffalo] CE; Buffaloe S
88.16   Buffalo] CE; Buffaloe S
*91.10   companions] CE; companion S

PRIMITIVE FORESTS OF THE MISSISSIPPI

93.38   venomous] CE; venemous S
94.13   beech] CE; beach S
94.20–21   excrescence] CE; excresence S

THE MISSISSIPPI

102.32   caving] H; carving K, M
105.23   flood, guided only] H; flood K, M
105.25   plummet] CE; plumet K

SPORTING IN LOUISIANA

106.24   qualifications] CE; qualfications S
107.1   Feliciana] CE; Felicianna S
107.22   nymphs] CE; nimphs S
108.16   day's] CE; days' S
108.19   sounded] CE; sonnded S
108.27   Feliciana] CE; Felicianna S
109.23   alligators] CE; aligators S (This same change occurs at its every appearance.)
111.1   minutes'] CE; minutes S

THE BIG BEAR OF ARKANSAS

112.35   hours'] BB, H; ~ ˌ S
113.9   And then] CE; and then S, BB; Then H

113.36   checkers] H; chickens S, BB
116.10   couldn't] BB, H; could'nt S
118.33   my own hunting] BB, H; myow unting S
120.30   ———.' My] H; ———.' my S, BB
121.39   Bowie-knife] BB, H; bowie-knife S

WOODCOCK FIRE HUNTING

123.24   hunting.] H; ~, S
123.31   Woodcock.] H; ~, S
 124.9   inhabit] H; inhabits S
124.38   says] H; say S
125.23   have] H; has S
 126.6   are] H; is S
126.8–9   synonymous] H; synonimous S
126.9–10   champagne] CE; champaign S

SCENES ON THE MISSISSIPPI

130.17   his incantations] M, H; hs incantations S
132.1   stopped] M, H; stoped S
132.6   on] H; in S, M
132.6   undiscernible] CE; undiscernable S
134.14   coolly] M, H; cooly S
*134.15   strangers] H; stranggers S, M

THE FIRST HUNTING TRIP OF THE STEAMER "NIMROD," OF "BARROW SETTLEMENT," LOUISIANA

137.2   crystal] CE; chrystal S
138.10   bow] CE; bows S

A PIANO IN ARKANSAS

140.12   Marryat's] CE; Marryatt's S
140.15   Marryat] CE; Marryatt S
*141.36   Pianos] CE; Piano's S
143.16   risen] H; rose S, M
144.27   it?] M, H; ~. S
144.30   ears] M, H; ear S

OPOSSUMS AND 'POSSUM HUNTING

146.4   dinner ony] IYS, H; ony dinner S
146.19   Shakespeare] CE; Shakspeare S, IYS, H
149.11   soared] IYS, H; roared S

A GRIZZLY BEAR HUNT

150.28   shot] M, H; *omit* S
150.29   Indian's] M, H; Indians S
150.31   wile] CE; while S, M, H
153.36   apparatus] M, H; aparatus S
154.13   infinitely] M, H; infinite S
154.15   protect] M, H; protects S

A STORM SCENE ON THE MISSISSIPPI

155.21   horses'] H; horses S
156.31   life,] H; ~ ˌ S
157.8   I, 'captain, I] CE; I captain, 'I S; I, Captain, I H

ROMANCE OF THE WOODS. THE WILD HORSES
OF THE WESTERN PRAIRIES

160.5   abrupt] CE; abrubt S
162.22   horses'] CE; horses S

THE AMERICAN WILD CAT

166.32   Ishmaelite's] M; Ishmaelites NSM, ATR
168.12   lose] H; loose NSM, ATR, M
168.19   passed] M, H; pased NSM, ATR
168.23   height] ATR, M, H; heighth NSM
168.25   if he] ATR, M, H; if NSM
168.25–26   huckleberry] ATR, M, H; huckelberry NSM
168.28   gobbler] ATR, M, H; gobble NSM
168.39   cap] ATR, M, H; clap NSM
168.39   braggadocio] ATR, M, H; bragadocio NSM
169.15   pettifogging] M, H; pettyfogging NSM, ATR

THE DISGRACED SCALP LOCK, OR INCIDENTS
ON THE WESTERN WATERS

171.30 ecstasies] M, H; extacies S
172.25 Choctas] M, H; Chocta's S
172.25 on] M, H; or S
172.27 starved] M, H; strawed S
173.8 in] M; *omit* S, H
174.4 Proud] M, H; proud S
174.26 Proud] M, H; proud S
175.19 seizing] M, H; sezing S
176.8 there] M, H; their S
177.2 hadn't] M, H; had'nt S
177.16 rise] H; rises S, M
177.33 It's] H; Its S, M
177.39 long-winded] M, H; ~. ~ S
178.19 fell] M, H; feel S
179.1 Then] H; then S, M
179.19 Ain't] M, H; 'Aint S
180.15 moccasins] M, H; mocasin S
180.24 riveted] M, H; rivitted S

THE DEVIL'S SUMMER RETREAT, IN ARKANSAW

181.16 mystery;] H; ~. S
182.15 surrounding] H; surounding S
182.36 potato] H; potatoe S
184.13 Brummell] CE; Brummel S
184.21 you couldn't] H; that couldn't S
189.23 route] H; rout S
189.31 years'] H; year's S

PLACE DE LA CROIX

192.6 Aragon] CE; Arragon K, M, H
192.16 Peter's] H; Peters K, M
195.32 incidents] M, H; incident K

MY FIRST DINNER IN NEW ORLEANS

203.38   magnificent] CI; magnificient G
203.39   the confused] CI; the the confused G
 204.5   unusually] CI, H; usually G
 204.9   as warm] CI, H; *omit* G
204.10   awry] CI, H; away G
204.11   dining] CI, H; ding G
204.16   looked] CI, H; look G
204.30   latter] CI; later G
 205.4   with the] CI, H; with G
205.20   beneficent] CI, H; benificent G
205.23   off] CI, H; of G
205.37   liberality] CI; liberalithy G
205.39   literary] CI, H; litterary G
 206.2   tremendous] CI; tremdous G
 206.3   buttons] CI, H; battons G
 206.8   him] CI, H; *omit* G

THE LOUISIANA LAW OF COCK-FIGHTING

207.21   where] H; where are S
207.30   itself] H; themselves S
 208.6   'stranger] CE; '~ S; 'Stranger H
 209.3   cock-fighting?] H; ~. S

THE WATER CRAFT OF THE BACK WOODS

210.19–20   aborigine] H; aboriginee SS, CI; aborigines M
210.35   torn] M, H; tore SS, CI
 211.8   deer] M, H; dear SS, CI
212.25   separates] CI, M, H; seperates SS
212.31   scroll] H; scull SS, CI, M
213.20   calabash] H; calibash SS, CI, M
213.26   buffalo] CI, M, H; buffaloe SS
213.27   lover] M, H; cover SS, CI
213.33   Imagination] CI, M, H; Imaginaton SS

THE WAY AMERICANS GO DOWN HILL

215.24	Alleganies] H; Allegany's SS, CI
215.43–216.1	Alleganies] H; Allegany's SS, CI
216.10	horses'] H; horses SS, CI
216.32	horses'] H; horses SS, CI
217.13	knot] CI, H; not SS
217.23	looked] CI, H; look SS
219.24	hoofs] CI, H; hoof SS
219.32–33	intellectual] CI, H; intelleciual SS

LETTERS FROM THE FAR WEST

For the convenience of readers, the number of each letter appears in brackets preceding the text. Because the only known copy of the *Intelligencer* issue carrying the first letter is damaged, the following words missing from it have been inserted on the basis of the *Spirit* reprinting:

223.4	*Fight*	225.3	such fun.
224.38	shall	225.3	airing his shins
224.39	"Black	225.4	restored, and we
224.39	nigger's	225.5	for our day's journey.
224.40	tent in	225.6	P. S. The
225.1	was all	225.6	was killed by the
225.1	all expecting		buffalo
225.2	us and the	225.7	letter, should read, "

223.2	*Philology*;] CE; ~. CI
223.3	*Anecdotes*] CE; *Anedotes* CI
226.28–29	a swab] CE; a a swab CI
228.22	regular] CE; regulaa CI
229.9	seemed] CE; seemod CI
233.29	turned] CE; tnrued CI
234.11	William.] CE; ~." CI
236.34	relief] CE; reiief CI
245.18	difficulty] CE; difficuly CI
248.25	eyes] CE; oyes CI
249.11	breakfast] CE; breakfaat CI

THE LITTLE STEAMBOATS OF THE MISSISSIPPI

255.2   were] H; was S, CI
256.10 was] H; were S, CI

BROKER VS. BANKER. SCENE IN A NEW ORLEANS COURT

257.20 defendants] CE; defendents CI (This same change in the
        singular form of the word occurs at its every appearance.)
257.20 counsel] CE; council CI
258.7   developement] CE; developyement CI

TRAITS OF THE PRAIRIES

259.40 that would] CE; that M
260.24 taste dulled] CE; dulled taste M
262.15 nelumbium] CE; melumbium M
262.21 nelumbium] CE; melumbium M
264.9   quiet] CE; quite M

PISCATORY ARCHERY

266.3   an] H; a M
273.25 bough] H; bow M
273.26 *nelumbium*] CE; *melumbrium* M; melumbium H

WIT OF THE WOODS

276.4   Pan] H; pan M
276.10 discovered] H; found discovered M
277.20 deer] H; dear M
278.10 wattles] H; wottles M
278.28 wears] H; was M
279.11 awry] H; away M
279.30 brown study] H; brownstudy M
280.39 bark] H; bank M
281.7   impatient] H; impatiently M
281.9   another. *Cluck*] H; another *cluck* M
281.23 note;] H; ~. M
282.1   beautiful] H; beautifully M

PICTURES OF BUFFALO HUNTING

285.38   start] H; starts M
286.10   speed] CE; speeds M, H
288.34   rigid] H; ridgid M
291.24   were,] H; *omit* M
292.34   were the] H; was the M
295.13   unwieldy] H; unwieldly M
296.36   beginning] H; begining M

ALLIGATOR KILLING

301.5   flesh like] CE; fleshlike M

CONCORDIA LAKE

310.38–39   vanilla-scented] CE; manilla-scented M

THE CHASE

*312.22   Dominion] CE; Dominions S
*312.24   under] CE; and of S
312.26   its] CE; it's S
312.38   tormentors] CE; tormenters S
313.13   leaps] CE; lerps S
313.16   ears] CE; years S
313.25   If] CE; if S
313.36   ecstasies] CE; exstacies S
314.7   this."] CE; ~.ᴧ S

ENEMY IN FRONT AND REAR, OR—
A BEAR AND SNAKE STORY

315.7   huntsman's] CE; huntman's DN
315.18   afflicted] CE; afflcted DN
315.24   impassable] CE; impassible DN
315.38   amalgamation] CE; amalgimation DN
315.40   became] CE; become DN
315.40–316.1   considerable] CE; considerble DN
316.30   days'] CE; days DN
317.23   sudden] CE; sndden DN

A TRADITION OF THE NATCHEZ

318.1 Indian] KG; indian MS (Forms of this word are capitalized also at every other appearance.)

318.9 Mexicans] KG; mexicans MS

318.10–11 hieroglyphical] KG; heiroglyphical MS

318.13 innate] KG; inate MS

318.18 impelled] KG; impeled MS

318.21 separated] KG; seperated MS

318.26 loveliness] KG; lovliness MS

318.39 Oriental] KG; oriental MS

318.40 idolatries] KG; idolitries MS

319.11 sacrifice] KG; sacrafice MS (This same change in forms of "sacrifice" occurs at every other appearance.)

319.12 altars] KG; alters MS (This same change in forms of "altar" occurs at every other appearance.)

319.17 Providence] KG; providence MS

319.21 settlement] KG; setlement MS

319.27 relics] KG; relichs MS

319.32 century's] KG; centurys MS

319.35 priests] KG; preists MS

320.1 priestess] KG; preistess MS

320.6–7 foreboding] KG; forboding MS

320.9 superstitious] KG; supersticious MS

320.12 existence] KG; existance MS

320.18 fulfilled] KG; fulfiled MS

320.18–19 fugitives] KG; fugatives MS

320.35 plaintive] KG; plantive MS

321.3 warrior's] KG; warriors MS

321.5 radiance] KG; radience MS

321.12 propitiation] KG; propitiacion MS

321.23 interminable] KG; intermidable MS

321.27 yet the] KG; yet the the MS

SIGNIFICANT POST-COPY-TEXT SUBSTANTIVE VARIANTS

This list records all significant substantive variants in Thorpe's reprintings of his sketches. For reasons discussed in the Textual Commentary, these include additions or deletions of single words, phrases, sentences, and lengthy passages; substitutions that provide different information, improve clarity, or avoid unnecessary repetition; changes in words that are spelled to represent the language of the frontier; and changes in punctuation that affect the meaning of a sentence. This list does not include differences in accidentals among texts otherwise agreeing with each other. Because the entries do not provide a complete history of the text, changes in punctuation that influence capitalization are not always noted. The significant post-copy-text substantive variants listed here include those in reprintings by Porter that influenced succeeding versions by Thorpe, those in the simultaneous reprintings of the "The Louisiana Law of Cock-Fighting" by the *Spirit of the Times* and the Baton Rouge *Gazette*, and those variants between the manuscript and printed versions of "A Tradition of the Natchez."

The reading of this edition is to the left of the bracket, to the right of which is a symbol indicating the text or texts having that reading. The revised reading or readings and their source follow the semicolon. The text cited following *omit* does not contain the reading to the left of the bracket. The curved dash ~, used in recording punctuation variants, represents the same word that appears to the left of the bracket, and the caret ⌄ indicates the omission of a punctuation mark. If an asterisk precedes the page and line numbers, the reading is discussed in Textual Notes.

The abbreviations identifying the manuscript and the publications that contain the sketches are the same as those used in the List of Emendations.

TOM OWEN THE BEE-HUNTER

83.3–4 ever noticed] S, M; never noticed beyond the immediate vicinity of their homes H

83.8 common] S; *omit* M, H

83.12 proper and] S; *omit* M, H

83.17–18 what does it amount to] S, M; how unsatisfactory their records H

83.20 present] S; present time M, H

83.21 tracked] S; traced M, H

83.25 own] S; *omit* M, H

83.28–29 and court the roseate hue of health] S; *omit* M, H

83.36 hat, resembling somewhat an ancient hive;] S; hat—M, H

83.37 ensconced in] S, M; encased by H

83.38–40 drawn; part of his "linen," like a neglected penant, displayed itself in his rear. Coats] S; drawn; coats M, H

84.12 ever] S; *omit* M, H

84.16–17 whose top contained the sweet] S; whose trunk contained the sweets M; containing sweets H

84.17 the possession of] S; *omit* M, H

84.22 at the top] S; *omit* M, H

84.23 thereof] S, M; of their honeyed treasure H

84.23 sounds of the] S, M; *omit* H

84.24 merrily] S; *omit* M, H

84.24 on the butt of the tree] S; *omit* M, H

84.25 gigantic] S; stout M, H

84.25 from Tom] S; *omit* M; of the tree H

84.25 the rapidity of their] S, M; their united H

84.26 sacrifice] S, M; victim H

84.28 founded] S; formed M, H

84.29–30 such, no doubt,] S; such M, H

84.30–31 I know not when I should have ceased my moralizing reflections] S; how long I might have moralized I know not M, H

84.34 were] S; were about to be M, H

84.39 At last] S; In the midst of this warfare M, H

85.1 bee-hive] S, M; bee-line H

85.1–2 and landing] S; *omit* M, H

85.2 Then] S; Now M, H

85.3　too] S; *omit* M, H
85.4　alarm] S; danger M, H
85.9　Don't holler, nigger,] S, M; Never holler H
85.10　grunt and] S; *omit* M, H
85.11　he did] S, M; the negro did H
85.27　and] S; and, like a politician, he M, H
85.30　smart] S; rich M, H
85.35　government] S; nation M, H
85.36　bees; exhibiting] S; bees. ¶Thus Tom exhibited M, H
85.38–39　Col. Bingaman, the Napoleon] S; Colonel Bingaman, the Napoleon M; the great men H
85.39　conquests] S; victories M, H
85.39　his] S, M; their H
85.40　Crockett] S; Crockett M; western hunters H
86.1　Moose hunt] S; bear-hunt M, H
86.3　blow he gave] S; of M, H
86.3　have] S; have also M, H
86.4–5　exploits] S; sports M, H
86.6　terrible] S; terrible, indeed, M, H
86.8　alone] S; *omit* M, H

A FRONTIER INCIDENT

97.5　obliged] S; indebted M
97.8　incident] S; adventure M
97.8　of them] S; in the army M
97.9–12　and . . . character] S; though all, in their way, can tell events so thrilling in their details M
97.33　warmest of hearts] S; warm temperament M
97.36　as naturally] S; *omit* M
98.9　inglorious] S; glorious M
99.5　thish-ere] S; this 'ere M
99.8　a friendliness and] S; *omit* M
99.18　Dick] S; *omit* M
100.4　regular] S; reg'lar M
100.7　this event] S; this—except M
100.8　across] S; *omit* M
100.11　pardon] S; overlook M
100.24　board] S; table M

THE MISSISSIPPI

102.3   are] K, M; are named H
102.12–13 cultivation . . . strength;] K; cultivation;" M, H
102.32   that] K, M; which but lately H
103.5   they] K, M; they continuously H
103.14   sink] K, M; sink and rise H
103.15   bottom] K, M; bed H
103.19   drive through] K, M; crush H
103.20   sometimes] K, M; *omit* H
*103.30–31 'snag.' ¶The vast] K, M; "snag." ¶The forests that line the
           banks of the Mississippi, and supply, without any appar-
           ent decrease, the vast masses of timber that in such varied
           combinations every where meet the eye, are themselves
           worthy of the river which they adorn. ¶Go into the primi-
           tive forests at noonday, and however fiercely the sun may
           shine, you will find yourself enveloped in gloom. Gigantic
           trees obstruct your pathway, and as you cast your eyes
           upward, your head grows dizzy with their height. Here,
           too, are to be seen dead trunks, shorn of their limbs, and
           whitening in the blasts, that are as mighty in their size as
           the pillars of Hercules. Grape-vines larger than your body
           will, for some distance, creep along the ground, and then
           suddenly spring a hundred feet into the air, grasp some
           patriarch of the forest in its folds, crush, mutilate, and
           destroy it; and then, as if to make amends for the injury,
           throw over its deadening work the brightest green, the
           richest foliage, filled with fragrance, and the clustering
           grape. ¶On the top of these aspiring trees, the squirrel is
           beyond the gunshot reach of the hunter. Upon the ground
           are long piles of crumbling mould, distinguished from the
           earth around them by their numerous and variegated flow-
           ers. These immense piles, higher in the places than your
           head, are but the remains of single trees, that a century
           ago startled the silence now so profound, and with their
           headlong crash sent through the green arch above sounds
           that for a moment silenced the echoing thunder that
           loaded the hurricane that prostrated them. ¶Here were to
           be seen the ruins of a new continent—here were mould-

ering the antiquities of America—how unlike those of the Old World. Omnipotence, not man, had created these wonderful monuments of greatness, with no other tears than the silent rain, no other slavery than the beautiful laws that govern nature in ordering the seasons—and yet these monuments, created in innocency, and at the expense of so much time, were wasting into nothingness. God above in his power could erect them. They were breathed upon in anger and turned to dust. ¶The vast H

104.2   narrow] K, M; comprehensive H

104.7–10   associated . . . *itself*:] K, M; suggests to the mind that the banks of the river itself are composed of this dark sediment which has in the course of centuries confined the onward flood within its present channel, H

104.12   down] K, M; *omit* H

104.25   world] K, M; world by its luxurious vegetation H

105.3–4   think . . . of] K, M; be confounded by astonishment, or excited by H

105.9   I might say tame] K, M; a dreary waste H

105.10   contemplation and] K, M; *omit* H

105.14   on, and on] K; on, and on, and on M, H

105.17   without] K, M; with scarce H

105.25   gone . . . sounded.'] K; in vain gone down for soundings M, H

THE BIG BEAR OF ARKANSAS

113.8   big Bar] S; Big Bear BB; Big Bear H (This same change occurs at 113.13. In *Hive*, Thorpe revised "bar" to "bear" every time the word appears either alone, in its possessive form, or in a hyphenated compound, with only two exceptions. Where the *Spirit* and *Big Bear* texts italicize "bar," Thorpe wrote "*bear*," and at 121.35 he wrote "B(E)AR." He did not change "bar" at 114.1 and 118.24. In three instances the *Big Bear* text capitalizes "bar" differently than the *Spirit*, changes which the *Hive* text follows: "Big Bar" for "big bar" at 117.22, "bar" for "Bar" at 119.17, and "BAR" for "Bar" at 121.35.)

113.13   dropped] S, BB; ceased H

113.24   speaking] S, BB; interrupting H

113.36   rolette] S, BB; roulette H
113.39   says] S, BB; says, I H
114.4   diggings] S; diggins BB, H (This same change occurs at 115.1 and 117.2.)
114.7   less] S, BB; less heavy H
114.8   weight] S, BB; size H
114.12   that he] S; that it BB, H
114.32   took] S, BB; tuck H (This same change occurs at 114.33 and 114.34.)
114.35   know] S, BB; knowd H
114.37   mosquitoe] S, BB; mosquito H
115.2   plentifuler] S, BB; plentifuller H
116.1   turkies] S; turkeys BB, H
116.15   been] S, BB; been very H
116.22   bear] S; bears BB, H
116.25   Mississippi] S, BB; Mississipp H
116.38   land] S, BB; 'pre-emption' H
116.39   such a piece] S, BB; like it H
117.4   Kentuck] S, BB; Kaintuck H
117.4   bisiness] S, BB; business H
117.6   stopped] S, BB; drapped in H
117.11   mounds,' said he, 'and *it*] S, BB; mounds, and H
117.12   mounds" ar] S, BB; mounds" H
117.26   In . . . but] S, BB; The evening was nearly spent by the incidents we have detailed; and H
117.36   them] S, BB; the words H
117.37   words] S, BB; way H
117.40   hurricane] S; Hurricane BB, H
118.17   marks on] S, BB; scratches on the bark of H
118.18   saw] S, BB; saw chalk marks H
118.25–26   considerable] S, BB; considerably H
118.30   Did] S, BB; Do H
118.38   them] S, BB; their meat H
119.32   was] S, BB; got H
119.36   this] S, BB; this shaky H
120.5   coming] S; he came BB, H
120.11   he] S; *omit* BB, H
120.25   friend—says I,] S, BB; friend—H
121.13   queer] S, BB; *omit* H
121.28   such things as] S, BB; of such things H

122.5　like] S, BB; as easy as H
122.16　mattrass] S; mattress BB, H
122.18　Sampson's] S; Samson's BB, H
122.18　it] S, BB; he H
122.23　come in] S, BB; guv up H
122.27　the story] S, BB; this story H

WOODCOCK FIRE HUNTING

123.3　ORIGINAL] S; *Tom Owen* H
123.4–23　The face . . . a description.] S; ONE of the most beautiful and "legitimate" amusements of gentlemen, is woodcock shooting. In the "backwoods," where game of every kind is plentiful, it is pursued as often as a necessary of life, as for the gratification afforded by the sport. ¶Persons living in the hotbeds of civilization, but who yet retain enough of the old leaven of the wild man, to love to destroy the birds of the air, and the beasts of the field, are obliged to eke out the excitements of the field by conventional rules, which prescribe the manner of killing, the weapon to be used, and the kind of dog to be employed;—and the sportsman who is most correct in all these named particulars, is deservedly a "celebrity" in his day and generation. ¶No sport is more properly guarded and understood by amateur hunters than woodcock shooting, and no sport is more esteemed. Therefore, it was that the announcement that there was a section of the United States where the game bird was hunted by torchlight, and killed "without the benefit of clergy," created the same sensation among the "legitimists," as is felt at Saint Germain's, because there is "no Bourbon on the throne"—a thrill of horror pervaded the hearts of many who could believe such a thing *possible*—while the more "strait laced" and deeply conscientious, disbelieved entirely, and pronounced the report too incredible for any thing but a "hoax." Yet, woodcock fire-hunting is a fact, although most circumscribed in its geographical limits, the reasons for which, will appear in the attempt at a description of the sport. H

350

123.30   most] S; so great a portion H
123.30   Louisiana . . . Mexico] S; Louisiana H
123.34   its pleasure with] S; alike its pleasure and H
124.5–6   takes place] S; is practised H
124.17   fine] S; excellent H
124.20   powder] S; ammunition H
124.28   *punched*] S; pierced H
124.39   in] S; into H
125.2–3   on . . . same] S; *omit* H
125.8   us] S; you H
125.9   in a sort of] S; with a H
125.20   and] S; and we have H
125.22   it is a good one] S; successful H
125.25   clubs;] S; clubs; while the negroes have thrashed them down by "baskets-full" with whips made of bundles of young cane, H
125.27   way] S; way, while endeavoring H
125.35   some] S; those H
126.1   it is] S; are H
126.2–3   this nocturnal . . . and] S; *omit* H
126.6   table] S; board H
126.9–12 As . . . Hunting.] S; *omit* H

SCENES ON THE MISSISSIPPI

129.1–4   It . . . country] S, M; As our magnificent Union has increased in population, the aborigines within the "older States" have become constantly more and more degraded. "The Government," as the most merciful policy, has taxed its energies to remove these red men from the vicinity of civilization, to homes still wild and primitive, west of the Mississippi. There, a vast extent of country is still H
129.17   unconscious] S, M; hopeless H
129.22   ages] S, M; age H
129.24   seeming] S, M; apparent H
129.31   boat] S, M; conveyance H
130.12   lay] S, M; were H
130.23   glazed] S, M; *omit* H

351

130.30   or] S, M; and H

130.31   a] S, M; no H

131.4   got] S, M; raised himself H

131.5–6   A . . . speak.] S, M; *omit* H

131.12   A . . . a] S, M; A smile lit up his features—his lips moved—and he essayed to speak. A H

131.24   nothing] S, M; nothing unusual H

131.33   discontented and] S, M; *omit* H

131.35   comfortable] S, M; contented H

132.2   late] S, M; *omit* H

132.3   dressed and] S, M; *omit* H

132.7–8   in obscurity] S, M; invisible H

132.10–11   looking . . . came,] S, M; *omit* H

132.16   it] S, M; the air H

132.25   discovered] S; *omit* M, H

132.34   and] S, M; or H

133.1   first] S; *omit* M, H

133.4   bar] S, M; sand-bar H

133.5   loud] S, M; *omit* H

133.34   and swore] S, M; *omit* H

133.37   wild] S; *omit* M, H

134.5   as . . . weight] S, M; beneath the surface H

134.8   Indians] S, M; Indian H

134.9   looking . . . coolly] S, M; heretofore an uninterested spectator H

134.12   a dead body] S, M; lifelessly H

134.15   Bar] S, M; b*ear* H

134.15   has] S, M; has a H

134.16   of] S, M; in H

134.18   Bar] S, M; b*ear* H

134.18–19   best of . . . *thar*] S, M; best Christian of the two, and a parfect gentleman, compared with the best copper-skin that ever breathed H

134.25   river] S, M; water H

134.32   pursued its way] S, M; again gallantly bore us toward our place of destination H

A PIANO IN ARKANSAS

140.9   with] S, M; to H
140.12   Capt. Marryat's "Diary,"] CE; Capt. Marryatt's "Diary" S;
         some traveller M; some literary traveller H
140.15   Capt. Marryat] S; said traveller M, H
140.25   before] S, M; previously H
140.27   a] S; per M, H
140.31–32 down east] S; north M, H
140.32   new] S; new and hospitable M, H
140.35   an indifferent] S, M; a very bad H
140.39   seemed] S; seemed very M, H
141.4   this was the Piano] S; that the piano made them M, H
141.5   One] S; In the midst of it, one M, H
141.8   with] S; with the greatest M, H
141.14–15 ladies] S; ladies with real sympathy M, H
141.16   Mass-sis-sip] S; Mass-is-sip M, H
141.16   has] S; have M, H
141.21   off] S; temporarily absent M, H
141.22   was the] S; was the only M, H
141.25   would have been glory enough] S; alone would have
         stamped him with superiority M, H
141.28   the village] S; the renowned village of Hardscrabble M, H
141.32   was] S, M; was therefore H
141.34   insensibility was] S; insensibility was considered M, H
141.35   thing as a matter] S; piano as a thing M, H
141.36   on] S; on, among other things M, H
141.40   screech] S; hoarse M, H
142.8–9 a . . . Pope] S; an abandonment perfectly ridiculous M; an
         abandonment that was perfectly ridiculous H
142.9   Now] S; Mr. M, H
142.19–21 visit . . . observed] S; experience in the fashionable soci-
         ety of the "Capitol," and with pianos, which he said M;
         experience in the fashionable society of the "Capitol, and
         ianos," which he said H
142.21   Cash,] S; Cash, to comfort him, that M, H
142.22   or] S; and M, H
142.23   put] S, M; pull H
142.28   Cash] S; Cash, mysteriously M, H

142.33   bars,] S; bars and M, H
142.34–35   this was] S; he beheld M, H
142.37   *that*] S, M; that strange and incomprehensible box H
142.38   toper . . . water] S; north wind to an icicle M, H
142.39–40   then wished] S; then, recovering himself, he asked M, H
143.10   his discovery] S; the moment M, H
143.10–11   for a moment] S; *omit* M, H
143.15   it] S, M; consequently H
143.18   New England] S; northern M; Northern H
143.19   received] S, M; received meanwhile H
143.29   *thick*] S; *thick-leafed* M, H
143.32–33   loud and long] S; much and loud M; much and loudly H
143.34   more familiar] S; exceedingly conceited even for him M, H
143.36–144.1   "Hope . . . Piano.] S; The evening wore on apace, and still no piano. The hope deferred that maketh the heart sick, was felt by some elderly ladies, and by a few younger ones; and Mercer was solicited to ask Miss Patience Doolittle to favour the company with the presence of the piano. M, H
144.4   instrument] S; machine M, H
144.8   Cash] S; Whereupon Cash M, H
144.14   spread] S; covering M, H
144.19   whisper] S; whisper now M, H
144.20   crowd] S; room M, H
144.21   the] S; a few M, H
144.22   not] S; not perfectly M, H
144.23   was.] S; *was.* The music ceased. M; *was.* The dulcet sounds ceased. H
144.24   and overcome with astonishment] S; by the music M, H
144.25–26   last . . . gallery] S; in your gallery once M, H
144.26   with] S; by M, H
144.27   bars and] S; *omit* M, H
144.27   turn] S; time M, H
144.28   to her eye-brows] S; to her cheeks, with confusion M; from confusion to her cheeks H
144.28–29   hesitated only a moment] S; hesitated, stammered M, H
144.30   spikes] S; nails M, H
144.31   his knees] S; the heretofore invulnerable Mercer's knees M, H

144.33–34   The . . . fashion] S; The fashionable vices of envy and maliciousness M, H

144.35   invulnerable] S; confident, the happy and self-possessed
M, H

144.36   at its shrine] S; to their influence M, H

144.39   bidders] S; bidder M, H

144.39–40   "Patent and highly concentrated"] S; patent, warranted,
and improved M, H

OPOSSUMS AND 'POSSUM HUNTING

145.1–2   Reader . . . a] S, IYS; An opossum was made to represent
the class of H

145.5   live.—] S, IYS; live. In their creation, H

145.5–9   become . . . introduce] S, IYS; shown a willingness, if necessary, to be ridiculous, just for the sake of introducing H

145.11–12   Mr. Walker's exclusive province] S, IYS; the details H

145.14–15   nature." ¶The] S, IYS; nature." ¶One of the peculiarities of
the opossum that attracts to it general attention, is the
singular pouch they have under the belly, in which their
young are carried before their complete development,
and also into which they retreat when alarmed by the approach of danger. ¶This particular organ contains in its
interior, ten or twelve teats, to which the young, after what
seems a premature birth, are attached, and where they
hang for about fifty days, then drop off, and commence a
more active state of existence. ¶This animal evidently varies in size in different latitudes. In Louisiana they grow
quite large compared with those inhabiting more northern
climates. ¶The opossum ranges in length from twelve to
fifteen inches, the tail is about the same extent. The body
is covered with a rough coating of white, gray, and brown
hair, so intermixed and rough, that it makes the animal
look as if it had been wet and then drawn through a coal-
hole or ash-heap. The feet, the ears, and the snout are
naked. ¶The organs of sense and motion in this little animal seem to be exceedingly dull. Their eyes are prominent, hanging like black beads out of their sockets, and
appear to be perfectly destitute of lids, with a pupil similar
to those of a cat, which shows that they are suited to mid-

night depredations. ¶The nostrils of the opossum are evidently well developed, and upon the smell almost exclusively, is it dependent for its preservation. The ears look as if they were pieces of dark or soft kid skin, rolled up and fastened in their proper places. The mouth is exceedingly large and unmeaning, and ornamented with innumerable sharp teeth, yet there is very little strength in the jaws. The paws or hands of the animal are the seat of its most delicate sensibility, and in their construction are developed some of the most wonderful displays of the ingenuity of an All-wise Providence, to overcome the evident inferiority of the other parts of the animal's construction. ¶The opossum makes a burrow in the ground, generally found near habitations. In the day time it sleeps, and prowls at night. The moon in its brilliancy seems to dazzle it, for under the bright rays of the queen of night it is often knocked on the head by the negro hunter, without apparently perceiving it has an enemy near. ¶The H

145.17	are] S, IYS; are, as might be supposed from our imperfect description, infinitely H
145.20	that hits him] S, IYS; *omit* H
145.21–22	seems . . . Frenchman] S, IYS; is, in fact, a harmless little creature, and seems to belong to some peace society, the members of which have agreed to act toward the world as the boy H
145.26	your own charitable] S, IYS; giving you an opportunity to carry out your destructive H
145.27–28	given . . . off] S, IYS; destroyed him, he will watch his opportunity, and unexpectedly recovering his breath, will make his escape H
145.29–30	of "playing] S, IYS; entitled "playing H
145.31	be] S, IYS; be well H
145.32	impossible,] S, IYS; impossible, then H
145.32	tap] S, IYS; tap on the body H
145.33–34	as beautiful . . . see] S, IYS; and be, according to all indication, perfectly dead H
145.38	dead] S, IYS; defunct H
146.4	thar's] S; There's IYS, H
146.6	one] S, IYS; me H

146.9   decateful] S; desateful IYS, H
146.10 did not] S, IYS; didn't H
146.13 did not] S, IYS; didn't H
146.15 devil] S, IYS; divil H
146.21 is extraordinary] S, IYS; is most extraordinary H
146.40 bretheren] S; brethren IYS, H
147.2   to it] S; *omit* IYS, H
147.8   animal] S, IYS; creature H
147.12 game] S, IYS; beasts H
147.17 animal] S, IYS; animals H
147.20 and] S, IYS; or H
147.21 years] S, IYS; years only H
147.26 Sittin'] S; Sitting IYS, H
147.29 to the ground] S, IYS; *omit* H
147.36 through] S, IYS; throughout H
148.37 bunch] S, IYS; protuberance H
149.23 song] S, IYS; melody H

A GRIZZLY BEAR HUNT

150.5   enacting] S, M; being enacted H
150.18 the exploits] S, M; the trophies of exploits H
150.26 as] S, M; as one formed of H
150.26 if he falls] S; if he fall M; slain H
150.31 destroy] S, M; break H
151.10 Apart] S, M; While apart H
151.16 cultivation. The unfortunate] S, M; cultivation. We are ac-
        customed to look with surprise upon the instincts of ani-
        mals and insects. We wonder and admire the sagacity
        they display, for the purposes of self-preservation—both
        in attack and defence. The lion, the bear, the beaver, the
        bee, all betray a species of intelligence, that seems for
        their particular purposes superior to the wisdom of man;
        yet, on examination, it will be found that this is not the
        case. For all histories of the human denizen of the forest
        show, that the Indian surpasses the brute in sagacity,
        while the white hunter excels both animal and savage.
        ¶The unfortunate H
151.19–20 uses the *sight* most extraordinarily well] S; uses the sight

most extraordinarily well M; is compelled by circumstances to cultivate his sight, to almost the same degree
of perfection characterizing the blind girl's touch H

151.22 seems . . . impresses] S; seems . . . impressions M; leaves
to him a deep and visible impression H

151.22–23 that . . . as unseen] S; that to the common eye are unseen
M; though to the common eye unseen H

151.27 behind] S, M; behind him H

151.29 directs] S, M; guides H

151.30 impresses] S; impressions M, H

151.34–36 one . . . itself] S; one because it is poor, and another because it is small, another because it is with cubs, another
because it is . . . itself M; for in those indistinct paths, are
visible to his mind's eye, bear that are young and old, lean
and fat. You look into the forest, all is vacant; the hunter,
at a casual glance, detects where he has passed his object
of pursuit, and grows as enthusiastic over this spiritual
representation as if the reality was before him H

152.2 him] S; *omit* M, H

152.4 methods] S, M; methods by which H

152.5 almost] S; *omit* M, H

152.9 if it comes to grappling] S, M; when you grapple H

152.17 until the] S, M; until awakened by the genial H

152.23 alive, if] S, M; *omit* H

152.24 his cave] S, M; this den H

152.28 one] S; *omit* M, H

152.28 best] S, M; stoutest H

153.4 empty] S, M; unoccupied H

153.6 this wise.] S; thus: M, H

153.8 the cave] S, M; it H

153.11 bear] S, M; animal H

153.12 a fat one] S, M; fat H

153.17 truthfulness] S; certainty M, H

153.24 no steadiness] S, M; steadiness H

153.40 is] S, M; sleeps H

154.13 protected by] S; to possess M, H

154.28 death] S; *omit* M; death H

154.29 such] S, M; such fearful H

A STORM SCENE ON THE MISSISSIPPI

155.2	travelling] S; travelling on horseback H
155.6–8	there . . . one] S; a silent and stifled atmosphere prevailed H
155.39	passed] S; pressed H
156.5	had] S; had once H
156.6	us, it] S; us. The cabin H
156.19	seemed] S; was H
156.21	surrounded] S; was upon H
156.23	some] S; *omit* H
156.25	was growing] S; grew H
156.28–29	grew . . . comfortable] S; feeling unusually comfortable, grew loquacious H
156.31	preceded] S; preceded, he said, H
156.36	other] S; other serious H
156.39	so,] S; *omit* H
156.40–157.1	After . . . changed] S; The quiet weather I spoke of, was followed by a sudden change H
157.3	flew] S; flew about H
157.5	way] S; way in which H
157.9	am a liar] S; can't speak the truth H
157.14	bakon] S; bacon and other 'plunder,' with which the boat was loaded, H
157.18	it like ——] S; harder H
157.19	as hard as he suggested] S; as well as I could H
157.21	would have done] S; *omit* H
157.22	half soaked to death] S; half dead H
157.24	Kentucky] S; Kaintucky H
157.24	what] S; what, stranger H
157.25	Mississippi] S; Mississipp H
157.29	its full] S; all its H
157.31	when] S; where H
157.32	downwards] S; downwards, apparently H
157.36	rain] S; water H
157.39	sometimes] S; *omit* H
158.1	forest] S; forest meanwhile H
158.2	muddy] S; turbid H
158.6	its] S; its most distant H

158.6–7 dark mountains,] S; mountains of H
158.10 full] S; momentary H
158.11 dying in the storm] S; in the agony of death H
158.15 you found yourself] S; you were, a moment after, H
158.19 descend] S; descend in gusts H
158.20 and snored] S; *omit* H
158.23 who . . . asleep] S; whom I thought in a profound slumber H
158.25 must] S; must be silent and H
158.25 dull] S; continued H
158.27 listening] S; interested in the prevailing dull sounds without H
158.28 gave a loud grunt,] S; *omit* H
158.34 are] S; ar H
158.36 left] S; stepped from H
158.39 *Mississippi*] S; mysterious river H
159.4–5 greenness, and freshness,] S; freshness and beauty H
159.8 gone] S; obliterated H
159.9 banks . . . ancient] S; banks were lined only with the unbroken forest H
159.9 stranger] S; stranger, while looking, H
159.11 obliterated] S; swept away H
159.12 about] S; about us H
159.13–17 NOTE . . . lost.] S; *omit* H

THE AMERICAN WILD CAT

166.9 plentiful] NSM, ATR, M; numerous H
166.23–24 in its mouth its victim] NSM, ATR, H; it in its mouth M
166.32 the Ishmaelite's] M; the Ishmaelites NSM, ATR; the hand of the Ishmaelite H
167.2 turns] NSM, ATR; turns out M, H
167.3 often] NSM, ATR; frequently M, H
167.4 takes often] NSM, ATR; will take M, H
167.10 are yelling at its feet] NSM, ATR, M; *omit* H
167.10 that they] NSM, ATR, M; *omit* H
167.12 seem] NSM, ATR; seem like M, H
167.14 hair standing] NSM, ATR, M; the hair stands H
167.15 ears pressed] NSM, ATR, M; the ears press H
167.17 when] NSM, ATR; and M, H

167.23 ghosts] NSM, ATR, M; ghosts vanish H
167.33 hound could] NSM, ATR; dog could M, H
*167.36 showed] NSM, ATR, M; gave IYS, H
168.9 desert] NSM, ATR, M; leap H
168.9 sometimes] NSM, ATR, M; Sometimes from negligence H
168.10 lodged] NSM, ATR; *omit* M, H
168.24 and then starting] NSM, ATR, M; it started H
168.25 leaped off] NSM, ATR, M; just jumped from H
168.28 rifle] NSM, ATR, M; gun H
168.31 visible, the cat advancing] NSM, ATR, M; visible in the cat; it progresses H
168.31–32 stealing] NSM, ATR, M; crawling H
169.1 own] NSM; *omit* ATR, M, H
169.4 sang] NSM; sung ATR, M, H
169.7 up rough, and tumble] NSM; ~, ~.~~, ATR, M, H
169.14 has] NSM, ATR, M; has all H
169.15 an old] NSM, ATR; a M, H
169.28 victors] NSM, ATR; victims M, H
*169.34 the] NSM, ATR, M; that a IYS; That the H

THE DISGRACED SCALP LOCK, OR
INCIDENTS ON THE WESTERN WATERS

170.5 forms] S, M; bodies H
170.10 if not] S, M; if not entirely H
170.11 grey] S; steel-grey M, H
170.17 no town at all.] S, M; "when it was no town at all." H
170.18 out] S, M; out by them H
170.23 insensibly] S; *omit* M, H
170.26 extinct and] S; *omit* M, H
170.28 flat-boatmen] S; flat-boat men M; keel-boatmen H
170.30 pursuit] S, M; pursuit of commerce H
170.33 kept] S, M; kept it H
170.36 warrior] S, M; warrior, therefore, H
171.4 to] S, M; to attract attention, or H
171.4–7 Obscurity . . . traditions] S; Obscurity has nearly obliterated the men, and their actions. A few of the former still
. . . traditions M; Death has nearly destroyed the men, and
obscurity is fast obliterating the record of their deeds; but
a few examples still exist, as if to justify the truth of these

	wonderful exploits, now almost wholly confined to tradition H
171.8–9	the notoriety of] S, M; more notoriety than H
171.12	Fink] S, M; *omit* H
171.16	It] S, M; The rifle H
171.29–172.6	light . . . people] S, M; light H
172.9	The] S, M; The beautiful H
172.11	as a . . . meanderings] S; with its meanderings as a child could be with those M, H
172.16	trigger done] S; trigger's M; trigger, did H
172.17	lucky] S, M; lucky then H
172.19	Who . . . 'em?] S; *omit* M, H
172.22	nigger] S, M; mule H
172.22	continue] S, M; continue this way H
172.28	Indian] S; *omit* M, H
172.29	dead . . . prairie] S, M; 'tack of rheumatism H
172.32	in those days] S; *omit* M, H
172.35–36	there . . . lived] S, M; a great many renegade Indians lived H
173.4	too was] S, M; was idle, and consequently H
173.11	who,] S, M; who, while H
173.17	together] S, M; joined H
173.17	they] S, M; the Indians H
173.18–19	an unfeeling] S, M; a thoughtless H
173.19	crowd] S, M; band H
173.31	filthy in] S, M; careless of H
173.31	these respects] S; this respect M, H
173.32	person] S, M; *omit* H
173.33	if] S, M; if still H
173.35–36	that . . . might] S, M; until . . . should H
173.38–39	it . . . lock] S, M; the revered scalplock a hawk's feather H
174.6	he got] S, M; *omit* H
174.7	of the matter] S; about it M, H
174.12	and from] S; and perceived from M, H
174.18	viewing him] S; reviewing him M; viewing Mike H
174.21	body] S, M; body were H
174.23	it] S, M; *omit* H
174.26	rifle] S; *omit* M, H
174.35	present] S; *omit* M, H
175.2	turning . . . fire] S, M; silently returned to the shore H

175.4   to the opposite shore] S, M; *omit* H

175.11   of it] S, M; *omit* H

175.11   ornaments,] S, M; ornaments, still H

175.23   around; like a fiend,] S; around like a fiend; M; like a fiend; H

175.28   man from] S, M; being from what he had been H

176.10–11   and carried] S, M; hurrying past H

176.12   of the situation which] S, M; which the situation of H

176.13   Indians,] S, M; Indians, even H

176.16   the worst] S, M; any kind of reception H

176.17   use] S, M; use with effect H

176.21   at his sides, and] S, M; *omit* H

176.30   in exultation of] S; exultation of M; exultation at H

177.2   why he] S; why, he M; why, he said that he would have H

177.28   moccasin] S, M; moccason snake H

177.28   that] S, M; and H

177.30   came] S, M; dar'd to come H

177.31   ask a] S; ask M, H

177.35   prehaps] S; perhaps M, H

177.35–36   Massissip] S; Mississippi M, H

177.36   so on until] S; and so on to M, H

177.37   I] S; I will M, H

177.39   withe] S; *omit* M, H

178.3   devils] S; divils M, H

178.3   thar] S, H; thare M;

178.14   lightning] S, M; lightning also H

178.18   one of] S; *omit* M, H

178.19   of] S, M; *omit* H

178.22   powerful] S; power M, H

178.23   finally] S, M; *omit* H

178.38   screams and imprecations] S; amid screams and imprecations that M, H

179.1   hell] S, M; h-ll H

179.13   antagonist] S, M; adversary H

179.25   mere] S; *omit* M, H

179.30   having] S, M; ever having had H

179.31   friend] S, M; comrade H

179.33   that claimed] S, M; of H

179.35   dead as it was,] S, M; still H

180.1–2   he, among other things,] S, M; he H

180.10–11 When . . . men.] S, M; *omit* H
180.11–12 was astir, and] S, M; *omit* H
180.13 the corpse of] S; *omit* M, H
180.14 disgusting, and required] S, M; requiring H
180.17 that covered it] S, M; *omit* H
180.22–23 from . . . on] S, M; was turned upon H
180.24 cat] S, M; cat's H
180.32 corpse] S, M; boatman H
180.33 as that of Mike's] S, M; for Mike Fink H
180.33 resigned] S; risked M, H

THE DEVIL'S SUMMER RETREAT, IN ARKANSAW

181.2 the Devil's] S; Satan's H (This same change occurs at 181.32, 182.21, 183.20, 186.22, and 187.21.)
181.3–4 the current of] S; aside the H
181.5 Ballston, or] S; Newport and H
181.16 composed of] S; environed by H
181.25 limb . . . body] S; gigantic limb H
181.26 some] S; *omit* H
181.33 which] S; where H
182.2 seems to be] S; is almost as H
182.4 ten thousand] S; myriads of H
182.7 Around] S; Amid H
182.13 Associated] S; Familiar H
182.23 He . . . and] S; For, while he . . . he is H
182.27 cabin] S; camp H
182.35 Wasps'] S; Wasp's H
183.2 resembling] S; characteristic of H
183.7 sucked] S; drawn H
183.9 was] S; were H
183.10 out,] S; out, it H
184.8 and went] S; and, therefore went H
184.12–14 and with . . . glory;] S; *omit* H
184.14 jinson] S; jimson H
184.15 larnt] S; l'arnt H
184.15 parfectly] S; perfectly H
184.16 larn] S; l'arn H
184.18 malitia] S; militia H
184.18 rigler] S; regler H

184.19 requires] S; takes H
184.24 nothin'] S; nothing H
184.28 nigh] S; nih H
184.29 prehaps] S; perhaps H
184.30 was] S; was upon H
184.36 knowing] S; knowin H
184.36 at that] S; on a H
184.39 rushing] S; running H
185.1   been] S; been a H
185.1   seen] S; seen a H
185.3   Hadn't] S; I hadn't H
185.4   very] S; *omit* H
185.9   sort a] S; a sort of H
185.9   slantindicularly] S; slantingdicularly H
185.10 sat] S; sot H
185.12 eend. 'Twas] S; end. It was H
185.13–14 without] S; without any H
185.16 rather] S; *omit* H
185.17–18 circumstances] S; carcumstances H
185.23 whar] S; where H
185.24 knowed . . . afor] S; know'd . . . afore H
185.25 Brusher] S; Blucher H
185.26 Tig] S; Tige' H
185.26 laying] S; lying H
185.32 with] S; on H
185.33 stepped] S; stept H
185.34–35 and he . . . me, when] S; and as he . . . me, H
185.37 leaped] S; leapt H
185.39 'narvious'] S; *'narvious,'* stranger, H
185.40 mad] S; *omit* H
186.12 *cartainty*] S; *sartainty* H
186.15 off] S; off, as he had said, H
186.23 at one time] S; often H
186.26 its roots,] S; roots, you are H
186.40 No idea . . . can be had] S; Nothing . . . could give an idea H
187.17 bear's] S; beast's H
187.18 h——l was] S; h-ll were H
187.21 angels] S; music H
187.22 out] S; *omit* H

187.22   On] S; Out of his lair H
187.24–25   but getting wind of them,] S; *omit* H
187.26   already] S; *omit* H
187.32   minutes] S; minutes necessary H
187.33   months] S; *an age* H
187.39   rear] S; ear H
187.40   common] S; usual H
188.4   nigger camp] S; political H
188.4   sartin] S; sartain H
188.11   A . . . approach, and the] S; On . . . approach H
188.23–24   One of . . . Herring] S; Bob Herring, and one of the hunt-ers, in spite of the danger H
188.24   his] S; their H
188.29–30   instant, the bear received] S; instant, received H
188.32   the Devil's] S; *omit* H
189.1   distant] S; *omit* H
189.7   he,] S; he, utterly H
189.14   afor] S; afore H
189.15   shoot] S; fire H
189.16   unsartin] S; unsartain H
189.19   dogs, God bless 'em] S; blessed dogs H
189.22   a] S; a huge H
189.24   Devil's] S; *omit* H
189.28–29   that . . . snow,] S; *omit* H
189.37   bear] S; the liver H
190.5   shoulder, "but I've] S; shoulders, "but I have H
190.6   dies] S; dies as H
190.7   virtue] S; vartue H
190.8   its] S; the caul fat and liver is H
190.12   similar] S; *omit* H
190.13   shall] S; shall ever H
190.15   Devil's Summer Retreat.] S; "Summer Retreat in Arkan-sas." H

PLACE DE LA CROIX

191.38–39   *The . . . Mississippi.] K; *omit* M, H
192.5   made] K; formed M, H
192.12   forests] K; woods M, H
192.16   splendor] K; grandeur M, H

192.26 instructer] K; intruder M, H
192.27–28 despondency] K; despondence M; despondence, when H
192.33 against] K; among M, H
193.1 seemed] K, M; seemed to him H
193.10 every] K; every other M, H
193.11 strength in] K; with strength M, H
193.14 sacred] K; *omit* M, H
193.15 or] K; or more M, H
193.20 thousand] K; thousand of those M, H
193.25 and] K; and now M, H
193.29 until it] K, M; and H
194.6 and nearer] K; *omit* M, H
194.7 hers] K, M; her view H
194.10 over Rousseau] K; in his face M, H
194.12 about him] K; about M, H
195.8 perfection] K, M; accomplishment H
195.10–11 not the bloody-minded] K, M; of a kinder nature than the H
195.23 formed] K, M; used H
195.34 mind] K; mind, to have occupied M, H
196.7 enlightening] K, M; enlightening and christianizing H
196.11–12 was sought] K, M; had been vainly sought H
196.12 difficult] K; indifferent M, H
196.17 any] K; any other M, H
196.18 bosom] K, M; breast H
196.28 in . . . death] K; with his life M, H
197.2 under] K; under the influence of M, H
197.14 the lodge] K; the Indian lodge M, H
197.21 seemed] K, M; appeared H
197.32 by] K; to M, H
197.32 stems] K; stones M, H
198.4 love-scene] K; scene M, H
198.7 whole tribe] K, M; Choctaws H
198.12 deeply felt] K; deep M, H
198.25 gentle] K; wild M, H

MY FIRST DINNER IN NEW ORLEANS

203.1 There] G, CI; No one told a story better than old Major Gasden—in fact he could detail very commonplace incidents so dramatically, that he would give them a real interest. He had met with a little incident on his first visit to New Orleans, that was to him a source of either constant humor or annoyance. Whichever view he took of the adventure, gave character to his illustration of it. ¶The "major," on a certain occasion, formed one of a happy party, and growing communicative under the influence of genial society and old port, was imprudent enough to call on several persons near and around him for songs and sentiments,—which calls being promptly honored,—the Major very unexpectedly found himself under the immense obligation of doing something for his friends himself; and as he could not sing, and hated salt water, he compromised, by relating the following personal adventure. ¶We give it as nearly verbatim as possible, but must premise, that from an occasional twinkle that we noticed in the Major's eyes, we have never been perfectly satisfied that he did not, to use the language of an Irish friend of ours, "make an intentional mistake." ¶"There H

203.2–3	dinner . . . speaking] G, CI; dinner, generally speaking," commenced the Major, "to make . . . way H
203.10	may] G, CI; may properly H
203.16	recollect] G, CI; remember H
203.17	eat] G, CI; ate H
203.21	intellect] G, CI; excitement of the intellect H
203.21–22	senses . . . all] G, CI; gratification of the senses H
203.22	the city] G, CI; New Orleans H
203.24	for] G, CI; for while in the city H
203.24–25	usual custom, my friend] G, CI; his usual custom, he H
203.26	plenty] G, CI; luxuries H
203.27	expectations and hopes] G, CI; anticipations of good living H
203.28–29	a . . . palate] G, CI; an interest to the gratification of my palate that I had never before indulged in H
203.29	fronting the city] G, CI; of New Orleans H
203.33	coursed] G, CI; crowded H
203.36–204.1	Orleans . . . dining] G, CI; Orleans. The dining H
204.2	dinners] G, CI; diners H
204.3	consequently was] G, CI; was, of course, H

204.4   hasty] G, CI; hastily-eaten H
204.5   uncommonly . . . dinner.] G, CI; in the spirit of enjoying a good dinner, for H
204.8   grow] G, CI; cool H
204.11   head] G, CI; top H
204.12   one, around] G, CI; round one, at H
204.13   The . . . table] G, CI; A single chair H
204.14   seated . . . chair] G, CI; appropriated it to myself H
204.15   not] G, CI; not endeavor to H
204.15–16 a kind of expression of] G, CI; the sort of expression which signifies H
204.16   way] G, CI; way, and happened to feel so too; and as I cast my eyes H
204.17   upon the] G, CI; at my H
204.17–22 and before . . . spoon,] G, CI; I paid no attention whatever to the cold stare I met with, as if intending to make me feel that I was intruding. ¶"In this excellent humor with all the world and myself, I asked the waiter with a loud voice for soup, hot if possible, and I found myself accommodated in the twinkling of a ladle. H
204.23   a] G, CI; an *extra* H
204.24–25 and I made the remark] G, CI; I accordingly made the reflection H
204.25   on the] G, CI; on my H
204.25   politely] G, CI; formally H
204.26–28 him . . . an] G, CI; him with great solicitude to follow my example,—and do justice to the viands before him. He suggested that he was troubled with a dyspepsia. This little conversation was received by the whole table with what I remember now, and then for a moment, thought was an H
204.29   from the one] G, CI; by a gentleman H
204.30   but . . . personage] G, CI; presuming I sat at the head. This person, however, H
204.31–32 that . . . bashful] G, CI; thought nothing more of the matter; at the same time feeling great sympathy for my friend on my right, whom I set down as a very bashful man H
204.32   tumbling] G, CI; trembling H
204.33–34 very . . . this] G, CI; was very beautiful indeed H

369

204.36 on my right] G, CI; *omit* H
204.36 observed] G, CI; observed to him H
204.38 famous for the] G, CI; growing quite celebrated for that H
204.39 agreed] G, CI; it was agreed that H
204.40 I then] G, CI; Thus encouraged, I H
204.40 them] G, CI; all present H
205.1   ate] G, CI; tasted H
205.1   then] G, CI; that H
205.2–3 dish . . . butter] G, CI; steaks in the chafing dish before us, but merely jerked off of the carcass, thrown on living coals of fire, and then while steaming hot, devoured with the simple addition of pepper H
205.5   another] G, CI; another unnecessarily H
205.6–7 hens . . . and was] G, CI; hens of a most delicate flavor followed after the meats; they were H
205.8   said; this] G, CI; said, and H
205.9–10 remarked . . . matter] G, CI; uttered, and my . . . matter were H
205.11–12 The . . . excited] G, CI; The *becasse*, as they were announced, excited my H
205.13 balls] G, CI; globes H
205.15 over and discovered] G, CI; over and over and discovered to my horror H
205.16 the bill] G, CI; it H
205.16–17 exclaimed] G, CI; ejaculated H
205.17 Our] G, CI; My H
205.17–18 exactly . . . else] G, CI; Exactly so.' ¶"I helped every body H
205.19 like] G, CI; as if they were alive and H
205.19–20 expressed the most astonishing] G, CI; a general display of the most cheering H
205.22 maunching bits, and] G, CI; munching bits of bread and other H
205.28 were] G, CI; were we H
205.29 I] G, CI; For my own part, I H
205.29–30 and in my] G, CI; and H
205.32–33 proposition . . . be] G, CI; suggestion of candles by an attendant proved H
205.33 drink] G, CI; glass H

205.34–35   Certainly . . . brim.] G, CI; Requesting all to fill to the brim, H
205.35   high, and] G, CI; on high, and thus H
205.36   as follows] G, CI; *omit* H
205.36–206.1   much . . . the] G, CI; much of the fine tables spread in New Orleans, particularly of this hotel, and of the enterprise of its host. I have heard nothing equal to their respective or joint merits (*great applause, the rubicund-nosed man breaking his glass in enthusiasm*). The whole of this affair is only surpassed in my experience, or most inflated dreams, by you, gentlemen (casting a sort of patronising look around me), by you, gentlemen,—in your social, literary, and scientific attainments'—(*tremendous cheering*). ¶"I concluded, in a halo of glory, with 'A health to our H
206.1–2   received . . . of the] G; received with tremendous applause judging from the consequences. Two of the CI; drank to the bottom, two H
206.3   three] G, CI; four H
206.3   flew] G, CI; rattled H
206.4–7   all . . . left] G, CI; with all who could go through the ceremony, I left the table, whereon had been eaten the best dinner of my life—where I had met the cleverest party ever assembled to my knowledge; such was my first dinner in New Orleans. ¶"It was nearly one o'clock at night, when I met my friend with whom I had parted H
206.9   was] G, CI; was still under the pleasurable excitement of my dinner, its effects were still radiating about my brain like heat from a cooling stove. I was H
206.10   thanked him warmly] G, CI; among other things exceedingly grateful to my sick friend H
206.10–11   a . . . Fine] G, CI; such a splendid hotel and to such good dinners. ¶"'Good H
206.11   exclaimed, with a groan] G, CI; groaned H
206.12–14   had a . . . hotel."] G, CI; eaten a good dinner? nearly dead from swallowing cabbage and pork.' ¶"The very mention of such gross aliment made me sick, and I asked him where he dined, with undisguised alarm. ¶"'In the hotel, to be sure,' was his reply. H

206.14 and] G, CI; and to convince him H
206.14–15 running commentary] G, CI; hurried description H
206.15 The] G, CI; The severe H
206.16 completely] G, CI; altogether H
206.16–17 twinkle . . . he] G, CI; mysterious meaning of my friend's eyes as he looked up, and H
206.18 and a] G, CI; and the dinner that had given me so much satisfaction was a H
206.18 at a . . . expense!] G, CI; at great expense, and under the immediate superintendance of celebrated *bon vivants*. H
206.19–20 dinner . . . vanished!] G, CI; party of strangers at the social board, vanished into thin air; the cause of H
206.20–21 and . . . fortunate in eating] G, CI; —fortunate, indeed, as I was in eating H
206.22–23 so . . . innocent] G, CI; too delicate to hint at any explanations that would, in their presence, inform me of my amusing H

THE LOUISIANA LAW OF COCK-FIGHTING

*207.13 burban] S, H; burbon G
207.21–22 statues] S, G; statutes H
207.24 himself] S, G; *omit* H
207.29–30 the expression] S; these expressions G; an expression H
208.2 came] S, G; come H
208.5 little] S, H; *omit* G
208.6 you have] S, G; you've got H
208.10 parfect] S, H; perfects G
208.10 cock] S, G; bird H (This change occurs at 208.11 and 208.14.)
208.12 puked] S, G; threw up his feed, actewelly vomited H
208.13 against] S, G; agin H
208.17 Perhaps] S, G; Prehaps H
208.18 perhaps] S; prehaps G, H
208.19 draw] S, G; draw on my purse H
208.24 started] S, G; stared H
208.29 and] S, G; then H
208.36 carried] S, G; waved H
208.38 not] S, H; no G

209.11   walked] S; walking G, H
209.14   a dam] S, G; an infernal old chuckel-headed H

THE WATER CRAFT OF THE BACK WOODS

210.1   among] SS, CI, M; amid H
210.7   another] SS, CI, H; another time M
210.17   and] SS, CI, M; and more H
210.17   have] SS, CI, M; have ever H
210.24   this] SS, M, H; its CI
210.30   searched in vain] SS, CI, M; fruitlessly searched H
210.34   be] SS, CI, M; be thus H
210.39   only the work of] SS, CI, M; the work of only H
211.5   on in its] SS; on its CI; in its M; on the H
211.7   leaped] SS, CI; leapt M; ran H
211.16   have] SS, CI, M; have accordingly H
211.25   migrating] SS, CI, H; emigrating M
211.28   are] SS, CI, H; is M
211.36   buffalo skin, when it is] SS, CI, H; buffalos' skins, when
           they are M
212.5   the most perfect of the] SS, CI, H; the perfect M
212.5–6   of the varieties] SS, CI; of variety M; the varieties H
212.9   will] SS, CI, M; will most H
212.11   boats] SS, CI, M; yachts H
212.12   they] SS, CI, M; their boats H
212.13   high] SS, CI, H; highest M
212.13   greatest] SS, M; great CI, H
212.26   blade] SS, CI, H; *omit* M
212.31   it is] SS, CI, M; it is quite H
212.31   inserted] SS, CI, M; inserted in order H
212.36–40 A . . . bark] SS, CI, M; But if to usefulness there can be
           added the highest beauty, then the rude clamps are dis-
           placed by the sewing together of the ends of the bark. A
           preparation is then made of deer's tallow and pounded
           charcoal, which is used instead of pitch to fill up the
           meshes of the seams, and the boat is complete H
213.1   cannot] SS, CI, M; can neither H
213.4   clear] SS, CI, M; cleave H
213.7   aided] SS, CI, M; aided but H

373

213.13   and then] SS, CI, M; the next moment— H
213.36   journeyings] SS, CI, H; journeys M
 214.3   then] SS, M; *omit* CI, H

THE WAY AMERICANS GO DOWN HILL

215.27   seemed] SS, CI; seemed ever H
215.28   reach] SS, CI; reach, but always to be near H
215.33   when] SS, CI; where H
215.36   they] SS, CI; he H
215.43   was] SS, CI; is H
 216.1   we allude] SS; we allude to CI; to which we allude H
216.3–5   How . . . pole] SS, CI; That we could live through such a night would have been deemed impossible, could its perils have been anticipated, before they were experienced H
 216.6   Pittsburg] SS, CI; *omit* H
216.16   and their backs] SS, CI; *omit* H
216.20   inventor] SS, CI; masters H
216.20   presses] SS, CI; presses to imagine H
216.24   most *in the middle*] SS, CI; in the centre H
216.25   frost] SS; Frost CI, H
216.31   sleet;] SS, CI; sleet; for H
216.32   shoes] SS, CI; shoes consequently H
 217.2   we are about to detail] SS, CI; about to be detailed H
217.11   Matter!] SS, CI; *omit* H
217.12   infernal] SS, CI; confoundedly H
217.16   sight] SS, H; light CI
217.20   smothered] SS, H; smothered fellow CI
217.28   conceived] SS, CI; conceived of H
217.31   either] SS, CI; each H
217.38   princess] SS, H; prince CI
 218.1   been] SS, CI; been most H
 218.4   they] SS, CI; it H
 218.8   the] SS; this CI, H
218.10   passed] SS, CI; *omit* H
218.14   difficulty in] SS, CI; difficulty," said he, "in H
218.15   in] SS, CI; of H
218.19   stage] SS, H; stage coach CI
218.27   married] SS, CI; wedded H
218.27   been] SS, CI; been married H

218.30   with the] SS, CI; with great H
219.3   One] SS, CI; At one H
219.4–9   sideways . . . again,] SS, CI; *omit* H
219.10–12   mountain . . . and the] SS, CI; mountain—and the H
219.12   lay] SS, CI; laid H
219.14   in the] SS; in their CI; them in the H
219.16   us] SS, CI; the stage H
219.17   we had] SS, CI; it had H
219.28   slightest obstacle, the] SS, CI; *omit* H
219.30   were] SS, CI; were then H
219.31   buried us beneath] SS, CI; hurled us on H
219.32   beneath] SS, H; below CI
219.34   an instant] SS, H; a moment CI
219.36   exposed] SS, CI; displayed H
220.1   so] SS, CI; *omit* H
220.2   until] SS, H; and CI
220.4   insides] SS, CI; insiders H
220.6   of] SS, CI; of ineffable H
220.11   nigger] SS, CI; darkey H
220.13   inside] SS, CI; insider H
220.14   do; if] SS, CI; do," said the driver contemptuously. "If H
220.14   the off fore] SS, H; that off CI
220.15   rut,' had] SS, CI; rut,' " he continued, "had H
220.16   back seat cushion] SS, H; of the back seat cushions CI
220.17   inside] SS, CI; insider H
220.18   one] SS, CI; we H
220.19   a] SS, CI; our H
220.20–21   the . . . travellers] SS, CI; more than my fellow-travellers, the terrible ordeal through which we had just passed H
220.25   so] SS, CI; *omit* H

THE LITTLE STEAMBOATS OF THE MISSISSIPPI

253.6   breathing like] S, CI; breathing out H
253.9   astonish] S, CI; convulse H
253.11–12   volume of] S, CI; *omit* H
253.18   slight] S, CI; *omit* H
253.21–22   that empty into bayous, that empty into rivers,] S, CI; *omit* H
253.23   geography, ever] S, CI; geography, never H

253.25   I found myself] S, CI; one finds himself H
253.25–26   I looked about me] S, CI; he looks about him H
253.26   I had got] S, CI; you are H
253.27–28   colossal . . . feet] S, CI; colossus—you find, on going on
           the boat, that your feet are H
253.29   my] S, CI; your H
253.36   spiteful] S, CI; spitefully H
253.39   big boat] S, CI; big steamer H
253.40   the boat] S, CI; the craft H
254.3   near it] S, CI; near H
254.6   a bundle] S, CI; a small bundle H
254.11   weigh] S, CI; way H
254.15   resented] S; presented CI, H
254.17   Being light myself I] S, CI; The two light passengers H
*254.19–20 boat." Dinner came on] S, CI; boat." ¶Captain Raft, of the
U. S. Mail steamer Emperor, it may not be uninteresting to
know, was one of those eccentric men that had a singular
ambition to run a boat where no one else could—he was
fond of being a great discoverer on a small scale. In one
of his eccentric humors, Captain Raft run the Emperor up
Red River, as the pilot observed, about "a feet," which in
the southwest, means several hundred miles. ¶Among the
passengers upon that occasion was old Zeb Marston, a
regular out-and-outer frontiersman, who seemed to spend
his whole life in settling out of the way places, and locating his family in sickly situations. Zeb was the first man
that "blazed" a tree in Eagle Town, on the Mountain Fork,
and he was the first man that ever choked an alligator to
death with his hands, on the Big Cossitot. He knew every
snag, sawyer, nook and corner of the Sabine, the Upper
Red River, and their tributaries, and when "bar whar
scace," he was wont to declare war on the Cumanchos,
and, for excitement, "used them up terrible." ¶But to our
story—Zeb moved on Red River, settled in a low, swampy,
terrible place, and he took it as a great honor that the
Emperor passed his cabin; and, at every trip the boat
made, there was tumbled out at Zeb's yard a barrel of new
whiskey, (as regularly as she passed,) for which was paid
the full value in cord wood. ¶Now, Captain Raft was a kind
man, and felt disposed to oblige every resident that lived

on his route of travel; but it was unprofitable to get every week to Zeb's out-of-the-way place, and as he landed the fifteenth barrel, he expressed his surprise at the amount of whiskey consumed at his "settlement," and hinted it was rather an unprofitable business for the boat. Zeb, at this piece of information, "flared up," raised his mane, shut his "maulers," and told Captain Raft he could whip him,—the pilot, and deck hands, and if they would give him the advantage of the "under grip," he would let the piston-rod of the engine punch him in the side all the time the fight was going on. ¶Raft, at this display of fury from Zeb, cooled down immediately, acknowledged himself "snagged," begged Zeb's pardon, and adjourned to the bar for a drink. One glass followed another, until the heroes got into the mellow mood, and Zeb, on such occasions, always "went it strong" for his family. After praising their beauty individually and collectively, he broke into the pathetic, and set the Captain crying, by the following heart-rending appeal:—¶"Raft, Raft, my dear fellow, you talk about the trouble of putting out a barrel of whiskey every week at my diggins, when I have got a sick wife, and five small children, and *no cow!*—whar's your heart?" ¶Dinner in due course of time was announced H

254.20   biggest] S, CI; largest H (This same change occurs twice at 254.21 and once at 254.22.)
254.23   steward] S, CI; steward would have done H
254.26   were] S, CI; war H
254.31   ever] S, CI; *omit* H
254.33   hour] S, CI; hours H
254.34   gutter] S, CI; ditch H
254.35   turned] S, CI; the pilot turned H
254.36   it] S, CI; *omit* H
255.2   us ahead] S, CI; it along H
255.3   in . . . going] S, CI; upstream H
255.4   our] S, CI; *omit* H
255.7   me] S, CI; us H
255.10   cultivatable] S, CI; arable H
255.13   and landing,] S, CI; "the passengers" landed and H
255.14   conceived] S, CI; dreamed H
255.14   glory] S, CI; glorious H

255.14–15 splendid] S, CI; splendidly-conceived H
255.17 we departed] S, CI; the steamer was again under way H
255.18 merged itself] S, CI; immerged H
255.26 two very] S, CI; the H
255.31 merged] S, CI; emerged H
255.32 went, the very] S, CI; swept, very much to the H
255.33 regular] S, CI; permanent H
255.38 hallowed] S; hallooed CI; hollowed H
255.39 kind] S, CI; tone H
256.1 owner] S, CI; owner of the wood-yard H
256.2 heap] S, CI; pile H
256.9 forth] S, CI; out H
256.10 expressive of] S, CI; expressed in H
256.12 gave me] S, CI; at this moment coming in sight, gave us H
256.12 shot,] S, CI; "wrath," H
256.13 enlarged] S; enraged CI, H
256.13 and great] S, CI; *omit* H
256.14 mere insects] S, CI; insignificance H

PISCATORY ARCHERY

265.5 without] M; without either H
265.29–32 *The . . . other.] M; *omit* H
266.6 upon the trees] M; upon the trunks of the trees H
267.6 would . . . foliage] M; taken from the forest would perceptibly alter the vegetation H
267.13 nights, perhaps, will only] M; nights only, perhaps, would H
267.40 where the fish were in] M; before the fish had left H
268.10–11 gaps . . . gives] M; opened his mouth and gave H
269.9 destroyed] M; taken H
269.10 pounds] M; pounds, in weight H
270.21–23 cord . . . quill] M; cord, about the size of a crow-quill, fifteen or twenty feet long, is attached to the spear H
271.6 turned quick] M; quickly turned H
271.9 only are] M; are only H
272.11 sporting] M; sportive H
273.19 England] M; our Northern States H
273.22 quickly] M; swiftly H

273.39   information] M; information regarding the early history of arrow-fishing H

274.1   "old] M; "invented by old H

274.5   differance] M; difference H

274.8   yearly] M; yerly H

274.8   inguns, and yerther] M; Inguns and other H

WIT OF THE WOODS

275.17   the] M; other H

275.26–27   and . . . strength] M; often makes the turkey an evening meal, while the weasel contents itself with the little chicks H

275.27   too] M; however H

275.33   season] M; season, therefore, H

*275.34–35   game. ¶The wild] M; game. ¶Independent of the pernicious influence of unfavorable seasons, or the devastation of the wild turkey by destructive animals, their numbers are also annually lessened by the skill of the pioneer and backwoodsman, and in but comparatively a few more years the bird must have, as a denizen of our border settlements, only a traditionary existence; for the turkey is not migratory in its habits, and its absence from any of its accustomed haunts, is indicative of its total extermination from the place where it was once familiar. ¶At present, the traveller in the "far west," while wending his solitary way through the trackless forests, sometimes very unexpectedly meets a drove of turkeys in his pathway, and when his imagination suddenly warms with the thought that he is near the poultry-yard of some hospitable farmer, and while his wearied limbs seem to labor with extra pain, as he thinks of the couch compared with the cold ground as a resting-place, he hears a sudden whizzing in the air, a confused noise, and his seeming evidences of civilization and comfort vanish as the wild turkey disappears, giving him by their precipitate flight, the most painful evidence that he is far from the haunts of men and home. ¶Turkey hunting is a favorite pursuit with all who can practise it with success, but it is a bird liberally provided by nature with the instinct of self-preservation, and

is, therefore, seldom found off its guard. Skilful indeed must be the shot that stops the turkey in its flight of alarm, and yet its wings, as with the partridge and quail, are little used for the purposes of escaping from danger. It is on their speed that they rely for safety, and we doubt if the best hounds could catch them in a race, even if the turkey's wings were clipped so that they could not resort to height to elude their pursuers. So little indeed does the bird depend upon its pinions, that they find it difficult to cross rivers moderately wide, and in the attempt the weak and very fat, are often sacrificed. ¶We have seen the wild turkey gathering in troops upon the limb of some tall cotton wood on the banks of the Mississippi, and we have known by their preparations that they intended to cross the river. There on their elevated roost they would set, stretching out their necks as if gathering a long breath for their, to them, prolonged flight. In the mean while, the "squatter," on the opposite bank, would prepare himself to take advantage of the birds' necessities. Judging from experience where about the "drove" would land on his side of the stream, he would lie concealed until the flight commenced. The birds would finally launch themselves in the mid air, as in their progress it could be seen that they constantly descended toward the earth,—the bank would be reached, but numbers exhausted would fail to reach the land, and would fall a prey to the insatiate wave, or the rapacious wants of man. ¶In hunting the wild turkey, there is unfortunately too little excitement to make it a favorite sport with those who follow the hounds. But the uncertainty of meeting with the bird, even if you know its haunts, and the sudden termination of the sport, even if successful, makes successful turkey hunters few and far between. ¶The cautiousness of the wild turkey is extraordinary: it excels that of the deer, or any other game whatever; and nothing but stratagem, and an intimate knowledge of the habits of the bird by the hunter, will command success. We once knew an Indian, celebrated for all wood craft, who made a comfortable living by supplying a frontier town with game. Often did he greet the villagers with loads of venison, with grouse, with bear, but seldom, indeed, did he offer the esteemed turkey for sale. Upon being reproached for his seeming incapacity to kill the turkey, by those who desired the bird, he defended himself as follows: ¶"Me meet moose—he stop to eat, me shoot him. Me meet bear—he climb a tree, no see Indian, me shoot him. Me meet deer—he look up—say may be Indian, may be stump—and me shoot him. Me see turkey great way off—he look up and say, Indian coming sure—me no shoot turkey, he cunning too much." ¶The turkey is also very tenacious of life, and will often escape though wounded in a manner that would seem to defy the power of locomotion. A rifle ball has been driven through and through the body of a turkey, and yet it has run with speed for miles. Some hunters have been fortunate in possessing dogs that have, without any instruction, been good turkey hunters. These dogs follow the scent, lead the hunter up to the haunts of the bird, lie quiet until a shot is had, and then follow the game if only wounded, until it is exhausted, and thus secure a prize to the hunter, that would otherwise have been lost. This manner of hunting the turkey, however, cannot be called its most legitimate form; as will be noticed in the progress of our chronicle. ¶The taste that makes the deer and fox hunt a favorite amusement, is not the foundation on which to build a true turkey hunter. The baying of hounds, the clamor of the horn, the excitement of the chase, the pell-mell and noisy demonstration, are all destructive to the successful pursuit of the turkey,—consequently, the H

275.35–38   peculiar . . . hunter] M; peculiar; he sympathises with the excentric habits of the bird, with its love of silence, with its obscurity, and it is no objection to him, if the morning is whiled away in the deep solitude, in comparative inaction, for all this favors contemplation worthy of an intellectual mind H

275.40   are] M; are, of course, H
276.3   Here] M; Herein H
276.6   note] M; sound H
276.6   sound] M; strains H
276.7   complaining] M; complaining notes H
276.7   chirps] M; chirrups H

276.10   or] M; or half H
276.11   decayed] M; decaying H
276.22   curious, when] M; curious; then H
276.38   wing . . . rifle] M; wing, or a small piece of wood, into which is driven a nail, and a small piece of oil stone (the head of the nail on being quickly scraped on the stone, producing perfectly the noise of the female turkey), and a double-barrel fowling-piece, H
276.39   The double-barrel fowling-piece] M; A rifle H
276.39   when] M; where H
276.40–277.5   plentiful . . . hunter] M; plentiful; and the person using it, as we have already described, depends upon the sagacity and speed of the dog, to rescue the wounded bird, for the turkey never instantly dies, except wounded in the brain H
277.6   indifferent] M; unskilful H
277.30   the fool] M; *omit* H
277.35   are] M; frequent H
277.36   their bodies] M; them H
277.36   they were] M; *omit* H
278.5   whether] M; whether it be H
278.11   although most] M; though almost H
278.21   rifle] M; gun H
279.3   rifle] M; deadly weapon H
279.21–22   peering . . . curiosity] M; and, with wondering curiosity, peering . . . insects H
279.34   and] M; and then H
280.1   poor] M; ruminating H
280.4–5   escaped . . . times] M; several times, as if by a miracle, escaped from harm with his life H
280.5   don't] M; will not H
280.8   catch] M; kill H
280.9   his own noise] M; the noise he makes himself H
280.10   thing] M; thing is H
280.10   naturally] M; *omit* H
280.14   killed] M; slain H
280.14–15   urchin's gun been overloaded] M; urchin overloaded his gun H
280.15   only escape death] M; come near being killed H
280.16   fellows] M; playfellows H
280.17–18   his last year's tail,] M; last year's "fan," H

382

280.18–19   He . . . and will] M; All this experience has made him a "deep" bird; and he will H

280.20   about,] M; *omit* H

280.22   are] M; are far H

280.25   married] M; newly-married H

280.33   stream] M; water H

281.6   solitary] M; solitarily H

281.10   gobbler] M; gobbler now H

281.13–14   they plunge . . . them] M; he plunges, until caution again brings him H

281.17   mind] M; heart H

281.26–27   flying . . . impatiently] M; impatiently flying over them H

281.27   open ground] M; an open space H

281.30   rifle] M; fowling piece H

282.2   head] M; neck H

282.11   rifle] M; bolt of death H

282.12   how] M; how vividly H

282.15   on] M; on, on H

282.16   gallant] M; *omit* H

282.18   rifle] M; gun H

282.18–19   its owner] M; the hunter H

282.22   supposed] M; *omit* H

282.22   and] M; and then H

282.24   wings] M; wings distinctly H

282.24   singularly plain,] M; *omit* H

282.27   The] M; Suddenly, the H

282.28   of the rifle] M; *omit* H

282.29   suddenly] M; rudely H

282.32   all] M; all—all H

282.33   he . . . body] M; our valorous lover has fallen lifeless H

PICTURES OF BUFFALO HUNTING

283.8–9   Where . . . is] M; The places where now are cities and towns, are H

283.33   never idle] M; ever restless H

284.13–14   animal sublimity before you] M; exhibited an animal sublimity H

284.19–20   against it] M; *omit* H

284.32   habit] M; propensity H

285.4   Indian Buffalo Hunters] M; *omit* H (The *Hive* text also omits all other subheadings at 287.20, 290.12, 293.13, and 297.22.)

285.5   ways to kill] M; methods of hunting H

285.9   among the aborigines, *the*] M; by the aborigines, considered as the *true* H

285.9–12   Cumanches . . . travelling] M; Comanches inhabit one of the loveliest countries in the world for a winter home— but when the heats of summer drive them northward, they travel H

285.13   under the] M; under every H

285.26   a] M; a grand H

285.28   priests.] M; priests. A solemn feeling pervades every thoughtful member of the tribe. H

285.28–29   finger . . . enemies,] M; scalp-lock derisively when he thinks of his enemies, now H

285.31–32   destroy . . . lively] M; destroy, and it is not until the fastings, prayers, and self-sacrifices are finished that the H

286.1–3   he has . . . instinctively] M; his motions are quick, and, at the approach of a human being, he instinctively takes the alarm, and H

286.32   eyes] M; eyes, lately H

286.32   are] M; are now H

286.34   take care] M; supply the wants H

286.39   little dress] M; loose garment H

287.3   to] M; for H

287.8–10   the two . . . emulation] M; these graceful Apollos pass before you, bounding gracefully along, and more than rivalling the beauty, H

287.11   they] M; there H

287.14   a . . . accomplished] M; an equestrian statue that art has never equalled H

287.18–19   on . . . death] M; onwards with redoubled speed,—they feel that a hurricane of death is H

287.29   crowded with and] M; *omit* H

287.34   will be seen browsing] M; browse H

288.1   to the ground] M; on their sides H

288.4   sleek] M; wild H

288.16   fearful response, they] M; bellowing response the buffalo H

288.24   was] M; is H

288.27   yet who] M; who yet H

289.3–6   The . . . inanimate] M; The old man compresses his mouth into a mere line; the eye is open and steady as a basilisk; the skin inanimate. The eyes of the young man dance with excitement, the blood flows quickly through the dark skin; and gives a feverish look to his lip and cheek H

289.19   ground] M; turf H

289.21   he] M; the bull H

289.33   will] M; will soon H

289.40   have been following] M; follow on H

290.1   have already commenced] M; eagerly begin H

290.5   pouch] M; paunch H

290.7   bodies] M; carcasses H

290.13   migrated] M; had settled H

290.17   the] M; the precarious H

*290.27–30   It . . . location] M; As might be supposed, the members of a party of adventurers once accustomed to the luxuries of refined life, and who had recently for weeks slept in the open air, congratulated themselves when they discovered upon the distant horizon the signs that mark the habitation H

290.34   all we found] M; the abode H

290.34   nearer] M; close H

290.36–37   people . . . horses] M; "family," which consisted not only of the human beings, but also of horses, cows, goats, and ill-bred poultry H

291.4   inhabitants] M; inhabitants alone H

291.14–15   somewhat . . . On] M; and on H

291.17   attended to] M; supplied H

291.31–33   with . . . our] M; finally appeared, whose bow-legs, formidable shocks of red hair, clothes of skin, and shuffling gaits, were the realities of our poetical H

291.37   were] M; were evidently H

292.10   notions] M; ideas H

292.14   had] M; enjoyed H

292.17   composed part of] M; infested the H

292.25   off] M; for H

292.37   be] M; be carried on a horse, and thus H

293.3 reposed the] M; hung H
293.17 animals] M; buffalo H
293.23–25 nostrils . . . helpless] M; nostrils, expanded by the associations around us; we grew merry at the thought of killing bucks, turkeys, and other *helpless, little* game, and
laughed so loudly, at the conceit of drawing a deadly
weapon upon a H
293.37 far off] M; distant H
294.5 any] M; any visible H
294.7 beastly-looking] M; wretched-looking H
294.10–11 rude . . . Indians] M; demonstrated use of all other weapons beside H
294.22 grace] M; grace, from the excitement of the moment, H
294.23 done honour to] M; have honored H
294.26 for] M; for especial H
294.31 Breeches'] M; "Breeches' " murderous H
295.1 muted] M; snorted H
295.7 with . . . him,] M; *omit* H
295.9–11 His . . . life.] M; *omit* H
295.14–15 Making . . . altered] M; He made no demonstration of attack, his usual expression of defiance had changed H
295.16 appeared . . . watch] M; roamed over the beautiful prairie,
and watched H
295.18 he looked] M; the dying creature gazed H
295.19 of his face] M; *omit* H
295.20 upon] M; from H
295.30 it was] M; the wild monarch H
295.40 horse's head was] M; horse carried his head H
296.5 from the] M; from the gay H
296.16 its own] M; the H
296.20 most] M; *omit* H
296.21 our] M; our most H
296.24 by some necromancy casting] M; had by some necromancy cast H
296.28–29 as we thought] M; ——— H
296.31 he] M; the Indian H
296.38 one] M; one on which H
296.40–297.5 There . . . antique art] M; The shaggy and rough appearance of the dead animal—the healthy-looking and un-

386

groomed horse with his roving eye and long mane—and the Indian himself, contemplating his work like some bronze statue of antique art—formed a group, the simplicity and beautiful wildness of which would have struck the eye of the most insensible H

297.8	Buffalo's body] M; buffalo H
297.10	at his] M; at the Indian's H
297.39	deer skin, Breeches,] M; deer-skin breeches; H
298.2	out,] M; out as H
298.13	harmless] M; harmless to one H
298.16	*tendo Achillis*] M; *tendon Achilles* H
298.20	party] M; party on H
298.23	given] M; given him H
298.31	the . . . *side*] M; and, as the animal always falls upon the wounded side, the mistake had caused the bull to become a stumbling block in his path H
298.33–34	The . . . him."] M; *omit* H
299.3	we were] M; surfeited as was the body, the mind was H

ALLIGATOR KILLING

300.3	seem to] M; *omit* H
300.17	The] M; But, alas! the H
300.29	taken] M; mistaken H
300.29	frequently] M; *omit* H
300.33	daily] M; *omit* H
300.35–36	taste grows more delicate] M; instincts become more subtle H
301.5	flesh] M; flesh of other living things H
301.13	It . . . mouth] M; The mouth is enormously large, and H
301.15–17	with . . . superabundance of] M; which, being ornamented with superabundant H
301.21	propelling . . . it] M; which propels it along swiftly in the water, and on land H
301.35–37	and . . . numerous] M; while the alligator, in its agonies of death, no doubt takes comfort in the thought, that the sun will hatch out its eggs, and that there will grow up a numerous brood of H
302.3	catching] M; watching H

302.8–9   that . . . pipe] M; which expands within them H
302.13   disposed of] M; disposed H
302.20   Louisiana,] M; Louisiana, on H
302.21   forest] M; forest trees H
302.23   covering nearly twenty acres] M; nearly twenty acres in extent H
302.25   most] M; nearly all H
302.29   mud] M; earth H
302.30   heat of the sun] M; intense heat H
302.36   of any size] M; *omit* H
302.38   mud] M; sediment H
302.40   sun] M; sun, soon H
303.1   sun] M; influence H
303.3   a] M; one H
303.6   if] M; if he was H
303.7   destruction] M; destructiveness H
303.8   throwing] M; throwing various H
303.26   that] M; who H
303.27   was made] M; made one H
303.36–37   nature . . . with] M; with which nature has provided the reptile H
303.38   thus compelled him] M; he was thus compelled H
304.3–4   alligator . . . plantations] M; alligator, when inhabiting places near plantations, is particularly destructive on pigs and dogs H
304.13   after] M; for H

A TRADITION OF THE NATCHEZ

318.23   west] MS; South-west KG
318.34   was] MS; was comparatively KG
318.37   take possession of] MS; occupy KG
319.1–2   all other nations] MS; the traditions of any other nation KG
319.21–23   industry . . . temples] MS; industry on which to erect their temples and bury their dead, the remains of which are so much admired to this day KG
319.28–29   foundations] MS; foundations of the mounds KG
319.32   trees] MS; trees of KG
319.34   smoking at their tops] MS; their summits smoking KG
319.35   this] MS; the great KG

319.39	God] MS; god KG
319.40	her] MS; his KG
319.40	greeted] MS; fell upon KG
320.2	taken] MS; regarded KG
320.17	in the struggle] MS; *omit* KG
320.23	away] MS; way KG
320.27	learn] MS; half forget KG
320.29	speak] MS; speaking KG
320.29	of the Natchez,] MS; *omit* KG
320.33	these were] MS; *omit* KG
320.39–321.2	and . . . fire] MS; and the altars, which had ever glowed with living fire, were cold KG
321.6	priests] MS; chief priests KG
321.25	undistinguishable] MS; undistinguishably KG
321.29	and] MS; and confidently KG
321.30	will] MS; will again KG
321.31	abandoned] MS; now desolated KG

COMPOUND WORDS AT ENDS OF LINES

The first list records all compounds and possible compounds hyphenated at the ends of lines in the copy-texts and gives the form of each as it appears in this edition. Where the decision to hyphenate or spell as one word could not be based on an appearance of the same word elsewhere in the copy-text or on its treatment in one of Thorpe's reprintings of the sketch, general familiarity with his style served as a guide. The second list records all words hyphenated at the ends of lines in this edition that appear in mid-line in the copy-texts as hyphenated compounds.

List I

85.1	bee-hive	151.5	sportsman
85.38	New-market	159.8	water-washed
99.5	thish-ere	164.29	deer-skin
99.31	windpipe	173.7	war-whoop
102.23	head-long	184.14	short-winded
112.31	-pressure-and-	186.1	wild-cat's
114.3	chippen-birds	188.8	undergrowth
114.38	cane-brake	188.30	well-trained
121.23	individ-u-	193.27	footpath
123.18	Woodcock	193.30	footsteps
123.34	cane-brakes	197.20	whip-poor-
124.27–28	warming-pan	197.23	buffalo-skin
124.30	broad-brimmed	200.2	steamboat
125.34	woodcock	200.24	straight-forward
132.24	whereabouts	200.37	fly-time
137.32	'me-li-	208.26	undertake
142.8	wheel-horse	209.13	cock-fighting
146.14	Irishman	215.4	spirit-level
150.30	whatever	216.39	whereabouts

221.12	frontiersman
227.30	Tar-pot-
230.25	ill–looking
237.11	-wah-me-
237.38	-wan-ja
238.22	-pot-wan-
240.33	-hum-bug-
242.10	Shallahrill
242.33	Tar-pot-
243.34	new-comer
244.4	-wan-ja's
248.17	-pot-wan-
250.18	-wan-ja
251.5	horsemen
259.23	herdsmen
259.37	horseflesh
261.33	stock-raisers
263.35	water-courses
263.39	sunshine
264.6	ground-flowers
264.11	never-failing
265.10	spring-time
267.25	arrow-fisherman

269.7	arrow-fisherman
269.33–34	arrow-fishing
271.35	ever-green
273.28	southwest
275.38	turkey-hunters
276.2	turkey-hunter
278.33	woodpecker
280.33	sunshine
282.5	semi-circle
283.20	Anglo-Saxon
284.28	war-path
285.35	well-trained
291.24	fine-looking
296.24	cornfield
298.33	whereabouts
301.23	nightfall
301.28	campfire
306.9	pleasure-boat
306.22	deep-mouthed
307.17	soft-shells
308.34	sunshine
309.13	brier-patch
316.37	earthquake

List II

87.38–39	-people-democrats
93.16–17	blood-stained
93.39–40.1	rattle-snake
112.24–25	half-alligator
112.30–31	well-known
116.26–27	cut-off
120.8–9	green-horn
128.2–3	pump-handle
144.22–23	Hard-scrabble
157.31–32	zig-zag
158.8–9	half-starved
178.29–30	war-whoop

201.4–5	ill-favored
208.30–31	cock-fighting
215.29–30	go-ahead
240.32–33	-poke-hum-
249.18–19	Tar-pot.
259.13–14	break-neck
267.30–31	air-bubble
268.21–22	arrow-fisherman
268.38–39	arrow-fisherman
277.16–17	turkey-hunter
278.38–39	turkey-hunter
285.28–29	scalp-lock

290.14–15	ragged-looking	305.15–16	thus-formed
290.35–36	dwelling-place	306.7–8	semi-palaces
297.35–36	fierce-looking	310.33–34	earth-dissolving
298.26–27	Ta-wa-	310.38–39	vanilla-scented
300.8–9	live-long